THE

LOGIC

OF SOCIAL

RESEARCH

Arthur L. Stinchcombe

THE

LOGIC
OF SOCIAL
RESEARCH

The University of Chicago Press

Chicago and London

ARTHUR L. STINCHCOMBE is professor emeritus of sociology, political science, and organizational behavior at Northwestern University. He is the author of nine books, most recently *When Formality Works: Authority and Abstraction in Law and Organizations* (2001), also published by the University of Chicago Press. In 2004 he received the Distinguished Career Award given by the American Sociological Association, and in 2003 he was elected to the National Academy of Sciences.

The University of Chicago Press, Chicago 60637
The University of Chicago Press, Ltd., London
© 2005 by The University of Chicago
All rights reserved. Published 2005
Printed in the United States of America

14 13 12 11 10 09 08 07 06 05   1 2 3 4 5

ISBN: 0-226-77491-0 (cloth)
ISBN: 0-226-77492-9 (paper)

Library of Congress Cataloging-in-Publication Data

Stinchcombe, Arthur L.
    The logic of social research / Arthur L. Stinchcombe
        p.   cm.
    Includes bibliographical references and index.
    ISBN 0-226-77491-0 (cloth : alk. paper)—ISBN 0-226-77492-9
        (pbk. : alk. paper)
        1. Sociology—Methodology.   2. Sociology—Research—Methodology.
    I. Title.

HM511.S75   2005
        301'.072—dc22   2004017206

Contents

Preface and Acknowledgments

THIS BOOK ORIGINATED AS LECTURES in a survey of methods for beginning graduate students in sociology, though some political science, anthropology, or engineering students found it valuable. The Northwestern Sociology Department was strongly methodologically diverse, and many of the department members used several methods. The first teacher in the course was Robert Nelson, whose earliest book was based on ethnography and ethnographic interviewing; he later coauthored several books based on surveys, and recently published one based primarily on archives: a tough act for me to follow.

I have preserved the oral style of the lectures, a style my brother William calls "academic Hemingway," because I believe the excessive formality of methodology books prevents methodologists from giving enough of the substantive context of the use of methodology, and enough of the "agent" character of the decisions about what to study by what methods. It is a deep fact of methodology that a good methodologist is an active agent with a purpose of finding out what is really going on in the world. If students do not hear a methodologist, but instead hear a theorem, they are intellectually impoverished by the teaching.

But the early history of the approach I took was based on an upside-down version of the "unified science" movement of my youth. Rather than trying to turn all sciences into physics, I have always tried to take different sorts of excellence and show that they had the same logic, or perhaps better, the "same intellectual strategy." Whatever was convincingly true in first-class ethnography, for example, had to be also true in physics, correctly understood. This is, of course, a utopian vision, not a practical plan. To start with, I do not know enough about physics to understand it my way.

This conviction was behind my first attempt to teach methods by teaching the fine exemplars of different sorts of excellent use of methods, with Neil Smelser. For ten weeks, we treated ten books, with him lecturing on the theory, me on the methods. Smelser is not responsible for any of the faults of this book, but the idea we developed in our team teaching has guided my many attempts to teach methods, from run-of-the-mill undergraduate statistics based on Lazarsfeld's collection of exemplars to advanced "exploratory" statistics courses at Berkeley. In the latter, most of the students had undergraduate mathematics degrees, but went on to write sociology of all different types.

What I have tried to add here is a systematic view of the underlying logic of the main methods in sociology, which also pervade political science, and are used widely in some parts of social anthropology and history, and among mavericks in economics. I stumbled around in logical tangles, and mystified a good many students who went on to do stellar work. That shows the trouble was with me, not them. I thank them for putting up with me, for discussion and critique, and I hope they can finally figure out from this book what I was driving at.

My closest colleague, Carol A. Heimer, has helped me with many discussions, but mainly by showing in her work what methods should look like at the end.

It will become obvious to the reader that my favorite methodologist is myself. It would be a suspicious methods book whose author had not taken his or her own advice. I have struggled with methods problems and invented new approaches (at least new to me) since my dissertation. There is, of course, a good deal of vanity in choosing oneself as an exemplar, and pride is one of the chief sins, both in theology and in scientific ethics. I apologize for choosing myself whenever I could think of no better example, and for the motivated blindness that has no doubt caused me to miss correctly identifying my betters.

Excerpts of previously published material are reprinted with permission of the publishers:

Arthur L. Stinchcombe, "Technical Appendix: The Logic of Analogy" and "Principles of Cumulative Causation," in *Theoretical Methods in Social History* (Orlando, Fla.: Academic Press, 1978), pp. 25–29, 61–70. Copyright 1978 by Academic Press, Inc. Reprinted with permission from Elsevier.

Arthur L. Stinchcombe, "The Conditions of Fruitfulness of Theorizing about Mechanisms in Social Science," *Philosophy of the Social Sciences* 21, no. 3 (1991): 367–388. Reprinted in Aage B. Sørensen and Seymour Spilerman, eds., *Social Theory and Social Policy: Essays in Honor of James S. Coleman* (Westport, Conn.: Praeger, 1993), pp. 23–41.

Arthur L. Stinchcombe, "Restructuring Research on Organizations," in *Information and Organizations* (Berkeley: University of California Press, 1990), pp. 358–362. Copyright 1990 The Regents of the University of California.

1 Methods for Sociology and Related Disciplines

What Kinds of Theory Do Sociologists Study?

THE CENTRAL PURPOSE OF THIS BOOK is to analyze logically and practically various strategies sociologists have invented to explore for, develop, or test theories of causation in social life. Almost all sociological theories assert that some social condition or conditions cause or produce one or more other social conditions. We have known since Hume that such theoretical links between causes and effects are not easily supported by observation. Sociologists have used four main kinds of solutions to Hume's problem of supporting theories involving causation. And they have contributed to the nearly infinite supply of reassertions that causation cannot itself be observed; one after another method has been attacked because it leaves the question of causation (like everything asserted about the world by all other theories in all sciences) somewhat uncertain. Our purpose as empirical workers of different kinds has been to make such theories as believable as we can, based on the evidence we can collect or create.

I will call the four main methods of addressing causal questions in social science by their common names: (1) *quantitative* regression methods (and their analogues) on systematically collected observations in the world, especially observations in surveys; (2) *historical* methods of studying time order and intervening processes between cause and effect in archives of various kinds; (3) *ethnographic* methods to penetrate deeply into sequences of actions and their context to provide evidence about action as it develops in its natural setting; and (4) *experimental* methods to verify that manipulations of causes have the effects that their natural analogues are thought to have, to verify "mechanisms" in the causal theories.

1

I shall elaborate the nature of these methods briefly here, before explaining why this book is organized not by the methods, but by the general logical problems the methods address in different ways. That is, there are no chapters on, say, ethnographic methods, but rather sections on a logical problem such as dealing with causes that are very complex products of one actor (say, an author) but that enter in a much simpler way into the life of another (say, a reader). Such patterns of causation pervade high culture: the arts, the law, medicine, and science. There is no reason that all the methods mentioned above cannot be used to address these patterns, but they have to deal with the same logical structure of investigation.

But there are different strengths and weaknesses, for different purposes, of methods such as surveys, which radically simplify the observations of the complex products before studying the effects, as we might expect from surveys of library use, and those that focus on the complex production process (say, of a book), starting with the author's background and setting and the historically developed genre in which he or she is writing. Although they are on the same theoretical topic, the sorts of things one finds out about that topic are different. Surveys might show that fundamentalists read more books than people of other religious persuasions, but that most of those books are on religious topics. Historical methods might show that narrative biographies of a person's life in different historical periods have been likely to produce sagas praising famous men at some times, family dramas acted out in a simulated living room on stage in other times.

1. *Quantitative.* The methods usually called "quantitative" in sociology have as their main technique eliminating the alternatives to a given simple causal theory that is weakly supported by an observed correlation, by examination of the relations among variables having relatively simple and abstract measures, such as can be created by a few survey questions. Such relations among variables are ordinarily collected mainly by surveys or other repetitive quantitative observations in "natural settings," rather than in laboratories. They do that elimination by showing that the pattern of partial correlations (or other partial regression coefficients) is not compatible with the alternative theories, but instead supports the simple causal theory at stake. They start, of course, by showing that the presumed cause is at least correlated with the presumed effect. But although Hume in effect already said, "Correlation is not [strong evidence of] causation," one of the possible theories that *would* produce the observed correlation is that simple causal theory. Each time one eliminates

one or more other theories of that correlation, one increases the likelihood of the simple causal theory. This is a very abstracted description of what is going on, so perhaps the following example will help.

Many of the advantages and disadvantages that children enjoy in school and in their placement in the labor market are summed up by the resources available in their family of origin, by the fact that their father or mother or both had good jobs, or at the other extreme that one or both did not have jobs or had bad ones. Consequently, one theory of the disadvantage in school and the labor market of African Americans is that their parents were disadvantaged in their turn by the low occupational standing of *their* parents, and so on back to the original forced occupation in plantation work in the slave system.

If that were true, then the fact that slaves set free before the Civil War were more often of mixed race becomes relevant. This was partly because planters and other slave owners more often freed their mistresses and "illegitimate" children, and partly because they more often freed household slaves, craftsmen, and slave supervisors, who were more often of mixed race. Consequently the "color" of a family (a very rough measure of mixed race) is a measure of early manumission of their ancestors. It also measures the longer exposure of ancestors under slavery to those aspects of majority culture that one learns as a servant, craftsman, or supervisor, even before possible earlier manumission. That is, generations since field slavery of a family, and so generations with higher human capital as valued in the United States, is roughly measured by color (for this process in the Caribbean, see Stinchcombe 1995a, pp. 138–152, 159–171).

The number of generations since rural servitude of families of American whites varies a good deal by where they came from. In the commercial farming environment in the Low Countries down the Rhine to northern Italy, and including England and the Seine valley in Europe, a modern "free peasantry" existed very early, with more feudal servitude in the interior plains, and more egalitarian traditional labor contracts in mountainous areas (except for some slavery, not of field slaves, in the Caucasus until the early eighteenth century). In central Europe coercive inheritable servile tenures in rural areas were decaying by the early eighteenth century, while in Russia serfdom was not abolished until the late nineteenth century. Temporary servile ("indentured servant") contracts existed in the American colonies well into the eighteenth century, and in Hawaii until the nineteenth century, though only a few of the indentured servants there were Hispanics.

The varying colors of whites do not map very well the history of families' liberation from servile tenures and the entailed human capital deprivation, so we are forced to lump "whites" all together here. Taking account of the mixture of sources of U.S. white immigrants, I would hazard an estimate of an average of about twenty-five to thirty generations, or roughly six centuries. The regression study design suggested below does not depend on this estimate; it essentially ignores all differences in cumulated human capital since servile conditions in family lines before the nineteenth century.

The accumulation of human capital in a family line in the generations since slavery or servitude might, then, be enough to explain the difference in achievement and placement between the races. This would turn the theoretical question from one of how far African Americans are disadvantaged by current practices, to how long their legacy of human capital has been accumulating. One would probably want to set whites at the value of the lightest category of African Americans for "color" (in effect saying that the effect of slavery erodes at periods over about ten generations). And another rough measure of that human capital deposit of generations since slavery and of other more recent causes of improved cultural legacies might be parents' occupational or educational position. The combination of estimating these two effects should better tell us which African Americans ought to be as well off as the average white person with a long period of accumulation of family-line human capital (by the coefficient of color, as manifest also by the coefficients of their parents' occupational and educational position).

Now partial regression coefficients could be calculated for several dependent (i.e., "effect") variables: the interviewed person's years of schooling, grade averages, and placement in the labor market, on three "independent" or "causal" variables: "race," "color," and "parent's occupational standing" (e.g., for the color variable, 0 for dark African Americans, gradually increasing to 1 for the lightest blacks and for whites; and for the "race" variable, 1 for all people with any African ancestors, 0 for those with "all white" ancestors).

Such an analysis would ask the question of how closely those African Americans whose human capital legacy was equal to that of whites equaled whites in educational or occupational achievement. If the "race" coefficient was very small, this would show that there was "no discrimination since slavery," just a slow course of "catching up" from the oppression of slavery itself. The quantitative result then pits one theory (that the causes of lower African American achievement are the slow accumulation of many kinds of human capital over generations) against another (that some factor like continuing discrimination explains the difference in achievement).

Conversely, if such controls did not eliminate the direct effect of "African American" versus "white," this would be good evidence that, in spite of our valiant calculation efforts, we cannot eliminate the effect of race discrimination. The alternative to the discrimination theory that has been eliminated is that African Americans who are "almost white," who have educated parents with good jobs, who therefore have evidently been accumulating a stock of human capital in the family nearly as long as whites, as well as having the occupational achievement in the previous generation representing that accumulated human capital, should have the same levels as whites of child achievement in education and in the labor market. The "discrimination coefficient" not being zero eliminates the alternative, "slow accumulation of human capital across generations." The analysis then would support the discrimination theory originally precariously supported by the correlation between status and race, but now in a much stronger position because some of its competitors have been eliminated as the whole of the explanation.

Such a strategy of regression elimination of alternative theories in quantitative data collected, often by interviews, with simple measures of many variables measured simultaneously (sometimes over time) will be called "quantitative" for simplicity. There is no inherent reason that historical, ethnographic, and experimental methods should not also be quantitative, but I will simplify the contrast.

2. *Historical.* Historical methods in sociology are mostly connected to comparisons of countries or of other social units. The point is to study sequences of conditions, actions, and effects that have happened in natural settings, in sufficient detail to get signs of sequences that are causally connected. In particular, such studies sometimes concentrate on *contexts* that change the meanings of actions or the conditions under which actions are carried out, so that similar actions have different effects in different times and places. A very good way to get variations in context is to compare times and places that have distinctive contexts.

A particularly important form of the causal pattern is what has come to be called "path dependency." For example, after the North American colonies had been organized by different companies, each company set up local administrations in America with varying powers to make local decisions in "legislatures." It was therefore easier to organize the postrevolutionary American government in a federal fashion. Many powers remained where they had been during the colonial period, in what were now the separate states but before had been the separate colonies.

In the nineteenth century, then, the conflict over slavery and its extension to the West took place in an environment in which both the South and the North had subunits, ones we call "states," able to raise taxes, already having militia organizations, having legislatures to organize themselves for war and policing, and the like. That is, being on a federalist path shaped the kind of civil war that one would have later, by having highly competent local "democratic" state governments on both sides. The Civil War then became, in the southern tag for it, a "War between the States." The context of the actions involved in civil war then was determined by the federalist path that one had been on previously.

But it is important to notice also that the nature of the "federalist path" was the continuing existence of institutional forms: persistent ways of organizing and validating social action. The context of the American Civil War in particular consisted of state legislatures with substantial power over labor relations (e.g., slave versus free), social welfare legislation (e.g., local hospitals), local coercive power (from county sheriffs and jails to state militias), schools, local banks, and the like. These then were institutional forms created by history that had continuing power and legitimacy, and so could be powerful causes in the 1840s and 1850s, and consequently in the political organization of the war itself.

Even after the Civil War in the United States, the southern states were reorganized with essentially the same boundaries, the same counties, the same laws and regulations except in the area of slavery, and legislatures elected more or less in the same way as before the war, and having the same local powers. After a while many of the same people were back in power, elected again. In some sense, then, history explains itself. Put another way, we do not know what causes of social action will be in a time and place without knowing what causes previous—that is, historical—action has placed there. In such cases, then, the causal picture is "inherently historical," because the causes are themselves historical creations.

Thus the keys to historical exploration of causal theories are penetration of the details of processes and sequences that in fact connected causes to effects over time, combined with attention to what deposits of causal forces are in a social environment, put there by past action (for a deep exploration of one method for thinking about this, see Bearman, Faris, and Moody, 1999). Then in turn their continuing effects would be shaped by new conditions later on in the sequence. To put it another way, the context of social action is shaped by the path history has taken, and is constituted in part by institutions, practices, and ideas that would not be causes at a given time at all, if history had not put them there.

3. *Ethnography.* In the early history of anthropological description of new peoples, the observer might see many things that seemed strange to him (or more rarely at that time, to her), all attached to a given "people." For example, one might find nomadic people dependent on herds of domesticated animals that supplied nearly all the needs of the people, which moved from pasture area to pasture area along with the tribe who lived off the herd. This is a special style of domestication of animals, and quite different from having animals in pens and barns and chicken coops.

He (she) might also find that such people held their pastures in common, so that all the herding units of a "tribe" in a locality could move among the pastures depending on the conditions of each pasture and the needs of the herd or of the people. But they might own the herds separately, rather than jointly like the pastures, in an extended family. Thus, nomadic herding tribes might turn out to have complex property systems, with pastures and herds owned in different ways, while in France where the anthropologist came from (on the average, nomadic tribes have been studied by the French or Russians more often than by other nations) the pastures and herds were owned in much the same way.

A good start on a causal theory might be that the one strange thing about domestication of animals entirely outdoors without fences, and another strange thing of no individual (only tribal) ownership of the main resource other than the herd (namely, pasture), might be causing each other. One might then try to see the connection, such as the possibility that one could not protect pastures from other tribes with only one herding unit, so family property of pastures might be indefensible, or that adaptation to different luck of the rains on different pastures might make an inflexible family property system fatal to the unlucky.

This might suggest other things to look into, connected to the defense of boundaries or claims on the meat, for example. The basic preliminary idea then would be that a group such as a "tribe" of nomads might be a system of interrelated causes, and that any one strange thing about them might explain another strange thing about them. Following out the details of actions and their interdependencies then might turn up good evidence of intervening causal links, supporting one or another theory.

Very often ethnographic study is combined with historical study, because it was by historical processes that the groups came to be autonomous units with many internal causes, and those causes came to be distinct from those in other groups. A very good early study that combined

ethnographic methods with extensive historical analysis in studying nomadic herding groups is Owen Lattimore's *Inner Asian Frontiers of China*
(Lattimore, 1967 [1940]).

A particularly important kind of cause that is hard to find by other
methods, but easy to find by ethnography, is an unusual saliency of some
cultural matter. For example, inheritance within the family of cattle rather
than private property in land might have many effects in many areas
of life. Other people than nomads inherit animals within their families,
but such inheritance does not often constitute nearly the entire basis of
family subsistence. Thus, one might expect nomadic herding societies to
have many features in common because of this special salience of herd
inheritance within the family line, but very little else (and in particular
not pasture land) inherited within families.

This may mean that inheritance of cattle has to create a herd attached
to a social unit that can supply quite a lot of work to keep all the herd's
components, and can support all the people in the unit that depends on
the adequacy of all parts of the work being done (Dyson-Hudson, 1966;
summarized on this point in Stinchcombe, 1983, pp. 36–46, 91–97).
Only in that way can the whole herd be maintained in good shape and its
components in good relations to each other and to the people. Patrilineal
herd inheritance with patrilocal marriage (the wife moving to the place
of the father of the husband, where then the husband remains) is one
system that tends to produce such units. The salience can be found by
ethnography.

4. *Experiments.* When it seems to potential experimenters that the
same sorts of processes create connections of causes and effects in a wide
variety of situations (and in particular within units of analysis; see chapter 6), these commonalities can be abstracted into mechanisms. Mechanisms are micro-theories. Then, if experimenters can manipulate the
causes in a special experimental environment where many other causes
and causal mechanisms are eliminated or randomized, they can verify that
such manipulations *can* produce the relevant effects. Such experiments
can often locate the core of a causal process that occurs, in mixtures with
other conditions, in the natural world.

It is central to the application of experimental results outside the laboratory that both the causes and effects demonstrated in experiments
be calibrated so that their sizes can also be measured in natural settings.
Thus, it is central to the application of theories of electrical energy to real
world economies that the electrical energy being used can be measured
and charged for, that the voltages can be adjusted to the motors or heating

coils being manufactured in actual factories, and so on. The voltages are calibrated on the same scale as voltages in a laboratory. That is why the science of electricity can be applied in power stations and refrigerators. In the same way it is central to the application of social experiments that the causes manipulated by the experimenter can be calibrated, as well as the effect. We need calibration not only so we know which other experiments are giving the same results, but also so that we can go find those causes and measure their sizes, and the sizes of their effects, in the world. Sometimes in the early stages of a science the calibration is "qualitative" rather than quantitative (see the analysis of Lawler and Yoon, 1998, in chapter 6).

The Formation of Methodological Factions

OFTEN SOCIOLOGISTS HAVE BORROWED METHODS from other fields that do not have the same emphasis on causal theories of naturally occurring phenomena. For example, census sampling theory was designed to do the job of a census: to estimate the sizes of populations and subpopulations. The number of people is a very small part of theoretical reasoning in sociology now. One would not want to do without the methods for finding that out. But to study causes we want to know the effects of distances between people (or groups) on causal variables, so that we can study the distances between them on effects that are due to those causal variables. The sampling of distances for maximum accuracy in estimating a causal distance and its effect on a distance of another variable is not efficiently done by the methods used for sample estimates of the sizes of various populations.

To get maximum efficiency in estimating a causal coefficient, for example, one usually wants to greatly oversample pairs of people (or pairs of situations, or groups) that are far apart on that variable. This is especially important if one wants to find whether the relations between causes and effects are curvilinear (as many, perhaps most, are). When nearly all the cases in a sample are close together, almost any curve is well approximated by a straight line; when cases are farther apart, the effect of curvature is much easier to find. Oversampling the extremes is a very bad way to estimate numbers of people, but a very good way to estimate coefficients or to fit curves. So sampling for most sociological theory should not be the kind the census uses. But when sampling experts move from the census to survey research centers, they bring the wrong methods for causal studies with them, and can become quite dogmatic about them. If survey research centers hired their sampling statisticians from among epidemiologists, interested in finding the causes of diseases or the effects of drugs in "natural" settings, they would find the design of causal survey studies much easier to accomplish.

Similarly, estimating the saliency of some cultural matter, such as how important family property in land is, compared to family property in animals, is much better done by listening to people in a nomadic setting talk about inheritance and noticing how much emphasis they put on it, how much it influences what they propose to do next.

If one asks nomads how important land is, they will answer, "Very." But that means one is controlling the salience of land by the question. Waiting for them to measure it in their own conversation is labor intensive, but it is better than getting the wrong answer. Family land is not always the core of inheritance from father to son in premodern societies.

In like fashion, the effect of federalism on politics in the 1850s and 1860s cannot be studied without the historical knowledge of how thoroughly the federal institutions of the United States had been built in the colonial and postcolonial period. And almost nothing about the causal process can reasonably be studied with survey or experimental methods. Even for the present, people would have a hard time answering how much of their total tax bill had been collected, and how much was spent, by state and local governments in the United States. They would also have a great deal of trouble with it in England, where the answer is very different.

The people in England would also have had very little idea in 1770 of how much of the taxes and how much of the expenditure in the North American colonies was assessed, paid, and spent there. So even if there had been surveys then, they would not have uncovered federalism in the Americas. The proportion of the budget that was collected, and the proportion spent, by the separate colonies was crucial before, during, and after the revolutionary war, and consequently crucial for what the Articles of Confederation and the "Federalist" constitution looked like. And that all meant that, in due course, the Civil War over slavery took place in a very different setting than it would have done without such legacy. There is no way to untangle that set of causes without historical research (and, of course, no easy way in any case).

Often sociologists specialize in one or another of the methods outlined above. They then often become dogmatic about the weaknesses of other methods and the strengths of their own. Naturally, practitioners of the other methods return the dogmatism. I have used all the methods except experiment, but I once tried to get money to do an experiment and failed. So naturally I am dogmatic in my conviction that all the methods are useful sometimes, and all are radically inappropriate for other purposes.

We are so far from what Hume would demand to establish causation—a method that would allow us to observe directly the cause having its effect—that anything any of these methods can turn up is precious. I will try to show why each method fills gaps in the others, to help us tackle the deep problem Hume posed. Aside from the discouragement of communication between scholars of different styles, this conflict among methods produces fruitless, and low-quality, epistemological disputes. What we need instead is new knowledge about the social world, and the causes and effects in it.

An Outline of the Argument

THIS SECTION GIVES A BRIEF INTRODUCTION to my view of the core logical problems in sociological methods, around which I have organized this book. Since methodology is inherently a more abstract subject than the substance of a discipline, I will try to bring many examples of each logical problem in each of the various methods outlined above. I will also provide some examples of studies or methodological arguments by practitioners of each of the methods, in shortened form so as to bring out the main contribution of the method to the logical problem being dealt with. Here, then, I will start by giving brief sketches of the logical problems that are the core of the book, using as many examples as I can conveniently crowd into a small space. My purpose here is not really to explain the logic, but to give an intuition of what will be found in the following chapters.

Problem I: The Centrality of Distances in Study Design for Causal Theories

THE BASIC IDEA OF THIS BOOK is that much of the methods discussion in sociology is crippled by the failure to realize that the fundamental things we theorize about are differences and, when we can manage it, distances. From a logical point of view, "differences" is a subclass of "distances"; the most powerful methods, when the situations allow us to use them, are those used where we can observe the differences in differences—that is, "distances" in the common meaning of the term.

For example, for most sociological purposes we do not care whether our sample of *units of observation*, such as persons or social groups, is representative, but rather whether we have a *good sample of differences among* units of observation. For example, if we are studying whether African Americans have a different musical culture, say, than white Americans, we would want to know the proportion of all the music that African Americans listen to, or sing to themselves, or create, that is different from the music listened to, sung, or created by white Americans. If we notice that the performers of country and western music are almost all white, we want to know whether that is a pervasive difference, so that African Americans do not listen to it, sing along with it, dance to it, or try to learn to play and write it. And we want to know the same thing for, say, blues or rap, or classical music. "Classical" music can almost be defined by the fact that one sits down and does nothing else at a live performance, so one might want to measure different distances to explain its audiences and their lack of interest in dancing.

One of the ways of getting a representative sample of differences, if we know what population manifests the differences, is to take a representative sample of the units of the population. However, as we will see in the long run in this book, that is not usually the most efficient study design for a great many purposes. One can get a good sample of differences and measurements on them much more efficiently than sampling most of one's sample units near the mean, where they have very small differences. In a representative sample, most of the units are near the mean on most variables, and so are not very different from each other. Therefore, they give very little information about distances. For example, if one wanted to know the proportion of performers of different races for different genres of music, it would be very inefficient to obtain a random sample of the population, take those few music performers we got among the different races, and ask them what genres they perform. Most people in a random sample are very near the mean number of performances, near zero. They are the same as all other people who perform no music, and therefore do not give us any differences in what music they perform.

Another application of this idea is that in order to study the effects of a variable that is deeply confounded with another variable (as, for example, black versus white race is deeply confounded with social class of origin in the United States), one has to "find" differences in race *that are not also* differences in class. The basic idea of multiple regression is that *the part of* racial differences in effects that are uncorrelated with a measure of social class (the "residuals" of race differences on the effect variable, given estimated equality on social class—that is, with the effect of social class taken out) are "purified" differences in race. For those residuals, distances between them are not also distances on social class as we have measured it.

Depending on the theory of race being studied, differences between Native Americans (perhaps distinguishing Eskimos from other Native Americans) and whites, between Asians and whites, between African Americans of mostly white ancestry and those with less white ancestry, between African Americans who grew up in the North and those who grew up in the South, between African Americans and whites whose ancestors all grew up in the cotton counties of the South, might give more illuminating differences by race. And such differences would be more informative than those obtained by random sampling methods.

For example, the experience of the civil rights movement for African Americans was very different in the deep South plantation counties than in southern cities, and very different in the South than in the North. From that difference in experience, one might expect that the notion that whites, deep down inside, really hate and despise black people might be much stronger among people who went through the civil rights movement in the rural South than among those who experienced it in the North (this would be a study of people who are middle-aged and old at the time of this writing). In such cases one would have to oversample the deep rural South civil rights participants and northern urban civil rights participants, to get at those differences. So the first problem of methodology for causal studies is to start from the beginning studying distances, rather than samples of people. The analysis of distances between units of analysis is treated intensively in chapter 2, and forms the foundation for chapters 3 and 4.

Problem II: Economy in Data Collection

AS IN ANY OTHER RATIONAL ACTIVITY, one does not want to spend more time and resources than necessary to get the relevant answer (or for any other purpose). This means that a scientific strategy, including a method of observation, is to be evaluated partly by how much effort or other resources it uses to get the relevant answer.

In general, finding new distinctions among phenomena or new mechanisms that have not been clearly formulated requires casting the net wide, and so requires cheap data collection that is not so focused that it misses relevant phenomena or mechanisms. "Naturalistic observation" ("ethnography" and "history" in the social sciences) uses cheap and relatively undiscriminating observation in surveying a field in which significant data are sparse, to find things otherwise unexpected (suggesting "new" mechanisms), or to find what is mainly going on (suggesting an area of social life where a mechanism, new or not, is especially relevant).

At the opposite extreme is expensive, high-resolution measurement of isolated, narrow phenomena in a highly restricted field of phenomena. This might be done in a laboratory. In a social science laboratory experiment the most common distance on a causal variable used in the analysis is a distance between "experimental group" and a "control group"; that distance is produced by actions of the experimenter. The expectation in such an experiment would be that nearly all the observations would be valuable, because each person in the experimental group is distant from any person in the control group along the same variable, and by the same distance.

Experiments are often used to investigate theories of micro-mechanisms that play a role in theories of large-scale phenomena; outside the laboratory the mechanism is rarely isolated from other forces. Most sociology falls between ethnography or history and experiments, with medium proportions of significant data and medium, "statistical" isolation of mechanisms. Investigating the way that federalism created in the American colonies affected the unified groups that formed within the Continental Congress and then in the Constitutional Convention would require scanning a great mass of archival data on action as it happened, while general hypotheses about how the experience of making decisions in subgroups affects the structure of decision making in plenary groups composed of those subgroups could be explored in laboratories. It is conceivable that mechanisms found in such laboratory studies might cause the historical sociologist to look especially hard at archives about the behavior of pairs who had served together in colonial legislatures before serving in the Continental Congress (an example of a study of state delegation behavior in the federal legislature is Padgett, 1990).

Since in general distances between separate observations give observations their theoretical power, increasing variance on the relevant variables (e.g., increasing the distance between experimental and control groups or oversampling extreme groups in surveys) and minimizing noise are central to economy.

Problem III: Using Data to Refine Concepts and "Measurements" of Concepts

THE CORE OF CONCEPTS IN SCIENTIFIC METHODOLOGY is as a *description of some differences* that observations may find. Most scientific theories are about relations between differences (e.g., differences or distances between values of a causal variable affect the differences in values, or in the rate of change, of an effect variable). Finding differences that make a difference is the core operation of developing a concept, and systematic observations of differences can help us to develop such concepts.

A central virtue that a set of concepts can have is high "exactness." By exactness we mean correct identification of exactly what phenomena cause the relevant other phenomena, and of exactly what they cause. Then, if such theoretical exactness can be tied to high resolution of observations relevant to a theoretical problem, concepts in the theory combined with observations of differences in the world add to the empirical content of the theory. The more exact the concept, the more exact the meaning of observations can be. Conversely, then, the more exactly concepts are adapted, by the development of exact methods of observation, to observed differences that do the work in the world, the more they will tell us about the theory in which the concepts are embedded.

This means that observations will have higher probative power, the higher the resolution or exactness of the complex of procedures for coding and measurement of the conceptual scheme. Concepts are only as good as the methods of observing differences in their values, and observations are only valuable if they measure what the theory calls for. For example, studying actions by studying attitudes is usually a low-resolution method. A central methodological device for developing a close relation between concepts and observational procedures is coherence (or "correlation") of measures, as a central clue to how to build exactness of concepts, and simultaneously to identify their observable measures.

For example, a loosely coupled organization whose parts are not coherent is not a good "case," because observations of its features do not predict much about ("are not highly correlated with") the behavior of the various loosely coupled parts. Observing subparts that actually connect causes to effects may improve both exactness of concepts and coherence of "measures." Getting the right units of analysis clarifies both theory and method, and it will show up in loosely connected systems, for example, by a closer correlation of measures taken on subparts (Stinchcombe 1990a, pp. 354–358).

Factor analysis and its relatives are a reflection of this "coherence locating" intuition of how one refines concepts, but the same broad criterion should identify units of analysis, as locations where causes are tightly tied to effects. Units of analysis are central concepts that often need improving, as will be seen in connection with the mechanisms within them, in chapter 6.

Problem IV. Contexts; Differences and Distances between Contexts; Contexts Shaping Causal Processes

MOST CAUSAL PROCESSES IN ALL SCIENCES have boundary conditions. But the way boundaries shape causes within them depends deeply on what is on the other side. Skins and mucous membranes are boundaries around people. But how skins and membranes function as boundaries depends on such conditions on their other side as temperature, clothing, what comes through special absorption processes in the various membranes (and on whether there is nutrition or oxygen to absorb). We usually talk about conditions beyond boundaries of causal processes as "environment."

In many ways the boundaries of social processes are even more porous, because central causal processes in social life are often shaped by meanings, and meanings are very dependent on what's outside, on what we usually call "context." Other causal processes depend on what the situation and the means of a person or social unit provide, as "opportunities." We often talk about this as "the situation" in the broad sense of that word, as in "the market situation." Other conditions beyond boundaries of a process provide causes that enter directly into social causation, such as darkness versus light determining the crime rate, sleep patterns, and the locked doors that often accompany sleep; locked boundaries facilitate sleep.

For all these reasons causal processes in social life depend on what I shall sum up as "context." An investigator often wants to spend most of his or her time and effort on elucidating a causal process. But the boundary conditions for that process are often determined in part by the "context." Usually, for reasons of economy, one wants to investigate the context only enough not to go wrong. But generally one needs to formulate concepts of the context, if only to be able to say something sensible about the generalizability of one's causal results. And sometimes there are theoretically interesting results to be had from the analysis of how processes differ as the context changes. Building concepts of context by looking at data on boundary conditions and environmental influences is therefore often central to the social science enterprise. Strategies for using data on such matters, and what data to look for and still not be defeated by not being able to study everything all at once, are the main subject of chapter 5.

Problem V: Using Data to Find Mechanisms and Processes; Relation of Such Process Concepts to Concepts of Units of Analysis

....

ONE EXPLORES PROCESSES THAT HAPPEN OVER TIME, the details of sequences that lead from a difference in one thing to another difference in something else, to study the mechanisms in theories. An important strategy is increasing the temporal detail of changes: in social science, participant observation, longitudinal survey data, and event history analysis all are methods to get more exact temporal detail, and so are especially useful in sorting out processes or mechanisms.

Quite often what we mean by "mechanisms" in social science is a causal connection *within* relatively bounded units that form coherent "parts" of a larger structure. For example, persons are parts of organizations and of social classes: rationality, emotions, habits, accumulated learning and competencies all may characterize either persons as members of organizations or organizations as members of markets or of political systems. Knowing how persons (or organizations) connect causes to effects helps predict aggregate behavior in larger structures, such as markets or public opinion. This involves locating the crucial lower level actors that have causal unity in the larger structure (e.g., firms are the main actors in most modern markets, though for Adam Smith persons were the natural units of markets).

The mechanisms that go on inside such lower level units predict their behavior. Thus, organizations collect accounting information to estimate "the bottom line" of a proposed line of action, while individuals rarely do such accounting to make their family decisions; firms usually have more permanent "preference functions" than people, partly because they do better accounting. Data can be used to locate units, and to describe mechanisms in those units that translate conditions in larger structures, through actions of the parts, into aggregate or collective behavior in those larger structures.

If there are instruments involved in making observations, studying the mechanisms in those instruments (e.g., what kinds of comparisons people can manage in answering oral questions on surveys, or what kinds of forgetting a social structure induces and when structural data will be inaccurately remembered) can improve the observational scheme. For example, it would be bad methodology to estimate graduate school attrition by asking professors how many students they can remember who dropped out, because individual dropouts are rarely discussed in departmental conversations and meetings and so are soon forgotten, and people do not remember their dropping out.

Problem VI: Testing Theories by Testing Hypotheses with Data

THE BASIC METHOD OF TESTING THEORIES IS to see whether or not their factual consequences are true. A combination of logic or mathematics and previously well-established ancillary theories (e.g., those embedded in measuring instruments) is used to "derive" hypotheses about what will be observed in a given situation (e.g., an experiment, a survey). Those hypotheses are then compared with the observations. The power of a test involves both the nature of the hypothesis (especially the solidity of its relation to the theory), its relation to competitive theories, its degree of resolution or exactness about what will be observed, and the like. In short, the amount one learns from "Theory T implies hypothesis H, and observations O imply H is false (or H is true)" depends on many features of H. Thus, the key to methodologies of all sorts, when used for testing, is to maximize the impact of H (and so of the observations) on our belief in T. We might call this impact the "observational power" of the hypothesis, or the "power" of the observations to test the theory.

For example, if a theory of educational achievement should have implications about how fast American children could learn the Uzbek language (a Turkic language of central Asia), but there are very few op- portunities to hear or read Uzbek in the United States, then naturally observed vocabulary size in Uzbek found in the United States would not be a powerful way to study the educational achievement. One can, how- ever, imagine experimental situations in which differences in the speed of learning Uzbek might decide between theories. The observational power of the first study of spontaneous learning of Uzbek would be very low. The speed with which people in an experiment learn Uzbek might be very powerful, because very few people in the United States would be odd cases in the experiment on the grounds that they happened to know a Turkic language. For example, an experiment to test whether people who were effectively bilingual as children learn new languages faster, using Americans for experimental subjects, might well rationally use speed of learning Uzbek as an experimental outcome.

A key feature of the "power" of hypotheses is their probability under competing theories. A "crucial experiment" is a hypothesis that is very unlikely under almost all serious contending theories, and very likely (or in the impractical extreme, certain) under the one being tested. In statistical reasoning in the Bayesian style, the likelihood of a hypothesis under alternative theories is called the "*a priori* probability" of the hypothesis. One learns most from the observations if their *a priori* probability, so defined, is very different from their probability under the theory being tested. A theory that predicts otherwise improbable hypotheses is more "testable" by testing those hypotheses. Another way to say this is that the degree to which a hypothesis is a "crucial experiment" is proportional to its "observational power," which in turn is proportional to the difference between the *a priori* probability of the hypothesis and its probability under the theory being tested.

Quite often the difference between probabilities under the different theories can be increased greatly by a careful study of the competitors, as well as one's own theory. In much of sociology, and even more of sociological methodology, the alternative theory is that the relation between differences could well have been produced by chance; statistical inference rests on a well-developed theory of the power of an observational scheme to reject any theory that implies that the observations could have been produced by chance. Often, however, chance theories are very weak, and hierarchical modeling is a way to improve alternative chance theories. The logic of hierarchical modeling is easily extended to nonstatistical methods. It is, for example, central to Becker's analysis of participant observation (Becker, 1958).

Problem VII: Using Data to Refine Theories

ALL OF THE ABOVE uses of data can improve the theories of the discipline. The overall objective here is to increase the empirical content of the "theoretical axioms" accepted in the discipline. We include as part of the "axioms" the definitions of concepts that implicitly assert "this is the core of what works." The more that is predicted by these axioms, the more exact the theories' predictions, the closer the fit between solid theories of their component mechanisms and the aggregate (or "comparative statics") theory, the wider the boundaries within which the theory applies (and the more the scope or coverage of the theory is derived from the theory itself), the greater the empirical content. Thus, if our theories still have "everything else equal" in their hypotheses, they have more content if they explain what, exactly, are the other things that have to remain equal in order for a hypothesis to hold.

But those theoretical axioms also include the clear identification of the causal units in the theory (e.g., what is it about individual people that, sometimes at least, connects differences in attitudes with differences in behavior); clear definitions of concepts and clear connections of these with methods of observing differences; clear theories of why the measuring procedures work (and consequently of when we will expect them not to work); great temporal and processual detail about the crucial causal connections, especially rates of change under different conditions and rates of equilibration after disturbances; clear indications, which one can look for in naturally occurring phenomena, that the mechanisms in the theory are what is mainly going on; and, *perhaps* most important of all, the elimination of falsehoods from the theory. Epistemology sometimes seems to imagine that falsification is all that is going on, which is some exaggeration but by no means irrelevant.

One should, of course, be careful about eliminating bits of theory just because they are known to be false under some conditions, if they work in the conditions at hand. Adding a condition (e.g., "at least it works in the United States": eight out of eight articles in the August 2000 *American Sociological Review* require that condition, in the sense that data about generalization to other countries is not given in the papers) to an axiom *is* an improvement of empirical content. A theory is valuable sociology even if it is only known to apply in the United States, and even if no rationale in the theory explains the assumed boundary. Of course, a theory is better if it either applies everywhere, or if the theory itself gives a reason why it applies in the United States but not in many other places.

In short, a theory, all of whose parts have been subjected to a gale of intelligently designed and analyzed observations, has the most empirical content. A central device for overall increase in empirical content of theory is to cycle between improving the theories, and then improving concepts and measures (with data) in the light of the new theories, revising mechanisms (so they are compatible with data on lower level units, for example), and deriving hypotheses to test again, then returning to refining theory.

Self-Evaluation

THE ULTIMATE TEST of whether a reader has understood this book well enough is whether or not he or she goes on to contribute a great deal to the empirical content of sociological theory about how the world works. Of course, any failure to achieve that purpose may be the fault of the book, or of the student. Let me try to specify some ways that students can gauge intermediate steps to that ultimate objective, by which they can judge the combined product of the book and the student.

The central criterion is whether a student, reading a professional paper in sociology or related disciplines, can specify hypotheses that, if true, would add empirical content to the theoretical contribution of the paper. These may range from suggestions for how to measure a causal or effect variable better; to what special conditions of salience of a cultural matter in the setting or group observed might make the causal process not work elsewhere; to significant historical circumstances at the time and place of the data; to an experimental design to see whether, for a central causal mechanism in the theory of the paper, manipulations of the cause actually produce the effects alleged.

Inventing new hypotheses that will have observational power for the theory at hand is the central skill to learn. Writing a critique of a professional paper from a leading sociological journal, saying how to do it better, is then the central operational measure of whether I have taught, and the student has learned.

2   Distances as Central to Causal Reasoning and Methods

The Minimum Piece of Causal Information Is Two Distances

OUR FIRST PROBLEM IS THAT ALL CAUSATION is a relation between a distance of some sort on a cause, and a distance of some sort on the effect. The methodological problem is to relate this elementary theoretical fact to observations, particularly of distances. If a cause, such as a year more of education, is to produce a three-point increase in a measure of labor market advantage ("social status"), then the smallest useful piece of information about the cause from the world must be a distance between two observations on education on different people (or difference in average education between different years within a society, or in average education in two different societies). Here we have different units of analysis on which we observe difference in education (people, years, and societies—see chapter 6 on units of analysis), but what is common to them all is that we can measure the distances on years of education between them. This gives us enough information to specify a causal difference, which then might have a measurable (or "observable") effect.

To see whether this one piece of causal information has a defined effect, we must have a difference in the effect (here status in the labor market) that can be measured between at least two units of analysis. That is, we need information on social status from at least two people, two years, or two societies, and those measures have to be in a "metric" so that the distances are comparable. We will choose our units of analysis so that they have causal unity and have mechanisms within them that transform causes into effects (see chapter 6 below). Thus, we need to have the same units of analysis for our measures of the distance between causes and the difference between effects.

Of course, the causal unity of a person is of a different sort than the unity of a year, or the unity of a society. It may therefore "carry" the cause of a year of (average) education into the effect of social status in the labor market with different degrees of efficiency. For example, the distances may work through different mechanisms. A year of education may give a *person* a competitive advantage in getting a better job, while average education in a *later year* may measure the creation of more jobs requiring higher education in the meantime.

There is no reason that the increase in jobs requiring higher education between years should be the same as the increase in numbers of people with that level of education, even though individuals within the society may get whatever good jobs there are only if they personally have more education than others. But manual workers in the later year may be able to use computer output in doing their work, because they have more education. Thus, whether the three points of status are attached to a year of education may depend on whether the distance is between persons, or between years, or between societies. But the main point here is that in all three cases, we can find a single piece of information about the effect of education on labor market status only with two distances, in cause and effect. This entails at least four observations, whether on persons, years, or societies.

Similarly, we may only be able to measure by ethnographic methods the saliency of inheritance within a family of a complete herd (with calves, milking cows, pregnant cows, and bulls). We may wish to argue that nomads whose whole society depends on the product of herds will have a higher saliency of such herd inheritance in families than will a society engaged in diversified agriculture with some domestic animals, while at the same time the nomads will have a lower saliency of family inheritance of land. We then need at a minimum one herding society and one agricultural society, and saliency from ethnography of herd inheritance and land inheritance in both, to have any information at all on that causal connection. The minimum piece of ethnographic information for causal inference also involves at least one distance on the cause (herding versus agriculture) and one distance on the effect (herd salience versus land salience in family inheritance). Of course, the study of the agricultural society need not be by the same ethnographer as the study of the herding society.

In a social psychology laboratory, we likewise need a distance between "the experimental group" (actually the cause is usually applied to individuals rather than groups) and the control group on the presumed cause manipulated by the experimenter. We also need a distance in some measure of the effect variable after the cause has been applied to one and not to the other. In historical research we will need a measure of the passage of time or the occurrence of great events (e.g., colonial America versus postrevolutionary America), and a measure at both times of the effects (e.g., a high level of organization of representative territorial sub-governments with taxing and spending power). (Note that here we have the somewhat odd situation that the cause and the effect are "the same" variable: we will come back to this point later.)

In all the methods, then, testing a causal theory depends on observing at least two distances, which means at least four observations, before we have a single piece of causal information. The whole question of efficient study design for causal studies is what kinds of distances we can observe, on what units of analysis. Consequently, some detailed consideration of the concept of distance and its relation to observations, units of analysis, concepts, theories, and the like is useful for getting an intuitive grasp of how different methods cohere into the "methodology" of social science studies.

Difference, Distance, Units, Causes within Units

A "DISTANCE" IN ORDINARY GEOMETRY implies two points at the end of the line or other curve along which distance is measured. The simplest form of a distance merely says that the two points are different, with no "metric" for the distance between them. Thus, when we speak of "experimental" and "control" groups in drug trials, we are specifying, for example, that the researcher has given the new drug for the experimental group, and given the best old drug for the control group. We think of this as a "difference" rather than a "distance." That is, we describe the distance *only* with the two end-points, rather than with any notion of different distances that might have numbers (other than perhaps one and zero) attached to them. This is in contrast to experiments in which, for example, different dosages (including zero) are given to different experimental groups. This design is common with animal trials to estimate optimal dosage, which involves estimating a causal curve, but is not common for the first main human clinical trials.

If the drug were given in different doses to more than two groups of people (as sometimes happens after the first clinical trials, for example, when trying to find a dose that has most of the therapeutic effect without serious side effects), then we could think of each group having different distances to the others. These distances would be the differences in size of the dosage. A difference is most usefully described as something that might be a distance in the size of the effect(s) if it were "properly calibrated." Experiments on different dosages are attempts at calibration. There is not much use in calibrating something if it does not have any effect anyway. Nevertheless, a casual glance into a handbook on pharmaceuticals will show a "recommended dosage," implying some attempt at calibration.

But now let us think about what we might mean by a "point" at an end of a distance, and more particularly two points. The two points needed to create a difference must be observations "on" something, a unit of analysis on which something can be observed, and that something might be different between two such units. We have already mentioned three common units of analysis in sociology: persons, years, and societies. For a given theory, we can think of these as unified units that have a "common" level of a given variable.

For example, individuals who take a drug in an experiment have a common level of "experimental"; each of them will have a different level of "therapeutic effect," measured on the individual person. Thus "person" is the unit of analysis that is thought to connect drug taking to therapeutic effect. Each person in the experimental group is observed to have a "drug taken" value on the causal variable, and varying levels on the "therapeutic effect." When the subjects in an experiment are people who make decisions for themselves, they may not be well disciplined about it; there may, then, be "errors of measurement" in the amount and frequency of drug taking.

The only unity in such an experimental group is its common level of drug taking; the experimental group is not a unified thing that itself connects causes to effects. The members of the group may not meet at all, and may only come in once every three months to have the virus level in their blood checked. The mean level of drug taking, and the mean level of therapeutic effect, are "only" statistical phenomena. We may think that the mean level of education of a society makes possible high productivity of the whole (e.g., experts can communicate by computer with manual workers), and so higher mean incomes. But we do not believe that the group level of drug taking for a disease is acting above the level of individuals to produce therapeutic effects. Still, taking drugs that lower the virus level in the blood of HIV-positive patients does indeed have a social, "epidemiological," effect of lowering the transmission rate of the infection.

The first feature of "points" at the ends of a distance is that the units of analysis are at those points. This means that in the theory being tested, such units are unified enough internally that they connect causes to effects. Groups are sometimes the units of analysis in epidemiology, but not usually in drug trials. For example, epidemics of communicable diseases have higher rates of new infections if there are many carriers of the infection in the group rather than few, but not so many that there is nobody left to infect. That is because groups have the kinds of interaction within them that communicates infection, and so constitute a unit of analysis with a given prevalence of the infection, which has an effect on the incidence of infection in the group. The drug trials for an epidemic disease will also have individuals as units of the disease; for example, the effect of HIV drugs on transmission of the virus from pregnant mother to child is sometimes tested in experiments.

One would want to test a vaccine on individuals who were in a group having an epidemic, so that one could see whether the vaccine reduced an easily observable infection rate. Thus, in the United States one would want to test an HIV vaccine on homosexual men, or on drug addicts using intravenous injections, groups in which the infection rate is high enough that changes would be observable. Since people may not agree to take a risky vaccine unless they think they might be exposed to infection, an epidemic may be the only condition under which a vaccine test could get sufficient consent.

Though we usually do not think of it in this way, a point at the end of a distance is, first of all, a node connecting cause and effect in a theory, which we conventionally call a "unit of analysis." If the effect of mean education is the total productivity of a national economy, one would want units of analysis that have a national economy to study the effect of average educational levels. Individuals would be the wrong unit; they would not have end points of the distances on causes and effects that provide us with relevant information. The manual worker who can read a computer screen makes the inventory control expert for a factory more productive, more able to have a complex and efficient control system.

In general, the clearer the units of analysis, the easier it is to measure the values of variables. Individual people and nations are popular units of analysis for collecting data about distances in part because they have clear boundaries. Connections between causes and effects are produced by internal processes in both. But this clear boundary is not a necessary feature of a good unit of analysis. For example, the Sun has very vague boundaries. But from far enough away its gravitation can be treated as a point, its center of gravity, and its mass can be considered the gravitational force concentrated at that point, and similarly for the giant planet Jupiter. The orbits of the planets are ellipses, and so the distance varies over the course of a planet-year. Therefore, for gravitational purposes the distance between them is, after Newton, pretty well defined. (Refined analysis requires us to consider that they both revolve around the center of gravity of the Jupiter-Sun system; given the far greater mass of the Sun, for most purposes that is not very far from the Sun's center of gravity.)

The "point" from which one observes the distance from one of the unit of analysis to another is always approximate. At some level the unity of the unit of analysis has to be theorized, as Newton had to theorize the center of gravity of a coherent stellar body, and of a two-body system such as Jupiter and the Sun, and how the concept of distance has to be modified to take account of the eccentricity of the orbit. Ordinary scientists often do not theorize their units of analysis, because the units are routine in the paradigm they learned as young scientists.

But someone (John Dalton, for example) once had to theorize that atoms were the units of chemistry, and that they had different valences and different masses, even though we now learn that in secondary school, and still regard it as natural when we retire from Dupont decades later. Particle physics shows that atoms are not actually "points," and modern chemistry shows that different atoms of the same chemical element have different masses, though in their natural form on Earth the ratios of those weights are often constant. But all that is an improvement in the understanding of the units of analysis found and theorized by Dalton, and much empirical work went into developing improved theories of what atoms were and why they were the right units of analysis for chemistry. The same general kind of theorizing and empirical study of why people are units of analysis for the studies of political attitudes or choice of risks have improved our understanding of market behavior and public opinion.

The theoretical nature of the "distance" identified between two such problematically defined "points" is even more problematic. This is supposed to measure both distances (differences) on the cause, and distances on the effect. But the processes that produce differences in effect from differences in the cause are themselves always complex. Many things happen to people differently if they spend a year in school than if they do not, and the differences are different for different people. Further, the causal arrows from education to good jobs are very much affected by what jobs people are trying to get.

For example, education's effect on success at a sales job seems to be minimal, while its effect on academic jobs is maximal. Sales jobs depend much on experience in interaction with strangers, while academic life depends on facility in reading, writing, and perhaps mathematics. In the business world, education has very different effects on getting "professional" jobs, such as accountant or engineer, versus jobs in line management (where seniority counts a lot), or versus jobs in sales (where amount sold counts a lot, regardless of seniority or education). Thus, the causal distance of a year of education depends not only on what a person does in that year, but also on what connects education to success at getting or holding jobs. It is clear from studies of the matter that these connections are different in different jobs, and in different countries.

The concept of distance seems moderately clear when we are studying Jupiter's orbit around the Sun, because gravitation is the main concept that connects them and has a well-described relation to distance (at these distances and masses), and the "end points" of the centers of gravity are well theorized. But when we think about what a year of education really consists of, and what three points on a status scale mean for the use of that year of education in sales versus engineering, it is not at all clear that we know what these distances are all about.

We deal with such problems in chapter 4, when we analyze how to approach defining concepts involving distances, like "education," "occupational success," or—particularly problematic—"race." The basic argument there is that we should use research to establish what concepts "really mean," and then should refine our observations so that we can be sure that the differences in our observations are really the distances we have theorized about in our causal theories. We want our concepts to "really mean" whatever it is that is causally relevant in a given situation, and what exactly it causes. Eventually we will come to a much more theoretical view of what a "distance" is. This in turn will suggest how we should think about study design. We want to be sure that we have well-observed distances between units of analysis on causal concepts so defined as to be exactly what is doing the causing, and well-observed distances of effect variables that, in their turn, have an exact diagnosis built into them of exactly what is being caused.

The problems of observing the distance on causes and the distance on effects are equally difficult. For example, the example given above suggests that social mobility into a job involving sales is really a different sort of thing, to be differently explained, than social mobility into a job involving engineering. This is redefining the thing being explained, so that a particular fact—that education is not very important in one of them, and is very important in the other—will not confuse our overall theory of stratification of a new generation as it depends on the stratification of the old, through effects of parents on the education of their children.

The very conception of distances as central to the most elementary piece of information not only requires at least four observations—two on the cause and two on the effect—but also requires us to have a theory of what kinds of units connect causes to effects (the "units of analysis") and what their boundaries are. We must also have a conception of what it is about the distances between observations on the causes that has the effect, and what it is about the distances on the effects that is being caused. There are two kinds of concepts that make the two distances matter: one describing the units of analysis that connect causes to effects, and another describing what it is about the distances that does the causing and that constitutes the core of the effect. (Chapters 4 and 6 provide extensive analyses of both kinds of concepts.)

Closer and Farther: Numbers, Lines, and Curves

I HAVE HINTED IN THE EXAMPLES given above that distances are often connected to numbers, such as the distance of one year of education or of three points on a status scale or of the millions of kilometers between Jupiter and the Sun. I contrasted experimental groups and control groups according to whether there was simply a difference between those who got the experimental drug and those who got the old drug, or whether there were differences in dosage as well, within the experimental group. A dosage is a number, a complicated number, usually a number of grams per kilogram of body weight per unit of time.

But for some of the reasoning in the examples, I merely commented on the difference—for example, asking if inheritance of herds within families was more salient in nomadic herding societies than in agricultural societies, and whether family land inheritance was more salient in the agricultural ones. In the case of a difference, we have no ranking of distances as near or far, but instead must work with a "dichotomy," cutting the total population into two groups. We may obtain stronger and more exact scientific results if we can distinguish distances as closer or farther. For example, for some purposes, gender is really a dichotomy, though "femininity" is not; it is important to rank distances on scales of femininity, but usually not on gender.

The distance of "a year of schooling" immediately suggests first that there is a difference between getting that year or not. But we also think that a distance between two people of one year is less than a distance of two years, and a lot less than four years. We may not want to say that all years of schooling are the same. For instance, in the United States the difference between grade ten and grade eleven has a much smaller effect on the duration of unemployment after leaving school than does the difference between grade eleven and grade twelve. And a worker with four years of high school earns less money than one with four years of college, on the average. But other things equal, a distance of two years is a farther distance than one, three farther than two (and so much farther than one), and so on.

The general tendency of quantitative sociology is to attach numbers to different distances, creating a "measure of distance" in which groups of differences may be ordered by size, and all recognized differences are thought of as being equal in size. We usually use linear relations among variables, so that nominally equal distances are assumed to create equal distances on the effect variable; we say then that "the relation is linear." The quality of the calibrations in social science is almost never good enough to justify the equality of distances, and the theory usually is not refined enough to tell what would be a good way of observing equal distances.

The linearity assumption is very often violated, in ways that are quite interesting. For example, it seems that one dollar is as good as another, and indeed if one has twice as many dollars one can buy twice as many tons of carrots (or a little more, perhaps, with quantity discounts). But to predict satisfaction with income, or to predict how much motivation an additional amount of money would provide, one should almost always use percentages rather than absolute numbers of dollars. If a person has $10,000 a year, and goes to $11,000, that is a distance of 10 percent; although the distance from $100,000 to $110,000 (likewise 10 percent) will buy ten times as many tons of carrots as a distance of $1,000, it seems to have about the same motivational effect or satisfaction effect. For example, to "give a generous raise" to a person earning $10,000, one might give an extra $1,000; to give an "equally generous" raise to one earning $100,000 will probably cost $10,000. That is why almost all equations describing salaries or satisfactions use logarithms of income or wealth in dollars, before measuring distances. Taking logarithms causes equal percentage differences to be equal. Thus, for sociological purposes, the logarithm of income or wealth is usually a well-behaved number with linear relations to other variables. In its raw form, income has curvilinear relations to almost everything, except tons of carrots.

Age is another variable where the unit of a year is almost always sociologically meaningless. Almost everything sociologically interesting has major discontinuities in the period between sixteen years and twenty-five years, where many "transitions to adulthood" take place, and again between about sixty and seventy, when many other "transitions" take place. Aside from nonlinearities in these transition periods, almost all sociologically significant activities show curved relationships to age. Examples are hours of child-care work, numbers of people in the household, sickness and handicaps, wages and salaries, equity in a home, probability of migration, and crime and other sorts of deviance (even automobile accidents, which apparently have a lot of "deviance" in their causation). It is almost always true that when a sociological paper has a linear treatment of age, it is because the authors have not looked at the data showing the curve.

The general point here is that the attachment of a number to an observation in causal analysis is a deep problem, and the problem is whether the distances between numbers measure the distances of the cause and of the effect. For most variables most of the time, almost any reasonable way of attaching numbers, treated as an equal-interval variable with linear effects, is better than a dichotomy, and there is not usually much difference when more nearly correct distances are properly calibrated. So age and income (and variables deeply confounded with them, such as education, seniority, or wealth), where the inequalities of intervals are pervasive and strong, are the exceptions. Equal intervals are almost always significantly wrong for those variables. Otherwise, carelessness in attaching numbers is aesthetically bothersome, but usually better than dichotomies. Almost everything in sociology is linear and additive, to a good approximation.

But after all, the equality of intervals in distances is a theoretical assertion about how the world works. That theory can be investigated. Often where it is important scholars will show that they have an intuitive grasp of those inequalities. For example, many histories of revolutions treat the prerevolutionary period a decade at a time, the revolutionary period roughly a year at a time (but crucial transitions between governments a day at a time), and postrevolutionary deposits of revolutionary "achievements and failures" a half-century at a time. (Recall my brief discussion of federalism in the United States in chapter 1.) Similarly, creating a dichotomy between "activists" or "militants" or "professional revolutionaries" may implicitly reflect the curvilinear effects of activity level in politics or social movements. Many effects of participation in a movement are strongly curvilinear with activity level. It would be better to treat activity level as a continuous variable with discontinuities or curvilinearities in effects, but that is often impractical. So a dichotomy may be better than hours of activities.

Proper calibration of unequal intervals is often impractical because the curves come in the extreme values of a variable, and the observational scheme does not reach the extreme values. Efficiency in sampling design is then necessary to do calibration studies, and the usual random samples in sociology are very inefficient for that purpose. One must oversample activists to calibrate intervals of activity level, oversample the homeless to calibrate poverty, oversample criminals to find unequal intervals in the propensity to violence, oversample wives and children of those with high propensity to violence to find unequal intervals in the effects of victimization, and so on. Ethnographies of extreme groups, or "clinical" studies of rare social-psychological disorders, are an especially important technique for identifying such discontinuities (a wonderful example, which combines ethnography and quantitative study, is Zablocki, *Alienation and Charisma* [1980]).

In later chapters I discuss some common techniques for dealing with the hypothesis that numbers attached to observations have unequal intervals or curvilinearities and discontinuities in effects.

The Centrality of Distances in Later Chapters of This Book

IN CHAPTER 3 we see that distances are central to economy in data collection because one should choose what to study in order to maximize *useful distances*. This is easiest to see when the central relation one wants to study is linear. One can get a very good estimate of the slope of a linear relation by taking, say, the seven largest cases on the "independent variable" and the seven smallest cases, taking the means of both these extreme samples, then computing the slope of the line that connects them. Furthermore, the t-test for the difference between these means will, in the average size sample in sociology, be reasonably near the significance level of the t-test of the regression coefficient. That is, most of the information that is in the large sample about the linear relation of the two variables is in the specially designed sample of fourteen cases. If only one knew how to sample those fourteen beforehand, one might collect the data for a good academic paper in a week.

But the general methodological principle that follows from this concentration of the information about causes in the largest distances between cases is that oversampling extreme cases is almost always rational. More specifically, for linear relations, one should always choose the next case for the sample to be the one having the greatest average squared distance from the other cases. If one already has a sample, then supplementing it with a few cases known to be at the extreme of one or more of the variables is always a great help in increasing the observational power of a study. (The best example I know of this is Stouffer, *Communism, Conformity, and Civil Liberties* [1955], with a large oversample of organizational leaders—leaders, he shows, have a much higher level of commitment to civil liberties.)

Furthermore if one wants to study the mechanisms of causation more intensively using ethnographic or historical methods requiring more work per fact, one would be well advised to start by scanning a large sample to find extreme cases, and to study several extreme cases on the variables of interest intensively. Ethnographers often make use of this strategy, by studying extreme deviants or people in extreme situations, and contrasting them implicitly with the people they meet in everyday life. (Becker, *Outsiders* [1963a], has several examples of studying extreme deviants; for an extreme situation, see Fox, *Experiment Perilous* [1974 (1959)].)

In chapter 4 I discuss how to conceptualize the distances between observations, and how to use data to improve observation of distances or end-points. If anything is a unified cause, then several observations of its value ("measures" broadly conceived) should give the same results. And insofar as it reliably causes a given effect, all of the various kinds of observations that might measure the effect should be correlated among themselves, and should also be correlated with all the good measures of the cause.

Consider, for example, the saliency among nomadic tribes of inheritance of the whole herd that can support a large family. We find that, as Chinese irrigated agriculture penetrated the valleys leading to the central Asian steppe, and the oases along the mountain chains to the south of that steppe, more "nomadic" tribes came to depend for their subsistence on payments in rice for military and political services and loyalties (see Lattimore, 1967 [1940], passim). We would expect various signs of decreasing dominance of herd inheritance, perhaps decreasing coherence of large patrilocal-marriage families depending on the herds, increasing salience of family political coherence and inheritance of political status. That is, the effects should hang together, and so should decline together with increasing dependence on products of agricultural land.

According to the theory, increasing dependence on agricultural land ought to decrease saliency of family herd inheritance, and increase saliency of land inheritance and inheritance of political position. There are hints of such developments in Lattimore (1967 [1940]). To this ethnographer-historian, looking for the central dynamics of social, political, and economic life along the boundary between nomadic and agricultural life, there was nothing inaccessible about the method of looking for correlations among indicators of effects, among indicators of the causes, or of all observations on both. He used data on a multitude of indicators of distinctive nomadic groups and agricultural groups, culled from an ancient text here, a walking trip with a Mongol guide there, a secondary source on the spread of irrigation in a third place, tales of European travelers to oases in a fourth.

In chapter 6, on mechanisms, I take up explicitly the problem of what happens in the distances, and especially what happens within units of analysis to make the distances causally effective. One of the central ways we can increase the precision and suppleness of causal theories is to look in detail at the mechanisms in them. Very often those mechanisms are "inside" the units of analysis. For instance, making explicit choices about whether each dollar spent on a thing is giving a dollar's worth of return, and comparing returns on expenditures so as to maximize, generally requires sophisticated accounting of both expenditures ("costs") and returns. Corporations do much more sophisticated accounting of both than do smaller businesses or families. Therefore, the central mechanism of economic theory, rational maximization, applies much better to corporations than to families, and so the theories of economics predict the behavior of corporate markets much better than the economics of consumption markets. Polls of "consumer confidence" are often the best one can do for consumption markets, while inventories play a theoretically well-defined role in manufacturing and wholesale markets. Asking consumers for an estimate of the total value of the inventory of stuff in their basement, attic, and garage would not predict much, except for the funny look they would give the crazy interviewer.

Chapter 7, on testing theories, focuses on developing the kinds of hypotheses that maximize the observational power of the observations. That is, we want hypotheses about observations of such a character that we will learn a lot about a causal theory from the results. Obviously the optimization of well-measured distances, dealt with in chapter 3, is central to that. But in addition we want to specify what kinds of observations maximize the rejection of alternative theories, by deriving exactly those observations from the theory we are advancing that are most improbable under alternative theories. Or in more naturalistic ethnographic or historical observation, we want to be able to recognize the rare observation that could hardly have occurred unless our theory were true. This is, of course, a new kind of distance—a distance of observations from those that would have been observed had a different theory been true. An observer of "naturalistic" life should have a keen eye for observed phenomena that have this special kind of distance from what would be true if the theory being supported were false, or vice versa.

Chapter 8 principally concerns using the results of observations to refine theories, so as to construct a line of continually better theories. We look in a new way at the results of previous chapters in which distances of various kinds are central. Though it is mostly implicit by this time, the notion that distances are central to methodology of all sorts still plays a role here, illuminated by the discussions in all the preceding chapters.

3   The Basic Structure of Economy in Social Research

The Centrality of Distances in Study Design

IN CHAPTER 2 I used mainly examples in which causal differences were differences among people, and associated them with the "variables" that are measured in surveys or censuses. But such surveys are very expensive to conduct, and it is very difficult to make them describe well a system of social action, where one person's acts depend on the acts of others. This method makes the measures easy to discuss as numbers, and the distances as differences between numbers. In this chapter I turn to the second problem, the economy of research design.

In addition to examples of reasoning about people, I have presented examples of reasoning about distances between societies, or within groups where an epidemic disease is prevalent so that the prevalence of the disease predicts the incidence of new infections. But it is not a simple matter to generalize a principle that one should look for extreme cases in a sample, or that one should study extreme distances with added care so as to explore mechanisms and the true meaning of distances. This chapter reanalyzes this and other problems by examining "economy" in study design. The basic notion is that every piece of information has a cost. The increasing value of an observation with increasing squared distance from the others already in one's sample does not have an immediate intuitive analogue to, for example, using a denser time sampling during times of revolution than in the prerevolutionary or postrevolutionary periods.

To take another example, consider an ethnographer collecting diverse treatments of inheritance of herds in marital negotiations, adoption of previous children of the in-marrying wife, the overall power of the head of the lineage over all his adult sons and grandsons, and the preservation of the herd in one piece by brothers herding jointly after the head of the lineage dies, until they are each ready to form a complete herd and a family to tend it. It is clear that we are studying an extreme herding-nomadic society, but it is not clear why we want to know all these things that indicate that it is high in saliency of family inheritance of herds, not of individual animals. It is obvious that these are the sorts of things historians and ethnographers should include in their study design, but the logical and optimizing principles are not clear. In this chapter we will try to expand to these other problems the simple principle whose application to regression analysis is so obvious. We will do this by taking explicit account of the costs of different sorts of data in different research situations.

Let me now give some examples of strategies and problems that occur in the "economics" of choosing among methods. I shall then return to some general points about the strategy of seeking extreme observations.

Differences among Cultures or Societies

INSOFAR AS SOCIAL ANTHROPOLOGY AND HISTORICAL SOCIOLOGY are involved in comparing "whole cultures" or "whole social systems," they also have the problem of figuring out what *differences* among cultures or social systems to "sample" and "observe." Many times the distances that one ought to concentrate on are quite different in different parts of the world or different types of societies. For example, much of modern historical sociology is concerned with what produces the differences among the government social welfare systems of rich countries (these are small differences in percentage terms). Usually the central variable to be explained is either their difference in generosity to the poor, or their difference in generosity to women who have not been fully employed (e.g., some governments provide pensions proportional to incomes having been earned in the labor market, much disadvantaging women who have worked as housewives).

The biggest differences among countries in overall generosity to the poor (and also in overall generosity to women, though there are great differences among cultures in this respect that are not related to societal wealth; see Charrad, 2001) are those between very poor countries and very rich ones. The problem for a researcher today is that we discovered that about five decades ago, and found a few mechanisms that explained it, though these were not very satisfactory. There is not much theoretical interest in those mechanisms anymore.

Among countries of intermediate average incomes, such as Cuba and Brazil, the big cause of generosity seems to be having had a communist government. Ex-communist countries have, at least on paper, much more generous policies. This may also apply among very poor countries, but it is hard to tell: mainland China certainty has more generous social welfare policies than India, for example, and the poorer Muslim countries in former Soviet central Asia seem to have more generous ones than comparable Muslim countries in Africa.

To sample differences in this comparative problem, one has to *choose which differences to explain.* The difference between Cuba and Brazil on generosity of the welfare system to the poor is to be explained by Cuba being ex-communist and so much more generous, which is a different cause than the difference between two rich countries of western Europe, such as the Netherlands and Switzerland. Between Switzerland, with a stingy policy, and the Netherlands, with a generous policy, there are roughly two variables: the power of the labor movement, stronger in the Netherlands, and the high proportion of all Swiss workers who are not natives or citizens. That is, the substance of the big differences between generous rich countries of western Europe and stingy ones is different from the differences in generosity between two medium-developed Latin American nations. The labor movement in Cuba is weak, at least in the sense that it cannot go against government policy, while that in Brazil is free but poorly organized, and both countries have a high proportion of native citizens.

Similarly, if one asks why unemployed people in India moderately often die of starvation, while this rarely happens in any of the other countries named above (Brazil, no doubt, would have the highest rate), the answer would be different yet: namely, that India is still one of the poorest countries in the world, and poor countries have very little redistribution from the better off families to the worse off. (Sri Lanka, with much the same cultural tradition and level of poverty, has almost no starvation, but many deaths in civil war.) The choice of which country differences to study determines the outcome of identifying the causes of generosity.

To turn from historical sociology to social anthropology, we find the same for studying differences *among* herding tribes (e.g., those in Africa versus those in central Asia) in social structure, versus studying the differences *between* herding tribes *and* horticultural or agricultural tribes within those areas. Central Asian herding tribes have sometimes herded horses (often mixed with cattle), while hardly any African tribes do; this often meant that the Asian tribes' economy was military, and depended on tribute from or plunder of agricultural tribes. Horticultural tribes, in both Asia and Africa, have a much higher ratio of land that is property of an individual or a family to land that is "common property" of the tribe. So if we choose to study differences within Africa between tribes that are herding and those that are agricultural (i.e., common versus private land tenure), we will get different cultural differences in economic matters than if we compare Asian herding tribes to African herding tribes (e.g., more Asian horse-based military tribes versus more African tribes whose subsistence is based on cattle, or camels, or goats and sheep). This is one of many problems that will occupy us in this chapter. We will go in a somewhat disorganized fashion through a lot of ways that information can be more or less costly, or more or less useful. Throughout, we will apply the general principle that we want to find the cheapest right answer.

Intensity of Observation

THE QUANTITATIVE MODEL OF RESEARCH outlined in chapters 1 and 2 supposes that one will pay the same attention to all the different cases: if one collects much information on some cases, one should collect much information on others. Throwing out most cases in the middle, as I have come close to urging, is merely the extreme of a variable of intensity of observation. It says to put the intensity of observation in the middle of the distribution on values of the causal variable to zero, if the investigator is interested in causes and does not have any of the curvilinearity, interaction, and deviant-case problems mentioned below. The ordinary theory of sampling says that one should know the same amount of information about all the units of observation, once one has decided to study the population of which they are members. But I have said already that we will find out more by intensive observation of extreme cases—of the Sun, for example—than by equally careful observation of all the members of the population or of the sample (of the Sun and planets, for example). If we pick cases by oversampling extremes, then we should use intense observation to collect a lot of information on the extreme ones. The reason is that extreme cases have more information in them that is not already in the average of the cases. In particular, they have much information on why they are not average, which is what we need for causal theorizing.

Let me first give a rough philosophical basis for this. Every entity is really a group of phenomena, and multiple observations on a single entity, especially if done over time, are really a sample of processes in or on that entity. We can learn a lot if we apply theories to say what will happen next, after one of the phenomena; what should be "in between" two observations; or how the entity will respond to a cause one way when one phenomenon is manifested, another way when another phenomenon is there.

Take the case of sunspots: how else but by their darkness might we judge the temperature of sunspots as compared to the rest of the Sun's apparent surface? No other bodies in the solar system have sunspots. We can consider *the set of phenomena associated with a given entity* (in this case the Sun) as a population of phenomena, in this case sunspot phenomena associated with a lower temperature we do not know how to explain. If we can penetrate the mechanisms of that one case, we might be able to go check it somewhere else—for instance, on another star. To come back to sociology, this suggests that if extreme religious groups, for example, generally seem to occupy more of the lives of their members than do mainstream religious groups, then we might study the special dynamics of those that occupy the whole of the lives of their members. We learn a lot about religions that do just that by intensive observation of one intensively governed "intentional community," or "commune" (see Zablocki, 1971). We can then go on to study a sample of more various communes (see Zablocki, 1980). Zablocki tried to find out the dynamics by studying the extremes, then to apply the dynamics to studying a range of cases. Wonderful stuff; too bad we are not interested in communes any more.

Let me again, for respectability, choose an example from another science, namely, geology. Roughly forty years ago the theory of plate tectonics on the Earth gained widespread acceptance as an explanation for the origins of mountain chains, for quite a lot of volcanism, for many earthquakes (especially the big ones), and for the magnetic stripes on the basaltic ocean floor that change polarity from one time of extrusion to another. By intense study of one case, the Earth, which was known to have tectonic movements, scientists developed many theories of its mechanisms and its symptoms. One such theory concerned convection currents in the mantle, where lighter hot stuff came up in one place and cooler, heavier stuff went down in another; scientists theorized that this could create very slow (centimeters per year) "currents" in the mantle even though it is obviously solid.

After much of this study, data about the surface of the planet Venus began to come in, by radar studies from satellites. The data showed that Venus has volcanism, but none of the symptoms of tectonic movements. To put it another way, almost all the mountains are volcanoes, but there are no "collision of plates" mountain ranges, such as the Rockies or the Himalayas, with a few volcanoes interspersed. By studying the Earth intensively, where plate tectonics was known to occur, scientists knew what to look for to see whether Venus also showed tectonic activity.

Similarly, Switzerland stands out among European states in having very ungenerous provisions for the poor in its federal-state welfare system. (Switzerland has many government powers concentrated on cantons, and because the country is so small, these serve as the first level below the national state apparatus. That's why I use the phrase "federal-state" to describe Switzerland's welfare system.) Japan stands out among the big, rich countries for its stinginess with the poor, except for poor Japanese farmers. But Japan has a very unified government, with few powers concentrated on the localities. One has the suspicion that a detailed historical study of each would show a lot, but that the two would show very different mechanisms causing stinginess. But a detailed study of Switzerland would be a good place to start in a theory of why the United States also has a stingy system. Japan might be a good place to study intensively to develop a theory of why Great Britain differs from the other highly unified states of Europe in having a much stingier system. (Sweden and Denmark, for instance are much more generous, as is Italy for the elderly.)

So once one has found a very extreme system, one can think of intensifying observations on that one case as sampling in a different population—namely, the population of phenomena on that one extreme. The purpose is to see the processes at the extreme. If one of the entities is much easier to study than the others, the same logic applies. We can study processes (sunspots) on the Sun much more easily than on any other star, and plate tectonics on the Earth much more easily than on any other planet. The second of these is a purely economic principle: study the entities where the data are the cheapest. One can afford a great deal more detailed study if it is inexpensive to get the data on a case. If the data are cheap, one can throw away a lot of data to sift out the few that tell what the symptoms of plate tectonics are. But the first is a purely epistemological piece of economic advice on research: study the entities that are likely to have the most information you do not already have.

Sparse Fields and the Expense of Getting a Grip on a Case

IN GENERAL IN SOCIOLOGY (AS IN GEOLOGY AND PALEONTOLOGY) each "case" is very expensive to come by, so if the researcher does not get a lot out of it, it is not very worthwhile. The low end of expensiveness per case is survey research with random samples, where each hour of interviews, done in person, costs about ten hours of finding the person. (See the appendix at the end of this chapter for more sampling troubles in sociologically significant samples.)

Good random samples, including good samples of extremes on some variables, are much cheaper in countries with complete and up-to-date population registers. If sociologists can figure out something to study in Norway or Denmark, they should do it. Telephone surveys reduce the ratio of finding time to interviewing time, which often more than compensates for the fact that the researcher does not find people who do not have easy access to a phone.

In general it is more expensive to find an extreme case than an ordinary case, but sometimes the reverse is true. For instance, being seriously ill is an extreme case. But sampling through a hospital, or a neonatal intensive care unit in a hospital (see Heimer and Staffen, 1998c, excerpted below in chapter 8), is actually cheaper than a random sample, once the researcher is "on the inside." But how researchers get the extreme cases depends on what they are studying. Getting access to criminal social activity; identifying all the people referred to in a historical document; learning the language, getting to highland New Guinea, getting empathy with the culture, and not dying in the process: all these are very expensive. Getting close to another star besides the Sun is very expensive indeed. And, of course, getting access to a big distance often requires twice as much work and expense, because the researcher needs two expensive extreme cases.

There is a reason, then, that much of experimental social psychology is about college freshmen and sophomores in large elementary classes in research universities, and that much of the rest of psychology once used laboratory rats as subjects. Good samples of the population are too expensive for subdisciplines and whole disciplines, when they need at least fifty reliable differences between experimental and control groups.

However, social psychology shows that people can learn a great deal if they sample "inefficiently" (e.g., getting only sophomores). *If* a psychologist can produce experimental control over the creation of differences in that bad sample, then unless *differences* between experimental and control groups are different for sophomores than for the rest of the world (i.e., unless there are "interactions among causal variables and sopho-morism"), social psychology is home free. In general, differences have more nearly the same effects or causes in different samples than is true of the values of variables on the cases. For example, in almost all countries in the world, as people go from being poor to becoming rich, they spend on food with the first new dollars or rupees, on cameras with the last, and on cheap cameras before expensive ones. That generalization is true in India as well as the United States, in Uganda as in Great Britain.

Nevertheless, we should be suspicious when a linguistics professor at MIT says that the upper limit of the number of a certain kind of gram-matical complexity that people can keep track of is about seven, when we ourselves have to read sentences twice or three times when they have two subordinate clauses with a couple of multiple-word adverbials—that is, four such complexities. One has a suspicion that perhaps it matters that seven is a number based on experiments with MIT students.

Finally, since what sociologists care about is differences, and they want the differences to be clear, they need to get *comparable* data on at least two cases. Quite often they cannot get data that are exactly comparable. The toughest case I have run into in my own research is the differences in the degree of oppressiveness of slavery on Caribbean islands. When I first looked at the subject some forty years ago, there was not much cheap data available in the form of secondary historical literature on most of the islands. In the intervening forty years universities grew up on the islands, so there were more historians who were close to the documents. This was coupled with greater U.S. foreign policy interest in the islands, and so more grants to study them. The amount of cheap data has increased greatly.

Stinchcombe Methods Slavery Short Version

From Arthur L. Stinchcombe, "The Constitution of the Data," in *Sugar Island Slavery in the Age of Enlightenment: The Political Economy of the Caribbean World* (Princeton: Princeton University Press, 1995), pp. 152–158. The text as given here follows the original very closely. The references are left in the text, though they do not appear in the reference list at the back of this book; they are here to suggest the method, not to teach Caribbean history. Similarly, references to tables in the original publication are left in. Two of the tables (4.1 and 5.1) appear on pages 304 and 305 below.

This appendix discusses the combined conceptualization and measurement process resulting in the evaluations of the variables on islands or on subgroups of slaves for Tables 4.1, 5.1, and 5.2. The data are "ecological," measurements of social structures, which tend to have higher reliability than measurements of individuals. But all of them are constituted by observations on several indicators, some of which are missing for each case, most of which are missing for some cases, and are sometimes derived from informal observation by historical actors or by historians. The data are closer to "diagnoses" than to "measurements." They are about named historical entities, so that experts in several of the islands can check for my errors, and future work can be better.

The first intervening variable in the text, explaining the practical daily deprivation of freedom in slaves' lives, is the degree to which an island had a "slave society" in the late eighteenth century. In Tables 4.1 and 5.1, this is measured by its presumed causes. The core meaning of this variable is the degree to which the island government has a disposition to react powerfully to suppress any source or symptom of slave free choice, regardless of costs of [that] suppression in other values.

My first judgment of this disposition was derived from a combination of: (1) defenses of slave society principles from defenders of slave domination as the principal end and purpose of island government, such as Poyer (1971 [1908]) for Barbados or Edwards (1801; 2, pp. 39–46, 150–186) for Jamaica, (2) accounts by unfriendly observers at the time, such as the liberal slaveowner Lewis (1929 [1815–1817]) for Jamaica, or the first civilian English governor of Trinidad, quoted extensively in Naipaul (1984 [1969]), or (3) from general scholarly accounts trying to identify features of harder and softer slave systems, such as Tannenbaum (1946) or Klein (1967) contrasting Spanish and English colonies, Goveia (1980 [1965]) for Antigua, Tarrade (1972) for the French islands with emphasis on Martinique, Bangou (1989) for Guadeloupe, Hoetink (1982 [1972], 1958, background chapters) for Curaçao and the Dominican Republic, Scott's background sections (1985) for Cuba, and miscellaneous sources for smaller islands.

The facts available on individual societies vary a great deal from case to case, since the different original authors were interested in different things, or had different theories about the same things. The facts ranged from passage of discriminatory laws against colored entrepreneurs in Barbados because entrepreneurial success might encourage insubordination among slaves, to slave right of ownership and sale of products from subsistence plots in Jamaica, to the colored mother of one of the post-slavery Presidents of the Dominican Republic being bought as a slave, later treated as married to her owner and free, without apparent formal manumission, to a burst of laws imposing new restrictions, for example against emigration or settling on mountain farms, passed immediately after emancipation in Jamaica (Holt 1992). These facts provide evidence about which islands had the most intensive slave societies, at a level of "global coding" of whatever is said about the island by its historians and contemporary writers, and is not formally used in the data here.

With this tentative set of contrasts, I then looked at data on economic and political history to see what could explain the variation tentatively observed. Facts about economic and political history were in general much easier to obtain more systematically than comparable judgments of negative polity responses to marginal slave freedom. As it turned out, features of the economic and political histories of the islands were apparently the big causes. This availability of better data on the causes than on the symptoms led to the unusual strategy of measuring the effect by its causes. Estimates for the three main variables at the level of islands (in Tables 4.1 and 5.1) of the degree an island had a slave society were constructed from varying information as available.

The dates of most rapid growth of sugar plantation development on the frontiers were shaped by the general ideas obtained from the S-shape of most growth curves, often modeled by the logistic. I also used: high slave imports; percent African and percent male of the slave population; high ratio of slaves to [free] colored. [Note that one must use data in the terms of recordkeepers in the eighteenth and nineteenth centuries, who did not choose their language to fit the political and racial sensitivities of the twentieth or twenty-first century; "coloured" then routinely meant people of mixed race who were free, but occasionally when it was clear that emancipation was not at stake, distinctions by color were made among slaves.] New plantations being opened only by substantial investments in roads to the interior measured a late stage of frontier development.

As a last resort or a check on uncertain judgments, I have used a high ratio of the population reported in the eighteenth century to modern population as a measure of being near the end of sugar development, a low ratio as indicating low development. For example, in the late eighteenth century Haiti had a population about five to seven times as large as the Dominican Republic, while now they are about equal. This indicates that Haiti was near the end of its sugar development, while the Dominican Republic's sugar boom was mainly in the nineteenth and early twentieth centuries. Since the time of sugar development is easily established in these two cases, the comparison on population growth since validates the ratio measure to some degree. When we use it as a check on uncertain dating, for example, in Antigua (which has a high ratio of eighteenth to twentieth century population), we can have some confidence that it was an old sugar island by the late eighteenth century, sugar having filled its niche before that time. These multiple sources, informally combined according to what was available, constitute the "timing of the frontier" variable in Table 4.1.

The proportion of the economy occupied by sugar when sugar had filled its niche is fairly well measured by the proportion slave when the frontier period was over, with three big exceptions. The first exception is that the peak of sugar production often came after emancipation: all of the Spanish islands but Cuba (the Dominican Republic, Puerto Rico, and Trinidad, plus Guyana, and one could make a case for Cuba as well). In that case one has to measure the exslave labor force and the free Creole [of African ancestry; sometimes the word *creole* or its cognates is used to denote whites born in the colonies as well, for example, in Louisiana] and coolie labor force after full development.

The second is that entrepôt ports such as Curaçao, Charlotte Amalie (on St. Thomas), Havana, Kingston, St. Pierre (on Martinique) or St. Eustatius (a Dutch Leewards island) produced economic value out of proportion to their (mostly free and domestic slave) population. Sugar production as a proportion of the economy on an island with an entrepôt is overestimated by the proportion slave.

The third is that on islands with much foothill land such as Jamaica, a varying but substantial part of the effort of slaves went into subsistence production. Some sugar slave labor produced part of its total economic production by producing provisions on such islands, and not all of their labor can therefore be counted as sugar labor.

For these reasons I have often used geographical correlates of low proportion sugar in the economy (e.g., mountains or insufficient rainfall predict low proportions [except when irrigation is possible]). I have also used demographic indicators other than proportion slave:

peasant or runaway slave populations in the interior; tobacco, coffee, or cattle exports; fishing or pearl diving villages; mining villages or metal exports;... shipyards, chandlery, forestry for ship timbers; or peddlers to the interior from market towns.

Conversely sugar booms after Spanish or French restrictions on sugar cultivation or trade were loosened either temporarily (as with the British conquests of Havana and Guadeloupe in the mid-eighteenth century) or permanently (as with the stabilization of independence of the Dominican Republic in the mid-nineteenth century, British conquest of Trinidad confirmed in 1800, French conquest of Haiti and British conquest of Jamaica early in the colonial period) show that the previous demographic and economic indicators did not measure the size of the sugar niche, because the boom indicates previously unexploited opportunities. The failure of the same types of conquest to produce the same boom effects on the British Windwards or Curaçao shows they did not have such large sugar niches.

I did not construct a formal algorithm to adjust for such factors, because formal algorithms would run aground on missing data problems. And sometimes a given indicator quite apparently gives the wrong result (e.g., Jamaica and Puerto Rico are about equally mountainous by the obvious indicators, but Jamaica had a fairly large sugar niche relative to the rest of its economy, Puerto Rico a small[er] one). This summarizes the construction of the data in Table 4.1 and its summary in the vertical dimension of Table 5.1.

The powers the empires granted to local island governments and the representation of planter interests in those government, the combination of which gives the dimension of local autonomy in Table 5.1, are usually quite transparent in general historical treatments. For example, good treatments are found in Geggus (1982) and Frostin (1975) on Haiti, Lémery (1936) on Martinique, Pérotin-Dumon (1985) on Guadeloupe, Halperin Donghi (1969) on Spanish America generally, Borde (1892), Naipaul (1984 [1969]) and Williams (1962) on Trinidad under the Spanish. There are thus usually multiple sources on the government of the important islands, especially the English ones. Sometimes, as with the Danish (now American) Virgins and Swedish (now French) St. Barthélemy, I have relied on quite casual histories. Great Danish or Swedish historians have not been very interested in these small islands. Some of the best scholarly history is written in English, but is very sparse, and most of that in Danish seems to have been written for tourists in search of their tropical roots.

The dependent variable which the two causes in Table 5.1 are supposed to be measuring is the degree to which planters could create internal processes, through socially well organized classes with clubs and intermarriage and concern for heirs, and through legislative discussion, to decide on planter interests, and to mobilize on behalf of those interests. Here, too, I first used scattered incidents to create impressionistic paired comparisons among islands on planter solidarity. For example, early in the French Revolution the Martinique planters agreed to the participation of the free colored in the polity, as demanded by Revolutionary France. The Haitian planters (and apparently also urban *petit blanc* revolutionaries on both islands) split apart on this question (cf. Lémery [1936] versus Geggus [1982] and Frostin [1975] on this). Similar incidents would compare Barbados versus Jamaica in rejection of royal governor intervention in law-making, and Danish St. Thomas versus St. Croix reactions to impending emancipation and to slave demonstrations. Sometimes the incidents involved extraordinary care for the stability of the slave system as a whole, as in the Martinican help to suppress a quite successful slave rebellion on Danish St. Johns.

I then looked for an available structural correlate for these differences. The best I found was the time lapse between my estimate of the peak sugar frontier growth period and the late eighteenth century (or whenever the incidents took place) controlling for the differences in the degree to which it was a sugar island. That is, most of the more organized planter classes and coherent planter policies in the contrasting pairs were farther toward the upper left of Table 5.1, the less organized ones toward the lower right.

I thought this was because building institutions of internal planter solidarity, especially unity in influencing the local government on the island, would take time and would work better when planters were living on the islands with families rather than planning to go back to the metropole with a fortune to marry. Resident planter families happened late in the sugar cycle, except in the Spanish islands where they were more resident than the government *peninsulares* from the beginning. But in the Spanish islands [planters] could not very well form their solidarities in island government councils, because they were mostly excluded from them.

For example, Barbados in the late eighteenth century had many more resident planters married to white women than did Jamaica, as well as more capacity to take power from royal governors, presumably joint results of the longer time since the sugar frontier period and [high] sugar dominance.

I then checked this indicator against similar incidents in previous periods. I also used incidents involving planter power after emancipation, used to introduce new limitations on now "free" exslave proletarians. The richest source for these last incidents was Holt's (1992) wonderful analysis of post emancipation Jamaica. I looked for the presence or absence of similar legislation and government activity on other islands, to judge their distance on planter mobilizability from Jamaica.

Availability of the central indicator of variations within islands of the degree of freedom of subgroups of slaves, rates of manumission, is deeply confounded with the degree of slave society in the government of the island. When a government does not create a deep divide between slave and free, it does not take an act of government to destroy it. So documented manumission works as a measure where freedom of individual slaves mattered most, on islands where the main role of government was to preserve unfreedom of slaves against a varying array of forces, including individual planter generosity to slaves.

On a tobacco farm in the northern valley of the Dominican Republic or in a copper mine in the Sierra Madre of eastern Cuba, slaves worked alongside masters and poor peasants. When in some contingency it became no longer worthwhile for owners to enforce the line between slave and free (e.g., if the vein of copper was worked out), the slave could wander off, or continue cultivation of a subsistence plot, and the government did not care.

In such cases I have substituted (informally) the indicator of the ratio of the free colored population to the slave population as a measure of what was probably widespread manumission. As outlined in Chapter 4 it is also a measure of the average number of generations slave lineages have been in the colony. This cause of high free colored to slave ratios would, of course, occur in the same places as we predict high informal manumission, where the sugar frontier had not recently brought in new African cohorts on a large scale.

Occasionally documents will happen to betray the fact that informal manumission has gone on and the government, in an ambivalent fashion, was eventually willing to let it stand, as in the attempt by a local governor to reimpose slavery on descendants of copper mining slaves in eastern Cuba in order to hire them out (probably to developing sugar plantations, Marrero (1978; 6) pp. 36–43—there was a bit of formal manumission by buying themselves and their relatives from the King as well, indicating that the non-manumitted slaves owned property and had "their own" money). I have then inferred manumission rates indirectly, with another cause of high proportion free unfortunately happening in the same places, exactly where we would most like to have the numbers to support our theory. (We must take what comfort we can in the freedom that they enjoyed, even if we cannot document where it came from.) We have predicted the distance between slave and free status to be lowest where contemporaries generated fewest numbers about manumission, and where a "normal" manumission rate would generate high ratios of free colored to slave populations.

For our purposes we would prefer manumission rates cumulated over slave lifetimes, like total fertility rates. What we have instead, even in the British islands just before emancipation, are yearly rates, usually accurate to only one digit because numerators are small. They are usually for age-heterogeneous groupings of the slave population which have however different age distributions, and usually age-standardized rates not readily calculable for the comparisons. These annual rates are based on more or less uncertain matches between the categories of censuses and the categories on manumission documents. We can guess that such rates are probably approximately a thirtieth or so of total lifetime rates, except for the young creole domestic female slaves who often got manumission by way of sexual relations. Their lifetime annual rates were presumably lower than they were when they were young women, so their total manumission rates would be overestimated by simply multiplying their rates at young ages. Higman (1984) is very much more expert than I where these data are best, so I have almost always accepted his word both about the estimates and about their degree of uncertainty.

For the rest of the analysis about [manumission of] subgroups of slaves, I have made my analysis here in the form of predictions in case anyone manages to create good data. But I have informally checked these predictions against what population data on color of free and slave populations was available, or against travelers' impressions of population compositions. I have paid no attention to travelers' impressions of the rates themselves, because I believe people's impressions of all sorts of social mobility rates are useless as evidence.

Still, not everybody who has worked on this now much richer history has studied the same thing on each island, so I had to cobble together information on the differences from data of very different quality and scope on different islands. It is not as bad as looking for all the intermediate types of hominids from 4 million years ago from a few bone fragments and trying to infer how they lived, what their evolutionary advantage was, when they might have learned to talk, why they walked on two legs and when, and the like. There each datum is very expensive indeed. But I had to make do with what I could get cheaply on many islands (as shown in Stinchcombe, 1995c; reprinted in this chapter with minor modifications). The main point here is that I was operating in a sparse field *for any particular indicator of my concepts* (that is, ideas about the variations of the processes of slavery and abolition). When one is looking in a literature for facts on countries, where the United Nations has not standardized the facts, one will have trouble. If the reader looks in detail at the many decisions about what measured what in the excerpt given here, many depended on was easily available. A sociologist's theoretical purposes are enough different from those of historians that I would sacrifice archival depth in order to cover the twenty or so main islands in the Caribbean with rough estimates of the sizes of the forces. On the average, historians look for much sparser, but more detailed, information on a particular island (or a particular colonial office in the metropole), in order to be sure for at least one island about a sequence of events.

The U.N. did not standardize things much before the mid-twentieth century, and it began with the big, rich countries. At about the same time, an attempt at standardization of observations on a lot of "primitive" societies was carried out in the Human Relations Area Files. But degree of oppressiveness of colonialism was not a principal variable in ethnography in those days. My book was all about the oppressiveness of colonialism, *and how the oppressiveness varies*. I had to have at least two cases *that were different* in order to get anything on what I wanted to study, if the units of analysis were to be islands. (I made an argument in the book that they are units, though more unified units when they are small than when they are large.) The historians who were interested in any two islands (one historian for each) that I ended up wanting to compare were, almost always, interested in different things, and so I had to make do with guessing the distances between the islands from details the historians reported for some other purpose. The excerpt given here tries to describe how I "guessed" from the data supplied by the secondary sources.

So when we have a sparse field of data on the differences we are looking for, we have to spend more time making use of each fact we can get. This usually requires much more intensive work on each case, such as looking for something in the nooks and crannies of a book on the right island but the wrong subject.

In these cases, Caribbean slavery or early hominids, our problem comes from the *sparseness of the field of data*—not necessarily the inherent sparseness, but very often a sparseness caused by expensiveness. For example, if we were willing to dig more canyons than nature has dug in the African savanna country below the Sahara, and to do it in such a way that we preserved the fossils, we could presumably find many more hominid fossil skeletons. Similarly, we could find many more dinosaur bones by running the Colorado River through a different part of the high plateau in the American West for 6 million years. Not bloody likely.

When we have a sparse field of data, then, either inherently or because of expensiveness of getting data on the differences, investigators must do more intense study of each case they have managed to find, taking many jumps with theory that they cannot find data to fill in exactly. We end up with a "case study" or a "small N study" in which we have to make a lot of theoretical argument about each crucial fact, because our observations are not quite comparable, and we cannot really tell without deep analysis which things caused what. Providing theoretical and historical context for each fact is more often possible in a book than an article. Books and articles enter in different ways into the discourse of a scientific discipline. The next excerpt, by Clemens and others, outlines these differences.

Clemens Books Short Version

Summarized from Elisabeth Clemens, Walter W. Powell, Kris McIlwaine, and Dina Okamoto, "Careers in Print: Books, Journals and Scholarly Reputations," *American Journal of Sociology* 101, no. 2 (September 1995): 433–494. Page numbers cited without further identification refer to pages in this article. The pronoun *we* in this summary means the authors of the article.

We study here the selection process for sociology journal articles and books whose publication was around 1987–1988, and the reception of those texts, indicated by citations in journals of all social science disciplines during the succeeding five years. More than half of the citations in social science journals were to books. The books we study in this paper were nominated for the most prestigious prize in sociology; the articles were all those published in some issues of the two most prestigious journals. Thus we study elite articles and elite books.

We will see that selection into the elite is different for articles than for books, and that the articles were mostly cited within sociology, sociological books mostly in the journals of other disciplines (though books taken as a whole, including books from other disciplines, were as likely to be cited in sociology journals as articles). The authors of elite books are generally more elite in status, seniority, and previous publication than the authors of articles, perhaps partly because nomination for the big prize is a tougher criterion than having an article in a prestige journal. The books studied were cited in journals of sociology and other disciplines about three times as often as the articles. However those few articles that were extensively cited in journals of other disciplines tended to have authors of high seniority, high previous publication, and from prestigious universities, like the authors of the prize-nominated books we studied. Insofar as books may be more likely to be cited in other books, which were not covered in the source used to count citations, three to one may be an underestimate of the larger impact of prize-nominated books. Insofar as the books may have been more rigorously selected as elite than the articles, the ratio of book citations to article citations may be overestimated.

Articles in prestige sociology journals were mostly quantitative. This was more true in *American Sociological Review* than in *American Journal of Sociology*. Ethnography and comparative sociology often use a wide variety of non-comparable facts which themselves have to be explained. They usually demand what sociologists call "qualitative methods." They also deal with the interaction of several or many people and organizations, in causal relations that themselves change over time. They tend to be published in books. Overall the most convenient summary measure is whether the methods are qualitative or quantitative. Books were about four times more likely to be qualitative as quantitative. Articles were about five times more likely to be quantitative than qualitative.

But it turns out that prize-nominated quantitative books are the most cited form in the journals of sociology and other social science disciplines, more than three times as likely to be cited than quantitative articles. Thus something about the book genre facilitates the wide reception of quantitative as well as qualitative knowledge. Quantitative books are more cited than either quantitative articles or qualitative books. This is especially true of citations from other disciplines. And the transmission of complex and heterogeneous facts about complex systems in ethnography and comparative or historical work depends more on books.

The patterns for selection of books to be published and the patterns of their reception were shaped by a process we call "sponsored mobility," a phrase borrowed from Ralph Turner. People on the inside of the publishing system, such as acquisitions editors and elite sociologists, actively recruit likely authors and book manuscripts for academic presses. Manuscripts that "come over the transom" from unknown authors without elite contacts are often ignored or just skimmed, to select those few to be published. This means that senior scholars with good reputations coming from elite schools have a better chance to get a book prospectus read by the editor and sent to a reviewer (and a better chance after publication to have book reviews written about it). The acquisitions editor was in turn recruited to be sensitive to what the educated public outside the discipline will want to read, and to arrange editing to improve readability rather than statistical rigor. The author's name was ordinarily known to the referees, and the editor hoped it would be known to potential readers. Young book authors got into this circle by being chosen and sponsored by one of the elite, or by exceptional good luck with an over-the-transom submission.

By "contest mobility" (also borrowed from Ralph Turner) for articles, we mean that young people and people from less elite colleges submit articles to the journal rather than being recruited to submit by book editors or elite sponsors. In journals almost all submissions are refereed in a "double blind" contest. The referees do not know the author's name, and the author does not know the reviewers. No one "sponsors" a paper. The editor, who does know the author's name, weighs the referees' reports. The journals have subscribers, rather than an article having separate buyers. No one has the job of making sure the article is readable across disciplines, but referees are unpaid judges of whether the article is important to the discipline and is methodologically sound. Formally speaking, then, graduate students and leading scholars have an equal chance to publish in this scheme. And contribution to the discipline rather than appeal to a generally educated audience is the main criterion of acceptance

For example, women have the same acceptance rate, once they submit a paper to one of these journals, as men do. But women, around 1988, were more likely to submit books than articles, and more likely to submit articles to *American Journal of Sociology* than to *American Sociological Review*. Much of the sex difference between books versus journals was due to much more than half of women authors of articles or books using qualitative methods, while slightly more than half of the men used quantitative methods.

There are then three main conclusions of this study, which apply to sociology in the late 1980s, and perhaps at other times. The largest difference between articles and books is methodological: articles are largely quantitative, books largely qualitative (though the most cited quantitative studies are books). The sponsored mobility regime leads to book authors being more senior, from more prestigious private universities, and they have had a more productive career before writing the book nominated for the prize. These books were more cited in journals of all disciplines than were the journal articles; each of the prize nominee books was cited about three times as much as articles, and this difference was primarily due to sociological books being much more cited outside sociology than articles were.

Theoretical Methods to Increase Economies in Data Collection

NOW I WANT TO TURN TO ONE OF THE MAIN STRATEGIES by which the value of facts, even precariously known facts, is greatly increased. Many theories of social phenomena are really aggregated constructions, made up of subparts, or small theories. Often facts are available that bear on the subparts but not on everything in the theory (for a general treatment of this relationship for network theories, see Gould, 2003, pp. 147–157). For example, in the excerpt on slave oppression given above (Stinchcombe, 1985c), I used a theory about *the amount of planter interest in oppression of slaves*, higher for sugar (or cotton) than for other crops, and a theory of *political solidarity of classes* (in this case the class of planters), to get my indicators. That is, there are two subparts, theories of mechanisms, in the bigger theory of the oppressiveness of slavery. The main methodological device is to get, from the literature, facts on those subparts, since comparable data on oppressiveness of slavery on different islands cannot be obtained.

First, there is a great deal of economic sociology about when people can use coercive power to get cheaper labor and high productivity of that labor. Many things are hard to do well with coerced labor, but growing and milling sugar happens to be one instance where coerced labor works fine. Further, since sugar took about five times as much labor per acre as the crops previously grown on the islands, planters needed to import labor from some population who could be got to come to the Caribbean. Roughly one-third of the people in the seventeenth and eighteenth centuries who immigrated (whites, African slaves, and indentured East Indians alike) would die of disease in the first few years there.

Planters *could* produce sugar efficiently with coerced labor, and they *needed* to coerce people to come there if they were not going to give them a good chance of getting rich (that is the way the empires had induced planters to come and die). This is a theory of the mechanism that would produce a high *interest* in coerced labor on the part of planters.

Second, there is a fairly solid tradition in political sociology on the topic of when a class group can get their interests reflected in the government. It yields a set of propositions about when an interest group has historically been able to act together in defense of its collective interest. One of the subsets of such theories is a theory of when social classes will be solidary; the most important part was first formulated by Marx to answer the question of why urban proletarians could rebel more effectively than most of the poor throughout most of history had been able to do.

In chapter 6, on mechanisms and units of analysis, I will discuss the building of this previous knowledge of the mechanisms that produce an interest in politico-economic oppression and solidarity of classes. The logic there will justify, in part, my choice of islands as units of analysis for the methodology presented here. For now, I want to point out that theories of mechanisms can often enable investigators to study something else on which they can get processual data to make a part of the larger argument. This approach uses the theory of the mechanism to allow them to get partial confirmation (or disconfirmation) of the theory by more intensive study of single cases where the mechanisms are more easily observed.

Astrophysicists can use a theory of the dependence of the spectrum of radiation on the temperature of the radiating body to learn much about stars from the example of the Sun; they can then use the knowledge gained to study stars that are far away and have varying spectra. Similarly, sociologists can study the mechanisms of solidarity of planters from Marx's theories about the solidarity of factory workers and *get more out of observations* on Barbados apparently being more oppressive than the Bahamas, or even than Trinidad and Isla Margarita right next door. This is because both kinds of scientists can supplement the gross comparison between units (whether islands or stars) with studies within units (e.g., why slave dock workers and slave prostitutes on Barbados were much less politically and legally oppressed than sugar field workers). The better the mechanisms in the theory, the more one can get out of intensive study of the convenient cases.

Theory Allowing One to Use Data from a "Lower" Level

THE KEY TO USING MECHANISMS to increase the amount of information obtained from observations of cases has to do, first, with what the theory of the mechanism does to the data and, second, with what it does to the big theory. The first is very simple: it multiplies the usefulness of comparisons, distances, *within* cases. Over time differences in phenomena within cases are especially useful, if the theory can tie them back to the social structural level we are mainly interested in. This is why historical study, especially comparative historical study, is so fruitful for sociological theory of gross structural variation between societies (e.g., between slave islands). It is also why a couple of years of ethnography on individual cases of "primitive" tribes is the basis of the richness of the sociology of such "tribes" in social anthropology. Such intensive observation, including historical studies where possible, has shown that we need to put the word "tribes" in quotation marks. By careful study of the mechanisms involved, and especially how they vary over time, we find that a "tribe" is merely an especially dense locus of networks of political and economic power that stretch both above the tribal level to other political entities and patterns of trade, and below the tribal level to lineages and other kinship structures. Thus, the theory of the mechanism can have important implications for the big theory.

The theoretical requirements for this to be useful are *both* that scientists can study the processes at the lower levels "within a case," *and* that they can connect it to the social structural problem. This second requirement means that one has to be able to connect the structure being studied to a set of "inputs" to the structure from "outputs" at a lower level of mechanisms within cases. For example, the general structure of the sugar trade and the technology of sugar production gave thousands of planters on different islands an intense interest in slave labor. This intense interest in slavery is an "input" to the level of analysis of island politics and international trade, from the lower level of individual planters. It explains pressures on the colonial office from Barbados and Jamaica, but not from the Bahamas, in the metropolitan country. But then the support from the empire level, proportional to the pressures for such support from the island, helps create variations between islands and between times on how intensely individual planters wanted slavery.

Then one has to connect the phenomena produced at the lower level to the structural thing to be explained—in this case, the agglomeration of interest in thoroughgoing oppression of slaves by solidary planters into reliable local government policy. This is where the theory of solidarity of planters comes in. Planters on a frontier island, where the labor-intensive cultivation of sugar was just being introduced, needed five times as much labor as before. They were intensely interested in slavery. But they did not have the time or intra-class social relations to influence colonial government of the island. So the agglomeration of the intense interest did not take place as effectively as it otherwise might have.

There is occasional data about how on Barbados the local (planter) council occasionally shipped the governor back to England, without the consent of the London Colonial Office. One might get more out of such data by observing that the planter interest in slavery was intense on Barbados, which had almost no nonsugar land, and that Barbados had the longest time for planter families to get established as a solidary grouping.

The Theoretical Penumbra and Exploratory Research

THERE ARE SOME TOPICS OF RESEARCH where almost any cheap fact can have value, and these are areas where the cheapness of facts should be a central criterion. Being by ancient inclination a quantitative type, I recommend that in the preliminary stages of a research project, a student should take calculator in hand and browse through the *Statistical Abstract of the United States*. Whatever a sociologist is going to study in race relations, for example, *has to be related* to something in some of the many tables there that have race as a variable. It is useful in scanning to keep in mind which cities of the United States have the highest proportion of black population. For example, when I worked on this problem many years ago, such cities included Atlanta, Washington, D.C., Detroit, and Baltimore. Keep in mind also the big cities where some other minority ethnicities or races are roughly equally important, such as Los Angeles, San Francisco, New York, Miami, or Honolulu. Then we can learn from the *Statistical Abstract* that Los Angeles has nearly equal median education for whites and blacks, and we are on the way to a theory and to how to study it. One fact involving two variables can be enormously valuable in starting one thinking along new, "researchable" lines.

Whenever an investigator notices something else that is different between Baltimore, Atlanta, and Detroit, versus other big cities, he or she may well have a hypothesis about the behavior of either whites in mostly black cities, or about African Americans in mostly black cities. I have picked cities to start with, but one should also look at the tables for the country as a whole about education by race and gender, about levels of welfare expenditure by states, and so on.

Sticking with race relations and quantitative data, one might next want to look at easily available data on other countries with racial or ethnic diversity. Quite often this is quantified in U.N. sources, but sometimes one will need to browse in the statistical abstracts of other countries. I recall, from about 1960 or so, that the distance in incomes (in percentages; i.e., in logs) between English-speaking and French-speaking people in Canada was then about as large as that between African Americans and whites in the United States. Presumably, if we are seeking a theory of race difference in the United States, it should at least be compatible with a society next door where the same amount of difference occurred, absent either race or slavery. That fact, updated, might take a half-hour to find—nothing like the amount of time it would take to find a historical document and interpret it, or to arrange an interview and transcribe it. Clearly, it is useful to know where to look for a half-hour for a big fact that has to be compatible with a theory of race and ethnic inequality in the United States.

Getting Unconfounded Distances

AS A FURTHER EXTENSION OF THE MAIN POINT OF CHAPTER 2, the most informative cases are those that have an effect of the main cause one is studying, "purified" of the effect of another. For example, most nomadic tribes live mainly on the milk or blood of the animals, rather than the flesh. We might want to say that they were more similar to Wisconsin dairy farms in the United States than to the mountain states ranches that raise cattle to sell to feedlots for meat. But more of the pasture in the West is public land than in Wisconsin, whereas herds are (nominally at least) inherited by the same legal arrangements as the land in Wisconsin. Thus the theory of nomadic tribes who live off milk of herds having public pastures but private herds seems to be reversed in the United States. While that shows that the milk—public pasture connection is not a law of nature, it poses the problem that the societies as wholes are very different.

The problem with this attempted generalization of the nomadic result is that commercialization of the whole economy (at least in this comparison) is deeply confounded with the differences among American states. A dairy farmer and a rancher are both dissimilar to either subsistence nomadic groups or subsistence agricultural groups. Dairy farmers do not need to live entirely off the substances produced for their diet by their herd; they can buy lettuce and mangoes at the supermarket.

Thus the apparent disconfirmation of the saliency of family inheritance of herds is due to not having information in this sample of modern and nomadic societies that studies the effect of consuming the milk separately from commercialization. In chapter 2 we avoided this problem by comparing African and central Asian nomadic groups during the times when they were dominantly nomadic and hardly at all commercial. We want to maximize the variation between milk-and-blood-using nomadic and agricultural technology that is unaffected by commercialization.

This is the key to what is called "orthogonal design" in the *design of experiments* literature. (The person who was most responsible for developing orthogonal designs, R. A. Fisher [1937], did not prove the efficiency of the design, which in his case meant equal numbers of cases in each cell of the cross tabulation of the dichotomous independent variables.) By the use of the term here, I mean the undersampling of cases near the regression line and oversampling of those far from it, until the two (or more) variables in the sample are uncorrelated. (This definition, for Fisher's cases, gives his result.) Fisher also did not advise designers of experiments that one should maximize distances among experimental and control conditions, perhaps because he was concerned with experimental variables that were known to have curvilinear effects.

At any rate, the comparable principle for regression analyses is to spend extra resources on cases that, in a regression of one independent variable on another, have the highest "residual." Merton called this "deviant case analysis," when talking about qualitative research (Merton, Fiske, and Curtis, 1946). Merton's point was that we learn a lot more about a theory if we intensively study the cases that do not fit. That is, one would want to oversample rich African Americans and poor whites, and spend more resources on detailed observation on those deviant cases. One would, however, want to compare them with likewise oversampled units of observation that were extreme on both—in this example, very poor African Americans and very rich whites. Thus one would be more likely to find mechanisms by detailed study of roughly equal numbers of four types of cases: very rich whites compared *both* with very poor whites *and* with very rich African Americans, and very poor African Americans compared *both* with very rich African Americans *and* with very poor whites. This is exactly orthogonal design, with the addition of the criterion that great distances provide the most causal information when the relationships are linear, and if the mechanisms are such as to produce curvilinear relations, the details of extreme cases should tell us why.

Similarly a comparative sociologist might want to have herding and agricultural tribes in Africa, and herding and agricultural tribes in central Asia, taking the extremes on economies, *and* extremes on the continental cultural and ecological environment. (The central Asian "steppe" is a cold semi-desert, surrounded by conquerable rich agricultural empires; the central African "savanna" is a hot semi-desert, surrounded by jungle on one side, desert on the other.)

Let us consider another case in which we may have "confounded" variables. Suppose we want to predict college students' evaluation of the teaching of the average teacher in their schools. We think there might be two main variables explaining the variation in evaluation: whether the teachers have a good understanding of what they are teaching, and whether teachers pay a lot of attention to students. We can call the first variable "scholarship," the second, "care."

If we start with institutions with full-time faculty (so that "care" does not go into the day job of people who teach nights), teaching loads indicate that colleges with fewer scholars (as measured by peer recognition) have more "care." So sorting out the effects of scholarship and care is difficult, because universities have more scholarship and less care, undergraduate-only colleges less scholarship and more care. The positive effects of each, whatever size they are, tend to cancel each other in both kinds of places.

There are, however, a few well-known liberal arts colleges with strong criteria of scholarship and intellectualism, but much evidence of faculty care for students. Reed and Swarthmore in the United States come immediately to mind, or Oxford and Cambridge in England, but there are quite a few others. And there are colleges that have very little scholarship but very large classes tended by a relatively small full-time faculty. These institutions are often descended from state-supported teachers' colleges or urban night schools and may have nationally rated football and basketball teams.

Before refining measures of "care received" and "knowledge well taught," one should design a study with an oversample of scholarly and caring liberal arts colleges, and also of large-class colleges with commuting students and very little peer-reviewed publication and little consultation with peers outside the college at promotion time. My own opinion is that the lack of such a well-designed study means we underestimate how much research and scholarship contributes to good teaching, and so do not understand the drift of students to research universities even when they themselves do not want to do research.

When Not to Follow My Advice on Sampling Extreme Cases Intensively

THIS STRATEGY OF OVERSAMPLING AND OVERSTUDYING extreme cases has three major difficulties: curvilinearity, interaction effects, and heterogeneous populations with different variances. These are all mathematical concepts, which means that the cautionary part of this chapter is more "technical" than the other parts about why extreme cases are interesting. But curvilinearity, interaction effects, and different populations at the extremes are also very theoretically interesting features of phenomena. The example discussed below, of the impact of age on childcare burden, and so on gender inequality, shows that central social policy issues of gender inequality depend on the mathematical features of studies for efficiently testing the main theories in sociology.

Curvilinearity

By curvilinearity, we mean in essence that differences on a cause have different effects depending on *where the distances are on a variable describing a cause*. Let us take age and the division of labor in the household as an example. Suppose we were to take married couples at the extreme of the age distribution to study the gender division of labor. The youngest, unmarried or married less than a year, would not have many children, and the oldest—say, those couples with both members over seventy-five—would not have many children still at home, so we would find low levels of differentiation of household work.

The big burden that women distinctively take up nowadays is care of small children, so to maximize the distances in childcare burden, one should study people who married two years previously, about half of whom would have no children, while the other half would have babies requiring maximum care. (The last time I checked, the median interval between marriage and the first child in the United States was two years.) Hours of care of children is, then, *curvilinearly* related to the duration of the marriage and to the age of the mother. If we sampled only the extremes, we might get very egalitarian division of labor among the very old and the recently married. This would not mean that age is not related to feminist beliefs and practice on who takes care of the children. Instead, it would mean that if there are no children, the main distinctive responsibility of women in gender inequality studies does not show up.

Two separate mechanisms are involved here: the young couples are usually *both in* the labor market and so not very different in home duties, and the old ones are *both out of* the labor market and so not very different in home duties. The differentiating variable, gender differences in the responsibility for small children, works mainly in the lower middle part of the age variable.

Practically every variable strongly related to age is curvilinear in age. This means that sampling only the extremes would be good only if one also had a sample with a substantial number of people in the middle. For most variables, one does not need very many cases in the middle to find that there is a curve, and the extreme cases still give a disproportionate amount of the information about what is going on. For example, one would not need much ethnography to find out that both spouses were often out of the house among young married couples, and that both were mostly in the house among retired people. This is a clear difference between the extremes. Others might be the amount of sickness, ownership clear of mortgage of their own home versus renting, low physical stamina versus strength, sobriety versus night life, having middle-aged children versus not, or having higher versus lower average education.

So when a difference of a given size (such as a year of age) has different effects, depending on where the interval of age starts (such as a year when young or a year when already old), then studying the extremes only does not tell us what we need to know. But there are many other variables where samples of the extremes and more intensive study of each sampled extreme would pay off.

Mathematical Interaction Effects

Interaction effects are a differently conceived example of curvilinearity. The central point is still that different differences of the same size have different effects. But instead of depending on the value of the variable itself for how much effect it has, as in the case of age, here we are interested in a variable that has a different size of effect because of the effect of another variable. (The logical basis of the importance of interaction effects in causal analysis is laid out in chapters 5 and 6, though not specifically discussed there; contextual effects and boundary conditions of causal processes within units of analysis often produce mathematical interaction effects.) For example, race differences may have a different effect on being stereotyped when a meeting of the races takes place in a southern plantation county versus a northern city. (Note that "interaction effects" means that the *variables* interact in producing the effect—not that individual people interact and react differently. The second is also true, but is a different truth.)

Let us return to the case of the age effect on the gender division of labor, and reconceive it as an effect of the age and gender composition of the children of the family. Older parents have, on the average, older children. But as children age during childhood and adolescence, the parental-gender composition of childcare work changes differently for boys than for girls. Many more fathers are involved in the recreational life of older boy children than in the recreational life of older girl children. Little League baseball games have more fathers taking and picking up children than do Girl Scout meetings, and girl children are rarely introduced into hunting and fishing by fathers. Even taking the child to a public rest room in an airport changes into a shared responsibility after boys are about three years old in the United States: after that age the men take boys to the restroom, women take girls.

Besides this effect of having an older child on the division of labor in the family, which is differential with the gender-age combination, total hours of childcare also decrease with the age of the child, and so statistically with parent age. Since it is disproportionately women who do childcare at all ages (e.g., a high school PTA tends to be dominantly female, even if the adolescent is a boy), the decline of total hours of childcare with children's ages decreases the difference in hours of childcare burden between the sexes, *because it decreases total burden.* Most of the total childcare burden is women's work, so when there is less burden, women get more of the benefit.

Now we have built variables out of the age and gender composition of the children, and we want to use this to explain differences over time in the degree of division of labor in the family—that is, the effect of gender on hours of work in the home. Gender has a larger effect when there are younger children, because there is more total childcare and women do most of it. Gender has a larger effect for older children when the children are girls than when they are boys, because men do a larger share of the childcare for older boy children, though women still do a good deal, while both general childcare and gender-specific childcare tend to be done for girl children by women.

Since the existence and the ages of children are correlated with age (or we would not have found curvilinearity of division of labor with age, perhaps), some of the curvilinearity that we find would be due to the interaction of the age-gender composition of children with parent age. Age has a different effect if it means that a boy in the family is growing up than if a girl is growing up. A parental year of age has a different effect if a child is going from the first year of life to the second, than if he or she is going from the fourteenth year to the fifteenth. Roughly speaking, in middle-class families in America, when a child is less than one year old, the couple (or the people they hire) need to provide fifty to eighty hours a week of childcare That goes down to about thirty to forty hours a week in the second year. From the fourteenth to the fifteenth year it might go down from ten hours a week to nine. If women do more of the total, whatever the total is, then women's excess work goes roughly from fifty to eighty hours a week to about nine hours a week (maybe to less for a boy child).

Here two different kinds of curvilinearity of the effect of age are confounded: simple age dependence on the theoretical meaning of a difference of a year of age (say, a year of learning more, or a year of brain cells dying off); and a child-maturation effect of a difference in a year of the child's age. The existence and ages of children are both highly correlated with parent age, and so is the number of dead brain cells. If one takes only the extremes of age to estimate the effect of age on the division of labor, one will miss childcare effects, but retain brain-cell effects. But unless one gets differences in the age-sex composition of the children of a household, as well as age differences in the division of parental labor for different child genders, one cannot sort out the two kinds of curvilinearity.

So one should probably have a theory that some more or less latent ideologies about gender and children would have most effect when the childcare burden was the greatest (an interaction effect of parent age and number of children on childcare burden, and so on inequality of work created by the gendered ideology of childcare). So if one wanted to explore which ideological elements had the most effect on what children do to the division of labor, one should select a sample of couples about two years after their marriage, when about half of them would have the lowest childcare burden or none at all, and the other half would mostly have the largest childcare burden, namely, a child of one or two years. This would be picking the point at which *the variance of the interaction effect* should be largest, and thus would be the best place to ferret out its mechanisms by intensive study. That is, when we have a theory of an interaction effect, we should oversample the extreme values *of the interaction effect.* Choosing a sample of people married about two years to study the gender division of labor would be following that advice.

Mixed Distributions

The next idea is a bit tricky, so let me start with an example from another discipline. The Sun is by far the largest body in the solar system, having maybe 99 percent of the mass of the system as a whole. Clearly, a piece of matter in the solar system would tend to fall into the Sun, and there are just a few minor cases of equilibria (orbits) that remain stable for quite a long time outside the Sun, namely, a few planets and comets.

Though Earth is not the smallest planet, it is small enough that we might sacrifice a bit of variance to get a good opportunity for detailed observation. So let us take the Earth as the smaller body in one of those multiple orbit-equilibria. Scientists have learned a lot of what is known about planets by studying the Earth. One problem is that the dynamics of the population of stars is quite different from the dynamics of the population of planets. So above the size and density required to start the hydrogen-to-helium nuclear reaction that mainly powers stars, there is a different heat dynamics on all stars than that on Earth or Jupiter.

For example, only above that hydrogen-to-helium boundary is there an outward light energy sufficient to drive interstellar gases and dust out of the immediate area of the star (i.e., out of the solar system); we see stars clearly because of that effect. Only above that level do stars exist with a lifespan of nuclear energies being generated that is measured in millions or billions of years, depending on how massive the stars are (bigger stars have stronger nuclear reactions, so burn out more quickly). Only at greater masses than the Sun, and so much greater than the mass of the Earth or Jupiter, do stars become supernovae, collapsing inward and producing the heavy elements.

In short, the bodies of the solar system consist of a distribution by size of planets, with nine major bodies and quite a few minor ones within that population. One might learn something by comparing Jupiter with the Earth, the biggest planet with the one smaller planet on which we have the most information. Then we have a single case, the Sun, of a member of another population, the population of stars, with a different distribution on almost all important matters. Many of the "laws" that apply to that population do not apply to any members of the population of planets, asteroids, moons, and comets.

In this example, if we take the extremes, we may get distances that have no clear meaning, because in the extremes we are getting into a distribution that has different laws. The Sun clearly got into its different population by being at the very highest extreme of mass in the system.

Quite often sociologists run into problems because cases that are very far from the main bulk of the observations seem to be following different laws. Frequently these cases seem to represent the law of mistaken data entry—a misplaced decimal point, for example. Presumably the laws of misplaced decimals are social laws, and it is a sociological, not a natural, fact that many errors are by factors of powers of ten.

But there is a whole subspecialty in statistics about ways of getting rid of such cases ("'trimming" the distribution, it is sometimes called). The basic idea is that if an observation is too far from the distribution of the rest of the sample (or population), the chances are good that it is really not subject to the theory being developed or tested by observations on the sample. If one is doing a regression problem, one may find that the observations on a single case are the main determinant of the regression line. To take a business example, most of the higher average profits of very large (oligopolistic) firms may turn out to be the very high profits of the very largest one of those firms. The average sociologist does not want to say that oligopoly has a big effect just because being IBM has a big effect. So he or she wants a device for throwing away the case "with undue impact" on the result. I do not think it is wise to throw away IBM, but instead would choose to study it intensively.

Another important case is also business-related: the volatility of the stock market (the over-time variance of prices) is largely due to about 2 percent of the cases that are apparently "naturally" highly volatile. Thus, our "laws of volatility" are mainly the laws of that 2 percent (they used to be known as "blue sky" stocks). If we want a theory of the volatility of the stocks most people own, we might want to throw away that 2 percent.

Looking at the problem another way, we note that it was intensive study of the Sun that first suggested many of the theories we have about what stars are, why they are different colors, what the spectra of very distant stars would look like if they were closer, and the like. One has to consider the point made by Merton about the deviant case (Merton's point applies in spades to the Sun): that one can learn a lot by detailed study of the exception. Similarly, if we want to study the volatility of the stock market, we may want to study especially the corporations, and the trading in shares of the corporations, that create volatility, and greatly oversample that 2 percent.

Another way to say this is that a sample of one, where that one obeys a different law, is much bigger than a sample of zero with that law. So Merton may have a big sample of a population that obeys one law, and a sample of one where he and his co-authors have one observation of a different population. If Merton is equally interested in both populations, he should collect an equal amount of information about that one as about the whole mass of the rest. He should try to collect as much information as possible on the only one he has in the second population. If one wanted to study why the Sun is so different from all the other bodies of the solar system, and what effect that has, one would optimize by collecting as much information about the Sun as one had about the whole other set of bodies.

"Nearby" Theories and the Value of Data

THE POINT HERE IS THAT near to the theoretical core of a research problem are other theories of the phenomenon at hand, whose implications the researcher needs to keep in mind. A theory of physical markers of differences between races should look at other racial differences than the black-white one where they started: for example, Tutsis and many Ethiopians and Kenyans are black like other Africans but differently shaped and living in a different overall social system (disproportionately the herding part). Chinese and Japanese are clearly racially identified in the United States and started out, like black people, working on plantations, but soon began to move to the cities, where they were small minorities. Native Americans are hardly identifiable because they are much intermarried in most of the United States, but in areas near large reservations they are quite racially identifiable. One's theory thus has to be compatible with the easy disappearance of the racial markers of Native Americans by intermarriage; with the change in meaning of racial markers of Chinese and Japanese so they are now disproportionately rich because they are professionals rather than because they are entrepreneurs or top managers (many more whites are entrepreneurs or top managers); with linguistic markers having the same effect in Canada as racial markers do in the United States. So the data one might get from cheap statistical sources on all these "racial" differences would elaborate the "nearby" theories to the researcher's theory about the strong meaning of being "black" for African Americans.

One of the most common problems in research is that we know a great many mechanisms that can produce the same result: discrimination on the basis of common physical appearance ("race"). For example, there is a theory of educational deprivation (historically this has been quite strong for Hispanics from Mexico, but quite weak for those from Cuba, with Puerto Rico in between). Then there is the theory of differential family solidarity (relatively low for Mexican Hispanics, American blacks, and Caribbean blacks, but high for Jews, Chinese, and Japanese). All these are competitors with the theory that racial prejudice produces most of the observed inequality.

The value of the extreme case, then, is that either it should give much support and information of the mechanism that works for the whole distribution, or it should give a start on developing further the "nearby" theory that explains some of the same phenomena. Sometimes it does both at once, for different theories. The mass of the Sun made the first calculations in the theory of gravitation much simpler, because one could ignore the small effects of the other masses. Studies of the Sun also suggested that some process of producing much energy must be characteristic of very massive bodies—a new theory.

The main point here is that when we move from a population of racially differentiated white-black interactions, to ones involving Native American intermarriages, or to ones between a young physician of Japanese ancestry treating a white patient who is an emeritus professor of sociology, we may be in a different population of race differences that have a very different causal structure—just as the Sun is not another planet.

Because one does not know in advance whether curves, interaction effects, or heterogeneous populations will be most important in a given case, or whether we have had the good luck to have a linear relation even at the extremes, we need cheap information about how to recognize and assess the likely effects of all of them. Then we can hone our ideas about our particular cases. Sometimes a researcher can add considerably to the believability of a mechanism that he or she found through deep analysis of a case or two. A relatively cheap study from the secondary literature of four or five other relevant cases could illuminate what one might study with special intensity about a very wealthy black physician, for example: adding a chapter on African Americans, Native Americans, Chinese, and Hispanics, each versus whites and Japanese, to a study of some feature of Japanese ethnicity in the United States, with perhaps a side glance at Tutsis and Hutus.

Process Data

....

THERE WILL BE A LOT ABOUT THE ADDED VALUE of process data in chapter 6. But let me emphasize again that sometimes a deep study of processes in the course of studying a few cases can add a great deal of information not otherwise available. Perhaps the classic case in the literature is Becker (1963c [1953]). By decomposing what marijuana users had to be able to do in order to become regular users and showing how social processes contributed to all those elements, that they tended to go in a particular order, and that the order made sense of creating the motivation and the competence, building on previous stages, Becker makes his readers believe that they understand the phenomenon. His readers will also be convinced that it very likely is much more general than the few groups he studied (he does not even bother to tell us how many), because the process data are so convincing. Becker's analysis of how to make single case studies of processes scientifically persuasive is given in a short version below.

Becker Short Version

Summarized from Howard S. Becker, "Problems of Inference and Proof in Participant Observation," *American Sociological Review* 23 (1958): 652–660. All page numbers without names attached refer to pages within this paper.

Participant observation is often used to find out what is mainly going on in a specific social situation, such as a medical school. A common kind of conclusion includes

> statements that some phenomenon is an "important" or "basic" element in the [setting].... [T]his phenomenon exercises a persistent and continuing influence on diverse events. The observer [for example] might conclude that the ambition to become a general practitioners is "important in the medical school" ... meaning that many particular judgments and choices ... by students and many features of the school's organization are arranged to take account of it. (pp. 657–658)

Thus what part of social theory (old social theory or theory invented by the observer) is relevant to the setting is problematic, until one finds out what is salient there. Thus, the main purpose of much participant observation is first to develop hypotheses about the dynamics of the setting; then to develop indicators of importance to social action of specific ideas, attitudes, or behavior; to verify such hypotheses; to build an overall model of what is mainly going on; and finally to write up the unstandardized and sequentially branching research process in a way that convinces a scientific audience.

In the exploratory phase of participant observation (or "ethnography"), the central problem is to locate tentatively what is important (what is salient in action) to the participants. Answers to survey questions about what is important are not good indicators because the observer's question makes a particular concept salient. When the investigator makes an aspect of the situation salient, we lose the information about the autonomous reaction of the respondent, and we may therefore get idiosyncratic answers not connected to saliency in the setting. The more embedded a symptom of importance of some cultural entity or action pattern is in the action system being studied, without being elicited by the observer, the more unlikely it is to be produced by the observer, or by the studied person's abstract ideas of what *ought* to be important. The hypothesis that something is distinctively important has to be developed for the setting, because different things are important in different settings. Thus, the hypothesis would be weakly supported by a survey question because that question is not embedded in the setting. The following is a ranking of observational features that are increasingly improbable *unless* an item observed is really important and salient in the setting.

1. Abstract survey questions, such as, "Are psychosomatic symptoms as serious a complaint as those with a biological basis?" (This belief is one of the things the authors observe about the culture of the medical students.)

2. A question by the observer about an action in the system (p. 654), such as "Why did you call that patient a 'crock'?" This is perhaps more valuable if observed before it is embedded in a theory, e.g., a theory that these medical students are studying to be general practitioners, not specialized psychiatrists, and biological causes are the central things such people can treat (p. 658). "The best evidence may be gathered in the most unthinking fashion . . . when the observer has recorded the item although it has no place in the system of concepts . . . for there might be less bias produced by the wish to substantiate or repudiate a particular idea" (p. 659).

3. Observing people spontaneously volunteering the cultural object in a way appropriate to its hypothesized importance, especially in interaction with others in the setting (rather than with the observer). The exception here is that sometimes there is a norm (e.g., a norm of cynicism) that requires misrepresenting the situation or one's reaction to it; then the true feeling may be better elicited in private (p. 655).

4. Observing the item whose importance is hypothesized in a quasi-quantitative way, being frequently spontaneously and voluntarily produced, apparently with the same overall meaning. This shows that the item is frequently involved in many different situations with many different actors when the same explanation of its use is appropriate (pp. 656–657).

5. Having developed (say) the hypothesis that symptoms produced by patients not biologically sick are rejected as useful training, the observer has systematically looked for contrary instances, and not found them. For example, the observer might look for contrary evidence by especially close observation of rounds on the psychiatric ward, and student reactions to these (example supplied here by ALS). Observing the lack of curiosity systematically observed on rounds, when it should happen, thus supports its importance in student culture.

Finding out the importance or salience of cultural items that are distinctive of a setting is a central objective of much fieldwork or ethnography. In the first phase of research, we cast our net wide, and select out items that are improbable in other settings. Almost nowhere else but in medical school are sick people called "crocks," and almost nowhere else in the educational system do people regularly study full time on the weekends, other than before final exams. Such unusual observations lead to hypotheses, poorly supported at first, about what is mainly going on, what is distinctively important or salient in the setting. The more improbable an event is elsewhere, the more likely it is to indicate something important and distinctive. But even if improbable elsewhere, if it rarely occurs in the setting, one occurrence does not make it highly probable that it is an important and distinctive symbol or action in the setting. Hence the next stage is a rough count of frequencies of "promising" indicators.

If an item observed indicates something important, it should be deeply embedded in many actions, come up frequently in conversations, and be associated with other items that may indicate the same general process. For all these things to happen to an item that is not important and distinctive would be highly unlikely. Consequently, the way to establish what is mainly going on in the setting is to work sequentially from hearing a patient called a "crock" toward establishing the whole complex of observations that show frequent complaint and avoidance of things that will not help a future general practitioner, as such a physician is conceived in student culture. Then, finally, one looks carefully for negative instances, in order to perfect the theory of the exact conditions of this importance.

Systematically organizing observations into degrees of improbability, and trying to find those spontaneous, frequent, action-embedded items of culture that most strongly and unequivocally indicate what is mainly going on, what is important and salient in the setting, is a strategy for making a participant observation study scientifically convincing.

Bruce Carruthers, in *City of Capital* (1996) and again in a shorter paper by him and me (Carruthers and Stinchcombe, 1999), breaks down the process of creating a market for the British national debt: first, the Crown borrowed from the British East India Company, and then that company sold stocks in its own corporation on the basis that the Crown would pay the debt. This process got around legal and administrative problems, and made a lot of aspects of the claims being sold on the debt more secure. Into this general picture he then fills in many processes (the origin of the stock exchange, the growth of the profession of market makers, the backing of Parliament for the Crown's debt by promising to vote taxes to pay it, and so on), so by the end we do not care that he has analyzed only one case. When then this processual evidence is supplemented, in the book, by evidence that the Dutch did it much the same way, but the other European powers did it differently and it did not work as well, the two kinds of evidence supplement each other's believability.

Context

ONE OF THE THEORETICAL PENUMBRAS of any given naturally occurring case is so big that I give it separate treatment in chapter 5: the "context" of causation. It is important in historical work, so I will discuss it in connection with Schneiberg and Clemens (forthcoming, 2004). In historical sociology one usually imagines that the whole context of the thing the investigator is trying to explain is likely to influence what happens.

If someone who looked like a Tutsi met someone who looked like a Hutu, and they were both born in the United States, they would treat each other as fellow African Americans rather than as members of ethnic groups so deeply opposed that they were both trying to commit genocide on the other, as in Rwanda. To interpret this meeting in the United States of individuals who in Rwanda would belong to two races but are members of the same race in the United States, we are going to have to find out a lot about the context of being a pair of African Americans in the United States. And if we then want to find out something about two people having the same difference in looks (Watutsis outside Rwanda look more different from Hutus than do those known as Tutsis in Rwanda) meeting in Rwanda, we would have to know a lot about the history of conquest, of colonial politics, of the proposed introduction of statehood, and perhaps democracy there. One cannot afford to spend to spend one's life on the context, or the book (much less the article) will never be published, and if it were, people would not be able to figure out the main point because it would be buried in contextual material. But for many purposes, one has to know a fair amount about the context of one's subject.

The answer is that one must get the main parts of the context with cheap data, helter-skelter, looking for anything that might be relevant in the readily available data—the *Statistical Abstract*, perhaps, for the United States, anthropology and political science monographs for Rwanda. This is just a warning of why there is a treatment of Schneiberg and Clemens later, and how it is related to the "economy of data collection." They give devices to tell when a sociologist has enough of the context.

My point here is that it is especially important to make research into the context of a causal process cheap enough that one can actually do it. It will often be necessary to explore the relevant context, because causal processes are often different in different contexts. But much of the reason that social science dissertations often take longer than the graduate school thinks they should is that the researcher gets buried in exploring the context. The logic of contextual research, and especially its contribution to the time and money spent on research, warrants its separate treatment in chapter 5.

Appendix
General Note on American "Random" Samples

....

MOST AMERICAN SURVEY SAMPLES called "random" are not random, so the apparent cheapness is sometimes an illusion. They are nonrandom in some ways that undermine their use for particular causal studies, but are usually all right—if inefficient—for other causal studies. They are modeled on census random samples *of households*, because the census uses a single respondent from each household to answer about the whole household. Social science survey samples usually choose *one* of the adults in the household randomly, to interview about his or her attitudes or behavior. So the probability of being in the sample is inversely proportional to the number of adults in the household. The census random samples are "better" in this respect only because they ask whoever is at home about all the people in the household, and depend on people remembering what defines a "resident" in the household, so that the data will identify each person with one and only one household. The census does not actually have to find all the people, at least for those variables that one can find out accurately by asking whoever is at home.

However, there may be people who occasionally stay at the house, but are out quite a bit, so it is not clear where they are "residents." Such individuals are grossly undersampled in both kinds of samples. People in institutions are grossly undersampled—for example, people in prisons, and there are many of these nowadays. People in the military abroad are undersampled in both kinds of samples. It used to be that college students who lived in dormitories were very much undersampled. But the census changed the method of identifying college students with households, and I'm not sure whether it worked.

In short, the connection between people and households means that various kinds of samples that are random samples of households may not be random samples of individuals. The question of whether people's adulthood (most survey samples are of adults, unless they study students during the school year) is well measured is also somewhat complex. One observes in census returns that too many people are ages of twenty, thirty, forty, and so on—multiples of ten. Not all people keep track of the ages of all people in the household to the nearest year. So we may not get all those whose ages are near the borderline between child and adult, or we may get some extras. People who do not believe the ideology of public service (generally communicated to them with something like, "You are doing a public service by answering our detailed questions on occupation, and please sign this consent form") are grossly undersampled; we study random samples of people with good attitudes.

The point of all this is that "random" in sociology is a term of art, and much of the artificiality is created by social processes that are of sociological interest. One should theorize these processes, rather than ignoring them (and rather than giving up on sample studies).

4 Using Data to Refine Concepts of Distances between Units of Analysis

IN THE PREVIOUS CHAPTERS we have assumed that we knew what a distance between two units of analysis (e.g., two people, two years) was about, and had only to say whether those distances were large, small, or zero. For example, some nations are much more important in science because they have many trained researchers, while others have very few. But within the United States, where there are many, some people are trained chemists and a few have won Nobel Prizes for their research, and many untrained people have never done a chemical experiment. Within the Congo, where there are few, those few can do the things that American scientists can do. So the distances between countries and the distances between people both have effects.

But when we look in more detail at a distance in "training" and ask why it predicts being able to do something no one has ever done before (Nobel laureates have to have done that), we realize that we do not know exactly what the distance between "trained" and "untrained" really consists of. At first blush we imagine "training" as learning to do what one's trainers can do, to think of what they can think of.

Reflecting on this a bit, we realize that when children learn a language, quite early on they can say sentences that they have never heard before. That is, both science and language are "generative," and training causes people to be able to do things they have never learned specifically to do. Something about human beings can connect training in speech *or* science into "generative" action, generating new lines of activity that they have, in some sense, "never learned." Similarly, something about nations with many scientists makes them able to institute programs to train scientists, and to do collectively huge projects that have never been done before, such as sending men to walk on the moon.

It is easy to say that the distance between chemistry in the United States and in Germany is small, and the distance between either and chemistry in the Congo is large. We do not know from that why, exactly, the highly trained countries can do massive things never done before. To do that, we need to develop a *concept* of generativity. One of the things that education does is to produce generativity. We need to develop methods to refine a concept of generativity (and why training causes it) before we can understand how the distances in training, between individuals and nations, produce these particular effects. A noble attempt to give a systematic account of what "training" for creativity is about is Collins, *Sociology of Philosophies* (1998).

The sociological habit of measuring education by years is not very useful. It is true enough that sentences never heard before become more frequent in a child's speech by about the fifth grade, that people rarely write all-new sentences end to end for twenty pages or more before about eleventh grade, and that people rarely make new arguments twenty pages long until they have about twenty to twenty-five years of education. But the years of graduate school in which the ability to write new arguments is "trained into" students are quite differently organized than the high school curriculum. These are not the same sort of years. A continuation of secondary education giving more secondary-level courses would be unlikely ever to produce Nobel Prize–winning research.

We need, then, to refine what a common-sense distance in years of education really is, in order to understand how it could have one of its important effects. We get clues from what "generativity" consists of in the early years, what different sorts of generativity there are in secondary school and college, and in graduate school. And we look for corresponding differences in what is learned in school, to see what causes generativity.

We started by observing one major effect of training, which is different from, say, the effect of obedience training for a dog—namely, scientific advances. Then we started looking for other effects that were similar to it, such as speaking sentences one has never heard before in grade school. This led us to distinguish learning characterized by "generativity" or "creativity." Then we looked for measures of this particular component of the effects of training or education, such as growth in the count of new sentences. Then we homed in on differences between years—that is, we looked back at our crude measure of causes, years of training, to what difference between years corresponded to differences in types of generativity. We found that seminars, assignments to do experiments, critical reading of recent advances in science, and the like are much more prevalent exactly in the training that produces people who create new science.

The basic argument of this chapter is that using data (in this case, fairly obvious data from one's own experience, now reconceived not as passing tests but as generating new things not on the tests) allows one to approach the core of a refined distance concept. Then we want to measure the core of the effect, distances on generativity in place of standardized test scores, as well as the core of the causes (e.g., seminars instead of lectures, critiques rather than summaries of textbooks, experiments rather than standardized tests) that could produce the differences in generativity that we have identified. The question of whether standardized test scores are highly correlated within grade with such measures of generativity, controlling the kind of education being received, and if so, why, is a different but also very interesting question.

We use data to converge on the exact definition of the effect variable to identify exactly what is caused by the causal variables: of all the things educated people do more than uneducated people, what is distinctive of the distances between the *new* things they do? Why, for example, would no one want to award a Nobel Prize for the best grade on a standardized chemistry test? Then we want to identify what it is about years that produces that effect, such as seminars, experiments, critiques, and the like.

Once we have identified these more precise variables *with the purpose of using data to refine concepts of distances*, we want to develop methods of starting with hypotheses stated in vague general concepts, such as years of training producing more new science. The distance between people within societies in scientific training is an obvious one. The average distance in levels of training of societies is partly a matter of adding up the greater training of individuals. But it involves employing those individuals to give seminars rather than lectures, to supervise experiments rather than to read summaries for accuracy, or to teach fundamentals rather than to "teach to the test." That is, creating research universities is only partly a matter of training the individuals who might teach in them. It also involves creating institutions that reliably, year after year, teach advanced students to be generative of new knowledge. That is, we simultaneously want to converge on an exact definition of the causal variable, training that causes generativity.

In this chapter, I start at the beginning of the convergence with vague general concepts, and I then show some examples of how one starts with these vague causal or effect distance concepts and refines them with data of different sorts. I then cover the basic logic of refining concepts at this low level, the level of distances between units of analysis. The following two chapters will concentrate on more difficult distances to analyze— namely, concepts of distances between the *contexts* of causal processes, and the differences in the concepts of *mechanisms and units of analysis.*

"Sensitizing Concepts" and Improving Them

INFORMATION ABOUT THE WORLD is useful in refining concepts about distances between situations, as well as between people or countries. Chapter 6 covers in more detail why situations as well as people and organizations can be units of analysis, internally coherent enough to transmit causal forces. Herbert Blumer (1954) called the sort of concept we start with a "sensitizing concept." He often used as an example W. I. Thomas's notion of a "definition of a situation." Blumer, following Thomas, thought that situations that were substantively identical could have quite different impacts on behavior within them, depending on how they were defined. One distance between situations, then, was a distance in how they were defined. He was one of the leading "symbolic interactionists." His basic idea was that concepts served mainly to tell researchers what to look for during fieldwork.

Blumer himself particularly liked concepts that sensitized people to a lot of different things (see Thomas 1967b [1923]). He believed that ethnography is primarily useful for exploring situations, finding out what people in them think, and only then being able to say why they act the way they do in that situation. I think there is a lot of use to such broad concepts as this, but I also believe that an exquisitely sensitive concept is one that tells researchers exactly what to look for, how to look, and how to tell if they are right. A good concept is also embedded in a theory that tells researchers that everything else they might look for is irrelevant to the cause (or the effect) that it is making them sensitive to. But to get from a broad, "sensitizing" concept to one that tells more specifically what to look for requires information.

The "definition of the situation" suggests, first, that there is something about a situation that the people being studied think of as outside themselves, and, second, that they think that something has its causes and effects out in the world. That is, the people reacting in a situation think that the definition is a reality. One possibility is that some of the apparent elements of the situation are really there. Thus, for example, it may really be true—as Howard Becker's medical students (and he and his co-authors of *Boys in White* [1961]) believed—that most students cannot find all the things they are supposed to find in dissection labs in anatomy. Yet the students themselves may define their task in that situation as learning enough anatomy for what they mostly are going to be, namely, general practitioners rather than neurosurgeons. They may or may not become primary care physicians; they may also be wrong in believing that general practitioners will not need to know how to find a particular nerve. But in spite of the realities, they may conclude that their learning task does not require them to be able to find the right nerve to draw for class in a particular corpse, where it may be some distance away from where the textbook illustration shows, and they may follow that "knowledge" whether it is knowledge or not. Becker and others' point is that this ignorance and error is structurally determined and then is carried by the culture, so is not a random residual.

That last proposition is the sort of thing Thomas, and Blumer after him, thought of as requiring us to theorize about the definition of the situation, rather than just about "the situation." The situation objectively is that the nerve is where it happens to be in this corpse, and the reality of the norm from the point of view of the anatomist would mean being required to find the nerve even though it was in an odd place. And it might be true that if the students found it in the wrong place, they might be graded down because the instructor did not think it *could* be there.

Microeconomics in principle believes that all one needs to know to predict a person's action in a market is "the situation," and any variation in a person's perception of the situation is put down to "ignorance and error." If microeconomists do quantitative econometric research, they usually put "ignorance and error" into the residuals of a statistically estimated equation—residuals that, being random, will be averaged out in macroeconomic outcomes. In the stereotypical microeconomics approach as taught in elementary courses, a theory of why people made the particular mistake they made, definition or not, is of no interest.

Institutionalized Definitions

SOCIOLOGISTS SPECIALIZE IN SHOWING that such definitions vary systematically, and that they matter. They cannot therefore be summarized as "ignorance and error." The medical students do not know where the nerve really is in *this* copse, because they hold in common the view that such details will not matter to them. But as I said above, *one* of the big things that determines what people see in the world is what is really there. It is no accident that graduate students at Northwestern University all will come to believe that no one can rent an apartment in Evanston below a number that would be, say, 30 percent of what a person working 160 hours a month at the minimum wage would earn. The reason they will come to believe this is the simple fact that people earning minimum wage cannot live in Evanston on what they earn.

Now the notion that people making minimum wage should not pay more than one-third of their income for housing is also a definition of the situation—in particular, a normative view of our public policy. The idea that people should not, instead of renting an apartment, build a stick-and-mud shack on somebody's lawn (which "isn't being used") is a definition of the property situation. The police will make the squatters tear down the shack. That, too, is a social creation; in some countries, such a solution would not bring the police down on the shantytown. In some, the police would come down only occasionally and unpredictably, when there was some sort of political ruckus about the building. The novel *Texaco* (Chamoiseau, 1997 [1992]) portrays such a situation in Martinique, a small French-speaking island in the Windwards in the Caribbean. In chapter 5, we will discuss in detail how to form concepts about distances between contexts, such as Martinique at the time of the novel and Evanston at the time of this book. Causes of definitions of a piece of land with grass vary between these contexts, so the behavior of police and squatters on "lawns" varies. The same causes do not have the same effects in different environments.

Parts of the definition of a situation may take on an air of "reality," even though their origins are social definitions. Thomas (1967a [1923]) gives many examples of different definitions that are socially or individually supported in different situations; from the title of his book, *The Unadjusted Girl*, one can tell that many of those are definitions of the differences in meaning of the situation of being pregnant. We sometimes say that such definitions are "institutionalized," meaning that ultimately they have social causes, but those social causes, *as far as the actions we are studying are concerned*, are "inevitable." Retrospectively, of course, we may question how institutionalized they were.

The most heart-wrenching cases are perhaps those of the Jewish community leaders who negotiated conditions, particularly the sending of people to "labor camps," during the Holocaust, and who occasionally got tried in court in Israel afterward, if they themselves got away. The "reality out there" was the Holocaust, as well institutionalized in Nazi Germany as the reality that one cannot build a shack on somebody else's lawn in Evanston. Unfortunately, the definitions of the situation by Jewish community leaders were factually wrong about what was institutionalized. We cannot predict very well what will happen, if we fail to refine the concept so that some definitions of situations are called "institutionalized" definitions. The institutionalized meaning of labor camps was extermination, whatever community leaders hoped the definition was.

To put it another way, "institutionalized versus uninstitutionalized definitions of the situation" is a variable, on which distances between situations can be observed. Different consequences follow in Evanston, where Texaco's property rights would institutionally exclude building a shack, and in Martinique, where such exclusion is a matter of political contest.

Blumer's reply to this "reality out there" argument would be that if investigators fail to recognize that lawns as private property, money as a social institution, and a landlord in the housing market having the right to set the rent are all social definitions, they will miss the variability out of which this definition of reality came to be "out there." It must remain "surprising" that nature ("a piece of land with grass") has become private property some places, a thing to plunder in others.

"Informal" Institutions

WE CAN THEN ASK OURSELVES about some of the definitions of situations that Erving Goffman studies, such as the "norm of civil inattention." This requires, for instance, that as people encounter a stranger while walking down the street, there is a distance below which they are required to turn their eyes away or down in a conspicuous way. If they keep looking beyond that point, they are implicitly asking the other person to make their acquaintance, or they are "staring." On a college campus one sees more violations of the norm of civil inattention in the first week or two of a new school year, or at parties during "rush" whose purpose is to give people a chance to get acquainted, or at what one sociologist called "body exchange bars" (Cavan, 1966).

People who do not want to form acquaintances presumably are more careful about "meeting people's eyes." Thus, one might expect that women would turn their eyes away or down earlier and more regularly than men do, because they are more at risk in several ways when getting acquainted with strangers. But when most people walk down the street, they are almost unconscious of this definition of the situation, and what its violation means. They may remember vaguely their parents' injunction, "Don't stare," but they may not realize that "staring" implies that they are willing to be spoken to.

Norms like these are institutionalized in a different sense than the ownership of lawns. Ordinarily there are no policemen to enforce them, they are not written out, and they are at least partly unconscious (I'd say unconscious most of the time, except when they create problems that one has to deal with). For example, celebrities have to get used to being stared at, and to adjust to the fact that a lot more people want to get acquainted with them than they probably want to be acquainted with.

Goffman would notice the ironies produced by such norms in places like sociological conventions; he once called attention to the instability of the norm for celebrities by telling someone that he would talk to them unless someone more important than they were came along. The norm at sociological conventions is that we are all peers, and anyone can talk to anyone, and some of us just happen to be friends. Of course, there are strong age-grading patterns in who is old friends of whom, and given the way reputations accumulate and last a lot longer than the merits they represent, there are very likely to be, "just by chance," groups of friends who are relatively famous older scholars.

The norm that people ought not to interrupt a conversation between old friends to make someone's acquaintance then creates an oligarchy, and that oligarchy is illegitimate by the norms of peer interaction that are weakly institutionalized at conventions. The norm that people drop their eyes is related to the norm that a groups of friends turn their backs on everyone else when they are talking, and cannot lower their eyes in the conversation within the circle of backs. Having one's back turned requires that others be civilly inattentive; this violates the norm of sociology conventions that we are all equal as sociologists.

That conflict of norms is a problem in the definition of situations that Goffman would be especially sensitive to, because he had studied and written books about those norms. He analyzed the circles-of-backs norm and the civil inattention norm at length in his book *Behavior in Public Places* (1963).

The norm that at conventions we are all peers is more institutionalized in sociology than in economics, statistics, or political science. The norm that we are all equal, but all of us talk to our friends, puts a person from another discipline in an awkward situation. Such a person is likely to have been invited by an elite member of the host discipline, because elite people have more interdisciplinary intellectual contacts and are more likely to have the power to invite. The visitor may find himself in the situation of knowing only that elite host. Everyone else wants to talk to such an elite person, and the stranger does not want the host to be tied down as his or her only friend. Yet the peer norm that anyone present is everyone's equal does not mean much if one has no acquaintances there.

The general point here is that by studying a subtype of institutionalized norm, the semiconscious norms by which behavior in public places is organized, Goffman came to see things that we would not generally see. It is one thing to say that, as Thomas's point was formulated later, "if people define situations as real, they are real in their consequences." In Goffman's view, people do not even really know what the reality is they are acknowledging. If we do not develop sensitizing concepts about that special type of subconscious norm, we do not understand why we are so lonely at other people's conventions.

So the methodological point is that we learn a lot more about what sorts of troubles people get into in public situations, such as a sociology convention, if we have sufficiently specified a "definition of the situation," including specifically "a situation requiring the norm of civil inattention." We can then go on to the norm that (a) we drop our eyes if we are facing a stranger, and (b) we do not demand the attention of someone who is in a circle of backs with ourselves on the outside.

Methodological Implications of the Examples

SO WE HAVE NOW GONE THROUGH A TWO-EXAMPLE SEQUENCE that started with a general sensitizing concept, "definition of the situation," that seems to take us in the direction of psychology: "Who knows how people will define a situation?" Then we noticed that some of these definitions have a high level of agreement, because the police come if homeless people do not define the lawn the right way, and because people do not have to provide apartments that workers on a minimum wage can afford. These definitions have a certain amount of solidity in Evanston, but as we go across countries, "squatters" have a different legal standing. The norm that "everybody has to have somewhere to live" is more powerful in Martinique. Put another way, we used observations about variations between definitions in "intractability" in the United States to see what made property "a hard part of reality," and then looked across countries to see that that intractability is not a law of nature, but a law of the United States.

Then we took up Goffman's observations about what norms create the patterns we can see when we walk down the street. We used observations about the first week of the academic year, and about the problem of circles of famous old scholars being inaccessible in a normatively "peer" environment at sociology conventions, to elaborate a more specific sensitizing concept about norms institutionalized without police. Finally, we used those conceptual notions to locate the almost unconscious conflicts among the relevant norms, peership and circles of backs, that we might not otherwise have been sensitive to.

Now let me make a methodological point about why we need participant observation, or ethnography. There is no way we could ask people in a survey, "When do you drop your eyes when meeting a stranger on a city street?" Nor, at a sociology convention, could we ask the ethnological question, "Why did the visitor and the conversational group of famous old scholars she was in, all turn their backs on the younger and less famous folks around them?" This is because the norms, and especially their fit in the situation, were at most semiconscious, more usually unconscious.

To collect data on the physical distance of civil inattention when meeting on the street, an investigator has to watch people. To study the recognition and incorporation into the circle of mutual attention of fellow old scholars, and the invisibility of the nonfamous young people who may be "staring," one may have to "experiment" by breaking one of the norms. And of course, the distances below which people drop their eyes, and how they do (or do not) break into a conversational circle, are matters that do not appear in historical documents. We can improve such concepts of interactional norms only by observation of spontaneously occurring action.

Extending the Notion

TO SOME DEGREE I HAVE POSED the reader with an impossible model here, because Goffman was the genius of my generation. So Goffman can walk down the street, notice when eyes disengage, figure out what norm would generate that, collect more evidence on the norm, and end up with a generalization of a special kind of sensitizing concept that fits within "defining the situation." So the advice is: Go be a genius, and it will all work out. Our job as methodologists is to turn what it takes a genius to do the first time into something that all of us can recognize and work on. So let me now try to outline the method that is involved.

The core of the method is to set out systematically to find the contrary instances. Investigators start with a concept that suggests that anybody can define any situation any way they please. Rather than making fun of economists for not acknowledging it, they look for cases where the people being studied seem to be right—such as that all apartments in Evanston are too expensive for people earning the minimum wage.

So the investigators then start to ask, what is the distinguishing feature of definitions of situations like that? They recognize that it is often coercive legal norms that specify what ownership means, why owners do not have to offer low-rent apartments, and why people cannot build on other people's lawns with corrugated tin. Then investigators might happen to read a novel on squatter settlements and the norms of a woman who was the leader of the squatters, and they learn that such property norms are not deep in the nature of the universe. For instance, they do not apply to Texaco property in Martinique at the time of Chamoiseau's novel. So in Evanston the norm is social, it is a definition of the situation, and it is coercive, but it might have been differently coercive if it was in Martinique.

Then the investigators start to look around for cases that fall within the class of "institutionalized" definitions of a situation, but not in the "coercive" (in the sense of police) part of that concept. As soon as they read Goffman and start watching people's eyes as they walk down the street, or observing a conversation among famous elderly scholars at a convention, they find that backs turned and being too close coming down the street reliably produce a definition of the situation so that eyes turn away or down or so that it is "impossible" to interrupt. Yet no police enforce street distances or leaving people alone when they are part of a circle of backs.

Then ethnographers notice the circumstances when people do *not* turn their eyes the right way. There are two main cases: children, who are then told by their parents, "Don't stare at people," and people trying to make new acquaintances.

In each case the investigators take up a preliminary concept, and then try to guess, by watching the exceptions, where the naive concept is supposed to work but does not. Thus one learns the defining features of a set of phenomena, tentatively summed up as a definition of a situation in which civil inattention is required. Or one learns when property law does not reliably define a lawn as a place where one should not build a shack.

This becomes a modification of hypotheses. We start with, "Definitions of the situation are easily changeable." It turns out that that generalization does not work very well: Nobody builds tarpaper shacks on other people's lawns because it is coercively defined as a situation in which, though there is no fence, people in Evanston know it is the owner's lawn, not the potential squatter's. So the definition is highly predictable, and real estate law on unfenced lawns is not easily changeable by a personal redefining. The condition is, however, a variable: namely, the degree of institutionalization of the definition of "my or Texaco's property." As Evanston people walk by, they glance at a piece of grass and define it as "lawn." But people in Martinique in the early twentieth century might glance, talk to the neighbors, and think, "Building site for my shack." In the immediate situation, the distance in institutionalization of "property" between countries causes differences in definitions of the situation, and so in behavior.

But a second condition seems to shift definitions of a situation of approaching someone on the street, from a distance from which it is all right to look at someone (e.g., 50 feet away), to the number of feet away where it is not (e.g., 5 feet away). The condition is a variable that asks how uncivil people are when they are "paying too much attention" to someone else. The reason it is different from an "institutionalized" definition is that it is not enforced very much, and then only by an offended person who says aggressively, "What are *you* looking at?" But we all apparently learn the norms involved in the principle of civil inattention early on, and most of the time obedience is either unconscious or only semiconscious. We say, "Oh. Sorry," when we realize that we have unconsciously violated the norm.

Ethnographers thus improve concepts so they are much more definite, even if it appeared in the first place that people can define situations any way they want. So when I start talking about factor analysis, which sometimes does the work of refining concepts by revealing what hangs together, remember Goffman finding out what hung together about where people subconsciously turn their eyes, with no factor analysis to help.

Distances between Situations

WE HAVE NOT YET DEFINED WHAT IT MEANS for something to be a situation, or for a situation to have a definition. We will leave for chapter 6 the unpacking of the intuition of what a situation is. We have, however, identified two dimensions or concepts of distances between situations: from coercively institutionalized situations, like property rights in American lawns, to less coercively institutionalized ones, such as grass in shanty-towns around cities in poorer countries. Presumably, there is a still greater distance from a lawn to a desert "no man's land," or *terra nullius*.

The second distance is defined by the semi-automatic application of unenforced norms, in this case the norm of civil inattention. Within public places there is a change in local physical arrangements (physical distance, a circle of backs) and in behavior governing attention (lowering the eyes, not listening and not interrupting). The key here is to find an unconscious or semiconscious norm that tells what distance between situations would give rise to spontaneous, not consciously coordinated, behavior of not attending. One way of elaborating that concept would be to collect data on what behavior of children elicits the parents' command, "Don't stare."

We found these two variables by a common-sense sorting of every-day experience ("everyone knows" that a lawn cannot be used to relieve homelessness and that people do not have to offer low-rent apartments) and the similarly common-sense portrait by a novelist of the urban slums of historical Martinique. Property clearly means something different for defining a patch of grass in the two places, and those definitions are coercively defined. A *terra nullius* in the Australian desert meant, coercively, that anyone could use it for their purposes. More specifically, the indigenes who had been using specific places for centuries to worship had no prior claim; as an "investment," a herding shack of a white man had priority.

What Goffman noticed was the continuity of meaning between three rather different situations in which attention is informally governed: looking away from closely approaching strangers, not interrupting a conversational circle, and telling a child not to stare. Concretely, these situations were distinct or distant from a pedestrian farther away, an elderly famous scholar wandering alone through the book display, and a child in front of the TV (it is okay to stare at characters on the screen). The commonality of meaning is inferred from the common effect of not attending to the business of others.

Quantitative and Qualitative Distances

THERE ARE TWO LOGICALLY VERY DIFFERENT MEANINGS given to the word *qualitative* (as contrasted to *quantitative*) in common discourse in sociology. In one of these a qualitative difference is simply a variable that has discrete states, so that male and female persons are "qualitatively" different in the sense that for many purposes, we do not want to distinguish degrees of maleness versus femaleness. The simplest sort of qualitative variable is simply a dichotomy, a binary, with only two states (say zero and one, for example: zero for male, one for female, in a variable we might call "female"). Another would be "state of origin," ranging from Alabama to Wyoming, with fifty values that do not behave as numbers, but rather as fifty ones and zeros, with each person having exactly one such value. The chemical elements in the periodic table of elements are such a category system, though just as states can be described by various quantitative features, such as population or percent urban, so elements may be described by quantitative values, such as valence or average atomic weight. Goffman would then classify people by a qualitative variable of "in the conversational circle versus out," and would notice many differences in their behavior that correspond to such a distinction.

The more complex concept of "qualitative" is a narrative account of a causal process. For example, consider a written account of the development over time of the conflict between North and South before the Civil War. Most narratives are constructed out of words that have categorical meanings, for example, that various states "voted to secede" versus not, perhaps followed by a narrative account of ambiguous cases, such as Missouri. What is logically involved in a narrative can sometimes be described quantitatively. Thus, for example, the development from infant to adult (qualitative) involves a person's increase in weight. But when we use the words, we usually describe many other variables than weight, often crucial to the narrative. We can radically simplify the narrative into the changes of a single (or a few) variables, which we then may present as a mathematical-looking graph, a "time series." Very often, then, "qualitative" means the investigator's description of many causes and many effects over time, and this is often associated with simplification of most of the variables into dichotomies on many variables described with words (such as "in the conversational circle" in Goffman, which he then wants to compare with "within speaking distance of an acquaintance on the street"). The two senses of the word *qualitative* are, in practice, usually mixed up together, and historians and ethnographers who write narratives very generally use words rather than numbers to write them with.

But this has little to do with the logic of narrative, and a time series graph is logically a narrative. Sometimes the translation into a quantitative variable can be illuminating, as in describing the degree to which some area is a "frontier" as "the proportion of all land in an area devoted to its most productive use under the technology of the time." A frontier, then, can be considered a continuous variable, which goes up with the importation of a new (e.g., sugar-growing) technology, then down as land is converted to the new crop. For narrative convenience, we may then divide that into "before active development," "frontier," and "developed" (see "Stinchcombe Slavery Short Version," in chapter 8). This implicitly quantitative variable may then be used in qualitative narrative descriptions of social and political life in nineteenth-century American history. For example, it is central to the narrative description of mid-nineteenth-century Missouri, mentioned above, that it was still a frontier (in fact, two frontiers—a cotton frontier and a grain frontier) at the time of votes on secession.

The following exploration of the logic of using qualitative concepts in causal arguments deals with the first meaning: namely, the simplification of variables into zero and one, present or absent, or into slightly more complex categories, such as state of residence, that are combined values of several such zero/one variables.

Exemplification of Discrete Variables

NOW WE TURN TO THE DIFFERENCE between qualitative and quantitative variables: in the simplest case, categories (qualities) versus numbers (quantities). In some formal sense, putting people in a job category like "skilled, propertyless, and authorityless" (Wright, 1978) is saying that all jobs of that sort are near enough to identical so we can ignore any other differences. For example, we might say that a keyboard operator who needs good spelling and six months of training is the same as a car salesman who needs a six-month apprenticeship in car talk and a fairly good background in arithmetic. In both cases the job has an intermediate level of skill, so that we may decide to call it "skilled," and neither worker is likely to own the means of production or to boss people around.

But we now have to decide whether these skills of car salesmen and typists are, or are not, to be lumped in with the skills requiring about four years of training instead of six months beyond high school—for example, primary school teachers and plumbers. We ordinarily call the first group "semi-skilled" and the second "skilled," when they are in the labor market and are male, though for Wright's purposes they may perhaps be classified together. If we do not think the plumber's four years of training really equivalent to four years of college with an education major, we will have to say why. And then, at the next skill level, do we need to distinguish the schoolteachers, perhaps to be called "lower professionals," from those with seven years beyond high school, like lawyers, or about ten to twelve years, like surgeons or pediatricians ("real professionals")? We see that a classification is a decision to ignore differences within a category. By accepting a category like "skilled," we decide to ignore the differences we have been distinguishing here.

By using the qualitative category "skilled," we are saying, first, that for certain purposes we do not want to distinguish by, say, the quantitative variable of years of special training, where we might count six months for typists and car salesmen as "unskilled" and so strictly analogous to those with no training, but we might lump together as "skilled" four years of teacher's college or of plumber's apprenticeship and seven years for a lawyer or ten for a surgeon. Second, we do not want to distinguish the dominantly female skills (typing, elementary school teaching, fine arts, and pediatrics) from the dominantly male ones (car salesman, plumber, lawer—though in law school classes gender no longer differs from the population—and surgeon). The logic of such analysis of categories and how to improve them is presented in "Stinchcombe Logic of Analogy Short Version," below.

The purpose of making a quality into a categorical variable is to ignore everything else that differs between cases in the category, because the investigators think the analogies they have made among their cases are *sufficient* for explaining the variables they are interested in. In Wright's case the categories are supposed to be sufficient to explain whether they exploit or are exploited (Wright, 1978). Of course, Wright knows that car salesmen make more than typists, plumbers make more than elementary school teachers, and surgeons make more than pediatricians, even on a per-hour basis (pediatricians and typists are at work fewer hours, on average, than surgeons or car salesmen). So presumably the women are exploited more.

To return to our concern with distances between observations: if we use categories, we set the distances within categories to zero. In its turn this categorical treatment sets distances to another category all equal. If we set both employed pediatricians and employed plumbers equal to the category "skilled, propertyless, and authorityless," and pediatricians in private practice and plumbing contractors into "skilled, propertied, and with authority," then we are saying that the employed pediatrician is the same distance from the plumbing contractor and the pediatrician in private practice who hires nurses and receptionists, and those two are the same distance from the employed pediatrician and the employed plumber.

The general experience with statistical treatments of the matter is that if one breaks continuous variables into three approximately equal subcategories, one does not lose much statistical power (except in small samples) because one is mostly throwing away knowledge of small distances, and those do not produce much difference in the effect variables.

Stinchcombe Logic of Analogy Short Version

From Arthur L. Stinchcombe, "Technical Appendix: The Logic of Analogy," in *Theoretical Methods in Social History* (Orlando, Fla.: Academic Press), pp. 25–29. This is a reprint of the original, with a few additions in brackets for clarity in this context.

Let us presume we have three objects, say General Motors, the Soviet Union [in 1978], and the set of pedestrians visible from State and Madison at 1:10 p.m. on some chosen Friday. Intuitively, it is clear that the first two are corporate groups, that part of their corporate activity involves allocating rewards and duties to members, and that they do this unequally. While no doubt our pedestrians are unequal, that inequality is hardly a stratification system that pertains to sidewalks near State and Madison. We therefore have the intuitive feeling that if we could understand why General Motors and the Soviet Union act alike in creating inequality, it might be causally solid knowledge about stratification, while the inequalities of the pedestrians come from so many sources that no one causal statement is likely to grasp them all. When Erving Goffman (1963) teaches us about the stratification of the pedestrians, the processes are mostly those about bleeding status from elsewhere into the signs one gives off as one walks near State and Madison.

Let our three objects be called X_1, X_2, and X_3. Then there is a set of predicate variables p_{ij} which can be used to describe such objects. For example, the first predicate might be p_{1j} = "does (or does not) the object j have collective production of goods and services?" p_{2j} might be, "does (or does not) the object have designated officials or written norms to admit people as members?" p_{3j} might be, "Do some people in the group eat more protein than others?"

For these three variables, General Motors (when it was object j) would have the values (does produce, does admit members, does have inequality of protein intake); the Soviet Union would have the same values; and the pedestrians would have the values (does not produce, does not have formal membership, does have inequality of protein intake). Or in more abstract notation, letting the first subscript be the variable number and the second the object number, we would have:

$$P_1 = (p_{11}, p_{21}, p_{31}, \ldots)$$
$$P_2 = (p_{12}, p_{22}, p_{32}, \ldots)$$
$$P_3 = (p_{13}, p_{23}, p_{33}, \ldots)$$

where

$p_{11} = p_{12} =$ does produce
$p_{13} =$ does not produce
$p_{21} = p_{22} =$ does have formal members
$p_{23} =$ does not have formal members
$p_{31} = p_{32} = p_{33} =$ does have inequality of protein intake

Then P_1 is the set of all predicates that apply to X_1 (to General Motors) [but the notation has not specified which values of that variable General Motors in fact had—that has been specified separately below the definition of the set of predicates that apply to General Motors], P_2 is all those that apply to X_2 (the Soviet Union), and P_3 all those that apply to the pedestrians at State and Madison.

The *analogy* between X_1 and X_2 is the set of predicates [whose values] they have in common, in this case all the first three (but not, for example, $p_{4j} =$ does object j divide profits in proportion to investments?). The differentiation between X_1 and X_3 is the set of predicates on which they have different values, in this case the first two ($p_{11} \neq p_{13}$; $p_{21} \neq p_{23}$; but $p_{31} = p_{33}$).

The concept that divides X_1 and X_2 into one class, and X_3 into another, is the set of predicates which simultaneously are members of the analogy between X_1 and X_2, and of the differentiation (of either) from X_3. Or in more formal terms [with the elements of the classes being predicates],

$$A_{12} = P_1 \cap P_2$$

(Read, "The analogy between objects 1 and 2 is the intersection of the sets of predicates [having the same value for both].")

$$A_{13} = P_1 \cap P_3$$
$$D_{13} = P_3 - P_1 \cap P_3$$

(Read, The differentiation of objects 1 and 3 is [the values of all predicates that apply to object 3, except for those that are the same for objects 3 and 1].)

$$_{12}C_3 = A_{12} \cap D_{13}$$

(Read: "The concept differentiating objects 1 and 2 from object 3 is the set of predicates [on which objects 1 and 2 have the same values] (their analogy) on which object 3 has a different value.)

The general object of developing concepts is to form interesting sentences. In a science we want interesting *causal* sentences. We will leave *causal* undefined here except to specify that it has to do with the application of predicates to an object at some time in the future.*

Suppose in particular we want to assert something like: "All corporately organized groups distribute status unequally." Since, while the pedestrians eat different amounts of protein, they do not have the money to buy meat distributed [to them] by other pedestrians, we might say the set of pedestrians did not distribute status unequally (this is an implicit definition of "to distribute status"). People will be treated differently on the street according to their age, race, physical condition, dress, etc. (see Goffman, 1963). Whether we want to call this "distributing status" is a purely verbal matter. If we do so, then we have to change the verb in the generalization to read something like "distribute status by collective decisions carried out by an administrative staff." Let us call this new predicate g_i having the values "distributes status unequally" and "does not distribute status unequally, though it may recognize status distributed elsewhere."

If we take the definition of "to distribute status unequally" as given, in such a way that X_1 and X_2 have it, and X_3 does not, then for the proposition to be true all the [predicate values] involved in "corporately organized" must be in the set that we have defined as the concept that divides X_1 and X_2 from X_3. Of course, many predicates other than those involved in "corporately organized" will be in that set differentiating General Motors and the Soviet Union from the group of pedestrians near State and Madison.

We can define the "causal fruitfulness" of the concept that differentiates objects X_1 and X_2 from X_3 as the set of all predicates that make causally interesting sentences ("predictions") with the concept. That is, the causal fruitfulness constitutes the respects in which the futures of General Motors and the Soviet Union are alike, and it tells us how much causal guts there is in the analogy we have formed between them [and the contrasts with the pedestrians]. But we want our concepts to be not only fruitful, but also economical. That is, if having

---

*This does not mean that I think the only "test" of a scientific theory is prediction. Many theories are easily disproved by disproving logical implications which have nothing to do with the future, however the future is defined.

their present constitution formed in the 1920s is irrelevant to a large part of the causal fruitfulness of the analogy, then we want to aim for a concept like "corporately organized" rather than one like "corporately organized in basically the same way since the 1920s," yet for some part of that causal fruitfulness (e.g., "distributes status unequally") it would be a mistake to go as far as "social order" defined as "a set of actions of people in which there is a positive probability that any one action will be oriented in its course by taking account of another action," for that would include the pedestrians at State and Madison.

Reducing the analogy between two objects (in contrast to at least one other) to its scientifically relevant predicates requires scientific work. Some of that work can be theoretical, provided we have some "regulatory generalizations" that tell us some predicates are more likely than others. For instance, in social science we may generally assert that: "Concepts involving the interactions and judgments of people are usually more economical (for the same causal fruitfulness) than those involving impulses, instincts, or mechanical responses to stimuli."

But the basic source of information for stripping away irrelevancy from an analogy is the examination of new cases. If constitution-forming during the 1920s is crucial for having a status system, then the king of France in the eighteenth century will not hand out patents of nobility. If mutual consciousness and mutual orientation is sufficient to affect status, then people should change their lifetime expectations of rewards and duties while walking near State and Madison. That is, moving from an analogy between two things to an analogy (or differentiation) between three or more whose futures are, in the relevant respects, the same, is the main way to "deepen" an analogy. An analogy is deeper: (a) the more the futures of two objects are alike, that is, the larger the number of predicates involving the future that are analogous; (b) the more causally irrelevant parts of the analogy have been stripped away, that is, the more other objects equivalent to these two [in respects captured by the concept] have similar futures.

It should be obvious that everything said here about deep analogies could equally well be said about deep predicates. In fact, we have carried along the predicate, "corporately organized," while outlining the analogy between General Motors and the Soviet Union, to communicate intuitively what the analogy of those two objects was really all about. The argument of this book is that this formal logical equivalence between an analogy between two objects and a (set of) predicate(s) defining a class can be used strategically.

Descartes' proof that algebra and geometry were really the same thing allows us to proceed either algebraically or geometrically, as suits our convenience. Likewise the equivalence of analogies and predicates allows our theory building to proceed either by causally significant analogies or by generalizations about classes. Our argument is that in historical studies it is often more strategic to work by analogies.

Similarly, we might classify a herding tribe more precisely by the proportion of all calories that come from sources connected to the herded animals (as opposed, for example, to calories from plots tended by the women and children back at the settlement, or gathering of wild root and tree crops by the women). It always turns out that the proportion due to women's and children's production is a lot more than the anthropologists noticed until they started counting, but it varies among tribes. By and large, tribes of camel herders work in territory where there isn't much food that can be grown in a garden, nor is there much they can gather. Camel herding tribes are thus "more herders" than those that herd cattle. Goats are easier to combine with some horticulture, and children often can tend them, so goat-herding tribes are often less "herding tribes." Anthropologists can partly subclassify, by noting which animals are in the herds, in "degree to which a herding tribe is a herding tribe." Camel tribes will be high on the degree variable, cattle and perhaps sheep tribes intermediate, and goat tribes more nearly horticultural. This turns the category into a more or less quantitative variable ("ranked with ties," or "ordered categories"). Anthropologists might start to make it truly quantitative by actually estimating the number of calories from plants and "domestic" animals versus herded animals.

But the logic of contrasting herding with agricultural tribes still ignores differences, even with a quantitative variable. If now a tribe is classified as "53 percent horticultural" because women's garden plots account for 53 percent of the calories, we may be ignoring the fact that men run everything, and they think their cattle are the center of the universe, and gardens are "just for women and children." A biological ecologist, interested in flows of nutrition in the local ecology, may want to ignore the men's attitude, and point out how important it is from a biological point of view that the herding tribe are omnivores rather than carnivores. A social anthropologist will note that all tribal politics and discourse about property rights is about herds and pastures, and no one (male) cares who owns garden plots.

Social anthropologists may or may not want to ignore variations in the ratios of calories from different sources, as long as the herding peoples are "herding tribes." When I began comparing African and central Asian herding tribes in a previous chapter, I was lumping them all together; if I had thought more deeply, I would have included yak herders in with the Asian ones. If I were an ecologist studying desertification, I would need to look at the calorie balance and what each source of calories does to the land and water. That is, what one wants to ignore depends on one's theoretical purpose, what one is trying to explain.

Lattimore (1967 [1940]) wanted to know when herding tribes go over from raising cattle to raising horses in central Asia, because that means they are off to the wars to conquer the horticulturists and take tribute from them. The reason he can infer this is that horses are quite inefficient as sources of food. But Lattimore's question about "inner Asian frontiers" makes the type-question one he had to answer: did he still want to count Genghis Kahn as a herder, or should he instead reclassify his tribe as military cavalry? In particular, does the distance between a herding tribe and a horticulture tribe predict the same thing when the herding tribe is herding horses to produce a cavalry rather than cattle, goats, or sheep to produce milk and cheese? Lattimore's answer is a resounding no.

But now let's turn to the quantitative variables. When investigators say that someone has ten years of education after secondary school (say, a Ph.D. or an M.D.), or twenty-two or twenty-three total years, and someone else has four beyond high school (sixteen), and someone else again has zero beyond high school (twelve), they imply that all years are equivalent. But we know that this is not the case. If students get three years of medical school, in the old days they could become an illegal abortionist, or perhaps a pharmacist. But getting those three years is nothing like getting four years followed by an internship or residency. Similarly, there is very little difference in income between those who get to the tenth grade and those reaching the eleventh grade of secondary school, but a lot of difference between eleven and twelve (that is, between not graduating and graduating). We know for sure that years are not equivalent in their effects.

When graduate students become teaching assistants, they will notice that a twelve-week quarter or semester of sociology teaches different amounts to different college students, and they may urge the weaker of them to try to qualify for the National Basketball Association rather than for graduate school in sociology. If twelve weeks of teaching is different for different students, then presumably a year is different for different students.

When I was doing fieldwork in Mexico as an assistant professor, I met a Protestant missionary couple who had learned their Spanish together in the same class. She sounded like a Mexican, and could understand what people were saying to her. He didn't and couldn't. He would be like the missionary father in Barbara Kingsolver's novel *The Poisonwood Bible* (1998) who tried to speak the local Congolese language, but had not caught on that it was a tonal language. The word for "holy" differed only by tones from the word for "poisonwood," a local plant that caused blisters. He did not understand why the local people burst into laughter when he talked about the Holy Bible in their language. A year of so of intensive Spanish was not the same for the missionary couple whom I met, and similarly, the years of study for the fictional missionary and his daughters learning a Congolese language were collectively not the same.

So different distances measured quantitatively may not yield the same effects. We have already run into this with age-curvilinearity, or with the qualitative effect of the gender of the child on the number of hours of child care that a father gives (more with boys), which produces different age curves for the division of labor in the family having boy children rather than girl children. When investigators measure something quantitatively and then use the quantities in predictions, they are really saying that the distances as measured have the same effect, that equal distances in the numbers cause equal distances in the effects. As we noted above, the abstractions in qualitative variables such as girl child and boy child also ignore other differences between them and put them all equal distances apart.

Sometimes investigators have a theory that some social process erases differences that would otherwise really be there. For example, the form of much race prejudice against, and also (perhaps therefore) of much race solidarity for, African Americans is that all people with any African ancestry ought to be classified together. Hardly anybody believes that one-drop rule about Native Americans in the United States. Even less does anyone believe that the *mestizos* in Mexico are the same as full *indígenos*. But for American sociology, we can ignore differences that would be crucial in Mexico.

The errors of measurement, of classifying things together that are really different, as long as they are close, just go into the residual, the error term; this only means we make a few more mistakes than we need to when predicting things. Most of the time investigators are not going to pay any attention to what information is still in the error term. If they ignore the information that the analysis machinery calls the error, they just lose an unknown amount of analytical power and a tiny bit of statistical power.

If investigators really wanted to know how education works, they would want to know why the distance from eleven to twelve years of education, or fifteen to sixteen, makes a much bigger difference than other distances. If they think education has to do with knowledge, such as whether a foreign missionary should attempt to preach in Spanish or in a local Congolese language, they would want a measure of knowledge rather than of years spent. But they do not lose much in the power of their statistical model if they ignore the fact that a year from eleven to twelve measures something different, or if they make some mistakes by estimating how much people know by how many years it took them to learn it.

The main thing investigators need to remember is that when they use a quantitative variable for anything, they are saying something about *the analogy between the distances* on that variable. For instance, economists usually want to say something different than sociologists about analogies between distances, so they almost always use logarithms of the raw numbers in their quantitative equations. That is, they take equal distances to be *equal ratios* or *equal percentages*, rather than equal numbers of units. The main exception is education, because unlike most other effects where distances matter less if they start bigger in the first place (i.e., if they are a smaller percentage), education has *more* effect on practically every variable, if people already have more of it. A peculiar thing, and one we do not understand, but even economists do not take the log of education, except in a fit of inattention.

I have started with the low end of a variable of "development of exactness" in concepts. Many sociologists might not recognize what the institutionalists or Goffman theorize about as sufficiently abstract and precise to be called a science. They might also fail to recognize that the analogy between General Motors and the Soviet Union, as described above, amounts to a good empirical description. And while I have talked in some detail about how categorical versions of variables that are really continuous throw away information, I have then taken much of the teeth out of that observation by saying that this rarely makes much statistical difference, unless one goes all the way to a word with only two categories, true or false. I now turn to the other end of development of concepts, by describing some "fundamental constants" in the physical sciences. By doing so, I want to show that the principles of converging toward more exactness at the hard end of science is the same as at the soft end in sociology.

The Opposite End: Exact Concepts

THE ARGUMENT OF THIS AND THE NEXT SECTION is that the process of concept development at both the soft and hard ends is one of *converging* toward exactness, by describing how one can observe more precisely those variations that have reliable causal effect. At the very high end of science this process involves what are called "fundamental constants." The use of *fundamental* here means that the constants (or other mathematical forms) turn up all over the place, and so it is hard to theorize about many things without knowing those constants. But the term *constants* means that the scientists can estimate them from physical phenomena exactly. Many of the constants are coefficients in equations that translate distances in one variable into effects on the movements of another variable. So to see what is at stake in forming concepts and then measuring them, what exactness really looks like (something that social scientists are very far from), it is useful to look at what physicists, chemists, and astronomers do when they are really serious about a number. So we look at the way fundamental scientific numbers (e.g., Planck's constant, the speed of light, the valence of hydrogen, the rate of expansion of the universe) get their authority.

The first feature of such numbers is that there are many ways to estimate them; a constant gets to be "fundamental" because different ways of estimating it give "the same" answer. In all different compounds, hydrogen combines in a way that shows a constant valence, by "acquiring," or "giving," or "sharing" one electron. Finding this out was an achievement, first made in a rough way by observing the ratios in which different elements reacted, and much later developed by integrating it with the theory of the combination of electrons and protons into different kinds of atoms. The idea of a "constant" valence of an atom of a given element was not immediately obvious. Most of the work done by Dalton in the first half of the nineteenth century was on the valences of atoms.

Often the early days of estimating such a constant are filled with questions of whether it is indeed a constant, of whether there are some systematic biases in the first ways of estimating it, or of trying to figure out how to resolve disagreements among the estimates. Hubble's first estimates of the rate of expansion of the universe suggested that the universe could be no older than about a billion and a half years, while several estimates of the age of the Earth suggested quite strongly that *its* age was in the general region of four billion years. Clearly, a constituent of anything one would call a universe could not be older than the whole. But the postulate that, whatever the value, it was a constant was partly confirmed when Hubble's method of estimating it gave about the same answer with observations on different stars. That is, though the method gave a wrong estimate, it gave consistent estimates, suggesting that the number was a constant.

Present estimates suggest that Hubble's value for the age of the universe might be off by a factor of around ten. Recent estimates of the constant using very distant supernovae instead of relatively nearby Cepheid variable stars suggest that it may not be a constant after all, since estimates based on nearby variable stars or nearby supernovae give different estimates than those based on stars farther away (which we observe as they were at an earlier time). That is, the question of whether or not the rate of expansion of the universe is a constant, and if so what that constant is, is a matter of scientific development, of refining measurement techniques and trying to figure out why different estimating techniques give different estimates. Scientists are still perfecting both the concept and the measurement by collecting data especially for that purpose. Imitating Hubble, we can start by being off on the effects of Goffman's circle of backs by a factor of ten, as long as we then set out to converge on the right answer.

A constant cannot have a great many estimates that converge unless the theory in which it is embedded has a great many consequences in many different empirical situations. Thus, the gravitational constant as estimated by Galileo with inclined planes, and tested by him (at least so goes the myth) for constancy by dropping balls of different weights to see if they hit at the same time, has implications for how much people and objects of a given mass should weigh on the moon, and so how far a given mass should stretch a spring there. Because of the way the post-Galilean (Newtonian) theory works, the gravitational constant being approximately constant *on the Earth* does not mean that it would produce the same weight of an object on the moon as it produces on the Earth. However, if an astronaut used a balance on the moon, a thing being weighed would balance the same number of weights on the moon as here, because a balance measures masses. It will not stretch a spring the same distance, because a spring balance measures weights.

Having several ways of estimating a constant also shows the theoretical scope of the concept it represents; those several ways provide the motivation for correcting or recalibrating each; and the convergence of the corrected estimates allows a high degree of accuracy of the abstraction, and allows that degree of accuracy itself to be estimated.

The estimates themselves can serve as tests of *the theory of the measuring instrument*, which often comes from quite a different branch of science than the one where the instrument is used. The theory of why a spring is stretched by attached weights comes from a quite different part of physics than the theory of why a mass would balance with the same weights in the other pan in all different gravitational fields. If the mass corrected for the gravitational field as estimated with a spring does not match the mass estimated with a balance, it may be because our theory of why a spring stretches is wrong. Thus, if fundamental constants have many independent estimates, this gives evidence of several ways in which they are fundamental: by having large scope, high correctability, high and estimable accuracy, and great usefulness in tests of other scientific theories.

This implies that fundamental constants are unlikely to be challenged, because there are multiple indications that one has the theoretical concept correctly defined and understands very well how it works in a wide variety of situations. Fundamental constants tend to be important in scientific research, to lead to new knowledge, *but* tend rarely to be challenged. This is the irony, then: that scientists have to use the certain parts of the science—the fundamental constants, for example—to find new things out. In particular, they do not want their measurements bouncing around, because they do not understand the measurement process and its instruments, into which they have built *other* fundamental constants.

The existence of fundamental constants (or of other, more complex mathematical forms) is a measure of a discipline's stratification of bits of knowledge by epistemological status. Jonathan Kelley, an Australian sociologist, used to define "Duncan's constant" (named for Otis Dudley Duncan) as "for anything of social importance, measurements on the father are correlated at 0.4 with measurements on the son." Sociologists immediately recognize this as a joke, moderately near to the truth for a wide variety of characteristics in a wide variety of societies, but far from what real scientists would recognize as a fundamental constant. And, of course, the exclusion of women from the estimate suggests that women's status has different causes and effects, so the "0.4" is not very "fundamental." That this is the best sociologists can do indicates that sociology is not as strongly epistemologically stratified into "solid and fundamental" versus "currently being investigated" as physics or chemistry.

But the contrast between Planck and social science concepts is *not* about what one does to improve one's concepts of what a distance is all about. What one does is, in essence, the same, whether one is working with Hubble's constant or the distance at which people have to lower their eyes or else appear to be "staring" (which is a constant in American society, but differs among societies). In either case, one uses data on how the world works to improve the concept. And one is already more exact in observing or "measuring" definitions of situations if one knows that some such definitions are institutionalized, some not, and some are usually unconscious, some not.

Criteria for Good Concepts with Good Measurements

LET US START WITH SOME OF THE FEATURES we look for in observations of the value of something described by a concept, if the observations are to be good "measures" of it. In the first place, there ought to be a *high correlation* of different measures of the same concept when applied to the same distances. When it turns out that some measurements of something that is supposed to be the same (according to the concept)—distances, the speed of light, Hubble's constant—are not the same as other measurements of it, then something has to be wrong with either the measurements or the concept. A similar strategy for a sociological topic is the "Stinchcombe Psychology of Rebellion Short Version." It shows that rebellion against the authority system of the high school is part of an attitude complex, which is related to behavioral rebellion and to the same causes as behavioral rebellion.

Stinchcombe Psychology of Rebellion Short Version

Summarized from Arthur L. Stinchcombe, "The Psychological Quality of Adolescent Rebellion" and "Appendix on Method," in *Rebellion in a High School* (Chicago: Quadrangle; reprint, New York: New York Times Press, 1964), pp. 15–48 and 186–191. All page numbers without further identification are to this source. References to tables are left in, though the tables themselves are not reproduced here.

The data for this study were collected in 1959 in a school in northern California. The task here is to demonstrate that rebellion against the rules of the high school is part of a complex of attitudes toward the school environment, including short-run hedonism; negativism; alienation from school authority, both formal and informal; and emphasis on autonomy by adolescents. Rebellion was measured by three criteria: getting sent out of class by a teacher, getting a flunk notice in a non–college preparatory course (that is, an "easy" course), and skipping school with a group of friends. There is a strong relation between rebellion and measures of short-run hedonism; negative attitudes toward conformity in general; belief that teachers, principals, and leaders among students conspire among themselves to do injustice; and claiming rights to make their own decisions on matters the school is unwilling to grant. If we show that all these attitudes are related to rebellion, we will have established that "expressive alienation" from the school is an empirical entity. We also show (in a "short version" in chapter 8, below) that not answering the questions in a survey given in a classroom is also a measure of expressive alienation.

> We are primarily interested in alienation from the social world of the school. Consequently, when we speak of "short-run hedonism" we mean a short-run hedonistic attitude toward that social world. All our indicators of short-run hedonism ask the student to express an attitude toward some aspect of the school. Whether or not the attitude of short-run hedonism is a character trait, and includes a short-run orientation to other social worlds, is of no concern here. (p. 16)

Among the aspects of short-run hedonism on which we have a question is that hedonistic people are bored when the meaning of the activity is expressed in long-run goals. In Table 1 the proportion of students who consider half or more of their classes "pretty boring" is tabulated against rebellious behavior. Rebels are more likely than conformers to find half or more of their classes boring, but there are no great differences among rebels that depend on how many offenses they have committed. Similarly, rebels are more likely to believe that work in class is not rewarded, and less likely to believe that grades are very or quite important to their personal satisfaction. That is, all indicators of short-run hedonism are related to rebellion, and rebels are more hedonistic.

"Negativism" describes the attitude that rejects all conforming behavior, but the only question in the study that measures it asks whether there are "too many squares in this school who would rather follow the rules than have any fun." Negativist attitudes are more common among boys than among girls, and rebels within the genders are more likely to agree that there are too many "squares."

The pattern of alienation from the status systems of the school varies between alienation from formal aspects of the system (e.g., teacher and principal authority) and more informal aspects (e.g., school "activities," athletics, and high-prestige cliques who run the informal life). By "status systems" we mean a socially established pattern of judgment of persons, with respect to their relative worth. A status system then includes at least the following:

1. A group of judges who allocate rights, duties, and rewards of the system according to their judgments of worth
2. A set of standards, more or less generally accepted, of criteria of value and worth for the purposes of the judgment in question.
3. A recognized process according to which people present themselves (or are presented) for judgment; some systems judge everybody, while in others one is only judged if one applies for judgment
4. Arrangements by which judges receive information on which to base judgment
5. A set of status or other rewards allocated by judges

Thus, for the grading system, teachers are judges, intellectual standards obtain, people signed up for the class get graded, teachers have the rights to give tests and grade assignments, and the grade on the transcript and parents', future employers', or college admissions officers' reactions are the rewards. For informal cliques of high prestige among students, members of the clique are judges, standards are vague and arbitrary but highly correlated with social class, people who want high-prestige friends make informal application to be judged by making friendly moves, and acceptance itself is the main reward.

> Table 5 reports the proportion of students holding that *teachers* did not allocate status according to intellectual merit, that "You have to get in good with the teachers in order to get a fair grade." [The] data ... show a sharp sex difference, with boys again more alienated. . . . The sex difference is explained both by the greater number of rebels among boys, and by their greater alienation from the classroom status system. . . . Rebels, particularly classroom rebels [as compared with truants], see their teachers as unfair. (p. 29)

Among the status systems examined, the more formal ones, such as classrooms, had more alienation among boys, while the more informal ones, such as the activities system, had more nearly equal alienation of the two genders; the ranking of students among themselves actually had higher alienation among girls, though this was not statistically significant. (Girls participated more in the informal systems, and those who participated—of either gender—were less alienated from them. Controlling for participation, girls were much more alienated from the informal status systems than boys.) For all the indicators of alienation from the various school status systems, rebellious behavior is related to alienation.

The general ideology of the school is that students are subject to school authority because they are adolescents, and therefore do not legitimately have the autonomy of adults. Claiming autonomy by claiming adult rights, such as sex and marriage, smoking, or owning or driving a car, are all denials of the age-grading ideology on which school authority is based. For these central indicators of adult claims to autonomy, we find very strong relations to rebellious behavior. The good behavior of college preparatory students is in large measure an agreement to extend adolescence, and the lack of autonomy of adolescents, well into physiological adulthood. The claim to early adulthood among girls largely took the form of a claim that it was all right to get married early, and dating behavior was strongly related to rebellion, especially among girls.

> We hold, then, that some students are characterized by a complex of attitudes and behavior toward the school environment named [here] "expressive alienation." Such alienated students are more likely than others to be rebellious—given the same opportunities, they are more likely to get into trouble. By establishing the correlation of rebellion to a number of other attitudes, we tentatively establish the emotional concomitants of this underlying state of alienation. The psychological state of expressive alienation, having as one of its manifestations rebellious *behavior*, has the following *attitudinal* manifestations . . . short-run hedonism . . . negativism . . . alienation from the status systems either created by authorities or closely connected to legitimate institutions . . . a culture of personal autonomy. . . . The establishment of a complex concept made up of inherently connected elements gives us more theoretical hooks on which to hang an explanation of rebellion.
> (p. 47)

If a proposed measure of a variable is not correlated with the others, investigators hope first of all that it is their measuring "instrument" that is wrong. The first measuring instrument for Hubble's constant was based on the empirical observation that for many of a particular kind of variable stars that seemed to be at about the same distance (e.g., that formed part of the same galaxy), their brightness appeared to be closely related to their period of variation. So one could perhaps (if that generalization held up) estimate the inherent brightness of that kind of variable star by its period, and so estimate how far away it was by the ratio of its apparent brightness on Earth to its postulated inherent brightness.

One can immediately think of problems with the measuring instrument, the first being that in Hubble's day astronomers did not yet understand why the stars were variable, and why brightness might vary with the frequency of variation.

Sometimes we have great confidence in our "natural" understanding of things—for example, that we can make a ruler with a stick of wood because wood stays the same size. It is important in a science to study closely that assumed fact about measurement. Everybody who has tried to move furniture built in wet climates to a desert (in a house without climate control) knows that wood does not in fact stay the same size, because their furniture does not fit together when the water goes out of it, unless craftsmen have built it so it will keep fitting in the desert. A steel ruler won't dry out, but at about 1500°C it will melt (just as the wooden ruler will burn). So who knows what trouble scientists will encounter when they use the brightness of Cepheid variable stars as a measurement. Being within a factor of ten, as Hubble apparently was, is not bad in that situation. But as long as people were working on measuring instruments, they continued to converge. So after considerable convergence, it looked as if Hubble's constant had been accurately measured, and was really a constant.

But it is always possible in science that the concept itself is wrong. For instance, it appears that many attitude questions that we ask about race prejudice, like questions about bussing to schools, measure primarily the attitude of whether the government ought to mess with us ordinary folks a lot, rather than whether African Americans ought to be equal. Answers to survey questions that favor bussing to integrate schools have especially measured, in the United States, an attitude that the courts ought to have the right to decide on bussing, rather than a belief that the people (the local elected school board) should decide according to what *they* thought was right. That is, such questions tapped into the attitude that contrasted the notion that lawyers and judges know best what is good for people, or at least what is fair, with the notion that the people know best what is good for themselves. And if they did not know what was best, it still was not right to coerce them.

That the people themselves were deciding in a way that was unfair to African Americans was hardly in the picture for many of those who opposed bussing. In the view of opponents of bussing, the law is supposed to do what the people want, more than what the judges think is fair. If the people want folks who sell marijuana to be in jail, while they want people who sell the much more dangerous drugs, tobacco and alcohol, to be viewed as upstanding citizens of the community, that's what they and their judges ought to do. And if the people want to go to their neighborhood majority-white school, the notion that that might be bad for African Americans is irrelevant.

We find out that a bussing question is not mainly about race prejudice by the same criterion that we find out the troubles with observations to estimate Hubble's constant: if attitudes toward bussing measure prejudice against blacks, the answers to survey questions on bussing should give the same observation of high or low prejudice as other measurements. The convergence or correlation among measurements is a criterion of whether they have measured prejudice well, and the fact that attitudes toward bussing do not converge with, say, attitudes about whether there should be antimiscegenation laws means that they do not measure the same thing. Many people who object to bussing are also against the government having the power to forbid them to marry a husband or wife they have chosen, but many instead favor antimiscegenation laws. If objecting to bussing were a measure of race prejudice, the first group should be very infrequent.

Similarly, the exposure of the two genders to the formal school system is quite similar, except that around 1960 they took different vocational courses, and girls took somewhat less science and mathematics. But girls were much more exposed to the stratification system of the informal and extracurricular system by participation. Participation presumably both measures and causes satisfaction with the informal system. Thus, when we measure girls' alienation from the informal status system, we are measuring two separate effects: the satisfaction effect of higher participation, and the alienating effect on girls of being a failure in a status system those girls think is more important. In the classroom system one cannot choose not to participate, nor can one avoid being graded. Controlling for participation confirms the notion that the more informal the system, the more girls will be alienated from it, while the reverse is true of boys. So the first thing to do if a hypothesized measure of a variable is not correlated with the others is to study the measuring instrument. First of all, one should think about it, and then collect facts that would be true if the instrument was mismeasuring.

Next, measures should depend on parts of the science that are quite certain. One of the problems of social science, for example, is that we have not studied and developed a theory about the differences between what people are in favor of, and what they want to government to do something about. And we have not studied or theorized about why girls participate more in extracurricular activities, and what effect their higher participation has on them. So when we have an alienation measure consisting of a grievance against that informal system, we have not based the question on a certain part of the science. In general, the theory of what we are doing when we ask a question, and so why it varies a lot from one situation to another, is not very well developed at all.

Uses of Exactness

IN GENERAL, WHAT ONE MEANS BY "EXACTNESS" of a concept or "precision" of a measurement has to do with what investigators wanted it to do in the theory. To take a famous example in physics, "black body radiation" was supposed to deal with the fact that, at a given temperature, a body will give off different intensities of radiation of different frequencies (Kuhn, 1978). What the physicist Max Planck wanted to do was to predict the *whole distribution of intensities by frequency* at that temperature (the mean of those frequencies is a good measure of the temperature of a body), and then do that for all temperatures. So the fact that Planck used some statistical mathematics of Boltzmann, another physicist, to derive that distribution (such a distribution is called a "spectrum") made him famous.

But the notion of a spectrum being what an investigator has to predict is a theoretical result. Planck's conception of the temperature of a black body as what explains the variation of intensities of frequencies (the "spectrum") emitted is not the sort of thing sociologists usually do. All ordinary regression analysis predicts only the means, not the distribution, for example. (If one takes the logarithm of the dependent variable, or assumes that the dependent variable has a Poisson distribution, the same coefficient predicts the mean and the variance, and so can be a mistake if the variance of the logged variable is not homogeneous; this means that there is no *separate* theory of the variance.)

There are many empirical consequences about the color of the Sun, for example, which has a surface temperature of about 5500°C, that are to be exactly reproduced by Planck's theory. The sun gives some heat in the infrared, and some considerable ultraviolet, but the ultraviolet received on the ground is much dimmer than Planck would predict. Without Planck, we would not look for ozone in the upper atmosphere absorbing ultraviolet, nor would we have noticed when the ozone went missing.

Most of the radiation given off by the Earth at around 20°C is in the infrared part of the spectrum, while both the ground and the water were heated by radiation with the spectrum of a body at 5500°C that emits radiation mostly in the visible light range. This fact, central to the "greenhouse effect" of water vapor and carbon dioxide, has to be produced by Planck's theory, down to the details of why the energy coming in is mostly not absorbed by the atmosphere, while much of that going out is absorbed. Planck's result was fundamental to physics because it was very exact about what distribution the two kinds of radiation ought to have, right down to the greenhouse effect, and gave the first (remarkably exact) estimate of Planck's constant. But the main comparison point is that exactness of the measurement of intensities of radiation at different frequencies gave Planck something very specific about variances to predict, and for sociology both the theory and the exactness of measurement are missing (there are traces of such a theory predicting variances in Coleman's mathematical sociology [Coleman, 1964]).

So the black body spectrum has to be an exact concept in order to do its theoretical job, and that concept has to have all (but only) what is needed to generate the results about the strength of radiation of all frequencies. An exact method of observation of the spectrum has to give us all the information we need to know, then, in order to get the temperature of the emitting body (e.g., of stars). By eliminating the expected infrared radiation from a star of a given temperature, and getting a residual of too much such radiation from a star, we then might get evidence of whether there is a lower temperature radiating body (maybe a planet) in that star's system. But in sociology, if there is a nearly blank place in, say, the income distribution between high officers of corporations and the CEOs, we have no theory of who, and how many, should have been there and what the equivalent of ozone was that blocked it out.

When Goffman tells us more exactly why young, nonfamous sociologists do not get to talk to old, famous sociologists at a convention, but I do, because they always have their back to the younger ones but not to me, it refines the concepts of attention governance. When we had only the "definition of the situation" concept, we could not figure it out. But clearly, it is not exact enough to estimate Planck's constant with, or to estimate what the variance (the "spectrum") of isolation by backs of different statuses and ages might be.

Principles of Refining Concepts of Distances

THERE ARE THREE MAIN PROBLEMS of developing concepts of the variables along which causal distances and distances of effects are observed:

1. To determine whether a single concept or multiple concepts are needed to describe distances, and if multiple, how to observe them separately
2. To specify the theoretical place or places in causal theory that the distance or distances so located play
3. To get hints from patterns of distances about what contexts and what causal mechanisms are at work

One or Many

Since sociologists mostly study causal relationships in the world as it comes to us, causal processes are normally mixed up with each other. "Years of education" is mixed up with "years of age," and so with different anatomies and physiologies; with changes in educational tasks and tests given by teachers in different years; with variations in summer and weekend experiences of people of different ages, genders, levels of wealth, or different parental education. The ability to say sentences never heard before, to make coherent paragraphs never written before, and to put such paragraphs into twenty-page papers with new theories and new evidence may depend on any of these distances.

Most novelists probably think their ability to write a new, coherent work comes mainly from experience outside school; most scientists probably think it comes from good scholarly training. We cannot sort out these theories (which involves finding out whether creativity in novels and creativity in science are substantially different variables) without unscrambling the distances associated with years of education *and* the distances between children's versus adults' ability to write new novels, or to write physics problems in new differential equations.

In this unscrambling, the key elementary logical observation is that if two ways of observing a distance between two units of analysis give the same result (for many units of analysis), then it is more likely that they measure the same thing. By "same result" here we mean that distances observed as big (or as one versus zero if they are categories, as gender or "corporately organized" are in our examples) with one way of observing are big with the other, and those observed as small (or zero) on one are small on the other.

The most common measure of this in the social sciences is some kind of correlation coefficient. So the most usual methods of testing whether several ways of observing (say, a series of "items" on a test or in a survey interview) is to study the pattern of correlations. Some version of "factor analysis" or of "canonical correlation analysis" or LISREL analysis, when used properly, can be used to study the hypothesis that a single variable (or two variables in canonical correlation) could have produced the observed pattern of correlations. All of these methods ask whether the big distances between units of analysis tend to be between the same units, and similarly for those that are small, by studying the patterns of correlation coefficients of some sort. Though they are usually applied to a matrix of Pearson correlation coefficients, they can be used with any reasonably well-behaved coefficients in a matrix of measures of association, such as differences in proportions for categorical variables. Thus, when we find that many attitude items whose surface meaning has to do with distances in race prejudice between people are highly correlated, we guess that there is an underlying (or "latent") dimension of race prejudice. The "factor" produced by those high correlations is, then, a good bet for a measure of a single causal variable that likely also has a single set of effects.

But when we find that attitudes toward school integration by bussing have differences that are not big when race prejudice is big, but instead fit with a set of correlated items that seem to measure how much interference with people's lives judges and courts should have, we then judge that we need two concepts, race prejudice and objection to intensive government by law. Big distances on one of these two variables do not occur between the same people that have large distances on the other. (The factors have an "orthogonal component," in the language of factor analysis.) They will, then, occur on two "factors" in a factor analysis.

Theoretical Place

Now suppose we find that there are reliable differences in the distances at which people turn their eyes away from strangers versus the distances at which they look away from acquaintances. We also find that when a group of people are turned toward each other and are paying close attention to what one after another of the group says, then most people outside the circle turn their eyes (and perhaps their ears) away. But when those people (the younger ones at the sociology convention) who turned away meet another person who also looks like a graduate student at the same convention, they soon form a pair or circle paying close attention to one speaker at a time. The distances in mutual attention between strangers and acquaintances on the street, and between those in versus out of a conversational circle of acquaintances at the convention, have similar effects. Eye contact, freedom to speak and to be listened to, allocation of attention to a single person at a time with associated turn taking, leave-taking rituals when one breaks off the high level of mutual attention, and a very low level of consciousness that one is following a delicate system of rules: all follow from these apparently quite different situations. And previous acquaintance seems to have a big effect on whether one looks at shorter distances or does turn-taking.

This says that "talk" is a mobilization and government of attention with a deep and relatively reliable normative structure, a secure place in the "definition of the situation." It is a quasi-institution, connecting acquaintanceship to attention governance, but mostly unconscious. An ethnographer who does not notice who can speak and who has to pay attention should take up a different method.

But this means further that a survey interview is a normative situation of "talk," and so is an interrogation in a police station, and the pitch of a used-car salesman. The Miranda warnings, the eager "May I help you? That Dodge is in very good shape," and the "Your responses are confidential, and will be published only as percentages not identified with any names—there are no right and wrong answers to these questions" all call on the set of norms about who should pay attention to whom, and what the norms of turn-taking will be. They are rituals of transferring from the situation defined as civil inattention to one defined as "talking to each other." The theory of what one can say and what one can ask in such conversations is therefore deeply bound up with the larger normative structure governing attention among strangers. Watch people's eyes to tell what is going on in any of these. And if an investigator is observing something with a police interrogation, a used-car sales talk, or a survey interview, it is the investigator's business to study the structure and norms of attention governance in that situation.

I take up in chapter 5 the concepts about the differences in context between streets, conventions, survey interviews, police interrogations, and used-car lots that make the norm of civil inattention work differently. For now, I want to emphasize that the distances observed in dropping one's eyes on the street and not interrupting conversational circles hang together, and many are found in all these situations. And the location of the distances in the theoretical role of semiconscious norms governing attention pervades them all.

Hints about Mechanisms

We want to refine concepts of distances because we believe that the distances in causes produce distances in effects. The verb *produce* here refers to causal mechanisms. So we find that rebellious behavior in a high school has a pattern of correlations with several attitudes that I called "expressive alienation." One of the components of that concept had to do with rejecting the implicit norm of high school authority, that one should put off adulthood until one is educated enough.

Since by the end of high school many of the students are bigger and stronger than the investigator, it is not obvious why any of them should put off being adults. The content of expressive alienation suggests that we need a mechanism in our theory that connects taking a college preparatory curriculum (a big predictor of good behavior and lower alienation), *through* an attitude that it is all right to be an adolescent for a while longer, *in turn* to good behavior at a school that has an age-graded ideology justifying its authority. Only if we get this mechanism right in the late 1950s are we likely to understand why, forty-five years later, oral sex is all right for college preparatory adolescents, but reproductive sex for them is pretty much reserved for after college. Heavy petting rather than sexual intercourse was the 1950s way of continuing to be adolescent though physiologically adult, and somewhat heavier but still nonreproductive sex is the trend in the first decade of the new millennium. The point is that if we get the concept of extending adolescence right in the first place, we will be able to redefine and recalibrate the measures with the changing times.

We will deal with the analysis of mechanisms and the improvement of their conceptual form in much more detail in chapter 6. But the technology of locating more exactly what observations measure a causal or effect distance between people or situations also gives us clues about mechanisms that connect causes to effects. At the very least, two different factors in attitudes, such as ones on race prejudice and ones on what sort of laws should be imposed by courts, suggest that we need two causal mechanisms when before it seemed as if one concept on race prejudice was enough for our purposes.

5　Refining Concepts about Contexts

THE APPLICABILITY OF ALMOST ALL CAUSAL THEORIES, in all the sciences, depends on "boundary conditions." Boundary conditions generally cannot be derived from the theory itself until late in the development of the theory. Up to that time one often uses a list of known boundary conditions under which the theory is known to work, but sometimes that list is, in essence, a list of proper names of known instances. For example, for a very long time in the history of astronomy the planets with internal coherence and apparently stable orbits formed a list, many of them known to the ancients as "wanderers," with proper names still found in the astrology column. For the development of the theory of gravitation, the solar system was a particularly easy place to start because the Sun was so much larger than any other body that its center could be treated as the center of gravity. Jupiter with its moons was a convenient early generalization because Jupiter was very large compared to any or all of its moons. Many of the early boundary conditions later had to be modified to treat binary stars, where the center of gravity was outside both bodies.

The named instances description of boundary conditions is an unsatisfactory theoretical situation, but often we do not want to go too deeply into the gravitational forces and collision histories that would create planets and their orbits, or into why they did not fall into the sun like the other 99 percent or so of the mass of the solar system. Planets and their orbits were the boundary conditions that were assumed. They were the *context* within which gravitational and momentum and tidal frictional forces work.

In the same way one may want to know for some historical causal process whether the common phrase in seventeenth-century France, *nulle terre sans seigneur,* should be translated as "no territory without a judge with jurisdiction," or instead as "no territory without a lord of the manor who also has other feudal privileges," or even "no territory without a person who can hunt on a peasant's land." One of them might be a step toward universal legal arrangements with some traditional feudal overtones, the other a division of claims on peasant incomes that brought into question the legitimacy of a feudal mode of production, another a grievance common to peasants in the records of grievances (*cahiers de doleances*) collected just before the French Revolution.

Many things about the meaning of property rights of peasants and landlords, and the king's authority, are bound up with the differences in the legal context suggested by the varying translations. For most purposes one does not want to go too deeply into the history, but only to be more or less assured that the seigneurial rights of the nobility were generally quite different from their rights as holders of landed property, and that this differentiation was more or less stable throughout the eighteenth century up to the Revolution. Most of the tangle of jurisdictions can be put aside for most problems of rural class relations and rural politics up to the Revolution, but are crucial for the dynamics of the revolutionary "abolition of feudalism" that John Markoff studied (1996). The times and places determining what a feudal phrase meant are thus crucial context for the causal analysis of what happened in the countryside during the French Revolution, because they were determinants of the interaction between the administration of law and property ownership in the old régime. They were not as important, and differently important, in the postrevolutionary context.

Sociology is pervaded by boundary conditions on its causal processes, and these conditions themselves vary over time and between places: sometimes very quickly, as a circle of famous old backs breaks up, sometimes over substantial historical time as with the differentiation of seigneurial and ownership land rights in old régime France. Contextual variations directly determine values of some causal or effect variables. They also determine the impact of variations in some causes on effects, and so produce different relations of causes to effects in one context than in another. In these complex causal situations dominated by boundary conditions, special devices are needed to use facts to improve concepts about variations in the context. This is true in all the sciences: concepts about skin and membranes in biology are developed in different investigations than concepts about physiology within them; concepts about plate tectonics on the surfaces of Venus and the Earth are very different for reasons that do not much bear on the role of the two planets' centers of gravity in the solar system.

Our job in this chapter is to take a few places in sociological theory where variations in context play a crucial role, to show how study of the facts combined with special logical structures can help us improve contextual concepts at the core of social causation. First, we will look at some of the clues in the presentation of scientific materials in the social sciences that suggest the importance of contexts to the causal situation being dealt with. A rough measure of the importance of context in the investigation, I will argue, is the ratio of words to facts in scientific publications, higher in books that have to deal with context than in articles and papers that can assume the context.

Then, moving on to the actual logical structure, we will deal with the determination of the meaning of symbols by the larger semantic and symbolic system of which they are a part. We will look at how to improve our approach to the meaning of symbols, in the sense of what their place is in a system of symbols. We will study Lévi-Strauss's use of facts about the place of a given symbol in many different mythical systems, which allows us to come to a better system of attaching meanings to symbols in a particular system, and consequently to interpret the meanings in particular local myths of a given tribe.

Then we will deal with time and place, central to the practice of historical sociology. Studying the meaning of seigneurial rights in eighteenth-century France, and consequently what the abolition of those rights meant in the French Revolution, requires that the place name "France" and the time (the eighteenth century) form part of our descriptions. The whole business looked very different in eighteenth-century America, a different place, where the "proprietors" of the colonies had quite different rights based on quite different arrangements among the king, Parliament, proprietors, and local governments, than anything that pertained to France. And France by the nineteenth century no longer had seigneurs at all, so arrangements of seigneurial rights did not "cause" anything. The problem of periodization and localization, and of improving concepts of period and place, is therefore central. For its place in the theory, the longitude and latitude of France and the astronomical definition of the time have nothing directly to do with our analysis of contextual effects.

Finally, we will take up the problem of institutional influence on organizations, a central problem of modern organizational sociology. Why do "autonomous" local school boards all across the United States create a very similar structure of elementary, middle, and secondary education, sharply distinguished everywhere from college and graduate school? The uniformity of organizations clearly has social causes, since in various ways English or French or Javanese schools look quite different—though they are coming to look more alike. We will also develop the concept of "mapping variables" that describe the variation in the impact of a context on particular units of analysis, and discuss how such concepts of variable impact can be improved by the study of appropriate facts. Such concepts of the mapping of units onto contexts also allow us to form more precise concepts of the environmental or context variables that shape the causal processes.

Concepts about Context, and Context-Specific Concepts

BY "CONTEXT," WE MEAN THE LARGE STRUCTURE that shapes the meaning or other causal impact of some particulars in a situation or system. For example, for people born in Uganda rather than the United States, almost everyone around them will be extremely poor by U.S. standards, they will learn as children a language that is not a world-language, and they will therefore spend a lot of their school life learning a foreign language. In addition, there will be a strife-torn environment (in the early twenty-first century consisting of civil wars on the north border and the Congo border), many of the most powerful political influences in the capital city will be international nongovernmental organizations that get their funding from outside the country, the roads to and from places where food is grown will mostly be unpaved, safe water will be expensive, and AIDS will still be an epidemic rather than a chronic disease as it mostly is in the United States.

The context of almost all the important causes in social life is very different in a very poor country. In some cases a cause may be present in the poor context, and absent or nearly invariant among the rich contexts. This means that many of the causes that will bear on the people in Uganda in an average year of their lives will be different from those in the United States. Some of the causes mentioned above will clearly have a different effect. On the one hand, Ugandans will spend a lot more effort in school to learn elementary English than will an American child, and therefore may have less time for other classes. On the other hand, those who learn English in school will be distinct from their less-educated peers in being bilingual by the time they are eighteen. Very few American students have learned in school by eighteen to differ from their peers by being bilingual. (In the United States in the first decade of the twentieth century, many children were learning to be bilingual in school because many of them were immigrants from non-English-speaking countries.)

Time and place are important indicators of context, so that an investigator does not know what education measures unless he or she knows what time and place is being investigated. In addition, very often one needs at least a minimal theory of context to understand where to begin one's work. In the United States since the conquest from the Native Americans, most religions have been organized in congregations. In Himalayan countries at present, and in ancient Rome, most religions were organized in families; one could say that in both places the male head of the family was the most important religious official. "Church membership" is a measure of something central to American religious life, but would not be an understandable question to ask on a survey in ancient Rome or much of the modern Himalayas. Knowing what question to ask about religion is a question of context.

The previous paragraphs have taken as sufficient empirical indicators of context only time, place, family versus congregational religions, or childhood language being a world language or not. But I have asserted that contexts cause things, both directly, as when being Ugandan compared to American reduces income of one's family and peers, and indirectly, as predicting different effects of a year of education on speaking a world language. Similarly, being Himalayan determines whether one's religion takes one out of the home to a professional religious specialist. If context causes things, and if we have to build that into our theories, at the very least as "boundary conditions" for our theories, then we need at least a rudimentary theory of it.

Yet for the sake of economy, we ordinarily want to spend as little time as possible on the theory of the context, so as to spend as much as possible on the main subject of the research. We want to know that, for a measure of theology and intensity of religious social influence, we can get by taking church membership and church attendance as sufficient in the United States. We also want to know that in the Himalayas we have to ask about family religious practices first, and then maybe a general name for the religious tradition afterward. One therefore has to interview the whole family on religious practice in the Asian mountains, but in the United States one can use, without interviewing the minister, a question on adherence to historically continuous denominations as a rough measure of religious practice. But *then* we want to get on with studying the impact of religious intensity and theology on, say, political behavior. It is someone else's job to ask for an explanation of the historical and social dominance of congregational organization in the Christian tradition. It is not a question for a modern political survey researcher: "Why did Saint Paul [or his disciple—the authorship is unclear] write to the Ephesians as a congregation, rather than to powerful family heads in the Ephesus?" But the consequence of this for the context—that one asks for an organizational connection to measure religious practice in the United States, but inquires about family religious practice in Himalayan polities—is essential for starting a study of comparative religious politics.

For historical sociology, the main indicators of context are time and place, and we spend a great deal of time in this chapter on the problem of periodization and the related issue of spatial boundaries. Periodization involves the question of which temporal boundaries are adequate measures of context, within which narratives of causation are likely to make sense. Outside a period, one needs to look for causes that were insignificant in the first period, and to find out the contextual features that make causes have different effects than in the period marked off by two dates. Clemens (1999), of which a short version is given below, deals with how to theorize such periodization (and also how to theorize the boundaries of geographical areas as contexts).

My choice above of the contrast between Uganda and the United States to study the impact of school-taught bilingualism, and then the United States around 1890–1920 for a comparable contrast within the United States, was not an accidental way to highlight the importance of context; time and place are of the essence to context, but need to be theorized and investigated. My example implies that the variable "bilingualism" is a context-specific concept. In the United States, it means that the bilingual people have in some ways a disadvantage, that they "wasted their time" before schooling, learning a language of little use. In Uganda, it means learning a world language besides the language routinely used by everybody in everyday life, and probably therefore being literate in both.

Similarly, a "herd" in a nomadic tribe means a way to get nearly everything needed for life, while in the United States it means a way to make money to buy things for a life. "Herd" is therefore a context-specific concept as well. A family owning a herd is the minimum condition for the family being members of the tribe in a nomadic society; in the United States it means getting access to pastures on public land to make a profit, where the fees do not cover the costs of administering and caring for the land. Here we have socialism for entrepreneurs, but not among Ugandan herding tribes; they have socialism for pastures within the tribe, but individual garden plots.

Again, a survey question about government-guaranteed health care means something entirely routine in Norway, something conservatives and socialists all agree on, while in the United States it measures a sharp break between left and right. So a great many "indicators" measure different things in different contexts.

Books for Context, Articles for Causation with Assumed Context

A ROUGH MEASURE OF THE IMPORTANCE INVESTIGATORS assign to context for their explanatory task is the ratio of words to facts when they write it up. Even within quantitative work, one finds papers that have up to four pages per table, explaining what is in the table and what that means for the argument as a whole. But a high ratio of words to facts is normally highly correlated with books as the style of publication. That is, usually the reason a social scientist writes a book (other than a textbook) is that it takes a great deal of work to explain what his or her facts mean, and only then how they bear on the scientific argument.

Such detailed explanations of the meanings of facts are almost always needed when the facts themselves are very scarce, so that much has to be made of each of them. For example, if there are only three pelvises of hominids of a given species in the fossil remains so far found, then any discussion of their problems of giving birth will require a lot of words. Humans have more difficulty giving birth than other mammals, including the other great apes. The question is when and why humans developed this difficulty. The usual theory is that it is related to the very large size of the human head, and also to the reorientation of the pelvis involved in walking upright. But to make sense of the facts on a hominid species that might have been our ancestor, one has to adjust this skeleton because it was a male, that one because it was in its early teens, and this other one because it might perhaps be an example from the following period, and it is hard to tell because only a few other bones of the skeleton remained. There may, then, be three actual pairs of measurements on the skeletons (skull dimensions and pelvis dimensions), and several pages of calculation, explaining assumptions, theoretical meanings, relation of adult skull size to the projected newborn skull size, and so on. Such processes as inferring anything about female pelvises from male ones depend a great deal on when and where the skeletons lived, since the amount of sexual dimorphism is variable among the various great apes and humans.

Much historical work (the field of paleontology that would study such skeletons is a historical subject, though the rocks keep the archives) falls into this situation of scarce facts, which have to be taken in context because they are "not quite on the right subject." Many ethnographic discussions of rituals are based on a single observation of a crucial ritual. For a lovely analysis of a rare case, see Clifford Geertz's paper on a failed funeral ritual (1973b [1959]). In that case, the religious official who conducted funerals refused to officiate because the person arranging the funeral was an atheist; this is an extremely rare observation opportunity, but everything that happened had to be interpreted in relation to the intertwining of religion and politics in Indonesia at the time. Paleontology from its beginnings often was written up in books; Darwin's *Origin of Species* (1872 [1859]) was a big book that was a short version of the manuscript he was writing. The even longer manuscript was to explain all the facts that supported or challenged his theory of natural selection as the main driver of evolution.

Let us then return to the paper by Clemens and colleagues (1995) (see the "short version" in chapter 3) on the uses of books and articles in sociology. There are two main kinds of context that are ordinarily explained in words in sociology. One of these is the subject of this whole book: namely, theoretical location of the reasoning and of the facts. The second is "other stuff going on in the same environment, that we are not mainly interested in, but that helps us to interpret the facts we get." This chapter is mainly about the second kind.

Now let us consider a book being contrasted with an article as having more room for giving the context of a fact. One of the reasons, then, that books travel more easily across disciplines than articles (Clemens et al., 1995) is that an article requires the *reader* to supply the context that gives meaning to a fact, while a book gives the *author* a chance to supply context. For example, for most of the quantitative articles in *American Sociological Review*, a reader must supply the unmentioned contextual fact that the "random sample" was of the U.S. adult population, that it did not include prison or jail inmates or inmates of other institutions, and that it contains data from one "time point" (usually a few weeks, or in "longitudinal" studies sometimes up to four or five years) in the very recent past. An experienced reader of *ASR* does not even have to be conscious of applying this assumed context, though if he or she is reading it in a European university, it may be irritating that American sociologists write as if they were universal.

I would guess that the ratio of text words to numbers in quantitative books is much higher than in quantitative articles (i.e., there is more text to explain each number in a book). Articles often have up to two or three hundred numbers in a table in which only three or four numbers and their significance tests (only the asterisks of the statistical tests are usually discussed, not the numbers used to merit asterisks, though these may be published in the tables as well) are discussed at all in the text. Even then the articles quite often give regression coefficients where the metrics of the variables are not explained, so one could not read the coefficients in the article if one tried; the reader is expected either not ever to try to export the coefficient to a different context, or to know what metric the variables are usually measured in. That is a scandal even in an article, but a book editor would never let it get by.

So articles are useful only to those for whom the ritualistic references to the literature supply enough context. The readers of an event history analysis in sociology, for example, know what chi-square will have been calculated, so what that number in the table coming right after the words "chi-square" is all about. The experts in sociological event history analysis, Nancy Tuma and Michael Hannan, had to write a "textbook" on event history analysis so that the average journal reader would know what the context of that chi-square was (1984, pp. 43–327). This is a context provided now by standardized professional training. The chi-square is of the opposite kind to chi-squares that one would have learned about in analyzing cross tabulations in the 1950s, as I did. (It is a "goodness of fit" chi-square, rather than a "badness of fit" chi-square from the 1950s. Unfortunately, the "badness of fit" chi-square in those days was called a "goodness of fit" chi-square, and no one was confused, because they had learned *that* peculiar semantics in graduate school.)

In chapter 3 I urged investigators to pay a lot of attention to each case in sparse fields, and identified history as investigating a sparse field of archives in which each important fact is very expensive. We would expect, then, that one would need a lot of space to make each fact as valuable as it has to be. Yet Clemens and colleagues (1995) show that *quantitative* books are (1) cited more than quantitative articles (indicating that context pays, especially in communicating across disciplines), and also (2) cited more than qualitative books (indicating that precision of observation pays). The theory of the measuring instrument for context, books versus articles, does not explain this. But it does tell us why almost all important historical sociology is presented in books, or else in articles that are quite a bit longer than the average quantitative paper.

Contexts to Study Meanings

LÉVI-STRAUSS (1969 [1964], pp. 2–3) has a penetrating paragraph on the importance of context for understanding symbols in myths.

> However [the interpretation of a myth] is approached, it spreads out like a nebula, without ever bringing together in any lasting or systematic way the sum total of the elements from which it blindly derives its substance, being confident that reality will be its guide and show it a surer road than any it might have invented.... Starting with a myth chosen... arbitrarily... I establish a group of transformations [of oppositions between symbols] for each sequence, either within the myth itself, or by elucidation of the isomorphic links between sequences derived from several myths originating in the same community. This takes us beyond the study of individual myths to the consideration of certain guiding patterns situated along a single axis [the "axis" created by starting with isomorphisms in the surrounding myths]. At each point on the axis where there is such a pattern or schema, we then draw, as it were, a vertical line representing another axis established by the same operation... by [similarities of patterns of oppositions in] myths that present certain analogies with the first, although they derive from neighboring communities. As a result, the guiding patterns are simplified, made more complex, or transformed. Each one becomes a source of new axes, which are perpendicular to the first on different levels, and which will presently be connected, by... sequences derived either from myths originating in more remote communities or from myths initially neglected because they seemed useless or impossible to interpret.... It follows that as the nebula gradually spreads, its nucleus condenses and becomes more organized [by more oppositions among its symbols and others toward the periphery of our vision, and by more similarities of patterns of oppositions from elsewhere]. Loose threads join up with the initial group and reproduce its structure and determinative tendencies. Thus is brought into being a multi-dimensional body, whose central parts disclose a structure, while uncertainty and confusion continue to prevail along its periphery. But I do not hope to reach a stage at which the subject matter of mythology, after being broken down by analysis, will crystallize again into a whole with the general appearance of a stable and well-defined structure.

I would argue that this indicates a Lévi-Strauss investigative process, modeled on what he thinks happens as a process to a body of myths among communicating tribes, for which he uses a context "cloud" as both a methodological and substantive metaphor. Lévi-Strauss had invented (or rather, borrowed from Saussure in phonetics) the opposition method of isolating the relevance of a symbol. Lévi-Strauss wanted to figure out the meaning of a given symbol in its local use. By carefully studying the symbols a given symbol was contrasted with in the body of myths of the cultural area being studied, then, an investigator can get a better understanding of what a somewhat vague symbol means. But Lévi-Strauss points out that this will also tell something about the symbol with which it is contrasted, so one's understanding of the context of the symbol grows at the same time, and in the same way, as one's analysis of its particular meaning. To use his metaphor, one gets a good idea of the shape of the cloud of symbols in myths each time one studies the meaning of some central symbol to which other symbols are contrasted often in the body of myths.

So an extensive explanation of the meanings of the other symbols in the myth being studied, by a precise observational protocol organized around contrasts for determining those meanings, allows one to grasp more exactly the total local context. Put another way, the more one knows about the context of a fact, the more exactly one can "interpret" the significance of that fact for the theory being investigated. And conversely, the more intensively one studies the environment of a particular fact, the more one learns about the contexts of other facts in the environment.

Empirical work on context is useful to make one more certain what local fact has to be interpreted in a book rather than an article. This is true also if the fact is quantitative, repetitively observed by a regularized protocol of observation or questioning. The better one knows that context through other precisely observed facts, the readier one is to write a book about it. So quantities whose context is thoroughly explained travel best across disciplines. This is the fact that Clemens and colleagues (1995) provide us, and that I have been trying to explain here. But in the course of that explanation, we have also built a theory of why historical and ethnographic investigations are more often reported in books than in articles, a fact also reported by Clemens and colleagues (1995).

Insofar as context determines what exactly is being observed, the reader and so the author need to study that context thoroughly before they both know for sure what was observed. This explains why investigators in disciplines based on expensive facts, such as history or social anthropology or paleontology, have to supply much context about their facts, and so tend to publish their work in books rather than articles. And this in turn explains why people outside the discipline will like to read such works even though they themselves do not study paleontology or African herding tribes.

Note that the paper by Clemens and colleagues (1995) is very long, and explains a lot about all the numbers in it. For example, that total citations of sociologists by people outside the discipline are of a comparable size to citations by people inside, and that books are more cited by people outside the discipline, is a really big fact about intellectual impact. If a sociologist is a book writer, and has a dean who is a biochemist, the article by Clemens and colleagues will provide some valuable context for interpreting a book on a curriculum vitae. Further, it is important to understand why quantitative books get more citations than the books we naturally think of when we say "books," the narrative histories or ethnographies.

We might include books without any numbers but that tell us, among other things, why numbers and formulas were crucial, and to call the numbers and formulas "quantitative," the point would be even clearer. A book like Kuhn's *Structure of Scientific Revolutions* (1970 [1966]), for example, is devoted to explaining the context of quantitative and mathematical "facts" in the history of physics. It is very widely read across the social science disciplines, as well as in history. Kuhn's book on black body radiation, which is full of mathematics if not numbers, is really good, even though it has not traveled across disciplines very well. Many people interested in the revolutions book will stop on page four of Kuhn's *Black Body Theory* (1978), when they see the first integral sign in an equation. So although the book supplies much context for each integral sign, it will not make a big splash. A deep division among social science disciplines is the criterion of whether the typical practitioner stops reading when he or she finds an integral sign; most of those who do not stop there are economists and statisticians, who do not usually put as much context into their writings as Kuhn.

The Relation of Context to Distances between Units of Analysis

THERE ARE THREE MAIN WAYS THAT ANALYSIS of variations between contexts is central to sociological methodology; the more these three conditions are fulfilled, the more likely it is that the ratio of words to the causal facts about relations between distances will be large.

The first such condition is very general: boundary conditions on causal processes are more practically important in some settings than in others, and for some causal processes than others. Thus, barriers to perception such as walls, doors, or the orientation of chairs in a classroom or auditorium are extremely important boundaries in social interaction, and often determine what situations are "units of analysis" in a social system. The classroom walls, closed doors, and chairs facing front, with professor at the front, determine that the capital equipment of a school or university is mostly buildings, because buildings form the situations in such a fashion that they are easily dominated by the person who has the most to say (or at any rate who gets to say the most). But such boundary conditions are much less important for the social situation of hikers, for homework, or for outdoor farmers' markets. The radical difference in interaction structure between one side and the other of a door-and-wall complex is an especially simple example of the importance of boundary conditions on social causation (e.g., who does and who does not learn to solve differential equations if they are or are not in class). But such boundary conditions have little to do with who buys what from whom in farmers' markets. What boundaries there are on social causal processes is a subject for investigation. Central boundary conditions in social life often determine the units of analysis in the social sciences: causal processes confined within persons make people units of analysis; legal boundaries often make organizations units of analysis because they make different processes happen within organizations than between them in the market; processes confined within rooms make situations units of analysis; processes confined within texts make the patterns in the text crucial determinants of cultural effects, and so make boundaries of texts create units of analysis for high culture. I deal with units of analysis and mechanisms within them in the following chapter. But the point here is that these boundaries form variations in contexts, between inside and outside, that crucially influence what goes on.

The second big determinant of the importance of context is that much social and cultural behavior is a selection out of a repertoire of possibilities, created by a larger cultural system. Thus, the "text" of a myth is a selection for a given narrative out of a set of symbols that have a meaning outside the myth, which then shapes in part what a symbol means within the myth. Similarly, the questions on a test, or the creation of an argument in a term paper, are different sorts of selections out of the material from a class, from its "factual" and "generative" content. The test is supposed to gain its meaning as a measure of competence in the subject, as reflected in the grade, by being a fair extraction from the cultural content of the course. Very generally, understanding the meaning of an act requires knowledge of the language in which something is said, a grading of the importance of topics in the situation (such as, "Will this be on the test?"), the special rituals at the beginning (e.g., the professor raises his or her voice) that mark the talk as being a certain sort of talk with its sort of attention-governance norm, the selection of people present and their roles in that situation compared with their other roles. All these are therefore reasons why the studies of cultural objects rely a great deal on context, and so occur primarily in books.

A third general reason is purely methodological. The sparser the facts, the less one can afford the error of interpretation that might come from "accidental" variations of context. For most purposes a fossil of a pelvis from a given period is an observation of a pelvis. For some purposes (e.g., birth troubles) it is crucial to know whether it occurred in a female or a male of that species and in a teenager or an adult, whether it was found in the first or second stratum above the datable lava flow, whether the species was knuckle-walking or upright. Similarly, one needs to know whether the context of a text in eighteenth-century France was one that made a key phrase emphasize the *seigneur*'s landowning quality, his legal jurisdiction quality, his inherited membership in the nobility, or his right to hunt on a peasant's land. If such texts are rare, then getting it right is important. This does not necessarily mean that the meaning in a particular case was an important cause of what was going on; it may just mean that the investigator will now know what *was* the important cause.

As a practical matter, many aspects of context vary a great deal from time to time and from place to place. Often these aspects are crucial for socially constructed boundaries, meanings, and the various determinants of how sparse our facts are. Our "second order units of analysis," on which we observe distances between contexts, frequently are times and places. The relations between times and places and social action are crucial to investigating distances between contexts. These can be very small scale, like the differences between the attention structure of a classroom, as well as of the halls outside, before and after class, or between large areas and centuries in historical causation.

Periodization and Localization in Historical Sociology

ONE WAY TO THINK of the central observation of Clemens (1996; see "Clemens Time Short Version," below) is that the context often changes its nature as the investigator pursues the study. Lévi-Strauss, in the passage quoted above, is assuming that the culture, the body of myth, will stay still enough for him to get the contrasts, one on each side of his cloud, and then get another, and another, until he has a dense network inside. Clemens is saying that historians have to specialize in time and space so that their contexts for their facts are reasonably steady, learnable in a finite period of time. But she is also saying that the things making up the context do not stand still either.

In meteorology, while an amateur observer is watching the wind in a thunderstorm knock down the chicken coop, he or she is not noticing that the wind is changing (growing stronger) because it is gaining energy from the ground being hotter than the air, so that energy is being poured into the thunderstorm from the bottom. Likewise, the context of a bread riot in the early 1790s in France may be that grievances were being formulated and collected all over the country in preparation for the Estates General to raise taxes. Only this change in context, perhaps, turned a rise in the price of bread into a grievance against the government that could start a revolution. But the Estates General being called is also the context changing from the king's scheme to raise taxes, to a possible alternative government of France, collected into Paris. The clear presence of an alternative government often leads to revolution. That, too, makes a bread riot much more dangerous than one a few years previously (Markoff, 1996).

So I am running away with Lévi-Strauss's metaphor of learning more about the cloud by studying an element (or rather, very explicitly, the distances between elements), but more about the elements by studying the cloud. We need periodization and geographical limits because context is important. *If* the context is important, *then* it matters that investigators keep track of its changes. But suppose someone watches the internal processes in the state of Washington, as Clemens did (the investigation is mentioned in the short version below, but is given in much more detail in Clemens, 1992). At the beginning of the period she studied, German social welfare innovations and trade union organization had not reached the Germans in Milwaukee (Clemens was comparing Washington to Wisconsin, among other states). This is crucial to the different development of "left wing liberalism" in the two states, a difference that made no difference at the beginning. That is, first the context changed in Germany, and only then in Milwaukee; after that, Milwaukee provided an alternative to the type of liberal movements that had meanwhile grown up in Washington. The difference became relevant at a later time, and the context of each state was different because of developments in the other.

Wisconsin could learn about women's movements from Washington, and Washington about unions from Wisconsin.

At the end of the period she studied, the Bismarck-period social-democratic innovations *had* reached Wisconsin, and so got into the American political arena. If Clemens had been trying to "control" the context of social welfare reforms by taking a narrow time period, she would have "lost control" over the context because at the state level, the context, partly made up of the other state, was changing fast.

Clemens (1999) tries to confront the logic of that problem of periodization as she met it in the book. I think her book on social welfare reform is the best book on the early history of American social welfare, because she recognized and dealt with a crucial fact about the context of social welfare in those days: it was done in the separate states in the United States, and in *the state* (i.e., the national or absolutist state) in Europe. Using *the state* in the abstract in studying those days thus missed a crucial aspect of the American historical context of social welfare, the federal character of the early American social welfare system (actually the German state is highly decentralized to *Länder* as well, which we comparativists often fail to analyze).

Clemens Time Short Version

Summarized from Elisabeth Clemens, "Continuity and Coherence: Periodization and the Problem of Institutional Change," in Fredrik Engelstad and Ragnvald Kalleberg, eds., *Social Time and Social Change: Perspectives on Sociology and History* (Oslo: Scandinavian University Press, 1999), pp. 62–83. Page numbers with no further identification are to this source.

Most historical work is organized into specialties of time and place. The idea is that context is important in all narratives, and time periods and places are convenient approximations to "constancy of context." Such a regression conception of "holding constant," however, requires a theory of what it is about a context that has to be constant, and how one would theorize that constancy and *its* change into a different time-period context. Historical social scientists need a strategy for using aspects of the narratives worked on (the social changes analyzed) to determine appropriate contextual constancy and contextual variation. ("Macroscopic" or *longue durée* change, too slow to be changing much during the narrative, is sufficiently well dealt with by periodization, for example). Within periods that are a small part of the *longue durée*, the microscopic or short-run changes in a particular monograph take place in a context one does not much have to worry about, and knowing enough about that context is manageable.

"Linked solutions to a continuing problem" provide Clemens with a strategy for identifying temporal and spatial limits to contexts. Thus Thor Heyerdahl sailed a reed raft across the Atlantic to show that ancient Egyptians had a set of linked solutions to the continuing problems of navigation, and that these combined were sufficient to allow one to cross the Atlantic. These included growing of reeds like papyrus, craft traditions of building reed rafts, crafting of useful sails and paddles, and navigation lore. The context then included the continuity of the problem of crossing bodies of water, the lack of timber for wooden ships (and so the lack of craft traditions of making planks and sealing the joints with pitch), and the continuity of crucial resources. For example, Heyerdahl believed the Canary Islands were outside this complex because navigators arriving there never established papyrus on the islands. Even though they may have been once in the larger project of exploration of the seas on reed rafts, this failure created a crucial spatial boundary between them and that system, which they could no longer cross.

The medieval Norwegians and Danes used planks and pitch to create a different set of linked solutions to navigation in the North Atlantic, a different navigation lore for the much rougher seas, and no boundaries caused by lack of reeds. Their project of exploration with their linked solutions had a different time frame, different crucial resources, and different geographical boundaries. Heyerdahl could come back to Norway to write a saga of a heroic navigator and join a different chain of linked artistic works. But he could never have brought new astronomical ideas or the notion of pictographic writing to the Maya, as he claimed the Egyptians had. Whether the ancients did so is a matter of some scholarly dispute, but Heyerdahl himself crossing in his reed raft would have found the Maya already with telescopes, clocks, alphabets, novels rather than sagas, and so beyond the period-place boundaries of the reed-raft linked solutions. (Scandinavian contrast example supplied here by ALS.)

Conceiving the changes at stake in the historical work as linked solutions thus points to the spatial boundaries of an interdependent development of action (e.g., reed-growing areas versus timber areas). But it also points to temporal boundaries (e.g., Egyptian sailing before the North European competitive marine shipping systems developed).

More important, it provides a positive analysis of how such boundaries might be transcended, by showing what aspects of the context are relevant. We can provide two versions of this approach from the literature. The first, from Kubler, uses the notion of linked solutions; the second from Sewell uses the notion of schemas. Clemens's summary of Kubler runs like this:

> The method begins with the identification not of periods but of projects that link a set of artists (or other actors) both over time and across social space: Every important work of art can be regarded both as an historical event and as a hard-won solution to some problem. It is irrelevant now whether the event was original or conventional, accidental or willed, awkward or skillful. The important clue is that any solution points to the existence of some problem to which there have been other solutions, and that other solutions to this same problem will most likely be invented to follow the one now in view. As the solutions accumulate, the problem alters. The chain of solutions nevertheless discloses the problem (Kubler, 1962, p. 33). (p. 69)

Or in Sewell's alternative formulation:

> Schemas refer to both "a given society's fundamental tools of thought" and "the various conventions, recipes, scenarios, principles of action and habits of speech and gesture built up with these fundamental tools" (Sewell, 1992, p. 708). The concept "schema" represents a point of intersection between theories of historical process and current institutional approaches to the study of organizations. See Powell and Dimaggio (1991b, pp. 22–27). (p. 70n)

An example with more sociological substance than reed rafts is the "fraternal order" model of organization in American nineteenth-century history. Fraternal orders like the Masons, the Elks, college Greek letter fraternities, combined solidarity and friendship for men outside the household; lack of religious or party-political affiliations; a tenuous affiliation, often largely ritual, with a larger structure with the same name; and locally determined purposes. This template was easily adaptable to many secular and "non-electoral political" issues: labor organization (e.g., the Knights of Labor), veterans' groups, college student housing, burial insurance, chambers of commerce, repression of blacks (e.g., the Ku Klux Klan), and even, with a change of gender, women's suffrage.

To show that there was an actual network of links among these "solutions" to a problem of popular organization, one needs narrative evidence. Initiation into craft unions with ritual secrets and secret handshakes, fraternal drinking places maintained by veterans' groups, a Masonic-like hierarchy in the Ku Klux Klan (rather than, say, belts in Asiatic martial arts [this contrary example supplied by ALS]) indicate a common organizational template.

Each such solution, as Kubler says, refines our understanding of the common and continuing problem. In a democracy the implicit convivial solidarity of various kinds of social segments can be organized for collective purposes, from drinking and college housing to continuing the southern side of the American Civil War after the defeat of the South.

The conditions for the continuity of the problem form the context relevant to the "project" of extending fraternal order solutions to multiple special interests. Before the Civil War, most popular political organization was specifically in one or another of the political parties or in local village and county governments. After World War II, national organizations often had "organizers" to create local "branches." Thus, the period within which we can tell comparable narratives of fraternal organization templates in special interest local groups is roughly the period 1860s to 1930s, especially in the more populist democratic states west of the Appalachians. Time and place, then, should be shaped by the linked solutions to the problem of translating local solidarity into special interest organizations, often using fraternal organization schemas of organizing.

Geographical and Temporal Boundaries of Context

CLEMENS (1999) ALSO ARGUES that there is a similar problem in marking off "the place" that forms a context. Geographical "specialization" of investigators, who think they have controlled the context by observing the Precolumbian Americas separately from Europe and Asia, may be all wrong. If boats of the sort built by Egyptians could cross the Atlantic from the Mediterranean, but might have trouble getting back, then middle America may have been part of ancient Middle Eastern civilization, without the Egyptians or the Mayans ever knowing.

My favorite example of misconceiving a temporal process by ignoring changes in geographical context involves American labor history.

If we look at the statistics of growth of union membership in the United States, we find that the two biggest bursts were *not* around the turn of the twentieth century, when the AFL got its start, or in the 1930s when the CIO was founded, but instead during World War I and World War II. That is, big causes of American unionization were in Germany and Japan, not in the United States. Since we do not really want Germany and Japan to be a main subject in American labor history, and we do not want the heroes of the War Production Board who strongly encouraged union organization in World War II to seem as romantic as Eugene V. Debs and the Pullman Strike, John L. Lewis of the coal miners and the steelworkers, and Walter Ruether organizing sit-ins in Flint, Michigan, we do not even really "know" this uncomfortable geographical fact in American labor history. Obviously the wars dramatically changed class relations, twice in the same way, a way that encouraged trade union organization. We have almost no theory about that fact, because it is outside the ken of American labor history. These geographical boundaries obscure the history of American labor relations. But since the War Production Board is not part of the same series of related problems and solutions, the processes of organizing during the wars need to be treated in the light of the radical changes in the context of unionization that war brought.

The context of the labor movement did not stay constant. The United States had quite a different stratification system during the wars than in peacetime. Japan and Germany, and to a lesser extent Italy and Austria, were a big part of the causes of that stratification reorganization. But U.S. labor historians specialize in the labor movement of a single country, most often the United States. Diplomatic history, even a war, is hardly their business. Yet how could labor historians not notice the huge waves of unionization *managed by the American national government*?

Now how do I know about those two bursts of union organization that, by and large, labor history knows not of? By looking in *Historical Statistics of the United States* and old *Statistical Abstracts*, where some bureaucrats or scholars had carefully compiled, as best they could, the numbers of members of unions in the United States. My abstracting away from the context that we all know about the American labor movement, and looking at the time series of union membership instead, but remembering the dates of the wars, showed inadvertently that the context of war fundamentally changed all aspects of American stratification.

The key lessons here are that one should look for a sequence of related problems and solutions, notice when they change to a different set (e.g., partisan mobilization in the early nineteenth century, fraternal mobilization in the later part, then NGOs after World War II), and mark "period" by those sequences. Apply the same criterion to spaces. Use those times and spaces to locate significant differences in context, and try to figure out what distances between those time and place contexts make them different.

Exactness of Concepts of Context; Institutions as Contexts of Organizations

WHEN WE WERE LOOKING at "period" as a measure of context, Clemens's argument was essentially that this was not exact enough as a concept of context to summarize neatly what we were trying not to pay attention to. We wanted a cheap way to "control" the context by "periodization." The basic advice of Clemens (1996) was to look for a series of linked problems or linked solutions through time and over space, and to choose periods or places defined by those links for the limitation of relevant context.

In the modern literature, we talk about linked solutions in terms of *institutions* that permeate the environment of some set of organizations or states. When the institutions manage to impose linked solutions or linked problems on a set of organizations, those institutions then become a context in Clemens's sense. Distances between the sets of linked solutions and problems then are distances between "institutions" that dominate in a given time and place. To concretize this a bit, let me outline the history of the multidivisional organizational form of large manufacturing firms in the United States, as analyzed by Neil Fligstein (1990; for the first period in his analysis he relies on Chandler, 1962). Then I will present Schneiberg and Clemens (forthcoming, 2004) in a short version, which outlines the strategies for collecting information on the impact of the context (i.e., the institution) on the organizations (the units that "adopt" or "fake conformity to" an institution).

Fligstein (1990) described two different periods in the adoption of the multidivisional form of organization of manufacturing firms: a first period in which there was not much outside pressure for this form of organization, and a second one in which manufacturing firms had difficulty in raising money and getting other types of resources if they did not have that form. A multidivisional form is one in which the engineering, marketing, and production of a given line of goods are organized in a single suborganization, the division, with a separate higher executive and budget, and control over the coordination of the specialists in each area. Divisions operate by specifying internally how they will reach the financial goals of the larger firm (this description comes from Chandler, 1962). Such divisions were, and are, controlled mainly by financial controls and career management of their higher executives by a central corporate office.

In the first (Chandler) period, the multidivisional form was *not* institutionalized for manufacturing. In the second period, the multidivisional form *was* institutionalized for manufacturing firms, primarily in their relation to the "context" of capital markets. In the first period, we would say that the causes of multidivisional organization were likely to be in the firm itself and in the markets for its products. If a firm did not have particular problems in coordinating production with marketing, or engineering with marketing, or engineering with production, then it would be unlikely to adopt the multidivisional form.

The environmental or contextual variable, let us say E, describes whether or not the capital market determined for some firms that they would be disadvantaged if they did not have the multidivisional form. The institution (external requiring of multidivisional forms) would have an effect on all large manufacturing firms when it exists (say, when $E = 1$), and would have no such effect when absent ($E = 0$). If the environmental variable is the popularity of the multidivisional form of corporation, as it was in Fligstein (1990), we need a variable that varies over time: E then has a value near zero in the early period that Chandler studied (1920s–1940s), and a variable nearer one in the later period. In the Chandler period, manufacturing corporations could be very respectable in the capital market having a centralized operations management, as Ford did. At that time, corporations adopted the multidivisional form only if they were active in several differently organized markets. Alfred Sloan made his fortune by imposing the multidivisional form on General Motors, which needed it. After that, every large manufacturing firm that wanted to get money cheap from Wall Street needed to have a multidivisional form.

Schneiberg-Clemens Institutionalism Methods Short Version

Summarized from Marc Schneiberg and Elisabeth Clemens, "The Typical Tools for the Job: Research Strategies in Institutional Analysis," in Walter W. Powell and Dan L. Jones, eds., *How Institutions Change* (Chicago: University of Chicago Press, forthcoming, 2004).

The first kind of evidence offered for the causal effect of institutions on organizations was showing similar effects on the organizations in spite of the variety of their conditions. For example, poor and rich states, dictatorships and democracies, all adopted organization of schools into primary, secondary, and college-university levels, especially after World War II. This showed that there was a norm for the organization of schools, so that, whether they had books and teachers or not, they were divided into primary, secondary, and college-university. This form was, then, institutionalized. The practice in the United States of dividing secondary schools by age-grade into middle and high schools was not internationally institutionalized.

Since these early days, methods to study institutional effects have developed in three main ways. Variations in the nature of institutions in different times or in different organizational fields should produce differences in external impacts on organizational forms and practices. For example, Fligstein (1990) argued that between 1920 and about 1950, the multidivisional form of large manufacturing corporations (meaning different products are produced by divisions that are much like firms) was not an institution. Therefore, only firms in multiple, differently organized markets had adopted the form. After that capital markets tended to demand multidivisional forms for large manufacturing corporations, so being in multiple markets no longer predicted adoption, and only large size, being a manufacturing firm, and dependence on capital markets did so. That is, variations in the strength of institutions should cause variations in the effect of institutional demands as compared with internal functional demands.

Second, variations in the links or causal pathways between institutions and specific organizations, or between organizations already conforming and those not (yet) conforming, should produce higher rates of adoption of institutional forms. For example, Edelman (1990, p. 1428) showed that firms with public contracts and public agencies adopt government-encouraged forms and obey new laws more quickly.

Finally, different contingencies of the cultural context, or different patterns of interaction, or different resources and competencies, at the boundaries between institutions and organizations should produce local variety in the effects of "the same" institution. For instance, Schneiberg (1999) shows that U.S. states with populist party political traditions experienced a conflict over insurance institutions between mutual versus stockholder companies, and other conflicts between cooperative versus entrepreneurial firms. This meant that new insurance, local retail, and farm produce marketing firms, depending on local political environments, had different pressures to adopt a mutual-cooperative, stockholder, or entrepreneurial model.

The key to all these elaborations of method is to get variation in the causal forces of institutions, to explain variations in adoption, conformity, or attentiveness to the institutions in the form of fake conformity. Thus, if at some times it becomes uncertain whether a firm's hiring and promotions standard will pass muster as fair to minorities and women, we may see in those times a great deal of activity of firms in creating affirmative action offices, attending to news of lawsuits or regulations, or setting up grievance procedures for accusations of discrimination (Sutton and Dobbin, 1996). We also learn from this example that "pressure" from institutions may be as much "posing problems for local solution" as it is "enforcing institutional standards."

The first successes of the new institutionalism were in explaining educational organization, the taking of children out of the family and out of "real life" to put them in environments specifically designed to teach. Unlike apprenticeship, failures in schools do not have immediate real consequences. So in the first institutional studies, the world culture explained an educational organizational field whose activities were "specifically inconsequential," except, of course, for giving teachers jobs and taking jobs away from children.

But these effects and others were larger and earlier if *the countries* had memberships in international organizations, had ratified international conventions, or depended on international aid or legitimacy. That is, the stronger the links between countries and the international system, the stronger the impact of world culture on local school policies. The lack of correlation between school policies and industrial and economic organization suggests that world culture had less effect in matters directly connected to markets and production. [This interpretation of the widely documented low correlation between economic development and school organization reported by Schneiberg and Clemens is added here by ALS.] Similarly, McNeely (1995) finds that nations belonging to UNESCO were "more likely to ratify the convention against educational discrimination." International links thus increase the causal force toward national conformity to suggested, but not yet institutionalized, aspects of world culture.

A similar argument at the level of organizational fields within countries shows that the "proportion of firms that have already adopted a particular model or policy" predicts adoption. This approach "raises questions of 'who is visible to this organization?'" or 'who are this organization's peers?'" Related studies show that "personnel professionals carry with them models of employee relations that differ from models promoted by labor lawyers" (Dobbin et al., 1994) (p. 16). That is, connections to different institutions predict adoption of different schemas.

But Sewell's schemas, of which institutions are collections, were intended to explain both conformity and pathways of innovation or "agency." Frank Dobbin's work illustrates the cultural mechanisms in creating new systems of organization in railroads in the United States, Britain, and France:

> Whereas much institutionalist research presumes the restricted extent of variation (DiMaggio and Powell, 1983) or the steady decrease in difference over time as nation states conform to world polity norms, Dobbin addresses the persistence of difference across industrial polities faced with a common technological challenge: the construction and management of railroads.... [R]ather than demonstrating convergence despite differences, Dobbin documents consistency within divergence. Britain's solutions to railroad problems not only differ from those adopted in France, but they differ consistently in ways that are informed by a distinctive model of industrial governance patterned after each nation's institutions of political rule. Second, attending to the persistence of difference across more than two cases, Dobbin addresses configurations of outcomes, breaking with the dichotomous logic of most diffusion studies where the only outcomes are "adopted" or "not adopted." Finally, he approaches the task of documenting models, scripts, and templates with the tools of a historian open to the diverse riches of archival sources.

Another strategy for documenting mechanisms of institutional contextual effects is to look at the differences between the public transcript of formal behavior and its informal, sometimes deviant, counterpart. Thus, "legal" regulation with punishments often produces "oblique resistance, political humor, private texts such as diaries ... private instrumental calculation, especially to 'work the system.'" When instead the schemas are regarded as sacred, so it is "unthinkable" to disregard them, and punishments are regarded as shaming those who have broken a taboo, we tend to find private diaries of a devotional sort elaborating rules, making everyday practices more severe and puritanical so as to become exemplary. Instrumental use of institutional forms, especially by authorities, is regarded as morally corrupt, unthinkable, or dangerous, even if unpunished. Thus different mechanisms of institutional conformity produce different kinds of private nonconformity or overconformity.

Thus, the four main strategies for studying institutional effects on organizations are: (1) to search for evolution of many organizations in a field in the same direction over time; (2) to search for different patterns of change of organizations in periods or places where different institutions reign; (3) to search for differences in the adoption of institutionalized forms between organizations more closely linked to institutions or to previous adopters and organizations more isolated from institutional forces; and (4) to search for evidence—for example, in informal cultures of organizations—of different mechanisms with which institutions induce conformity.

The basic idea of Fligstein (1990) is that E, the pressure to have divisions, was high after Chandler's (1962) book, and articles touting the multidivisional form in the *Wall Street Journal* and *Forbes* magazine. That is, the E variable (pressure on manufacturing firms to have a multidivisional form) varied over time, and after it was high, it produced homogeneity of form among large manufacturing firms.

Many of the firms with very large capital value during these periods were banking firms, which did not have to coordinate engineering or production with marketing. In neither period was there any special tendency of these firms to have divisions controlled financially by central offices. This is a "mapping variable," let us say, m. The mapping variable m is up near one for big manufacturing firms, so that all such manufacturing firms will tend to have great pressure from capital markets to become multidivisional *after* it becomes the fashion; m is lower among big retail firms or financial firms. That is, after the environmental variable, E, the "institutionalization of the multidivisional form," gets high, it will have a big effect on all big manufacturing firms. When m is high (that is, among manufacturing firms), then whenever E gets high the multidivisional form will be homogeneous among that group.

Those manufacturing firms that are in multiple markets organized differently will tend to get multidivisional forms. Such firms will get them, most likely, before they become fashionable. Like General Motors, they would and did go looking for Pierre du Pont to serve on their board of directors so that they could import the multidivisional form first developed at DuPont; GM then allowed Sloan to manage the introduction of the form from DuPont. There was no separate pressure from Wall Street.

So as a first approximation we have as the form of Fligstein's (1990) institutional argument one that looks like this:

$$f = K_1 mE + K_2(\# \text{ of markets})$$

where f is the pressure toward the multidivisional form, the Ks are constants to tell one the units in which one measures f, and in relation to the units in which one measures m and E and (# of markets) (see Stinchcombe, 1968, p. 204). Then m is the mapping variable that is near one for large manufacturing firms that raise money on Wall Street (and so near zero for small manufacturing firms and for nonmanufacturing firms), E is a variable that is near one for firms after Chandler moved from a professorship of economic history at Johns Hopkins to a professorship of business history at the Sloan School of Management at MIT, and near zero before.

Now the nifty thing about Fligstein (1990), and Schneiberg and Clemens's (forthcoming, 2004) analysis of it, is that following their analysis, we have specified much more exactly the mechanism of institutional (i.e., contextual) causes. The first notion is to divide environmental effects into two variables: a mapping variable for the unit of analysis (firms) that measures, essentially, how vulnerable the unit is to the environmental force, and a second environmental (here, institutional) one for variations in that force.

Here we see analysts adding information about what features of the organization affected make it vulnerable to an external institutional force (being in manufacturing and raising capital on Wall Street), and what variations over time (in this case before and after multidivisional form was fashionable) there were in the institutional force. This strategy can lead to observations that much more exactly mirror the mechanism that does the work of contextual causes. But that in turn is because the investigators have developed the concept more exactly. An environmental force almost always affects some units more than others, so m, the mapping variable, is always appropriate; "m everywhere one" is just an extreme case. If the environmental force does not vary, then the mapping variable does all the work, as when nations adopt international forms more quickly if they are members of UNESCO. But if the environmental force does not vary, it is not very interesting. Fligstein (1990) showed convincingly that the environmental force, the institution, varied over time.

Notice also that this specifies a more exact thing that we may want to know about the "context," so that Schneiberg and Clemens (forthcoming, 2004) suggest we are not supposed just to call the measure of institutional vigor a "period." We have to specify our periods for Fligstein's temporal analysis of the multidivisional form so that they will have an effect on big firms, on manufacturing firms, and in the appropriate period. So Fligstein (1990), and then Schneiberg and Clemens (forthcoming, 2004), have a much more exact specification of "institutional theory" for the purposes of relating it to specific data than the form given in the usual references, such as the canonical paper by Dimaggio and Powell (1983).

The correlation between having a multidivisional form and being in several markets goes down from one period to the next, which shows we need a concept of an institutional force toward the multidivisional form, reducing the variance to be explained and so the correlation coefficient. We observe that this correlation was only ever high, and the proportion having a multidivisional form was only high, among manufacturing firms. It is therefore appropriate that Fligstein (1990) used the sample of the Fortune 500 largest manufacturing firms. Thus we have developed a much more exact concept of the institution of multidivisional firms, with the two components of variation on whether the form is institutionalized, and a mapping variable that says it only governs large manufacturing firms, by looking at the facts about contextual causation.

Concepts and Variables about Contexts

INSIDE THE APPROPRIATE BOUNDARIES within which a particular theory applies, the conditions are "context" for that theory. Ordinarily some causal forces come across such boundaries, so that Lévi-Strauss finds that the meanings of symbols in myths have come across the boundaries of tribes within which particular myths exist, and from the tribal culture into a particular telling of the myth to an anthropological fieldworker. Yet the composition of those symbols into a particular myth has many internal causes, the causes of the previous choices of the myth teller guiding succeeding ones, and many effects on aspects of the internal organization of the myth, such as the ritual uses of the particular myth in circumcision ceremonies or in weddings or in rituals of war and raiding.

For most purposes we want minimum information about the larger mythical environment, just enough to understand what a particular myth is telling about; we want to focus, for example, on its effect on the status of the circumcised boys or girls. So we want the boundary conditions of the meanings of symbols simply to stay still enough for us to figure that out. Lévi-Strauss himself wanted also to give a general theory and method for studying mythical systems as wholes.

Similarly, we want to know enough about the history of the context for multidivisional firms to know that one could raise money for a big manufacturing firm without such a form up to about 1950, so only being in multiple markets mattered in the causal account, but that after 1950 this no longer mattered because firms in manufacturing had to have them. We probably do not want to know how Wall Street came to believe in multidivisional firms for manufacturing after 1950, though we may fill in, rhetorically, uninvestigated causes like Chandler becoming famous and articles that may have appeared in journals we do not routinely read.

Clearly, scraps of theory about the environment may be useful. The elementary theory that the supply of share and bond capital for very large firms through national or international financial markets is likely to be important, so that anything that is widely believed in those markets is likely to be institutionally powerful, will help us know where to look. The flow of capital from savers to large investors is a boundary condition, determining where large corporations can exist. One would not study small retailers' response to that part of the environment, unless they were part of a major corporation's franchise system. But in general, scholarly and theoretical depth of understanding are not very important. Reading the news the organizational managers read will be an empiricist way to get at what context one needs.

The basic logical starting point that Clemens has given us is that one needs to look for a series of connected problems and solutions over time, to see evidence in what one is explaining that it depends on conditions obtaining in that time (and in those places). Starting with the problems tells us where to look for the causes in the environment that need to be there for such problems to recur. Starting with the solutions tells us where to look for the technologies and cultures that provide the repertoires of possible activities embedded in the solutions. The sequence then gives us clues to the boundary conditions. Chandler (1962) found the problems and solutions in the four major corporations he looked at in his book on the multidivisional corporation. Fligstein (1990) found a sequence of solutions without the problems, suggesting that the boundary conditions, the context, had changed. This is a fundamental guide to how much context one needs. This, then, is the point at which one goes back to the principles of economy in research design, laid out in chapter 3.

Summary on Concepts of Context

ENVIRONMENTS OR CONTEXTS have effects on people and on social relations and interactions, so one has to have at least a minimal theory of environments. At the least one needs to have a theory of the boundary conditions under which the causal processes being studied work, boundaries of the generality of the causal theory.

Further, some units of analysis are more affected by particular contextual variables than others, so we need concepts to map contexts onto the units they affect. Everyone knows that situations defined as funerals and weddings are more affected by the religious environment, different among the world religions, than are business transactions. People behave more religiously at funerals than when signing contracts, though the rituals of a real estate closing in the United States could be thought of as honoring several aspects of the civil law, and the rituals of sterility in a hospital operating room confer a scientific *mana* on the sterile instruments and a ritual scientific dominance for those who have scrubbed and donned sterile gloves (nonsterile people and things are untouchable). Different contexts are called up for different ritualized happenings; we would say situations are "mapped" with a zero-one vector onto religious, civil law, and medical-scientific contexts. A death on the operating table would have all three mappings, on religious, legal, and scientific contexts, and so would vary with variations in each of those contexts.

Almost always contextual variables vary from one time to another and one space to another. Clemens (1999) argues that, for a given theoretical purpose, a good way to approximate the temporal and spatial context onto which some social practice should be mapped (the equivalent of defining concepts of period and place in historical methodology) is to locate the practice or the relationship in which it is embedded as part of a series of solutions to a continuing problem, or as part of a series of problems that have common solutions. Then the birth of the sequence of solutions or problems is a good tentative identification of the period and space whose context needs to be studied, and a tentative specification of what it is about a period and place that makes it the relevant context. Thus, one uses data on social practices to refine concepts of context, appropriate to the purpose. For example, Fligstein (1990) uses the detachment of the practice of divisionalization of manufacturing firms from the problems to which it was originally a solution (being in multiple markets) to identify his periods by the degree of institutionalization of the multidivisional form. In the new period it became a solution to the new problem of having a form institutionalized in the market for investment in manufacturing firms. And the place to look for the difference was largely on Wall Street in New York (rather than, e.g., the Bourse in Paris), and in the new practice of promotion of financial experts to chief operating officer of such firms.

Schneiberg and Clemens (forthcoming, 2004) turn this basic method into a way of identifying periods in the development of methodology for studying institutional effects on organizations. A set of linked solutions to the problem of explaining the forms and practices of organizations defines the periods of methodology to investigate and develop institutional theory. For example, similarities of organizations with different causes bearing on them (e.g., schools in different countries) are attributed to institutions that must be there to explain nonresponsiveness to varying causes. Then institutions are considered as varying from time to time. Some organizations are identified as having higher values of the mapping variables that indicate, for example, greater exposure to international institutions. If they change faster toward institutionalized solutions to their problems, it is evidence both for effectiveness of the mapping variables in indicating channels of influence, and the character of the institutions that are so channeled.

All such methods are generalizable from the field of organizations to any other environmental effect. For example, in the Ukrainian-Russian steppe between the mountains and desert to the south and the forest to the north, the rainfall decreases fairly steadily from west to east, because of the southern mountains casting a rain-shadow, so most of the moisture in the air comes from the west and is carried east by winds from the west. As one goes east, then, agriculture becomes more precarious, and herding by nomadic tribes becomes more dominant. As in the United States, the lower the average rainfall, the more years the crops fail, and usually the more radical the farmers are. But also the lower the rainfall, the harsher the competition between nomads (or ranchers) and arable grain-farmers. Thus, if one uses as a mapping variable whether the enterprise is peasant farming versus nomadic (or rancher) cattle raising, and the environmental variable of average rainfall or proportion of years of crop failure, one can predict a good deal about the date of Russian conquest (later with less rain), the radicalization of the farmers (more radical toward the east in Russia, toward the west in the United States), resistance to settlement by herders (but not farmers), increasing toward the east in Russia.

This will come as no surprise to any general Russian historian, or any student of nomadic central Asia (see Lattimore, 1967 [1940]). The methodological point here is that Lattimore fits as easily as Fligstein into the logic of environmental variables (varying here primarily with space) and mapping variables (varying here with Russian versus Turkic ethnicity, settler versus nomadic, among other things). A historian or anthropologist who ignored variations in rainfall context, and the mapping of the effect on nomadic versus settler populations, would soon be out of a job. But one does not have to become either a meteorologist or an agronomist to understand enough of the context. The logic of contextual analysis remains the same.

6 Units of Analysis and Mechanisms: Turning Causes into Effects

THE DISTANCES OF CAUSES AND EFFECTS in chapters 2–4 are between units of analysis, and if we allow contexts to be units of analysis, that is true of chapter 5 as well. The two measurements or observations that give us each of those distances are observed on a unit. We have talked of units of analysis as turning causes into effects; units are the nodes of a network graph of causes and effects, of "path diagrams." Units of analysis were situated within contexts: the contexts determined how the causes behaved, within the context's units. I have spoken briefly about boundaries around units of analysis as determining what causal mechanisms operate within them, or determining the limits within which they operate, to produce effects that we observe.

Units of analysis have to be sufficiently unified, sufficiently bounded, to turn causes into effects, and to permit one to observe the units' features, or features of inputs and outputs to them, so as to know how distant they are from other such units. Processes within those units are the *mechanisms* that turn causes into effects.

Thus, in situations of mutual presence and interaction, people oriented to each other can create definitions of what is going on, "definitions of the situation." These definitions include such matters as who is in a conversation with whom and who is excluded, as indicated by conversational circles of backs. They then have consequences of who will get acquainted with whom. For example, a large classroom lecture situation may produce acquaintances among students before and after class, but not during, while wandering in the book display at a convention may create many new contacts.

The situation, with internal government of attention, talk, physical arrangements, and visible signs of roles in the situation, such as uniforms or turned backs, is a unit of analysis, because it has within it mechanisms that turn causes into effects—for example, attention governance into acquaintance. Situations then can be described by variables, most often two-valued, one vs. zero variables described in words, and distances on those variables may be causes and effects.

Situations can be arranged into larger structures. The class schedule of a university is such a structure, probably more important than the stratification of the population of the university into paid and paying, faculty versus students and staff, and the like. The class schedule is arranged so as to produce lecture situations, seminar situations, changes in the obligations of teachers between semesters by scheduling them into situations, and changing syllabuses specifying student obligations to those same situations. Without altering the status of very many people, one can have quite a different organization of the activities of thousands of people from one semester to the next. Professor-student social relations are created and destroyed on a large scale by changing the structure of situations, and the relations of students and faculty to those situations. Only the registrar's office, and their computer, knows the whole structure.

The program of a convention is also the central formal structure, with its officers and committees peripheral to everything important, their official position announced in most situations only by the ribbons they wear, without situational effect.

A person is also a unit of analysis that makes decisions with his or her rational faculties, forms romances with his or her hormones and rational faculties combined with readings of responses of others, and has a schedule of courses that defines his or her formal role for this term. Turning decisions about courses into attendance and homework and grades, making acquaintances with potential for romance after class, and calculating the derivative with trained reason are unified into causes and effects by processes within the person.

The social ties within a network are units of analysis; a tie can be described by such variables as whether it is a marriage or not, whether it is symmetric or not (e.g., the relation "brother" is symmetric, the relation "father-son" is asymmetric; for an extensive study of this difference, see Gould, 2003), whether or not the people have a contract covering the flows in the tie, and so on. But a two-person relation is merely the simplest form of a network. A network can be described by concepts on the character of the ties within it (e.g., a kinship network has relations of marriage and descent), or by structural features, such as the average number of links it takes in a network of physicians to reach one who keeps up with new drugs (Coleman, Katz, and Menzel, 1957). Persons who make up the nodes at the ends of social relations in the network graph can also be described by their structural position, as in the variable of how many links it takes for *each* physician to reach someone who keeps up with new drugs.

A poem is also a unit of analysis, with its meaning, its meter, perhaps its rhyme or alliteration scheme formed into a unit. The causes of a poem and of its features are in the social world of creation. In the United States it usually has no reception, because Americans do not read or memorize poems, except for song lyrics. The world of creation is linked to the world of such reception as there is by use of the same language, by the various causes of publication and the distribution of published text, by its potential place as the lyrics of a song. One might describe a poem by a variable, lyric of a song versus not, and make predictions about its reception, the amount of money it might make, and whether one might dance while listening to the lyrics.

A poem transforms causes in one social world into possible effects in another largely by being a coherent cultural pattern, formed in one social location and ending up in another, or sometimes nowhere. Its inner coherence is largely formed in the world of "high culture," the place where complex cultural patterns are formed. That coherence makes poems and other cultural patterns, such as laws, scientific and mathematical discoveries, newspapers, and television programs, into units of analysis in sociology. Those units may be described by variables (usually qualitative ones described in words), having mechanisms of meaning and "fit" in a cultural system, and producing effects (or their absence) by their features relevant to their reception and use.

Organizations are held together by legal boundaries, by authoritative communication systems within them, by incentive systems that make people work at organizational purposes instead of their own, by a focus on information about the narrow parts of the environment that they use to produce and sell goods and services. The ordering of such internal systems and boundaries consists of variables describing the mechanisms by which organizations transform prices of raw materials into finished, marketed products, or transform students with high grade averages into physicians, or blow up buildings and bridges in Afghanistan or Iraq and beg other countries for aid to help rebuild them. Organizations, therefore, are units of analysis that transform causes into effects, by means of causal mechanisms within them.

Many of the causal mechanisms that sociologists study are ones that cross the boundaries of units of analysis, creating lasting changes in the internal structure of those units, and having effects over the long run. For example, the power of financial institutions makes their beliefs about how large manufacturing corporations should be organized create divisions in many corporations. Divisions cause raw materials to become priced commodities differently, as noted above. (For a more detailed analysis of institutional boundary processes that make organizations units of analysis that respond to institutional environments, see Heimer and Stinchcombe, 1999.) The general point here is that mechanisms are likely also to occur outside, or across, the boundaries of units of analysis used in any particular study.

It is often very useful to get an idea of how the mechanisms within units of analysis (say, within a situation) are affected by the causes, and produce the effects. To do so one needs to study mechanisms and processes within those units in more detail.

For example, if John Dewey was right when he argued (most extensively in Dewey, 1938) that rationality is usually only elicited when our habits and routines do not work, then much of the mechanism of rational decisionmaking that dominates economics is an observation about habits, rather than an observation about rationality in the "thinking" sense of the word. An investigator who thought that Dewey was more right than, say, Gary Becker might do detailed observation of signs of conscious thought and analysis in choosing a book in an airport to read on the plane; not much thinking there.

For another example, the patterns of turn-taking that constitute the polite conversation bounded by the circle of backs are detailed mechanisms that shape whether people in the circle do or do not get acquainted. Everyone has been in such conversations where only one person talks, and acquaintanceships are formed only as the group breaks up, as one shares disgruntlement with whoever else is going in the same direction.

The purpose of this chapter is to analyze the interrelated logic of the mechanisms that connect together causes and effects by repetitive processes, and the units of analysis within which such connections occur.

The Interdependence of Concepts and Units of Analysis

WHEN WE SAY THAT A BUNCH OF PEOPLE have a given class position in the Erik O. Wright (1978) system—say, of skilled but otherwise propertyless and authorityless workers—we are saying two things. First, we are saying that every pair in that three-variable category is *analogous* in having the quality of being skilled and in *not* having the quality of "propertied" or "having organizational authority," in the neo-Marxist sense of those words. They may have a house and an expensive car, and they almost undoubtedly will have a pension plan that they themselves do not manage but that makes a profit and that they will eventually benefit from. But in Wright's system as in Marx's, that does not make them "propertied" in the sense of exploiting others. In the Marxist system a private pension plan that invests workers' savings is exploitative, of course. Its high returns in old age depend on invested money giving profits or interest, hence on exploitation. We do not generally, however, call all people with private pension plans capitalists in the Marxist sense, for reasons we need not explore here.

Second, they are analogous in being "people," but it turns out that this is a special concept. For these people are the sort of unit that might have "skilled, propertyless, and authorityless" *or some other value* such as "skilled, propertied, and sitting on the board of directors" in the Wright system. A baby cannot have the other values on those variables, and cannot be skilled, and if a baby is propertied but unskilled and without authority, all the consequences that follow from being an exploiter in Wright's theory do not follow until he or she grows up. Wright's class scheme cannot describe a baby, and if we stretch it so it does, then the consequences do not follow. Likewise, until about the 1950s there was no sense in which the variable "citizen of what country" applied to New Guinea highlanders. The reason we do not define the variables so they apply to all these other folks is that we want the unit of analysis, the unit on which we observe the value of the variable "class" describing that unit, to be the kind of unit that connects causes to effects in that theory, and so can vary on the variables that are causes and effects. Babies do not fight the class conflict. Similarly, New Guinea natives did not fight international battles.

So the key here is that in order to have a causally relevant difference on a Wright kind of class, investigators have to have units that *can* have that kind of class, and can have the consequences of being that class. We do not bother to think about babies in the Wright class analysis, because they are not "persons" in the sense relevant to the theory.

People have to be analogous in the respects that are needed to carry skills and own property, and *also* to have differing values on the variables that are Wright's effects—for instance, they have to be able to have incomes that are larger and smaller. It turns out that "income" means "earned individual income" in Wright's scheme, for which family income is sometimes the best available proxy. Most of my pension income now is capitalist income in a certain sense, coming from my pension fund. But I am unlikely to be a capitalist in Wright's class system, because I do not have ultimate authority over other workers who have to be made to work hard for me. Since I am not a direct exploiter, but a *rentier capitalist*, some of the consequences of being a capitalist in the Marxist sense do not follow in my case.

So Wright's theory defined "people" as modern economics does. People start being people for an economist when they can own property and make decisions about it, and when they can earn incomes. In other words, an "assumption" of modern economics is that "people" are over eighteen. Hardly ever does economic theory have a baby maximize anything, by equating marginal cost with marginal revenue. Economists do not tell us at the beginning of Economics 101 that economics is a science of adults, so if we are interested in children we should learn a different theory.

It is more explicit in political science, for political scientists changed their samples for voting studies from all people over twenty-one to all people over eighteen when the voting age moved a few decades ago. Political science is also a social science of adults—though sometimes its practitioners study how children are turned into citizens (unlike economics, which does not have a subdiscipline of "economic socialization" to turn people into decisionmakers). This is not the sort of thing students learn in chapter 1 of a political science textbook, either. Wright does not "know" that he learned from economists and political scientists to think of the world as made up only of adults.

The main point here is to show that we *need a double set of analogies to give an "operational definition," a description*, for a variable. The variable "herding tribe versus horticultural tribe" implies an analogy among "tribes" as all being the sort of thing that "has a technology," and then a variable that says this thing-that-has-a-technology has a herding-tribe technology. If we look closely we will find that "herding tribe" does not include the United States or even Australia, though those societies have enormous herds of cattle, sheep, and even, now, kangaroos in Australia and buffalo in the United States.

But the herding technology of the United States does not connect having herds to the features common to herding tribes. Anthropologists will not learn a lot about the United States, but they will learn a lot about the

Nuer and the Karimojong in Africa or the Mongols in Outer Mongolia by reading Numbers and Deuteronomy in the Bible, books dating to a time when the Jews were evidently herding tribes. A "tribe" for this variable has to be the kind of thing that is dominated by its technology. The theory does not apply to societies that have ranches hooked up by railroads to feed lots, which in turn are connected to packing plants that are connected by railroads and semi-trailers to supermarkets, because such societies are not dominated by the organization of social life to take care of and live off of herds.

That's why we do not pay any attention really to Moses's biblical genocide: try to remember when anybody gave a sermon on one of the verses that tell about it, or on the verses giving all the complicated stuff about asking for passage across some other tribe's land and being willing to pay for the water the cattle would drink. Moses's talk communicates immediately that this is not a part of the Bible that is like modern-day life on an Idaho ranch. We generally skip over Numbers and Deuteronomy, books that talk about all that. This also makes the variable "genocide" into a different concept in a different kind of theory than the theory of the Holocaust or of the killing of millions of Ukrainians in the 1930s by Soviet authorities.

I had a friend who was a teacher in the high school where I did field-work for my dissertation. This teacher had a small ranch in Idaho, and he moved his herds from summer to winter pastures and back by truck. The government arranged his passage by building a road and collected the taxes on his truck to pay for the road: this does not sound like asking to buy passage and water from a foreign tribe, and wiping them out if they do not grant it.

Besides the analogies among tribes that can make them either herding or horticultural, investigators need the analogies among herding tribes: they speak all different languages, in East Africa they are often taller than the horticultural tribes but are about the same height as some horticultural tribes in West Africa. But for most social anthropological theories, none of these things matters. These are not the differences we are interested in theorizing about.

The comparativists also need analogies among the horticultural tribes that live among the herding tribes. They need to know, for instance, that the animals of the herders are by and large grass eaters, but for horticulturists more likely pigs. (Why did the Jews in the days when they were herding tribes develop a norm that Jews did not eat pigs?) Herding tribes as units "own" in a certain sense the rights to the grass and water they need, but the herds themselves are usually owned by large kinship groups. These groups regenerate their herds by not eating them much, but instead living off the milk and blood so that they can keep the herds going over the generations. They trade with nonherding tribes for many of the things they want and need by selling off a few animals, though the amount of trading varies with their location. Property in herds almost always passes in patrilineages, but property in grass and water passes in tribes. Most horticulturist tribes are analogous to each other by not owning their central subsistence land in common, but instead having the same lineage unit owning the land and the animals raised on it.

When in the Book of Exodus God killed off the firstborn animals in the herds of the oppressive Egyptians, rather than trampling down the Egyptians' gardens, we pretty much know that God was acting on behalf of a herding tribe. That was the way a herding tribe would understand getting even with every family. Trampling down the grass of a herding tribe just made the herders range a bit wider. For a herding tribe, trampling down the growing crop does not mean that they will not eat that winter; it does mean that for a gardening tribe.

So there are many things that go with being a herding tribe rather than a horticultural one, and not many of those things go with the United States or Australia having a lot of herds. So the United States, in spite of all its cows, is not the sort of unit of analysis that goes into our theory of herding tribes.

Thus a complex theory of what the unit is that "has a technology," or that "can be an owner in authority over workers," or "can be a voter" is involved in the conceptualization of the causal situation. Further, people often get into theoretical difficulties if they do not think about the units of analysis. In fact, only big manufacturing corporations have a sufficiently varied set of product lines to have divisions that have different markets; financial and retail corporations do not routinely have product lines with different markets. Only big corporations are dependent on the central financial institutions of Wall Street, where the multidivisional institution was strong. So the Fligstein (1990) theory is about the Fortune 500, not about capitalism in general, or firms in general, or "modern society." And it is not about herding tribes, which rarely raise money on Wall Street.

The key idea here is that units of analysis are also concepts, having analogies between units that make them able to carry causes into effects.

These analogies include having similar mechanisms within them, and having similar boundary conditions and processes, such that the causes can get in and the effects can get out. Likewise, there may be degrees of being that sort of unit, as when camel-herding tribes are more dominated by herding technologies than goat-herding tribes, and Idaho ranchers teach school in California in order to support their ranch. Herding tribes and Idaho ranches are analogous in that both have to get the herd to summer pasture to get the animals through the dry season.

Concepts of units of analysis can also have distances between units, like other concepts. Much of the time we hope that a simple dichotomy between, say, adults or businesses that can make contracts versus other entities, which might define units of analysis of economics, will be close enough. But those distances, like the age of a human or the proportion of all calories from herding, can tell us what variables and causal connections between variables will be useful in analyzing concepts that constitute units of analysis. That means that data may help us improve concepts of units of analysis.

But in particular, the data will need to bear on whether the causal mechanisms that transform causes into effects obtain in those units of analysis. If my pension-fund capitalism does not make me believe that I have an interest in increasing the rate of exploitation of workers, or that I should support anti-union policies, then pension capitalism does not create the same effects as owning and running a business. That is a problem with a too-simple concept of the variable of being a capitalist, as someone who has capital invested.

But if I were a baby, and could not yet be taught what a union is, I would not even be in the running for being a capitalist in Wright's sense; I would simply not have a value on the variable "capitalist or not." We can presumably, if need be, try to talk to a wealthy baby about unions, to show that they are not yet ready to be units of analysis in Wright's theory of exploitation and its relation to class and politics. That the baby cannot understand about unions means that it is not the kind of unit that *could* connect cause to effect in this theory. A rational action theorist might agree with the law that a firm is a "person," for his or her purposes, and the theory would work better because firms are more rational than people. But they would not even think of including babies.

Often people vary their units of thought, if not exactly their units of analysis, in the middle of their reasoning. See the "short version" of Abbott (1992), below.

Abbott Short Version

Summarized from Andrew Abbott, "What Do Cases Do? Some
Notes on Activity in Sociological Analysis," in Charles Ragin and
Howard S. Becker, eds., *What Is a Case? Exploring the
Foundations of Social Inquiry* (Cambridge: Cambridge University
Press, 1992), pp. 53–82, 228–230. Citations with page numbers
only are to this source.

Sociologists write about people's social action in two main ways.
In most writing in quantitative papers, variables such as "increasing
control at work" get "in the heads of cases," but the variables cause
the effects in those heads, such as "work itself becomes the terminal
value." In some writing in quantitative papers the people having high
control themselves do the action, such as "realize that their productivity depends less on the identities of the employers," for example
(the quotes here from Abbott, 1992, are originally from Halaby and
Weakliem, 1989, pp. 553–554).

We need an indicator of whether the people or organizations are
thought of as a scene within which variables act, or as actors who take
account of the variable and produce the effect. Only in the latter case
is the humanity of the thing that transmits causes a "thing theorized."

One can look in an article for the predicates in sentences with
a verb indicating action. Then one asks whether the subject of the
verb is a variable (which means the case is thought of as an arena),
or people or organizations (case thought of as actor). Applying this
method to the first three papers of *American Journal of Sociology*
in November 1989, we find that people act when the sociologist is inventing new theory; variables act when the old theory works well. In
most sentences in the first two quantitative or "positivist" papers, the
case is a scene of the action of variables. "The worker need not be seen
here as acting or thinking, but merely as the locale for the variables
doing their thing" (p. 54).

But when a variable fails to act as theory expects, or when the author is developing new theory, the people or organizations act. "For
anything unexpected, however, the level of real narrative [where people or organizations do the acting] rises, both in the number of steps in
the narrative chain and in the replacement of variables by the [cases]
themselves.... [N]arrativity again rises for the unexpected and the
authorial" (pp. 57–60).

What then do cases do in standard positivist analysis? For the most part, they do little. Narrative sentences usually have variables as subjects.... When cases do do something, it is generally conceived as a simple rational calculation. All particularity lies in the parameters of calculation. Since only the parameters change, there are no complex narratives; narratives are always one-step decisions. There are no real contingencies or forkings in the road. There is simply the high road of variables and the rest—which is error. (p. 62)

In the third paper analyzed (Bridges and Nelson, 1989), the "unexpected and authorial" occupies most of the paper. Bridges and Nelson describe how it came about that the Washington state civil service discriminated against women in pay. The civil service trade union opposed splinter groups bargaining for themselves, and so opposed women's groups pushing for equal pay for women. Women's grievances therefore went to the splinter groups, which were ineffectual. The union then became an effective bargainer on the men's pay grievances, partly because the employer's representatives they bargained with were themselves senior men in the civil service, partly because women's grievances were sidetracked.

The reason this narrative account with cases acting took most of the paper is that it had several actors: the union, the women workers, the women's splinter groups, and the senior men on the other side of the table. The process by which men's grievances more often got effective remedy, those of women more often ineffective remedy, itself developed over time, in court cases, bargaining sessions, and internal political battles in the union. The case as described in the paper became more complex to contain the interactions of multiple parties. Those actions in their turn were driven by different interests and different foci of conflict at different times, with changing and contingent conditions of action. In the paper the case became, as time passed, a case of a different sort, different in many ways from other American states and other civil services and other unions. The quantitative analysis in this paper showed only that the qualitative complex process actually had the consequence alleged, discrimination against women.

Thus, within the positivist quantitative papers, and between them and more historical papers, theoretical unexpectedness, authorial claims to originality, and complexity of the theory of what was going on within the cases all produced real narratives. Only then did cases become the subjects of verbs of action.

If we examine papers or studies where time, and therefore a "narrative," is explicitly involved, there turns out to be a comparable difference between "events" conceived as units that either happen or do not, and events conceived as developing over time. "It is one thing to describe the courses of ten battles, and quite another to identify the turning of the tide in a war" (p. 64). In quantitative "event history analysis," events are simple cases with no internal action, described only by the time at which they happen, and variables that act (i.e., cause the probability of the events) in the time interval before events happen. In the development of an event such as "the allies winning World War II," as described by a historian, many shifts and changes between 1939 and 1945 shape what kind of event that was, what its internal development on the two sides of the war and the separate theaters and national governments involved was, and consequently what actual sequences of action brought the end into being. The narrative tells what the event really was. Then, of course, the nature of that event shaped what consequences followed for occupation governments, for the development of the Cold War, and so on. (World War II example supplied here by ALS.)

Thus the presence of narrativity about events is produced in much the same theoretical situation as the narrative of "What do cases do?" except that the time intervals between events are the "cases as arenas" in quantitative papers, an aspect of the narrative in historical analysis.

Investigating Analogies and Their Causal Meaning

ALL THIS IS NOT JUST LOGIC-CHOPPING, or pretending that Wright would be embarrassed because he did not notice his theory was all about adults, not about children. The reason I make the point with a simple and obvious example is to show that if we think about, rather than intuiting, the qualities that produce agents able to hold property and to spend money or to vote, we will find that many of those qualities occur in other social entities besides adult persons. For example, pension funds and corporations all can hold property and spend money; in the United Nations, countries rather than people vote. Then we start asking questions about what are the kinds of things that have property, competencies, and so on. We will soon notice that some corporations own property that they use in production, but not all corporations depend on their property for their corporate advantage (e.g., law and accountancy firms instead depend on their skills). Some firms are in the property management business, so they have authority on behalf of capitalists, like Wright's people with organizational capital (jobs where they boss people on behalf of capital), but do not own the capital and do not exploit many workers.

That is, some corporations and partnerships are themselves capitalists in Wright's sense of employing labor, and some are skilled and some are not, but neither he nor we would want to ask them their household income in order to estimate the size of the Marxist stratification effects of being in authority over workers or having a skill advantage. This is an automatic blindness to potential effects of corporations' positions on Marxist variables, due to our not thinking about what makes an adult person the kind of unit that connects skill to family income, and therefore not thinking about what might make a law firm such a unit, or about what would be a good observation of the effect (Dewey, 1938).

Usually, one will get the narrow question of what makes an adult, but not a baby, a "person," right by intuition, without thought about what constitutes a unit that turns skill into income. But thought is in the long run a more correctable process than intuition. And the reason we may need correction of thought is that *some* of the variables that are consequences of "class position" may operate the same way for firms as for people. There is a system of differences among corporations that are analogous to the differences among "economically active" people. So there is a question of whether, say, law and accountancy firms are in conflict over anything like a collective bargain between them and those who hire them, like those of skilled workers (high skill, low organizational capital, low property rights). Do they form something like craft unions to defend their turf and their collective wage rates for "billable hours"? In what respects is the American Bar Association like the Carpenters' Union? Do law and accountancy firms have profit rates comparable to those firms that also exploit or manage skilled workers, such as construction firms? Are their entrepreneurs (partners) recruited from among the skilled workers? In short, do these corporations differ along what are apparently "the same" variables that "carry" the same causal differences into the same sorts of effects? Having assumed that the units of Marxist theory were persons, one might underestimate how far firms are stratified in the same way as persons into more versus less exploited, with the same effects.

The main point here is that one needs to choose as one's units of analysis, on which variables are observed, units that have the capacity to turn causes into effects. The mechanisms that turn causes into effects then have to be captured by the concepts that have formed the units of analysis. Economists, psychometric testers, behavioral political scientists, and Erik Wright all routinely choose adults or children who can read and write as their units of analysis without thinking very deeply about the choice. But if they were to think about it more deeply, they might find out things they do not find without thinking. Not only may firms be like people in a theory of exploitation, but also juries may be more intelligent than twelve people separately reading the crime news, because processes that make individuals think better may also be at play in the activities of listening carefully to evidence and discussing its meaning, as juries do, and that may make juries more intelligent than people. A psychometrician may not know what to do with that hypothesis merely because he or she never thought about why persons should be the only unit of analysis. The average jury may be two standard deviations smarter than the average person.

Analogies between Distances as the Core of Analogies between Units of Analysis

WE STARTED BEING INTERESTED IN UNITS OF ANALYSIS because we could observe distances between them on causal variables, and we are interested in mechanisms because they translate distances on causes into distances on effects. I have just argued that we should pick units of analysis such that they have the right causal mechanisms inside them. This implies that we learn about choosing units and theorizing about mechanisms by learning more about concepts of distances, and as we learn more about mechanisms and units of analysis, we learn more about the distances.

So let me go back to the variables—say, the "skill" of workers that makes Wright distinguish them from those who would fall into the "reserve army of the unemployed" if they lost their jobs. A housewife can be a skilled worker, for example, in the sense that he (if a "househusband") or she cooks recipes that many other housewives could not cook as well; notices earlier the symptoms of the children's sicknesses that might be dangerous and arranges to get them to the doctor; knows which foods are high in saturated fats, and so on. There is a stratification by skill in housewifery, the same as there is in machine shop work. Why is Wright not interested in that?

Would he propose to us a way to tell whether a machinist and a housewife who knows her way around a lot of cookbooks are at the same level of skill? No, because he has a theory about labor and capital market statuses at the core of his work. So units not in the labor market, or variables describing skills of such non–labor market units, should not have the same effects.

Wright is willing to consider that housewives are similar to proletarians and exploited by their husbands, but not that some are more skilled than others. I'm sure this is partly that stratifying housewives by skill seems to be defending middle-class childrearing and cooking, and deprecating the poor even as mothers and cooks. But partly it is that we do not think of the average higher living standard of more skilled housewives (presuming that middle-class wives have a higher living standard "in return for" housework and would rank higher on such a measure of skill) to be a higher "wage" paid by the husband, their exploiter, because of their labor market power due to their skill. (The correlation between husbands' and wives' education is around 0.6, which is very high for sociology; courting men and women who control a job as "my wife" or "my husband" are apparently as sensitive to "human capital" as employers are.) We do not want the feminist movement to have a "skilled workers' caucus" the way the United Auto Workers had, nor would we expect it to admit those few men who cook better, and detect children's symptoms earlier, than most women do, to that skilled housewives' caucus.

But aside from the ideological bad temper that I am showing, there is a sensible reason we do not want to do it. We do not think that the difference between a skilled and unskilled worker in a factory or on a construction site is *like* the difference between a mother who has read a lot about child care, child development, and pediatrics, and who has forty-seven cookbooks in her kitchen (I counted the cookbooks in our house for this point, positivist that I am). We do not think the analogy in skills has analogous effects. It does not have any appreciable effect on the variables that Wright wants to predict. But we are better off thinking about it, because it *might* have had such effects. Presumably there is *some* reason that professional husbands with a high-wage position as wife on offer in the courtship market much more often choose wives with the same education as themselves, or higher. Presumably there are reasons that highly educated women with a position as "physician's husband" on offer will marry an educated man. If that is not due to the same causes as higher wages of the educated in the labor market, then we need to distinguish potential housewives from potential teachers or real estate agents, as different kinds of units of analysis.

In short, the analogy between distances among housewife skills and distances among construction worker skills does not really hold;

proposing it is just sociological troublemaking. We will not want to classify people in a housewife role as being much like a machinist, nor would we predict with that same categorization that the skilled housewives among us will join craft trade unions to bargain better with the employed spouse and exploiter. There is a better reason to suspect that law firms are like carpenters than that housewives are. But a good methodologist will reflect on that choice, and will note facts that suggest that *something* similar is going on in the two situations. That is, he or she will explore what kind of a concept of the unit of analysis will properly distinguish those effects of education in marriage that are similar to, as well as those that are different from, the effects of education in the labor market.

For another example, let us consider the adoption of e-mail among senior citizens isolated (as many are nowadays) from their kinfolk (I owe this example to a student, Michaela De Soucey). The kin often work in organizations that provide desktop computers. The kin are more likely to be busy when the seniors have leisure, so a telephone conversation is not really convenient. The kin then know the advantages of not requiring coordination of schedules in order for a message to get through, and have someone to consult when their e-mail does not work. The seniors do not have that richness of technical environment. So we ask for our research project whether "units of analysis" in a study of computer use should include, say, both professors and seniors. Across university departments, the computer-technical richness of the social environment varies between the humanities (potential poets rarely make their living as part-time programmers), the social sciences (where packaged programs are routine, but not routinely created), and the physical sciences (where ordinary scientists started routinely writing their own programs in the 1960s).

Senior citizens vary according to whether they have kin living far away, whether the retired wife or or husband will be home to receive calls and coordinate phone contacts, whether they are on good terms with any of their relatives, whether they themselves learned to use a keyboard in a previous clerical career, whether they are male and unlikely to contact relatives anyway. That is, seniors vary primarily in their need for e-mail for the kinds of contact they routinely make, rather than varying in whether or not they are in an interpersonal environment of easily available and cheap computer competence. In a study of the causes and effects of senior isolation from kin, and their attempts to solve that problem, we should use the variables that primarily differentiate seniors, and we should sample seniors.

When studying the impact of technically sophisticated interpersonal environments, we should leave out many of the family situation variables, and instead study variation among units of analysis that have computer-using or nonusing environments. Therefore, we should have as our units neither seniors nor professors (except, perhaps, for sampling convenience), but instead variations across departmental environments in a university. The selection of units of analysis, then, depends on which distances one wants to study, and vice versa. If the units are interesting because old people are more likely to be isolated, then one chooses the variables determining isolation, and e-mail as a solution. Or the variables may be interesting because the specialists in information technology do not want to talk to clients about their problems. For example, at Northwestern in 2003, the set of alternatives for contacting people by phone for computer help, listed as the "help line" in the university directory, *does not include* the option of talking to the help desk, where people will answer questions on computer problems: this strategy is ingrained in the culture of information processing, that one is wasting valuable time talking to a user. Further, the location of the help desk is not listed in the phone books prepared by the information-processing division, so without informal knowledge one cannot easily go around the nonfunctioning phone contact system to get face-to-face help. One has to solve computer problems within the department, and so departments and their associated computer histories become the units of analysis.

We study the distances that we want to study, as informed by the mechanisms we think might connect causes to effects, and use that knowledge of the distances to be studied to choose the units of analysis. Then we may refine that analysis about distances by facts about the mechanisms (such as a telephone answering system on the help line that prevents the help desk from having to give help), to locate boundary conditions for learning to use e-mail: if potential users have to get in contact with the help desk to get out of trouble, they are isolated.

To go back to chapter 2, what we principally need is an analogy among differences or distances—it is the differences that we want to have the same impacts on differences in the effects. So the kind of thing we need to know is whether distances on causes of the variable and distances on the effect variable are comparable *among our units of analysis*. Try to think of a distance on an effect variable where the distance between two members of a household as housewives is comparable to that between a professor and a teaching assistant, between a physician and a nurse, or between a machinist and a semi-skilled worker on an assembly line. Or try to think of the causes of those within-household gender-professional distances (say, on cooking), and see whether these look like the differences between how one becomes a doctor and how one becomes a nurse. It is clear that the differences are different, but thought is required to figure out what those differences in differences are all about. Which means that it is hard to figure out what kind of unit of analysis in the sociology of work a housewife is, and which theory of exploitation she might be a unit of analysis in, which has skill differences not in the labor market in it.

But sometimes in the course of building a theory, one wants to study the mechanism to be embedded in the units of analysis of a larger theory. For example, one may want to know whether one should regard mechanisms within persons, due to their past history, as creating emotions that are then embedded in transactions and determine their outcomes, or whether instead the basic causal unit is the transaction, the competitive situation, that produces the emotion (see Gould, 2003, for a macroscopic argument that competitive situations determine emotions). Studies can be designed specifically to see what mechanisms can connect two variables together, and consequently to determine what the correct selection of units of analysis is.

An Example of a Mechanism Paper

IN THE *AMERICAN SOCIOLOGICAL REVIEW* for December 1998, Edward Lawler and Jeongkoo Yoon discuss experiments on a mechanism by which networks can produce, among members of the network, "biased" trading patterns. This is because trading patterns themselves, under some conditions, cause close emotional ties that in turn preserve them (Lawler and Yoon, 1998). This is a mechanism stripped to its elements, and the elements are represented by manipulations of independent network and transaction variables in the laboratory. The distances on the independent variables are between experimental and control groups. These distances in the paper are named for their experimental group treatment, when they are really distances between experimental and control groups. The authors never say that, but their "regressions" have independent variables in which (apparently—they do not say) the experimental group has a value of one, the control group the value zero. This failure to say the metric of their variable does not matter, since they do not expect us to go out into the world to measure their independent and dependent variables. Their metric for the distances is arbitrary from the point of view of the science. It would be completely off the point for a referee to object that they did not show how to measure the experimental or effect variables in the real world. Ordinarily, in the physical and biological sciences, the distances on the variables manipulated in the experiment are measured on a metric that can also be measured in the world, so such theories represent theories of the world, not just mechanisms that might be used in theories with their own measuring scheme.

Lawler and Yoon give unstandardized coefficients, even though they are meaningless without the metric, because they have forgotten that they did not tell us the metric of their causes; they did not tell us the metric of the dependent variable, either. The crucial number for the argument is the t-value for the statistical inference, yet they do not give the reader enough decimal places of the coefficient and the standard deviation of the error for the reader to compute the t-value, and they do not give the t-value, but only the probability of the null hypothesis.

Methodologically, this means that the generalization into the larger world is qualitative: if one gets causal variables in the world that are qualitatively like those in the experiment, then perhaps the mechanism they have demonstrated as working causally with manipulated variables in the laboratory might be operating, so then one should build that mechanism into the theory.

In short, Lawler and Yoon are so thoroughly in the mood to say that this is just a mechanism whose basic idea may have application elsewhere, that they assume it is arbitrary whether the parameters they estimate make sense, as long as their sign and probability level are correct. If arbitrary, why say what the numbers represent? And so they do not identify the metric of the significant parameters, because one needs meaningful distances of both cause and effect to know what the dimension of the parameters would be.

Similarly for their statistics. Lawler and Yoon do not actually tell us enough about the computation of the tests for us to do the calculations, even if we had enough decimal places in the coefficients and standard errors, and if they told us how many degrees of freedom the tests have. The degrees of freedom should be the number of cases they have, minus the number of parameters they have. For a one-tailed test to be significant at the 10 percent level, one would need to have three cases more than the number of parameters to get significance for a t of 1.72, which is one of the ones they actually give. (It looks to me as if they have 15 or 16 degrees of freedom in the denominator, but I may well be mistaken— such a one-tailed test would be significant at the 5 percent level when the t equals 1.72.) My point here is only that presumably what they did to conduct the significance test was valid, certainly at the level they say and maybe at a much higher level because they have more degrees of freedom. But there is no reason to get the level right for a test that one is not going to use except as a qualitative guide in theorizing. This suggests that the results will be valuable in a qualitative way if they are true, and they seem to be true.

The mechanism more specifically is that some networks produce some pairs of people in positions of equal power, because each has alternatives to trading with a given partner (the one with whom they are equal) that are equally good. Then the causal theory is that those people in "equal" relationships will (1) exchange more, (2) like each other better, (3) think the relationship is solid and important, and (4) reproduce the relationship when the restrictions on trading with everybody are removed and they could reorganize their trading network entirely. These results should not follow (or at least should be weaker) when the people are in relations of unequal power. Further, the difference between equality and unequal power should be less if the subjects in the experiments are induced to think of the whole network as a unified, interdependent unit.

Also, in their description of their method (especially the middle paragraph of the first column on p. 880), the authors do not let their actors take the lowest bid, which would tell one of the subjects some information about whether the bid from an exchange partner was too high or too low. They are stuck with the deal even if somebody else gets a higher or lower price. Otherwise put, network structure matters more if there is no "auction" or "competitive bidding" to clarify matters and set a market price, so Lawler and Yoon provide an experimental situation that has no market price in it.

That is, they are *not* trying to simulate trading in the market, where one person's price depends on what others offer. The authors want to be sure people do not create a market price, so that their experiment can produce differences in profits. To put it another way, since they do not want to say empirically how important the network effects they demonstrate are, they do not allow market structures to "take their natural strength and see how strong they are compared to networks" (as, say, Carruthers does in chapter 7 of his book *City of Capital* [1996]).

In particular, the contradiction to their theory in the italicized portion below table 5 in the paper may be due to people not knowing they are being exploited by the powerful people. On pp. 886–887 Lawler and Yoon show that increased frequency of interaction in unequal power relations also produced positive emotions (in real life this might be called the "loyal servant hypothesis"). This in turn produced higher cohesion in the network. "It appears that the frequency-to-emotion-to-cohesion process is more broadly applicable than we initially assumed" (p. 887). But note that the experimental conditions (see p. 880, col. 1) do not allow the less powerful subjects to know that "A" is more powerful. "Subjects do not know how much profit other companies received at different agreement levels." So this shows that the authors are interested in exploring a mechanism, not a network in which people can usually be expected to know a market price. And inequality does not have its predicted effect when people do not know that inequality could have been more equal.

Another thing that shows the "theoretical mood" of the paper is that the people are named for their network positions in the text, and the names turn out just to be mnemonics. When we are given data about the people, they are not called by these mnemonics, but instead called by letters of the alphabet. It also turns out that nothing about the people— for instance, nothing suggested by the connotations of the mnemonics—is in the text on the results. The people do not appear by their own letters— they only appear in two-letter combinations denoting relationships with certain network structural features.

In the real world, of course, people have names, not a vector of two-letter descriptions of their various ties. Here, then, we are in a theoretical situation in which we want to strip people of any features that might be connected to their names. And this is a deep feature of the experiment. The experimenters hope they have randomized between the experimental and control groups so as to isolate the mechanisms of networks sometimes creating unequal, sometimes equal bargaining powers, which may produce emotional effects. Such emotional effects would not be expected to be isolated, in real life, from the qualities of people, and so not from their names. For instance, older studies show that in a car showroom or used-car lot, men get better bargains than women do. So in real life qualities of people cannot simply be summarized by initials specifying what kind of network situation the bargaining takes place in; the gender that might be communicated by their name would have a bargaining influence, but not one explained by network position. The same used-car lot that might offer a lower price is across the street for the woman as well as for the man, and both could buy the *Consumer Reports* service that gives information about market prices. They are in the same network position, but are still not identical in bargaining power.

In short, everything about Lawler and Yoon's paper shows that it is intended to be a theory of mechanisms, which can then be embedded in theories like Mark Granovetter's about how networks shape labor markets (1974), or Wayne Baker's (1984) or Bruce Carruthers's (1996, chap. 7) that study social relations in stock markets. Occasionally the theoretical parts of the paper betray that there is a level of mechanisms involving how people as people react to success in forming transactions, but that is to explain why the social mechanism works the way it does, connecting the structure of the network to how relationships in the network behave.

In some sense, then, the mechanism here suggests that market relations have emotional (and therefore sociological) effects. That is, such features of network relations as the solidity of personal relations among market participants may be an outcome rather than a cause of the bargaining situation. This is a fundamental theoretical point about processes in markets: one is more likely to become friends with business contacts if one is in a bargaining position of approximately equal power. Whether this happens frequently in real life may also depend, for example, on whether one is a woman or a man talking to a salesman on a used-car lot. There are no metrics in this experiment that can be used to compare the size of gender effects to the effects of how far it is to a competing used-car lot, or how many used-car lots the customer has already visited, or whether the customer has equalized his or her power by consulting market price information from *Consumer Reports*.

The mechanism here is much the same sort of thing as what Blumer calls a "sensitizing concept," though it is a concept of how causation may work rather than of what variable one ought to be looking for. In short, it is a very abstract mechanism, making us aware that business relations may have emotional effects that depend on their economic structure, which makes it a "sensitizing mechanism" rather than a "sensitizing concept." (See the analysis of what we mean by "mechanisms" in "Stinchcombe Mechanisms Short Version," below.)

Five Main Kinds of Mechanisms and Units of Analysis

The Structural Hole

The paper by Lawler and Yoon (1998), discussed above, is an example of mechanism development in one of the main strands of mechanism-thinking in sociology—namely, the development over time of social networks, and the causes and effects of the structures of networks. The type-finding in everyday social life is one done by Sheila Klatzky (1972, pp. 73–81) in kinship systems. For a variable like, "How long ago was the last time you saw your sibling?" it turns out that a big determinant is whether or not the respondent sees the parent often. Parents connect children together in life as they do in kinship diagrams giving genealogies. So whether or not people have a relation to their sibling does not depend on them and the sibling alone, but on whether they have a parent at all, and whether that parent brings them together.

Such a mechanism is no doubt to be explained by the behavior of siblings and of parents, and how that varies with what the other people in the kinship network do. But Klatzky (1972) did not have to have those "deeper" mechanisms to make her finding function to explain the patterning of kinship relations. There is a big correlation between contact with parents and the strength of ties between siblings, and that's enough for it to work as a mechanism. One might find features of parents that would make this less true: for example, if (in the British phrase) the parents "couldn't organize a boozeup in a brewery," then they might not bring siblings together because the parents could not create an occasion for them all to come. Nevertheless, once we have a mechanism that lack of contact with parents creates a "structural hole" in the network, then the consequences of the structural hole create a network mechanism. This is then the first common type of mechanism explanation in sociology.

Individualism

The next type of mechanism is individual behavior, which we saw sneaking into the network mechanism example (individuals having positive emotional reactions to equality in bargaining). Jon Elster, probably the leading philosopher of the social sciences, advocates mechanisms located within the individual under the name "methodological individualism." He basically says that we should not be satisfied with reducing larger social structures to network mechanisms, for example. Instead, we should go on and reduce the network mechanisms to individual preferences, individual possibilities, and individual choices among their possibilities in terms of the preferences (e.g., Elster, 1987).

Many of the people who defend methodological individualism—thinking that all mechanisms should have the connections of cause and effect through individual people—also go in for analyzing individual behavior in terms of preferences, possibilities, and choices. There is a high correlation between a theory of *individual rationality* as the central mechanism and *methodological individualism* as the preferred form of choice of units of analysis. I think this is a mistake of not reducing to the logical minimum what it takes to connect causes to effects. Networks clearly can do that, and other processes besides rational choice ones can do that.

But to stick with the mechanism of rational choice, the data show that organizations are usually more rational than individuals; families are more rational than their members; people are more rational in organizational or family roles than when they are acting on their own behalf. People collect information better, calculate more, write things out more, and so on—all the symptoms of rationality—in organizations and in other continuing groups, such as families. I believe this is partly a deep social-psychological fact—that people are more rational when they are talking to someone else than when they are following their impulses. But we could argue instead that it is an individual mechanism that people use different criteria in being rational when they think they are acting on behalf of another person or organization or on behalf of an institutionalized value. (The Heimer and Staffen [1998b] concepts of "responsibility" as a concept and a mechanism, discussed in the concluding chapter, suggest this.)

Rational Choice

In the name of methodological individualism, many sociologists introduce the mechanism of rational choice as central to explaining social life. Rationality is a mechanism that connects *changes in the situation* (say, by changing prices or costs of products), of an individual or organization, to *changes in individual choice*, by way of knowing the (stable) preferences and possibilities (e.g., the income) of the individual. The characteristics of the individuals that matter are their preferences and their view of the situation. Most usually, rational choice theorists assume that the preferences and possibilities are the same before and after the change in the situation, with some minor caveats. That is, preferences and possibilities are predispositional at the level of individuals and firms, and one knows them from behavior of the individual before the changes in the situation. The Lawler and Yoon (1998) mechanism, discussed above, shows that the assumption that having business dealings does not change preferences is sometimes false, over even the very short run.

In some sense in economics and most rational action analyses, the individual's own characteristics play little role, because high autocorrelation of preferences or "lifetime expected income" is assumed. To put it another way, when a rational action is a unit of analysis, it does not act but instead merely translates one feature of the situation (e.g., changing relative costs) into another (e.g., changing mix of things bought). Thus, contentless rational action theoretically creates contentless individuals carrying it. Methodological individualism in its rational action variety counts individuals only as arenas in which changes in the situation, operating through stable preferences in the individual, affect other variables, such as expenditures. A person with predispositions and possibilities is a unit of analysis constituting an arena that turns a lower price of peas relative to carrots into buying more peas and less carrots, reliably time after time, whatever his or her identity or history or social relations, and regardless of whether he or she liked the last transaction that came through the network.

Rational action methodological individualism is in some sense an "individualism" without any individuality in it—perhaps that's what makes it "methodological individualism" rather than "individualism" *tout court*. In individualism as a moral system, for example, we assume that individuals are unique. That they have a proper name and social security number that is unique to them is a morally important fact. For example, I put my own name on the front of this book, though I can think of other people's names that I think would cause it to sell better. I do this not to maximize my income or any other rational purpose, which might lead me to put Aristotle's name on it to sell it better; putting my own name there is definitely an individualistic action, and if I were Aristotle, I would put that name on the front.

The general lesson to be drawn is that choosing the unit of analysis is an empirical matter, involving the relation between the boundaries of the unit and the boundary conditions of the mechanism at work. If the accountants behind a rational choice create accounts constructed in excruciating detail for an organization, and if that is sufficient to cause buying an investment, then choosing the individual who signed the check as the unit of analysis is feather-headed. So organizations are another kind of unit of analysis, to which often the mechanisms of rational action apply.

Situations

In some sense rational action theory, from the point of view of causes, is a theory about situations rather than about individuals—situations described, for example, by relative prices. But sociological situational theory argues instead that situations have a definition of what is supposed to be done in them, and that definition is what determines what is done, often more or less independently of the character, preferences, or possibilities of the individual people. Further, situations are bounded by the range of things that can be attended to and responded to, in developing a definition of the situation. These boundary conditions make a situation a unit whose features determine connections of causes and effects, within which interaction mechanisms have immediate effect on people's actions.

For example, consider the proportion of my time I spend reading and writing in the classroom, as compared with the time I spend reading in my office. Every reader can predict that I will read less while in a classroom. Students who come to see me usually find me reading or writing, and I go back to that activity when they leave; their coming into the office changes several variables in the situation, and in particular what both of us may do later. It is appropriate for me to read a book in a university office, but it is not appropriate for me to read a book in the classroom during class—not even to read out loud to the students.

What is strongly governing here is that we all know what is appropriate to a classroom, and the teacher reading is not appropriate. In secondary school, American students can sometimes get away with doing their homework for one class during another one. By college, however, the norm against even students reading something else in the classroom is very strong. I do not see any other way to learn the variations between situational norms than with fieldwork or relatively loose experimental methods. Even in experiments of situational variations, it seems to me that an investigator often needs "fieldwork"—for instance, relatively unstructured questioning of subjects afterward, whenever they did not act as predicted

Patterns

Still another kind of unit of analysis that has a central place in sociology is a "pattern," such as a particular arrangement of the symbols Lévi-Strauss studies into a myth, or the larger "cloud" pattern of meanings and contrasts that he uses in that interpretation. A pattern is formed by a mechanism such that any particular symbol or sensory stimulus that is a bit of a pattern—a word, for example—has to be interpreted in terms of the pattern or context before we can understand its causes or effects.

To determine the fate of the poem discussed above, for example, we have to know whether it gets its meaning in part from being the lyrics to a song.

Very simple examples of how patterns make pieces of culture have different meanings come from how phonetics distinguishes among words. Thus, the same contrast between phonemes (here vowel sounds) makes the English words *bite* and *bit* different, as makes *height* and *hit* different. The meaning of the same phonetic contrast in the two cases, however, is completely different because it occurs in a different context, formed by the other letters (the consonants) in the words.

The different spellings of the same phonetic contrasts (for example, *i* with final *e* versus *eigh* for the long *i* sound) show that historically these meaning distinctions were marked by quite different phonetic contrasts than they are now. That is, the causal-historical story that produced the same phonetic contrasts was different in the two cases; *height* a long time ago had different consonants in it, that disappeared from oral language as the vowel contrasts developed.

The two meaning contrasts conveyed by *bite* and *bit* (namely, between *bit* as the past tense of *bite*, and between the verb *to bite* and the noun *bit*, meaning "a little piece or morsel") can maybe be untangled sometimes by whether the words function in the grammatical context as a noun or a verb. Then perhaps one has to go further to the overall semantic or topical context to tell whether a noun refers to a bit of dirt that fell out of the dustpan onto a clean floor, or "a bit of breakfast," a "morsel."

None of these contrasts between *bite* and *bit* has anything to do with the contrast between *height* and *hit*, except that they sound the same. The differences sounding the same has no consequences for the social life in which the contrast in sounds occur. Such pattern-dependence of the social content of a similar physical difference in sounds makes social life inherently "cultural." And it explains why one cannot study the distance in meaning between *bite* and *bit* with a regression equation that also explains the distance between *height* and *hit*. The first methodological example of mechanism thinking about observational strategies below is in this cultural style, in which the observation of the pattern contrast of "texts" is central to the problem of explanation.

Associated with such patterns are special kinds of boundary processes that produce a "text," in the modern sense of a unified cultural product that can be transferred with some degree or other of common meaning between one person and another, between one age and another, and so on. Thus, some causes in the creative world of production of cultural objects produce a bounded pattern, which then becomes an object with various effects in various worlds of reception, or becomes an object with no reception, forgotten. This system of interrelations among patterns is the subject of the section of this chapter on the methods of study of the mechanisms of creation and reception of complex cultural objects, "texts" in the broad sense of that word.

The units of analysis are then the places where mechanisms connect causes to effects. Hence a list of useful mechanisms is inherently connected to a list of convenient units of analysis. It is only sometimes useful to think a lot about the mechanisms; for instance, a much simpler analysis of mechanisms within the person is appropriate to quantitative papers than to narrative papers (see the Abbott "short version" in this chapter). In the "short version" of my paper on when it is economical to think about mechanisms in social science, I am always implicitly, and sometimes explicitly, talking about what the units of analysis should be and how they should be conceived.

Stinchcombe Mechanisms Short Version

Summarized from Arthur L. Stinchcombe, "The Conditions of Fruitfulness of Theorizing about Mechanisms in Social Science," *Philosophy of the Social Sciences* 21, no. 3 (1991): 367–388. Reprinted in Aage B. Sørensen and Seymour Spilerman, eds., *Social Theory and Social Policy: Essays in Honor of James S. Coleman* (Westport, Conn.: Praeger, 1993), pp. 23–41. All page numbers with no further identification are to this source.

Much of the popularity of rational action theory in economics and the other social sciences is due to rational acts by individuals or organizations being an easy intuitive mechanism, which can translate macroscopic forces that act on those individuals or organizations into macroscopic effects. Rational action theory also has an ideological advantage, presuming that what people choose is what brings them the most welfare, and that markets provide the means by which everyone can choose whatever they can afford, given the constraints of costs of production and trade. But this ideological advantage can be destructive—for example, if richer whites choose to segregate poorer blacks and not to provide adequate public services there.

The purpose of this essay is to remedy the narrowness of rational action theory by "developing one other main kind of mechanism (which I will call situational), by mentioning a couple of others, and by showing that it is epistemologically respectable under quite a few conditions to do without mechanisms altogether, or to make do with quite inadequate ones." First, I will define a "mechanism" by its function in scientific research:

> As I will use the word, *mechanism* means (1) a piece of scientific reasoning which is independently verifiable and independently gives rise to theoretical reasoning, which (2) gives knowledge about a component process (generally one with units of analysis at a "lower level") of another theory (ordinarily a theory with units at a different "higher" level), thereby (3) increasing the suppleness, precision, complexity, elegance, or believability of the higher-level theory without excessive "multiplication of entities" in it, (4) without doing too much violence (in the necessary simplification at the lower level to make the higher-level theory go) to what we know as the main facts at the lower level. I will be talking mostly about mechanisms at the individual or the situational level that make theories at the social structural level and at the level of longer time spans more supple, precise, complex, elegant, or believable. (pp. 24–25)

If we consider rational action of individuals as used in economic theory, "any good M.A. student in psychology has no trouble inventing experimental situations in which the great majority of subjects will violate the most ordinary axioms of the theory of rationality as usually used in economics. Recipes for inventing such experiments could be adduced from the work of Kahneman, Slovik and Tversky ... (1982), Zajonc (1980), or ... Fouraker and Siegel (1963)" (p. 25). But this makes little difference in most mass behavior in a market because the deviations are minor; the risks in the future are poorly known anyway, so how people misjudge them makes them little more wrong than they would otherwise be. For example, professional investors and ordinary people did equally badly in predicting the mass failure of dot-coms in 2000–2001, so small mis-estimates of small risks would have made no difference. Besides, the rational actor betting on the future is a persuasive image, even among people who lost their shirt from the irrationality of their speculative investments.

> The core of the definition of a mechanism is the definition of lower-level units of analysis which have causal unity. By this we mean that the units of analysis are places [or things] where a given kind of causal forces

(I will usually call them *inputs* because we are interested in how the larger system functions and are using the smaller units of analysis to explain) are connected to their effects (I will usually call them *outputs*). 'What are the causal unities that can form strategic units of analysis?' is an empirical [and therefore ultimately theoretical] question. . . . I think the four main kinds of causal unities in the social sciences, making up units of analysis in which mechanisms operate, are (1) individuals, (2) social actors that can be treated as individuals (such as firms), (3) situations, and (4) patterns of information [such as languages]. (p. 28)

One such unit of analysis, as analyzed in more detail by Erving Goffman (1963), is a "situation."

By a situation I mean a time and place in which there is continuing communication or interaction such that the actions and communications of one person are facts to which the others respond, and such that some "objective" features of the situation come to be defined in a common way by the people therein. What is crucial about a situation then is that the same people act differently if they are inside the temporal, spatial, and communicative boundaries of the situation than if they are outside those boundaries. . . . [For example] it is useful to break down the processes by which a criminal goes to jail into the [series of] situation[s] producing an arrest, then the indictment, the plea, the trial, the conviction, and finally the sentencing. Distinct sets of people are oriented to distinct facts and information about the facts, distinct incentives, distinct possible outputs, in each of these situations, but all of them have to come off right to get a criminal in jail. [Each therefore is a unit that connects causes to effects in a distinct way.] (p. 29)

Andreas Papandreou (1958) provided a good analysis of how the "sometimes true" character of economic models makes the theory more supple (the phrase comes from Coleman, 1964, pp. 516–519). He calls a structure made up of theories of mechanisms a "model." In the clearest of models, there will be a statement of empirical conditions that are assumed for the model to hold. Thus, for the statistical mechanics of gases, physics started off with a *list* of substances that, under known conditions, were gases: air, oxygen, hydrogen, water [at sea level] above 100°C. Under those conditions, then, the mechanisms of statistical mechanics held. Later on this list was turned into a theory of when the intermolecular bonds that made water or other substances sometimes liquid would give a more exact specification of the conditions, because they were part of the theory itself rather than just a list of conditions under which it seemed to hold. Similarly, Papandreou argues, we can specify conditions under which rational action theories in economics apply: for example, well-defined and stable currencies; prices specified in public; many buyers meeting many sellers, all knowing these prices; and standardized commodities. Such a model with specification of conditions is more supple, for the conditions can be tinkered with to suit many different failures, such as the difficulty of knowing whether a given used car is a lemon (a failure of standardized commodities).

> Obviously either way of using mechanisms—building them into theories by specifying general empirical conditions under which they hold, or using them as models for which we have a list of some conditions under which they hold and some conditions under which they do not—makes the theory more supple. . . . The following proposition summarizes the general point [here]. Mechanisms are likely to be a useful part of a theory to the degree that we can specify the boundary conditions at the macroscopic level, within which the mechanism at the lower level has a simple structure. That is, the better we can specify when exactly the sometimes-true theories we use for mechanisms are in fact true, the more likely it is that the mechanism will be a fruitful part of the theory. (pp. 32–33)

If, however, we have a good theory at the aggregate level that has a lot of support, but we do not know what mechanisms produce the individual behavior of which it is composed, then providing what Elster calls (1987, pp. 11–12) "just so stories" of what they might think does not help us. For example, if we know that Polynesian sailors have elaborate canoe magic for their sea-going craft but not for those they use in the lagoon, and we also remember an old hymn with the line "Oh hear us when we cry to thee/For those in peril on the sea" (Whiting, nineteenth century), we suspect that high uncertainty and risk in a line of activity like sailing the high seas may produce magical institutions. Rational action theory does not have much to say to us here, and the historical connection between sailing small boats and magic does not apply to great modern tankers so we cannot now study the anxieties of sailors and watch them build magical institutions. Thus, we have no individual-level mechanisms that help us build a better theory, but the theory itself works perfectly well at the historical collective level. This suggests the following proposition:

> Where there is rich information on variations at the collective or structural level, while the individual level reasoning (1) has no substantial independent empirical support and (2) adds no new predictions at the structural level that can be independently verified, theorizing at the level of mechanisms is a waste of time. (p. 35)

Even when one needs individual-level mechanisms, the actual mechanisms may be much too complicated for the structural purpose. For example, fecundity, the capacity to have children, has many mechanisms in individual psychology determining the amount of sexual intercourse, many mechanisms in physiology determining the likelihood of a fertilizable egg being present, many mechanisms determining the rate of miscarriage, the mechanisms that connect nursing a baby to reduced fertility, and so on. A very useful, fully empirical summary of many of these mechanisms is the curve that describes the number of children born at each age in an early-marriage, monogamous, non-contracepting population with ample food and shelter for everyone, such as some Hutterite communities. Even if we do not have some of the component mechanisms in our theories, a convenient summary of everything that determines the possibilities of human reproduction is a good starting point for analyzing social behavior that might limit fertility below the fecundity level. How important a limitation of fertility was late marriage in early modern Europe, or how far did contraception decrease the relative frequency of births after couples had as many children as they wanted, or how many sons who did not become senators would ancient Romans have had, who have therefore disappeared from the historical record? Such questions theoretically depend on the monthly hormonal cycle of women, the climacteric beyond which men are less likely to reproduce, and all sorts of physiological factors. But a mechanism summarized in a fecundity curve from the Hutterites is a convenient empirical approximation for all these mechanisms, until endocrinological theory catches up with our theoretical needs. Such reasoning often substitutes for lower level theories, being a sort of "empiricist mechanism" that serves the function of a lower level theory. This may be summarized by a proposition:

> Mechanisms may be useful in a theory at a higher level even if they are quite unsatisfactory as theories. A very sketchy knowledge of causes of

the observed fecundity curve [or of a tendency in organizations to appoint committees to recommend structural changes when a firm is losing money] may be perfectly adequate as long as whatever is going on at the physiological level [or the level of administrative practice] reliably continues. (p. 37)

Mechanisms will work at the aggregate level only if they satisfy three criteria:

1. There must be large variations of aggregate-level causes that change the conditions for the mechanisms to take hold. For example, if large variations in rainfall cause large variations in the supply of wheat, large price changes between years will take place, but in irrigated agriculture without much variation from year to year it takes much larger droughts to affect prices.
2. Such variations in aggregate variables must have large outputs at the mechanism level. For example, a large increase in the complexity of calculating costs of particular products in very large diverse firms may not affect the price mechanism, because although almost no one can manage such calculations, firms can hire a few accountants with high quantitative scores to set up a cost accounting system for the complex problem. So the large cause does not get through to the market.
3. Unless all units of analysis in which the mechanism functions at the lower level act alike and simultaneously, the lower level response will not aggregate nicely into an aggregate result.

This results in another proposition: At one point in his analysis of revolutionary movements, Leon Trotsky summarizes this point by saying, "To a tickle people respond differently, to a red hot iron alike."

Theories of mechanisms will be more fruitful if they are shorn of all but big effects, and of all effects which do not depend on variables that have big variations at the aggregate level. Even then, if there are compensating mechanisms [such as hiring accountants] that prevent variations in the macroscopic effects from having structural or collective outcomes, some big effects may be omitted from the mechanisms.

In sum, then, "assumption mongering" about the unbelievability of mechanisms in a theory is usually not very productive. The theories embedded in the mechanisms do not have to be true or adequate to work. "If we can specify the range of conditions at the collective level within which the conditions for the simple functioning of the mechanism are satisfied, then the mechanism becomes a theory rather than a model" (p. 39). But then it does not matter that in many other conditions the "assumptions" do not hold, as long as we keep the conditions straight. There is no point, however, in adding mechanisms if we do not know how they respond to macroscopic forces; we are not served by theories of the sort infamous in nineteenth-century anthropology, of the anthropologist imagining what the savages might have thought, the sort that Elster calls "just so stories." But if one knows how individual-level mechanisms work, as we may know for fecundity in demographic theory, then knowing what physiological or other mechanisms are embedded in those empiricist mechanisms may do no good.

> Finally, it will tend not to be useful to have a mechanism with small and delicate effects that can be easily wiped out at the aggregate level. . . . What one needs is mechanisms that translate large variations in the conditions of the microscopic level unit due to variations at the aggregate level, and producing large outputs which cumulate in some simple way at the aggregate level.
>
> The overall conclusion is that it is very often useful to think in terms of mechanisms, and very often not. It depends on the scientific situation whether there is much mileage in going microscopic, and what kind of microscopic theory will be useful.

A Basic Mechanism with Variants: Complex Cultural Objects, Their Creators, and Their Users

THE FOLLOWING SECTIONS ANALYZE a fundamental mechanism of "civilization," in the sense of the development of complex cultural structures (here we will call them "texts") produced by experts or artists and influencing many people directly (as in adopting a technical innovation) or indirectly (as in being subject to laws whose texts they cannot read). High art or complex music, science, or law are examples of the aggregate structures whose basic mechanism is the production of "texts." The mechanism has three basic parts: (1) the creation of a stream of complex cultural objects, texts, by specialists in such objects; (2) the transmission of such texts to other social locations at which there are varying structures of reception; and (3) the processing of such objects for local purposes in the sites of reception. Thus, laws and novels (1) are created in different sorts of worlds, (2) are transmitted along different paths, and (3) are received and "applied" in courts or in airplane reading, respectively; yet despite these differences, the common structure of the mechanism makes the comparison between them fruitful.

The simple version of this mechanism is a process in which a complex object (we will call it a "text" although it may be a picture or a statue) is created in one social world. In the creative social world models of texts (we will call the models "briefs" in "genres") are developed, and the creator of a complex text develops a more or less unique brief for his or her creation. For example, the particular complex cultural object the reader is reading is a member of the genre, "methods textbook," but it is slightly different from other methods textbooks because I have a different brief for that genre of text than other authors do. It is written in the same creative social world as other methods texts, and received in the same set of classes as other methods texts, and is written by somebody good but not great at mathematics. That social world, and in particular the creators of a particular text, intend that work for an audience where the text is received and enters the minds or activities of members of that audience (we will call this, following Griswold, 1987, "reception").

The social relation between the creators in creative worlds and the audiences produces a discourse, shaped simultaneously by the nature of the creative world, the nature of the texts produced, and the nature of audience reception. Bodies of discourse may be more or less isolated from other discourses on the same subject. For example, in the early history of European art, writers of religious works, painters of religious paintings, architects of churches, and parish and cathedral clergy all aimed at audiences of believers. The discourse was different because the social worlds of creation differed, because the "texts" differed, and because believers used the texts differently in forming their own lives. For example, believers rarely "confessed" to authors, painters, or architects.

Similarly, scientists at leading research universities are often promoted only for those writings designed to convey new knowledge to other scientists. Textbooks or popular science writing "do not count." The discourse differs because "the same" scientific material is oriented to different audiences. Similarly, scientists do not ordinarily read textbooks to improve their own research; instead, journal article discourse conveys new knowledge useful to other scientists so *they* can produce new knowledge. That is, scientific papers are discourse that serves the world of creation, not the world of reception. Journal editors assume that the reader already knows everything needed to read the article *except* the new knowledge—including the techniques, the theory, the mathematics, and why the question the paper answers is "interesting." This is the discourse that a great scientist has to influence. Whether an undergraduate could read the paper, or even less whether the congressional representative who votes to pay for the research could read it, is of little interest in the promotion process.

The special character of mechanisms in the sociology of "high culture" (e.g., literature, art, science, law, invention, theology, and biblical studies) involves the connections between two radically different social worlds, the worlds of creation and reception. That relation is reciprocally involved in the constraints of the discourse between them, as when scientific journals have a restricted audience of other scientists, who are themselves motivated by their incentives to advance knowledge with an article of their own. The textbook discourse in the same disciplines has very different constraints; the rewards come from a different place, since the texts of such books are immediately recognizable as textbooks by the experts and immediately downgraded as "not true measures" of the merits of the author. The same is true of the evaluation of jazz musicians when they are jamming and the audience is other musicians playing with them, as opposed to the evaluation by a lay audience where the reaction of the audience is of "commercial" interest only (Becker, 1963b). This means that the musical discourse is different in the two situations; no dreaming of a "white Christmas" in a jam session.

Methodological Strategy on Texts, Discourse, and Reception

THE KEY TO SUCH A COMPLEX MECHANISM, by which high culture influences daily life and audience reactions influence high culture, is to break the variables into sets having to do with the different parts: worlds of creation, audiences and reception processes, and segregation of bodies of discourse. We then have partially separate creative histories, separate receptions, and separate patterns of features of the texts to work with.

We ask, for example, how the creative world of scientists, where the important audience members are largely other creators, differs from the world of novelists, where audience members may be used to non-novelistic genres like traditional episodic sagas, but not themselves writers of either sagas or novels (see "Griswold Short Version," below). We can also ask how works from the nineteenth century are received in the twenty-first. For example, some nineteenth-century poems are part of a canon taught in literature courses and subject to interpretation by teachers who are at least quasi-expert in the literature of the period, versus pieces by the same poets which are, perhaps, of "equal merit" but not part of the routine curriculum. Or we may want to know how the discourse of psychoanalysis was shaped by the high level of education and verbal fluency of the patients of American psychoanalysts, and so was isolated from the experience of working-class neurotics, and also from the discourse about insane asylums. Or we may want to know how journalists in the nineteenth century conceived their jobs, so that a twenty-first-century historian knows how to interpret a newspaper clipping from that century.

We will start with an analysis of a classic methodological piece by Wendy Griswold (1987) on the relation between the worlds in which paintings and novels are created, and the worlds in which they are received. This should give us some clues about what kinds of variables we need to look for to differentiate creative worlds and creators' place in them, what kinds we need to characterize different worlds of reception and the people in them, and what kinds of variables differentiate patterns of discourse.

Then we will return briefly to the analysis in chapter 5 of the differences in creative processes and audiences for sociological books versus sociological articles, a variable describing variation among texts with "the same" substance. Finally, we will wander around a bit in law, in other sciences, and in the applied sciences, to explore the usefulness of the mechanisms of "creation-text-reception" in understanding the sociology of these parts of high culture.

Objects and Actions, Griswold and the Artist-Audience Relation

THE GRISWOLD PIECE (1987), of which I have made a "short version" (below), has as its topic the sort of mechanism discussed above. Two different action systems—that of the author or other artist, and that of the reader or viewer—are connected by a complex cultural object. Her basic situation is that a novel, for instance, may take up to a year's work to write and to get into shape for publication, sometimes more, sometimes less, and is read in a few hours to a week's worth of free time. The object, the novel, is a text produced by the author's action system, and is a complex project that has a complex social "recipe" and the "charge" or "brief" of the creator (the individual realization of the "recipe" or "genre" by the author).

There is, of course, a lot of trial and error to make the object fit the brief of the author (to "realize" the brief). The action system of the reader into which it enters after being published is quite different, with different purposes, competencies, levels of attention, or attitudes toward the experience of the object.

The system of "refereeing" articles submitted to scholarly journals allows us to see the overlap between the worlds of the author and the reader. The referee is supposed to be a reader who partially takes up the role of author. Both editors and referees qualify for the job in part because they have been authors. The referee, at least in sociology, is supposed to suggest ways in which the author might more adequately (for a given audience) reach his or her goals of communication, or might go back to his last to do more research and thinking to build a better object for the next try.

Griswold Short Version

Summarized from Wendy Griswold, "A Methodological Framework for the Sociology of Culture," *Sociological Methodology* 17 (1987): 1–35. All page numbers without further identification refer to this piece.

The creation of a cultural object, such as an altar painting, a romance novel, or a poetry competition at a Moroccan wedding party, involves a complex intention by the creator; the intention has social elements in it. An analyst should be able to create a "brief," a set of requirements and purposes, for that creative project by analyzing the social setting, the artistic traditions, the biography of the artist, and the features of the object itself. The complex intention of the artist may be inferred from its causes (e.g., the common desire of a patron in the Renaissance commissioning a painting to display his [more rarely her] wealth by gilding, so that gilding became part of the brief), from evidence of its intended effects, from the process of production, or from the structure of interactions with clients or fellow artists during production.

The brief ordinarily includes common features of the genre of the artwork. For example, "an altarpiece must represent a recognizable scriptural passage, it must be instructive, it must be clear and memorable, and it must reflect the fame and wealth of the client who paid for it" (p. 6). Seven of the sixteen elements Griswold extracted from Baxandall's (1985) chapter on a Piero della Francesca altarpiece are directly related to this description of the genre (pp. 6–8). For example, it was common for the client to specify the amount of gold or silver gilding, to show his wealth, as specified in the last element of the genre description, and by the Baxandall description of the brief. But other elements go into the analyst's hypothesis about the complex brief describing the creator's intention: the width of the altar, Piero's expertise in the mathematics of perspective, his habitual use of rose color to indicate importance, his study of Donatello since the last time he himself had painted angels, and the like.

In contrast, the intention in "reception"—the reading, looking at, or listening to the cultural object—tends to be simpler. Jauss (1982) suggests seven features to be analyzed, such as the history of the genre, the work's place in literary history, and how the work affects the "social horizon" of the reader (p. 10). The main methods for studying reception are broad comparisons of social groups, where the responses added or counted up are number of readers of a book, museum visits, prices paid for paintings, and other simple indicators.

All this apparatus has actions in creating or receiving the cultural object and its meaning, and the social organization of production and consumption of cultural objects. There is, at this place in the argument, no strategy for connecting the culture to wider aspects of social life, such as social classes, regions, artistic circles, or political systems. The key conceptual link to do this is the idea of a "genre"—a pattern of meanings of objects connected, on the one hand, to the formation of the creator's brief, and, on the other, to a place in social life (Rosmarin, 1985), such as "altarpiece donated to a church by a rich client of the painter."

Thus, a genre is simultaneously a class of briefs for creating objects, and a class of uses and social locations of those objects' reception. The brief always has more features than are included in the genre. The social locations likewise always have more connections and more associated meanings than are specified in the genre. Therefore, the description of the genre, as a methodological concept for the researcher, has to be shaped so as to explain the connections of some particular cultural objects to some particular social locations. A "genre" is a unit of analysis in an observational scheme for describing the patterning of discourse, including the creation and consumption of complex cultural objects.

For example, gothic romances written by Nigerians for the Nigerian public moderately often have endings that do not fit the overall narrative structure of the novel; they do not "end" the novel in the way romances are usually ended in the genre. Such novels are connected to a social location, middle-class Nigerians, with a strong narrative tradition with a discontinuous or episodic character, like the genre "picaresque" in English. (One might imagine such sagas as romance novels modeled on television "soap operas," where the last episode in the series does not collect the threads developed during a television season. [This example supplied by ALS.])

The genre of romance novel was originally shaped in a particular novel-reading social location (England and the United States). But now it is selling to a public used to episodic narrative structures. The original genre may not fully shape the briefs of Nigerian writers of romances, and this may not bother Nigerian buyers of romances who do not necessarily expect the last episode to "finish the romance."

The methodological point of this example is that, without the strong development of the genre concept, classifying together the briefs of English and American romances, the specific deviations of some Nigerian romances from the genre would simply be individual variations (e.g., "James Joyce and some Nigerian romance novelists use episodic structures" [contrary example supplied here by ALS]). The strong tradition of episodic narratives in a specific social location of Nigeria would have no place in the explanatory scheme.

So for Griswold (1987), sociologists take interest in the "text" for its implications for the relation between the two action systems of the author and the reader (or other user) of the object. The text—in the sense of what is actually in a given painting or novel or other work of art—is socially significant in part because it is a result aimed for in the action system of the author or painter, who is trying to make a text that will talk to the reader. Griswold is interested in the recipe or "brief" the author uses, the "genre" he or she is trying to create in, as well as some special features due to social forces on the specific text, such as Piero having studied Donatello.

Back to Books versus Articles

A SOCIOLOGIST WRITES VERY DIFFERENTLY in an elementary textbook than in a monograph intended for his or her colleagues and for scholars in other disciplines, as the "short version" of Clemens and colleagues (1995) implies (see chapter 3, above). The sociologist will also have a different recipe for writing a chapter of a book than for writing an academic article, because less of the context is assumed—that is, more is written into the text—in the chapter than in the article. So in sociology "book chapter" versus "article" is a concept differentiating genres; they are ordinarily separated in one's curriculum vitae. Similarly, there are different action systems for the reader as well. One of these is "do nothing." Potential readers do not know what is inside the book, and if nobody else has told them the book is good, they generally will not read it at all. The author's vague suspicion that the book was dropped in the well and nobody heard the splash is very discouraging.

This applies even more when deep sociological insight is built into a novel, a different genre yet for sociological writing. For example, the titles of novels do not tell much about the contents, while a sociological book should have a descriptive title, not a cute one. Take Barbara Kingsolver's novel, *The Poisonwood Bible* (1998). Readers will not even know what the title means until they are well into the book. The title does not tell the reader that the book is about the sociology and personal experience of missionary life in the Congo, about the political science of the missionary preaching under a government where the CIA will arrange to assassinate the elected president while the United States preaches democracy, and about missionaries who teach democracy but do not want to have the village vote on whether to have Christianity (in the novel the chief insists, and they vote not to have Christianity; the fictional missionary was more convincing on democracy than on Christianity, I guess).

I have told several potential readers of the book that it is the best of a great novelist, and they should read that and everything else of Kingsolver's they can get their hands on. Kingsolver is also the best sociologist I know of writing on the race problems of Native Americans and now, along with Doris Lessing, among the best on the varieties of colonialism. So it looks as if writing novels is another method in sociology, and I think that's right. In some sense a realistic novelist, to be convincing, has to invent social action mechanisms that the reader will, at least sort of, believe in.

The action system that built Kingsolver's book took years; she apparently was in the Congo when it was a colony and in the early independence days when it was Zaire. After that, perhaps one could say she was building up to the competence to write *The Poisonwood Bible* by writing lesser novels. In Griswold's terms, Kingsolver was working on a "project with a plan," a recipe or "brief" for the text. (Griswold presents several examples of briefs in some detail.)

Now our question is, how do we build a theory and an associated method for dealing with objects created by such complex action systems (and then run the risk that no sociologist will take time off from his or her serious work to tell students it is a great novel)? Griswold wants to study the relation between objects created by such plans, which are classified together into genres, and the social life of the readers. Clearly, part of that relation is that many readers do not read her work at all, perhaps preferring Kingsolver.

The methodological principle of Clemens and colleagues (1995) is to pick an indicator of distances between genres, such as between sociological articles and sociological books, and to explore backwards to differences in the creative worlds in which they were formed (e.g., differences in the refereeing process, or in the amount of context supplied for each fact) and the social locations of reception (e.g., that books are read and cited in other disciplines, articles within sociology). Sociologists themselves cite many books, and they are often the work of authors outside sociology.

Reception versus Production

MOST WORKS OF ART, most items of scholarship, most thoughts about a case by a lawyer, do not get any significant reception. The lawyer may be heard in the courtroom, but not beyond. Most legal reasoning does not get into an appeals court where precedents are set, just as most novels do not get into the syllabus of literature courses (see Griswold, 1987, on "canonization").

Suppose some prospective authors do not think that a particular bright idea they have had is going to go anywhere, perhaps because their own brief for it does not justify the investment (it's just not something they want to devote their lives to). In most scholarly fields, for example, there are moderately clear boundaries for an author between a brief aiming for an after-dinner speech, versus one for a serious enterprise where the text might have a long future. A long-term project may then be cut back for an after-dinner speech, or for a presentation at a convention, or to bury in a review of someone else's work (to make a dense paragraph, thus increasing the interest of the review). That is, one modifies the brief for that piece of work, given how it has turned out and how the author has turned out, so the fit is better. After seeing the after-dinner speech, the author may give up the long-term project.

If the author is a real genius those offhand pieces may be of permanent value; if the author is a dud, they will make long, dull books longer and duller. But even genius may not guarantee wide reception. If people can pay attention to, say, an average of thirty or forty works of art a year, and they are inclined to tell someone else about three or four of them, and people hardly ever take their advice, then most things from a world of creation will not go anywhere.

Randall Collins (1998) calls this the "law of small numbers," when it applies to the central topics of philosophy at a given time in a given network of mutually attentive philosophers. He says there is only mental and social room in a group of philosophers to pay intense attention to about four or five major problems, and if there are already five problems agreed on, then there is no room for a given author's sixth. The same thing applies across the board: not all appellate opinions are cited in other appellate opinions, for example, so some are created to be worthy of being precedents (every appellate court's "brief") but do not actually get to be precedents.

So most complex objects of culture, produced by hardworking artists and authors with a brief, do not really have any "reception." One of the general methodological problems of cultural studies is that nobody wants to study the artistic failures much, and the same happens to dissertations that never get cited in the sociology of science. Though it is methodologically sound to have equal size samples of exciting and dull works, it may sink interest in one's article or book of intellectual history that half of it is about dullness.

We need to have a control group in the sociology of culture, "things that did not go anywhere," for our analyses of the cultural causes of cultural reception to be adequate. I have a book or two that I will only get sociologists to read if it is a member of such a control group—for instance, my book on how to run government-owned industrial plants in South America efficiently (Stinchcombe, 1974). I thought it complex and innovative. It turned out that even though those were socialism's glory days, American socialists did not want to know how to run socialist steel plants efficiently; nowadays the IMF is on the way to making socialist steel plants, the species I was studying, extinct. I did not write the book to be a good example of a control group of failed complex cultural products.

Another cause of nonreception, noted both by Collins and by Cynthia and Harrison White (White and White, 1965) on the origins of the impressionist painting movement, is that if a social system of authorship training and support of cultural producers results in more objects (e.g., by training many painters in the multiplying French academies of painting), and if there are the same number of things that can be best-sellers, then more of the works have to fail.

But the main point of Griswold in introducing us to the action system of reception is not so much to give us a sociology of diffusion of artworks or texts, as to get at the causes of changes in the (reception) meaning of texts—otherwise put, changes in the relation of the writers' products to the reader over time or across groups.

In the first place, even the most serious reviewer or referee for a cultural product spends a lot less time than the text producer. But even things well reviewed may go nowhere, among those not deeply concerned. If the books that investigators consider excellent on the topic of their library research project have not been checked out by others, that may predict that the investigators will find out for themselves how to write a failed book.

Scholarly Citations as Evidence of "Serious" Reception

ABOUT THE ONLY PLACE where reception versus nonreception over time has been studied systematically is in the over-time citation patterns for scientific articles. It turns out that the growth of the number of scientists (and so the total number of citations) for a long time just about balanced the average decay rate of citing older papers (i.e., the decay of the proportion of all citations referring to articles of a given date of birth), so that the average number of citations to old articles was just about constant over the years.

But many of these citations, however frequent, do not actually mean much. Let me give an extreme example. There is a current of cold surface water that comes across the south Pacific eastward at about 40°S, and then part of it comes north up the coast of South America. The northward part used to be called the Humboldt Current, after Wilhelm von Humboldt. But the entry in my old *Encyclopedia Britannica* tells the reader to look for "Humboldt Current" under "Peru Current," and the latter article says parenthetically that the Peru Current is "also called the Humboldt current" but does not even tell which Humboldt it was named for. Well, that's somewhat different from the original "brief" in naming the current: of creating a permanent "citation" to honor a great man who first documented it. (Captain Cook knew earlier that he had crossed the current, by figuring out from the Sun that he was farther north than dead reckoning would have put him. But he did not study it as Humboldt did.) The encyclopedia tells the reader only so that he or she will not get confused by its two names. By now, obviously, the "citation" to Humboldt is, at best, a ritual one.

Part of the change in meaning that took Humboldt's name off the current is that most people do not know how difficult it was for sailing ships to tell when there was a current, and which direction it was going. That is, the sociology of reception of "finding a current" has changed radically, because currents are no longer hard to find and do not mean much of anything for navigation.

Griswold gives good examples of changes in reception of works of art, but the generalizations evidently apply to works of oceanography as well. More important for Griswold is that the important action system for the receivers is itself subject to all sorts of causes of intellectual or appreciative action, of passing on meanings to others. So one can study the variation in meanings of texts over time or between social locations by studying the variations in action schemes in which reception takes place.

In a footnote Griswold suggests that "canon formation" is a major problem in the sociology of reception. "Canon formation" is the creation of an official history and norm about what is valuable in works of art (or science, or law, or theology; the word *canon* comes from theology). This usually comes to sociologists in the discussion of "paradigms" in the history and sociology of science, and in particular of our own science. Kuhn's idea (1970 [1966]) of how a scientific "brief" becomes a "paradigm" through "exemplars" calls for the imagery that Weber used to describe "charisma": the exemplar's realization of the brief has to be "specifically extraordinary." A paradigm is established by "specifically extraordinary" scientific work—what we often call a "work of genius."

In a field of cultural objects and their creators, the history of objects may itself change the action implications for reception, by canonization. For instance, one is quite likely to write, for a dissertation, a biography or an analysis of a lifetime of work of someone who is canonized. That generalization applies as well when the canon is a scientific "paradigm"; Kuhn himself writes about Galileo, Planck, Einstein—scientific heroes.

The writing of textbooks also influences reception. For example, I first learned factor analysis by reading a textbook on the subject, but I didn't get the intuition behind it very well at all. The basic idea of most factor analysis textbooks is that after taking out the main thing the researcher was trying to measure, the next things to look for are *uncorrelated* factors. Suppose I throw together into a factor analysis program different measures of social stratification position. Then I would take out the first factor, presumably a general measure of occupational social position. But the "mathematical" idea that another factor found in stratification—say, property ownership—should be uncorrelated with occupational social position seems ridiculous. This is raising a mathematical trick for sorting things out into a reification in the world that almost seems *designed* to distort the world. So I went back to read the original work on the subject, written by a psychologist, L. L. Thurstone (1935). It turned out that I could get the intuition there, and from then on I not only taught factor analysis, but also taught it differently from the textbook. The point is that I originally missed the exactness of the scientific purpose that gave meaning to the criterion of orthogonality (uncorrelatedness) by reading it in a textbook that conceived its job as teaching the mathematics, not the science. If a student does not understand the reason for something in the methodological literature, he or she should go back to the relevant classics that got people excited about it in the first place. A textbook is like canonization, except that the original often disappears into dullness.

Griswold's general point is that canonization is a special process that changes the meaning of the original, by changing the social determinants of the brief. In my example, the textbook author writing after canonization produces a mathematicized textbook rather than solving a deep scientific problem of developing concepts. The purpose of studying the original in psychometrics is to learn why it was great, and why it influenced the future history of the genre of psychometrics after it was written. The original will tell the student why there are textbooks in factor analysis; the textbook writer does not have to show that.

Canonization changes the value of the work from a future anticipated in the brief of the author, to the brief of a literary historian or a methods teacher. The reasoning then is that if one takes the meaning of any artistic or scholarly or legal work from a modern presentation of the canon (for example, from a set of courses on the subject), and contrasts it to the best reconstruction one can make or find for the original meaning, one has measured two distances on the object: the difference between the brief of the canonizer and of the original, and the difference in time and space between the literary historian or methods professors and the author.

Interpretation

THIS BRINGS US TO THE PROBLEM of the sociological analyst's relation to the cultural object. Suppose I am a sociologist without a law degree working at the American Bar Foundation, where many of the social scientists do have law degrees. The problem is, what standard I should hold myself to in knowing *what the standard legal interpretation is of the laws I want to analyze?* When I wrote a paper on the sociology of the law of evidence, and Richard Lempert told me he thought I had the law of evidence wrong, the paper went into the waste bin. A brilliant sociologist, Lempert also has a law degree and writes law review papers on the law of evidence. If he said I had it wrong, the chances that I was right and could find support for my view were close enough to zero to be not worth pursuing. The notion that I would know better than he did what the appellate judges were up to was ridiculous. There is a level, then, at which a scholar from outside cannot stand up to people who know.

Griswold calls this the problem of "comprehension." She says the sociologist might argue that "one rich interpretation is as good as another," so that as long as my view of the law of evidence has a lot of implications and some supporting quotations, I should disregard Lempert. Or a sociologist could take up the position that he or she has "no business interpreting culture anyway" (Griswold, 1987, p. 17 n. 9). This last is more or less the position Robert K. Merton takes up in the sociology of science: that we have to accept the scientists' own judgment of what is good science, or what is new enough to be an innovation.

Harriet Zuckerman, for example, would read the scientific papers for which Nobel Prize winners had been honored, and some relevant secondary treatments, before going to interview the Nobel Prize winners themselves (Zuckerman, 1977). But she would not get into epistemological arguments with them the way Bruno Latour would have done (see Latour and Woolgar, 1979). If I were to use Zuckerman's strategy, I might admit the possibility that, say, some untrained people like me can "comprehend" the law of evidence better than others, but not as well as a specialist in the topic. The Latour tradition argues, not that the sociologist is so smart as to have a contrary opinion to that of a real expert, but rather that the natives themselves—let alone the sociologist—do not understand their own culture because there is really no "right" interpretation. The methodologically correct position, as I understand the matter, is a bit of both: the sociologist of science has to know what is going on intellectually, but also has to admit that real scientists will know better, and that they do not agree among themselves about anything on which research is still going on. They usually agree to nearly everything that is in an elementary textbook.

The sociologist of science who comes the closest to Griswold's (and my) position is Michael Mulkay; readers can get a good idea of what the scientists think they are doing from work where he is at least the coauthor (see Edge and Mulkay, 1976; Gilbert and Mulkay, 1984). Gilbert and Mulkay show that scientists believe that most of their views actually represent the consensus of the field, and that their opponents think the same about their own view, and each thinks the other is isolated; it isn't that the scientists disagree with Mulkay, but that they disagree with each other about what that consensus is. But I would argue that if Gilbert and Mulkay had not attempted to understand the scientific issues were, so that they would know that one picture of the consensus was truly different from the other, they would not have been able to construct that argument.

Incidentally, I think that the tendency for people to believe that social constructivism has epistemological consequences—if it is socially constructed, then the truth is irrelevant—is all wrong. For example, if I am at the head of the table in the seminar room, I can count the number of people on the left side of the table. "Left side" is of course a social construction, and we would see that if the table was round or the room was crowded, it might be hard to define "left side" exactly. A "person" is also a social construction, and I might not count someone who entered the room briefly to get the book he had left behind, while I was counting, even if he entered on the left side. But most people in the room would agree anyway on the number of people I counted. There is still a "fact" there, which represents what most of us would think of as the "reality." And I can get that fact right or wrong.

I would argue, then, that we can all agree on empirical procedures for ordinary circumstances that would tell whether I was right or not, and that when we did that and got (maybe) the same number, we would all agree that what I said was true, regardless of the social construction of "left side," "person," and "true." I think Latour has led us astray by an irresistible inclination to epistemologize. I think, in general, that a sociologist pontificating on epistemology is a sign of weakness: I'm guilty again as charged.

Early in this chapter, I used as an example a paper in the December 1998 *ASR* that proposed a mechanism and tested the mechanism *in the abstract* in an experiment. I did this to help readers recognize papers that were trying to develop a mechanism. One could find the same symptoms in James S. Coleman's big theory book introducing individual rational action as a mechanism (*Foundations of Social Theory* [1990]) and, in less extreme form, in George Homans's *Social Behavior: Its Elementary Forms* (1974). Abbott (1992), given in a "short version" above, discusses how to tell when a reader is reading a run-of-the-mill paper about how social variables work, versus when the author is about to introduce a mechanism ("theory") to explain the deviant results he or she has gotten. He uses as a clue whether the positivist authors start talking about mechanisms *within* their units of analysis (usually individual people). When the author starts guessing what people might have been thinking, or with whom they were comparing themselves, then he or she is talking about mechanisms *within* the units of analysis, instead of the variables describing the distances between people or other units of analysis. The simplest test is whether people or variables are the subjects of the verbs.

So the reader here has had instruction in genres of sociological writing on both sides of the mechanisms literature, so as to recognize when an investigator with a structural problem is proposing a mechanism in the test about the structure, and when he or she is trying to show that a mechanism in the abstract really seems to work out even in manipulated laboratory situations, which are made abstract enough so that the rest of the social structure cannot get in. In the latter case, all the people are As and Bs instead of "executives" or "African Americans." That is, the reader and Abbott and I can agree on the symptoms in different contexts of sociologists talking about "mechanisms." This is all socially constructed, and we learn from each other how to talk "mechanisms talk." But that talk either is, or is not, a symptom of mechanism reasoning, just as the number of people on the left side of the table is or is not a reproducible fact.

In my failed book on how to run socialist steel plants, mentioned earlier (1974), the reader can find a recognizable "mechanism" argument about how the rapid growth of a firm (together with a few other assumptions) produces: (1) a high promotion rate, and so (2) a high rate of production of bureaucratic-promotion rewards, (3) to induce people to pursue careers by working hard and responsibly, and (4) to induce people to educate themselves for good work. Presumably that mechanism would produce different investments in preparing oneself for a career in a field of, say, American agriculture, where downsizing would be a major social process. And I believe that when the reader comes to that discussion in my book, he or she can recognize the signs that it is "following the brief" of introducing a mechanism.

Explanation by Interpretation

THE BASIC IDEA OF THE EXAMPLES GIVEN ABOVE, of reading what a "genre" is in sociological writing about mechanisms, is this: *if* researchers have set themselves up right in Griswold's first three parts—if they have gotten the author's intention or "brief" right, gotten it to fit into the "genres" of the analysis of the relevant artistic world as a whole, and gotten the variation in the place of the reception in the life plan and social relations of the reader or interpreter of that text—and if they have studied the segregation of genres (such as textbook versus article), then the researchers will have lots of "hooks on the variable explained" in studying the causes of high culture. Abbott used interpretation of the switch to talking about what people thought in positivistic articles, then confirmed it in talking about an article at the opposite extreme that used talk about what people thought all the way through. I used a similar strategy to say why the Lawler and Yoon paper (1998) and my chapter on South American steel plants' career structures were both mechanisms papers. Those features that the researchers identify in that process will tell them what to be interested in, in the author/cultural object/reader triplet, so as to be ready to hook social locations, historical periods, cross group variations, and so on to the explanation of particular roles of complex cultural objects. If the researcher gets the "brief" wrong, as apparently I got the brief of an appellate judge writing an opinion using the law of evidence wrong, then an expert in writing about such briefs will be able to say that I was singing sociology, maybe, but not getting the tune of the law of evidence. That is, one can show that an interpretation is wrongheaded.

In general, then, "comprehension" or "interpretation" of texts, of the elements of the discourse, is the method of finding what the variables are in the discourse itself, the body of communication between the creation and the reception of complex cultural objects. The analysis of the total complex in which it is embedded helps in analyzing the discourse, the "interpretation" of the cultural objects. In the law, it is ultimately the appellate courts that get to say what the right interpretation is.

Summary: Methods for the Sociology of High Culture

QUITE DIFFERENT SOCIAL SYSTEMS MANAGE THE CREATION of complex cultural objects and their reception. Consequently, the methods for studying them must involve different variables, describing the sociology of creation, the sociology of reception, and the sociology of bodies of discourse composed of texts transmitted.

The first set describes variations in the process of production, in the social world of creation. The variables specify such things as the flow of resources (who pays for creation, and what are their motives), the sources of feedback about the work's quality, originality, acceptability to receivers, how the creators are recruited and socialized, the complexities of the chosen genre, and so on.

The second set of variables describes variations in the system of reception, such as whether the receivers are experts or lay people (e.g., science versus literature), how they pay for the use of the object, whether the receivers are fleeting or reception is a part of a style of life, whether experts (curators, professors, appeals court judges) decide what the naive receivers will consume, and the like.

The third set of variables describes distances between bodies of discourse that connect these two worlds, the flow of texts. Is sufficient context provided in the items of the discourse for naive consumers to get the complexity? Are there collections of canonical works in museums or edited volumes, to produce a core consensus on the genres? Is there a high ratio of "fad" consumption of new subgenres (as in fashions or advertisements; see Menger, 2002)? Is the consumption organized in authoritative interaction situations, such as court hearings (for an analysis of how the structure of reception of law in lower courts shapes the substance of American law, making it different from English and Continental law, see Kagan, 2001)?

Because the mechanism here has three different, coherent systems in interaction, it generates conceptual and observational problems in three main domains: that of creators, of cultural objects, and of receivers. This threefold character makes it easy for scholars in the area to talk past each other. More often than in other fields they talk nonsense across the lines between systems, which are tied together in the mechanism but not very well by methods.

But the methodological disunity of the field is not mere ignorance of the right methods. The right method of identifying the relation between a genre and a particular creator's brief for his or her own creation has nothing much to do with observing the variations between whether (say) the law received by jurors in an authoritative courtroom differs from the law of those same jurors in a family dispute over who gets to use the father's computer, though both may be based on the legal concept of "property."

But the mechanism that ties these problems together—of creation, transmission, and reception of complex cultural objects—also ties the various appropriate methods together. A wise student of creation of such objects would do well to examine methods for studying reception and for measuring qualities of flows of discourse containing the complex cultural objects. The same holds for the other elements, changing the changeable parts.

The general point here is that a single overall mechanism, the creation and transmission of high culture, generates three main kinds of units of analysis in the transmission of complex cultural patterns. While all of these have to do with the interrelation of meanings, and the pattern (more or less purely exemplified in the text) is core to them all, as a practical matter one studies the creator of the text, the text transmitted, and the reception of the text, each in a different fashion, with different objects on which one observes distances. The meaning is core to what happens in all three, of course. But one studies the creation of appeals court opinions, the documented appeals courts decisions as a body of discourse, and the working lawyer and judge in a lower court, by different methods with different units of analysis. And there is some similarity in what one has to know about the same sorts of units of analysis of different bodies of high culture, such as literature, sculpture, law, and science, because they have a similar basic mechanism, one that Griswold (1987) has laid out for us.

Bargains as Social Systems and Creators of Social Orders

ONE KIND OF LASTING SOCIAL STRUCTURE is a bargain. Like a flow of discourse between creators and receivers, a bargain ties social systems together. For example, tenure in a university is a bargain between a worker and an employer, but the very word implies that it is supposed to be a structure that will be valid in the future. If the bargain actually holds, it will be a component of social structure for a good long while.

In a paper in the *Annual Review of Political Science* 1999 (Stinchcombe, 1999), I argued that the process of constructing a government that can end a revolution is a process of some (and early on, often several) authorities making bargains with (and between) important interest groups, and making those bargains believable, so that the bargain has a long-term existence that is worth something to the parties involved. This in turn makes it to the advantage of those interest groups to sustain that authority, to build it into a government, so that *its* future existence is more believable, so that the government can make more bargains with more interest groups. That is, because bargains are mechanisms whose internal structure changes causes into effects, they are units of analysis for some purposes. These units of analysis can be built into structures of concluded bargains, which can be postrevolutionary governments.

Ordinary bargains can also constitute the structure of the real estate market, in which systems of bargains among contractors and between general contractors and clients can create buildings, rental contracts or sales can turn those buildings into profits and rents, and the profits and rents can pay off the original loan for building the building paid for by a mortgage bargain.

Features of these bargains can be variables in the analysis of various kinds of behavior, so that contracts backed by blueprints as descriptions of the product to be produced can go into court in the way that a verbal agreement to tile one's bathroom for the cost of time and materials plus 35 percent for overhead cannot. They are units of analysis that can be theorized and on which distances can be observed, in the way discussed in previous chapters.

For instance, one of the bargains central to the Bonapartist regime (in postrevolutionary France, around the turn of the nineteenth century) that sustained Napoleon in power was the Concordat with the pope. On Napoleon's side, the agreement retained in their posts both the "non-juring" priests (those who would not take an oath to the revolutionary government), and also the revolutionary priests. In return, the pope was to restrain the more enthusiastic antirevolutionary priests from their rebellions against the new government, to accept that the priests would be sustained out of money that came from the state rather than from Church-controlled funds, and not to require the return of church properties taken by the revolutionary government. This bargain, in its essence, lasted for a little more than a century.

Here two people, standing for two organizations (as persons they are not the ones delivering the goods in the agreement; their organizations are, and this is evidenced by how long the agreement lasted), building a social structure, a bargain, to get benefits from the exchange. People are units of analysis in the constitution of the bargain, but the bargain itself has a continuity of structure that outlasts the people, and continues to turn causes into effects for a century.

The agreement on properties was essential for a second bargain: that all property rights obtained during the Revolution (specifically, property rights to former Church lands) would be confirmed and defended by the

Napoleonic government. This meant that at least those bourgeois who had bought Church properties or properties confiscated from antirevolutionary nobles would not oppose either the Concordat or the Napoleonic regime. The unsold properties of nobles were returned to them, but the aristocratic properties bought by the bourgeoisie were also guaranteed by that bargain.

These two bargains—between the Church and the French government, and between the government and the bourgeoisie—were "mechanisms" that sustained what we might call the first postrevolutionary government, though Napoleon and his followers defined it as a continuation of the revolutionary government. Furthermore, the first bargain gave a crucial input to the second bargain. So it is useful to explore what connections between cause and effect make bargains continuing features of larger social processes or units, which stabilize bargains so that they can be units of the structure of universities or postrevolutionary regimes.

Let us divide this problem into four parts:

1. *The communication of preferences and "interests" of the parties to a bargain.* Only in this way can one identify the possibilities for satisfying each one's interests by actions of the others, which those others are willing to undertake if they in turn get their interests served. (This is analogous to the "consideration" in contract law, what each of the parties gets from the other in the bargain; the point here is that it takes communication of interests in order for the parties to find out what would be a "consideration" for the others, and so eventually for a judge to agree it was a consideration.)

2. *A sufficient agreement among the parties about the actions that can be carried out, the ones they are bargaining about, and their relevant causes and effects.* They have to agree on an analysis of the relevant part of a possible future of the world. Then the interests will be realized in the future. (This part is analogous to the contract law description of "performance"—for example, a construction blueprint is a description of a proposed performance on which clients and construction contractors agree. The point here is that both must believe the performance can be done.)

3. *A government, often partly internal to the bargain and partly external (for example, in the courts) that manages the incentives of (1) and whatever other incentives are created externally or internally.* This assures people that the relevant parts of the bargain will be carried out, disputes will be resolved by agreed means, and the agreement can

be renegotiated if necessary (this is especially prominent in bargains to set up corporations or nonprofit entities).

4. *A social arrangement for the bargain not to be interfered with by outsiders.* (This is analogous to "property rights" in the law of contract, or "legal personality" that allows corporations and marriages to sue and be sued).

Communicating Interests

People cannot come to an agreement with others without knowing what they themselves want and what the other person wants. One standard way of communicating one's interests is a "request for proposal" (RFP). This describes what an organization has come to believe its interests are, which it can best pursue by making a bargain. A constitutional convention is equivalent to an RFP, except that the interests involved are not ordinarily clearly specified. However, for the U.S. Constitution, a long set of *Federalist Papers* was written, trying to persuade people that a new constitutional bargain should replace the Articles of Confederation. The authors laid out considerations about what would be in the interests of various sorts of people. Obviously, in this constitutional set of bargains, the setting up of a government to carry out the bargains was the essence of the matter. The same is true of negotiations to set up a corporation, or to reorganize such a corporation in a basic fashion (as described by Alfred Chandler in his chapter on General Motors in *Strategy and Structure* [1962]).

Similarly, to reorganize a corporation after bankruptcy (see Carruthers and Halliday, 1998), according to bankruptcy law in Britain and the United States, is also primarily a matter of setting up a new government for the failed corporation. The new government for the corporation is very different in the two countries, in Britain much more often dissolving the corporate charter. In either case, we expect there to be a lot of talk, even formal speechmaking, in the negotiations.

In such speechmaking or negotiations, people lay out what they are interested in, or why they think some particular proposal in the bargain is not in their interest. Almost everybody agrees for political bargains that this "debate" in legislatures and in newspapers is central to the "consent of the governed." Much the same thing is true in contracts. The courts are quite suspicious of any contract in which one of the parties did not get to speak or have any input into the terms of the contract (usually called "contracts of adhesion"). But sometimes such contracts of adhesion are implicitly dependent on the consent of the governed.

For example, when a corporation "goes public" and starts to sell its stock, the firm takes advice of investment bankers and others about how to set up a bargain such that a lot of people will want to get in on it, and will be willing to pay for it. The investment bank's advice shapes the prospectus of the corporation. So the issuing of stock is arranged on the presumption that unless the bargain is in the interest of potential investors, they will not buy it. The threat of their not buying it is then, in some sense, their "participation" in the negotiations, their way of making a speech. That process, however, is surrounded with precautions of the Stock Exchange and so on, which make public what the bargain consists of and what its risks and liabilities are.

In other words, the character of bargains, and their stability, depends greatly on the process of communicating what people want out of a bargain. There are various formal social institutions by which people can express what they want out of bargains, but there are also informal ones. For example, a modern decision to get married often involves a relatively long courtship, perhaps of the form of living together, in which people generally discuss at the very least whether and when they want children, whether both people are going to have careers and if so where, how they think they would support the children and possibly buy a house, whether all their money will be thrown into one pot or whether they will keep some part of their money separate, and what kind of wedding best symbolizes how they want to present themselves to their kin groups and to the rest of the world. Different people, of course, choose to negotiate about different things. From the pattern of divorce statistics, it is clear that some things are still being bargained over in the first years of marriage, because after the honeymoon period the divorce rate is much higher in the first year than in other years. Since the people had to be somewhat happy with the bargain so far worked out in order to get married in the first place, it is quite rare for the marriage to fall apart in the first few months. But then, as money and sex and babies start to bite into freedom, the agreement may fail. Nowadays in the United States, it will fairly often turn out that the first year or two of marriage was really an extension of courtship, and now that it comes down to it, at least one of the people does not want to have children with the other.

Performances

A bargain is a proposal about something one party is going to do to the world in the future, while the other is to do something else (at least to pay for it). The purpose of a bargain is to wrest from the world the benefits that will make the bargain worthwhile for all of the people in this contract together. This proposal or "project" is the core of the bargain. This means *either* that the people agreeing regard the "performances" as quite unproblematic, *or* that they figure the tiny government they are setting up will be able to deal with the uncertainties. Since in businesses there are quite often bankruptcies, and since parties do not always comply with contracts, some bargains end up in court or in arbitration. Similarly, since marriages sometimes end in divorce, this means either that folks were wrong about what it took to change the relevant little bit of the world, or they were wrong about what they wanted out of the bargain.

Obviously, some part of this is technical—for example, it may not be possible to build on a given piece of land for the cost specified because it turns out there is a buried gasoline tank that has to be removed and the polluted earth replaced with clean. Technical mistakes are quite often found in military alliances. It sometimes turns out to be technically impossible to win the war the bargainers thought they were going to win; at least one of the coalitions must have been wrong about the future for the war to happen. The only war I know of where one party knew they were going to lose is the Finnish war against the Soviet Union during World War II; Finns fought to get a better bargain at their defeat, and they got that.

But usually the biggest parts of the performance risks are misbehavior of the parties to the bargain, or market risks to the values produced or to the costs of the performances, or political changes that make it more expensive or less valuable to do what was agreed to.

The bargain about performances generally has two key parts. The first is the specification of who agrees to produce what effect in the world, along with guarantees and punishments of various kinds (especially by not getting paid for it) if that effect fails to be produced. Thus, for example, a blueprint is a technically complex document that describes in great detail what the contractors are supposed to be producing. Not all the necessary detail is there; some of it is in the building code, some in the standards of the professional engineering societies, and so on. But the basic idea is that it is the building contractor's risk if he cannot produce the effect described in the blueprint (Stinchcombe, 2001, pp. 55–75). But when trouble occurs (quite often because the blueprint is wrong), there is usually a process to rebargain, to have somebody in charge of continuing the work while the rebargaining is taking place, or to have an arbitrator if the people in the bargain cannot agree.

The second part of the bargain about performances is the division of risks. For instance, if the contractor produces the building and no one wants to rent the offices in it, that is normally the risk of the client, not of the contractor. In some very big projects nowadays, the contractor for building a particular part takes a share of the equity in the overall result for part, or all, of its payment; for instance, a portion of the equity of the corporation that markets the power generated in a huge dam and hydroelectric power project might be the payment to the builder of the generators. The contract is supposed to provide for that particular division of risks—the contractor hopes the profit on the equity will be more than it could have charged for the work, and the other owners of equity hope that the contractor will figure out how to integrate his work more effectively with other contractors so as to generate more profits for all of them.

In a marriage contract the description of the performances is not so clear. For instance, if the marriage has a baby that is badly damaged, there is a lot more work and expense and a lot less joy in it (Heimer and Staffen, 1998a). In such a case, often the husband does not do any of the extra work, does not compensate the wife for hers, and may even leave the marriage, divorcing his wife and getting out as cheaply as possible. One of the favorite divorce tricks is to get a child support requirement that exceeds the present value of the husband; the husband then goes bankrupt, and is forgiven part of what has now turned into a debt rather than a responsibility.

The important thing here is that bargains require two or more parties to agree on a part of the nature of the future; they may have the idea that the future will come out more in favor of themselves than of their bargaining partners, but the picture of the future has to be pretty solid or the two sides will not agree on the benefits and how to divide them. Consequently, institutions that provide solid views of the future, that provide ideologies of what is coming in the future and how it will be created by human action, of how reliable people are, of how reliable the larger environment is, will determine how stable bargains are, how easily they are formed, and hence what kind of a mechanism bargains are in the researcher's theories.

Government

In general, people can do better on anticipating how to create things in the future if they can agree how activities, benefits produced, punishments or rewards for good behavior, and adaptations to what the world brings in should be governed. The question of which risks belong to whom is central to this. But often it is better to work together to minimize the damages than to make sure *one of the bargainers* in particular does not pay for them. This is especially true of bargains that are expected to be very long term, such as starting a corporation or taking out a mortgage on a house or getting married. If people can agree how to adapt, how to resolve disputes without going to court, how to take their own side in an argument without everybody else getting furious, how to keep people from bugging out, how to find out what is going on in some objective fashion, then a bargain will be a more solid structure once it exists, and will therefore be more likely to come into being.

Even small time periods and small uncertainties create a need for government. For instance, a produce manager in a supermarket puts fruit on offer at a given price, and in the United States the customer gets to inspect it. But if the inspection includes pinching the fruit too hard, then the next person gets a bruised papaya because *the first customer* bought a different one that he or she was willing to bruise, because he or she was going to eat it right away. This means that a government of inspection has to be built into the produce department's apparently simple bargain. In the nature of the case, if customers can trust the greengrocer to be on the clients' side, the greengrocer can inspect the fruit to test ripeness with the least possible damage, because he or she knows exactly how to tell. I used to buy from a produce dealer I trusted, a woman in an Australian market, and she kept the fruit behind the counter. I would tell her when I was going to eat the kiwis, and she would pick them out by very soft pinches. I was better off for giving consent to that kind of government, but it obviously required some social conditions for me to trust it. It would be to her short-run interest to sell me overripe kiwis, or ones that were too green to sell in this week's market.

In the United States, I would start with the assumption that the produce worker or manager was on the store's side, and would sell me green fruit because it looked prettier. That would save all the labor of answering customer requests for good judgment. The point here is that even tiny governments vary with social conditions, here conditions that determine whether a produce seller will be skilled enough, will take the time, and will be honest enough to give kiwis that will be ripe at the right time.

So trust in the government of a bargain is crucial. That is especially true of bargains people hope are lifelong, like whom to marry, or what sort of constitution of the national government looks good enough in the 1780s, especially bargained so northerners would not take southerners' slaves away. In the latter example, remember that the Articles of Confederation did not provide any mechanism for anyone to raise an army to free the slaves. To get the South to agree to a government that could do so (we know it could because it did) required that the constitution be federalist, and that in particular slavery be a state and local matter. (The *Dred Scott* decision took away the power to abolish slavery within northern states, and then the Civil War took away the power to approve slavery from the southern states.) The North in the 1780s would have had either to fight the South to abolish slavery (and probably lose, since the North was not an industrial power at that time) or to agree to states' rights. Because the future is uncertain, one's best bet is to play the game not as if it were game theory, but rather in such a way that, whatever comes up, the government will worry about one's own welfare, if not the welfare of the slaves. So they chose states' rights in the 1780s.

Bargainers often have to look for the informal government of the bargain to understand it. This is more true, the more long-lasting the agreement is. Thus, long-term investments, such as the ones that allow someone to build a steel plant, have to have a plant government one trusts to take stockholder or bondholder interests into account, before anyone invests in *either* learning the skills of managing a blast furnace, *or* investing money in steel company stocks. If one is a worker, one may not be willing to invest in learning the skills and staying in the plant, unless the steel company's internal government includes a union to defend worker rights. Turnover is costly in the steel industry, which has one of the highest capital-labor ratios of all manufacturing industries. One look at a steel plant shows that the capital cost goes in part into huge steel-producing furnaces. If a worker loses a day's production of one of those 80-foot, steel-producing machines by being new on the job, the company loses a lot.

So the labor contract, the "citizenship contract" (the U.S. Constitution), and the marriage contract end up being more about consent to the form of government than about consent to the terms of trade; one calculates statuses over the long run rather than the benefits as of next week. Of course, one judges whether people are on one's side or their own side in governing things, in part, by what happened this last week.

The Structural Niche of a Bargain

One tends to think of "property rights" as being of the nature of the "law of trespass," which keeps people from coming onto owned land if they would do damage to the owners by so doing. But more generally the law of property is about preventing people from interfering with anything of value, and in a modern economy most things of value are created by contracts, not by pieces of land. At any given time, the main values will be ones of continuing bargains, so the law of property has to be mostly about bargains. Law schools often teach "property and contracts" together. And the fancy stuff in the law of property turns out to depend on the contracts clause of the U.S. Constitution, not some special property clause. Perhaps this is the central reason that the law seems so mysterious to people: they can't get used to the main valuable things being promises of one person to another about a house, rather than the house as a material object. Protecting against interference with those promises is what the law of property does. The law will also protect the owner against trespass, though even that will turn out to be more complicated than a nonlawyer would think.

Similarly, in old days people could be prosecuted or sued for "alienation of affection," violating a marriage contract. This did little, if any good. But the point here is that to understand a contract, the investigator needs to understand what the behavior of other people ("third parties") toward that contract will be. Another person who whispers sweet nothings to one's wife was once an "interfering" third party.

The same is true of any other kind of bargain. For instance, there used to be a definition of the integrity of politicians that ran, "When he's bought, he stays bought." Most of us would support outside intervention (e.g., a criminal investigation) to undermine this bargain, unless we happened to be one of the buyers or the bought. To put it another way, the more one's stake in a bargain is like "property," defended by third parties like civil court judges or policemen, the more stable it is likely to be. Spouses not being able to sue for alienation of affection probably makes marriage less stable, but presumably most of the marriages it would have saved would not have been a good bargain anyway.

This whole set of examples of prevention of "outside interference" is intended to show that a bargain is a different thing if everybody else has agreed not to interfere with its performances, or with the benefits to various people that motivate it, or with the powers of government in the face of uncertainty created by the private contract. So when we look at Napoleon's concordat with the pope, we have to think of who might intervene in that contract, how it would look to the Protestant states Napoleon was about to conquer and whether he would violate the Concordat in those states, and in particular whether those states, especially England, the Netherlands, and Prussia (all then Protestant states), would invade or defeat France and impose conditions contrary to the Concordat.

Summary on Bargains

A BARGAIN CREATES SOCIAL EFFECTS out of the "private" interests of the parties. In order to understand what kind of mechanism it is, we have to understand the conditions under which it has the effects postulated. Those conditions are that people understand their own interests and enough of the interests of others to make a bargain and to anticipate that it will be carried out because it is to the benefit of the others; that they think the manipulations of the world involved in the promises in the bargain are actually possible to the people involved; that they think a government can be created, with materials in the surrounding political and social structure if necessary, to adapt the bargain to contingencies; and finally that they believe the interventions from outside the bargain, from the society at large, can be controlled. *In those cases,* then, we will expect to find that bargains are central to the nature of the social structure. We will expect the mechanism to work worse, or with different consequences, when these components of the mechanism are not in place. To be a sociologically useful concept, it is not up to us to "decide" whether to assume the prerequisites of the mechanism are in place; the requirements are all social conditions, which themselves have to be explained, and on which it is moderately easy to collect data. Variables on the degree to which these conditions obtain, and variables on what the content of the bargain is, are observations on the bargain as a unit of analysis.

A lot of the philosophy and political science of the eighteenth-century Enlightenment dealt with how to establish things like governments subject to the consent of the governed, and whether that was even possible (a century later Lincoln was still, at least rhetorically, doubting its possibility at Gettysburg). A lot of the development of the common law concerned the noninterference of governments and other outsiders in the agreements among businessmen, and between them and clients such as tenants on their lands or in their houses. A lot of Weber's theory of the origin of capitalism, especially in his *General Economic History* (1981 [Ger. 1923, Eng. 1927]), is about the historical origin of these conditions in which bargains among citizens would be the primary instruments of government of social action. And a lot even of feminism today is a study of the conditions under which women and children will get to agree to the conditions under which they will live, free from arbitrary authority of their husbands and fathers. So this whole set of things are at the same time central to the mechanisms of social structures constructed of bargains, and central to the liberal vision of the world.

Methods to Study When Bargains Hold

BARGAINING MECHANISMS HAVE FOUR MAIN CLASSES OF VARIABLES, from the four main conditions that make them stable, that make them hold for long enough so that both (or all) members of a bargain are better off because of the bargain. We can observe variations in the causes of all four:

1. How good is the knowledge in bargaining pairs or groups of each other's interests and capacities?
2. How well can the parties control the execution of the performance bargained about?
3. How much adaptability of the continuing bargain is built into the governance of the bargain?
4. How well do general social and political arrangement prevent outside interference with the knowledge, the execution, and the governance of the bargaining?

Knowledge of Needs and Competencies in the Market

Knowledge of others' interests is determined by variables like freedom of speech, social valuation of honesty, an advertising structure that has information about the products in the advertisements, institutions of audit and credit rating, the capacity of bargainers to commit whomever (or whatever organization) they represent to performances and payments, the capacity of both sides to monitor and hear gossip about patterns of behavior that indicate important interests and other commitments of the counterparty.

Prediction of Parties' Performance

The second set of distances we need observations on are those about the security with which people can predict the outcomes of their own actions. These fall into two great classes, commonly called technological and institutional. The ease with which a moderately strong rock can be shaped quickly by combining steel, portland cement, gravel, and water makes the structural integrity of buildings of all well-designed shapes and sizes possible and predictable. The law of property, condominium, and rental; of mortgages and checking accounts; and of fire insurance makes the system of continuing bargains in the real estate market predictable, turning all that concrete into a long-lasting capital asset.

Of course, this predictability is itself highly variable. Squatters' property "rights" are often overturned by bulldozers, and bulldozers have an easier time with wood and corrugated tin shacks than with concrete skyscrapers. The reason one can write of the end of revolutions being the result of solidifying bargains is that revolutions can be defined as instability of the institutions that make bargains stable, often instability due to making the performances of political actors unpredictable; political actors in revolutions cannot manage the performances they promise because political institutions do not behave predictably.

Government

The central observation on the internal government of bargains, the adaptation of the bargain to changing conditions and risks, is perhaps that of Max Weber in his analysis of cities. He argued that "autocephaly" (as opposed to "heterocephaly") of cities—having a city's chief local authorities be, not princes or appointees of princes, but individuals locally selected and empowered—was central to the growth of civil law. Local groups of merchants could then create a law that allowed bargains to be struck and governed. The purpose of civil law in its turn was, and is, to allow pairs or groups of bargainers to set up governments of the bargain (Weber, 1968b [1921–1922]), to adapt it to local conditions and to the risks it faces, to specify who is to control what, and who is to bear various risks. Weber's early work was on the legal creation of the *societas maris*, the marine partnership, an early form of corporation government for a "venture," a trip in a cargo ship. It divided the risks, the responsibilities, and the rewards among the partners (the ship owner and the captain were always among the partners). Responsibilities for dealing with risks were central to such governments (Weber, 1924 [1899]). It was, so to speak, a bargain that, for the purpose of the trip, made the captain the prince, but it was central that the investors and cargo owners chose that prince and set up the conditions under which all would act.

To oversimplify, then, government of a bargain is for the purpose of responding to risks or changes in any of the performances and values embedded in the bargain. This means that government of bargains must vary with the nature of the risks to be governed. Insurance issuers need to be organized differently than ships, and both of these differently than guilds of goldsmiths, because the risks and conditions for profit are different. The key observations are those that measure variations in the substance of risks, and those that measure arrangements to manage and divide the risks (a good analysis with many examples of observations of risk divisions and their government is Heimer, 1985).

Exclusion of Interference

If good fences make good neighbors, it is because a neighbor's cows in one's corn interfere with all one's corn contracts. If the internal government of bargains has to vary with the risks to be borne, then the external government, the "defense of property," has to vary with the nature of interferences with the bargain. This holds whether the "property" defended is that of a public enterprise, a family, or a business enterprise. The more finely adapted the property regime to the dangers of interferences with the bargains, the more the bargains are likely to become long-lasting features of the social structure. For public enterprises, the requirements of the property regime for a park, where "trespassing" is the whole purpose, are different from those for a drinking water reservoir, or a school, or a street repair crew.

Similarly for businesses, the interferences of piracy are different from alloying gold with cheap metal, and both of these differ from a conspiracy between a ship captain and a distant shipyard to overcharge for insured damage to the ship. What it takes to defend property depends on the uses of the property in the bargains. Therefore, the stability of bargains depends on flexibility of property law (or its equivalents, such as goldsmith guild regulations) to respond to those interferences that matter. Developing methods to study a structure of bargains therefore requires one to design observations to measure distances between them in the interferences that matter most, and distances between property regimes relevant to those interferences.

Bargains matter to economics when they have prices for specified goods and services that are comparable between different bargains; the goods and services cannot be comparable unless the degrees of risk associated with them can be known and provided for. But otherwise the social structure of standardized goods—which enables people to find out what others want and what they can deliver in return, makes them able to produce and transfer the benefits involved in the bargain, allows them to build governments to adapt the bargain to changing situations and risks, and excludes those interferences by others that would undermine the benefits of the bargain—is only of incidental interest to market equilibria, because it is "nearly everywhere" achieved. Economists, then, can "assume" all this. Bargains, and networks of bargains, both of which construct a beneficial system of action of the parties, are delicate social structures. We have described those methods above. But the methods for studying them are not the same as those for studying the equilibria of outcomes when they are successfully made sturdy by social structures; the equilibria are found in economics.

The variables that predict the stability or instability of bargains, and the observational tools that find distances on those variables so that one can do research on them, therefore pervade the sociology of markets, of governments, and of families. Creating observations measuring distances on the determinants of bargain stability is central to sociological methodology.

Mobilization as a Mechanism

MANY SOCIAL SCIENTISTS STUDY SOCIAL MOVEMENTS to see where new social structures come from. Social movements start out with weak access to resources that make social structures go, and have to recruit people on grounds of "belief," or "grievances that demand new remedies," or "solidarity with troubles of others." These are small causes when they remain personal, but can be strong causes when organized. The assembly and unification of these small causes is often called "mobilization." Or to simplify, mobilization is a crucial mechanism for creating social movements. Special methods emphasizing the networks among people that can be channels of mobilization and unification of social movements are involved in this mechanism. The first two sections of this chapter were devoted to a mechanism of the creation and diffusion of cultural patterns and to the forming of social structures as a deposit of rational bargaining; the third section is centrally organized around network mechanisms.

Social Movement Theory and Diffusion Theory

IN SOCIAL MOVEMENTS THE SOCIOLOGY of microscopic interpersonal relations strongly interacts with macro-sociology. A person almost never "joins" a social movement unless personally asked by someone else, and most often the recruiter has a close interpersonal tie with the joiner, as a family member or a close friend. Fundamentally everyone is recruited to social movements by "networks," in the strong sense of a structure of interpersonal ties between people who trust each other.

The same holds true in the adoption of innovations; in some sense, almost every social movement is an innovation, and supporting it is the same as adopting it; thus, the sociology of mobilization is almost the same as the sociology of the adoption of innovations. In both cases, the main "function" in the theory for the interpersonal tie of trust is to transform something abstract—in particular, something that comes from a cultural frame ordinarily foreign to the adopter or mobilized person— into something that fits into his or her life. To fit, it must be presented in, adapted to, a framework in which it makes sense and which gives it motivational power. A "frame" is called an "apperceptive mass" in *Gestalt* psychology.

Such a mechanism is facilitated if the frame of the adopter or mobilized person is as a "seeker," someone who is looking for a new religious experience, new commitment, or a different kind of tractor for his or her farm. It still usually takes an interpersonal tie to convert an abstract theology or a notice in a cattle breeding magazine discussing a tractor into a new experience the person will recognize. Essentially every adoption or mobilization is a particular transformation of the movement or innovation into the sort of thing an individual can understand. In some sense we are back with the novel people will not read unless someone gives them the notion that they would like it, by describing it as an example of a genre they are addicted to, or telling them how great this particular book is though in another genre. The same sort of thing has to be done, usually by an interpersonal tie, for a new version of hybrid seed corn (Grilliches, 1957), or a freedom summer where college students go south to break down Jim Crow (McAdam, 1986; McAdam and Fernandez, 1988).

Many of these networks of interpersonal trust are created in other social movements; for example, one-quarter of all early civil rights activists integrating restaurants had socialist mothers (Pinard, Kirk, and von Eschen, 1968). The socialist movements of the mothers' generation made their children more easily mobilizable for a somewhat similar movement in their own generation. The centrality of black churches in the civil rights movement generally, demonstrated by Aldon Morris and Mary Patillo-McCoy (Morris, 1984; Patillo-McCoy, 1998), showed the same pattern—those mobilized for Christ could be mobilized for civil rights. If some people become used to transforming abstract ideas into something they trust in one social movement, they have a structure all set up to translate new abstractions into new commitments in the same environment of trust. So the more civil-rights-tinted organizations one is already in, the more one is likely to join a new one, and to recruit other people to a new one.

Even tame social movements like the American political parties of the present day are an environment in which seekers of political enlightenment can find someone to trust to translate an uneasiness into a movement. People's uneasiness with liberals can be transformed into hatred of communist Cuba, support for tobacco farmers, and support of anti-abortion legislation pushed by Jesse Helms, first within the Democratic party, then the Republican party. Political parties are structures that routinely connect interpersonal networks to social movements on abstract issues. The same apparatus can translate first this, then that, then another issue into a social movement, connecting the same people and networks to the same political party with multiple strands. The greater participation of politically active people in social interest groups, then, is due not entirely to interests mobilizing political activity, but also to political mobilization stimulating interest group formation.

So the relationship turning something Jesse Helms works on seven days a week into something constituents do on a few afternoons a month near election time has a sociology much like that we heard about from Griswold. Every novel is an innovation—if it is not and the customer has read it before, he or she will not buy it. One may, however, "buy" Jesse Helms again and again and again in different contexts, in much the same way that one's friends connect one to new novels as well as to the ones one already read at their suggestion. Such repeated mobilizations ended up being against Cuban tobacco because it was communist tobacco, rather than because it was competitive to North Carolina tobacco; the last was a lucky coincidence.

At the macro end of social movement analysis, the great sociologist nowadays is Charles Tilly (see, e.g., his *Vendée* [1964]). He has done the most to bring network methods into the interpretation of social and political history, because he knows a lot about the political and cultural context in which information and mobilizational activity flow along networks. From the mechanism end, rather than the macro end, I will try to put together ideas that may help us build theories of mobilization into social movements, so that we can build methods. Then we can transfer them to adoption of innovations, or selection of novels, or conservative and reactionary movements during the French Revolution.

The grand structure we are trying to build would be a sociology with network mechanisms, and social movements as network structures constituting units of analysis, easy to study because of our methodological work. This is the overall problem Robert Redfield, the anthropologist, set us a few generations ago: the relation between "the great tradition" and "the little tradition" in culture generally. By this he meant the inter-penetration between traditions carried in particular oral cultures (carried by interpersonal networks there), and those carried by the high culture of current reading and writing (created by creative networks there).

For example, the "gander in my lady's chamber" in English folklore gets there mainly in the little tradition. The poem about ganders and chambers is learned from mothers and fathers by children who have never seen ganders and call chambers "bedrooms," and this little tradition is connected to the great tradition through children's books for oral passing on; one knows one is in a little tradition when a three-year-old who cannot yet read corrects the parent who is trying to skip a bit. But within that great tradition there will be authors and editors and illustrators in networks creating books for parents to read to their children, with the goose in the illustration.

If the great tradition is, say, the Republican party or the Baptist church, the little tradition is what the member or senator says recruiting others, the one who ties together the others' interests as tobacco farmers with hatred of Cuba, or instead the one who ties different black people's Old Testament imagery of leaving bondage in Egypt to objection to bondage in the American South. That is, networks that form little traditions within a great tradition also have (less frequently used) network ties to the great tradition. They attach new cultural and social movement material to the same kind of local subculture as the networks that carry children's tra-ditional poems with words like "gander" and "chamber," domesticating them to fit into a child's life that has no ganders or chambers.

"Seekers," "Cosmopolitans," "Other Adopters," and "Opponents"

THE BEST PLACE TO START METHODOLOGICALLY is with a rough classi-fication of types of "recipients" of influence from the network, by the type of frame they already have toward the subject matter at hand. I will divide them into four groups.

Seekers

I adopt the word *seekers* from the literature on recruitment to extreme religious groups: cults, spiritualists, fundamentalists in the North (in the South the great majority of fundamentalists are recruited as children through family ties), charismatics or Pentecostals in the Catholic church.

It is common for sociologists of religion, as well as the recruiters, to use the term "seekers" for people who seem to be "looking for something" to complete their spiritual life. Seekers turn up as curious onlookers to cult meetings, especially meetings devoted to evangelizing.

Cosmopolitans

From Robert K. Merton (1949) I will adopt the concept of "cosmopolitan" (versus "local") to describe those people who are oriented to networks and other sources of information above the local level—for instance, magazines, newspapers, or books—and who have interpersonal contacts outside the locality. Locals, in contrast, collect information from interpersonal contacts mainly at the local level. The point is that the receiver's framework, which makes cosmopolitans receptive to information from elsewhere, evaluates information from nonlocal contacts, including even written contacts, as more important. Cosmopolitans tend to influence local mobilization through interpersonal contacts at the local level, but bring to those contacts a "more complex" culture learned above the local level.

Other Adopters

By "other adopters," I mean people not especially prepared to adopt or be mobilized (especially locals and nonseekers, then, rather than cosmopolitans or seekers), who are recruited "only" through local ties, such as the children of members of a cult as opposed to seekers, or ordinary church members of black churches at the beginning of the civil rights movement.

Opponents

By "opponents" I mean those who are resistant to solicitation, or to urgings of family members who are converted, because of their previously developed frames that reject the social movement or reject the sort of people who carry it. Thus, from socialization as a socialist I was by no means open to influence from a friendly elderly southerner I knew in Mount Pleasant, Michigan, who urged all sorts of racist ideology on me, or from another fellow, a co-worker, who proposed to report me to the FBI because of my socialist arguments with him. I was already their opponent before I got into interpersonal contact with them. I do not think my anticommunist contact ever reported me to the FBI, but someone did. The agents interviewed friends of mine, but obviously had already concluded that I was a naive young man who did not know any better, a misguided liberal. Guilty still.

The chief differences here among the "local nodes" of networks, the determinants of the causal impact of network contacts in recruitment to a movement, are those that make people receptive to, passive, or rejecting of relevant influences coming through the interpersonal network. This is a variable that determines which people and which links constitute different sorts of nodes in that network, those that receive and pass on movement material, and those that stop its movement.

Note that there are two sorts of variables here: ones that describe the nodes by their probability of transmission along the links they are nodes for, and the ones that describe what sorts of ties they have. A "cosmopolitan" is defined both by being the sort of person who reads, and the sort of person who has local ties through which he passes the information on. The cosmopolitan farmer who reads about cattle breeding, who talks a lot to the veterinarian about what sorts of cattle are best for what purpose and about artificial insemination and other techniques, who joins up with a breeding society that keeps records of blood lines and displays his cattle there is a likely adopter of some sorts of innovations long before his other local friends; in particular, he is more likely to ask his veterinarian to do artificial insemination for his herd. The cosmopolitan node may be a family; in the beef ranching family I know, it is mainly the wife who reads, and the son who is a veterinarian, so they have a functionally cosmopolitan family although the husband-father is mainly a local. He introduces innovations in cattle breeding into the local community anyway. Similarly, the seeker may end up bringing along his or her children to the cult.

The first part of the methodology for studying mobilization, then, is to develop observations that measure distances among people (or organizations) that classify their readiness to be mobilized or to be adopters (see the analysis of Trotsky and de Tocqueville in "Stinchcombe Time Short Version," below), and their connectedness to others who can be recruited.

The growth of such systems of links can form social movements of various kinds that have lasting effects. But how they pattern themselves so that they grow into massive changes in social structures over historical time is a rather different methodological problem. Such network processes are what Trotsky called "molecular processes," which transform grievances into revolutions—his figure of speech for "mechanisms."

Molecular processes change one compound into another in chemistry, so they are the "mechanisms" of chemical reactions at a macroscopic scale. Trotsky was interested in the "molecular processes" that resulted over relatively long periods in the creation of social classes and parties representing them, dual powers that could challenge the older governments, and other large movers of history. Some of the uses of such mechanisms are suggested in the "Stinchcombe Time Short Version."

Stinchcombe Time Short Version

Summarized from Arthur L. Stinchcombe, "Principles of Cumulative Causation," in *Theoretical Methods in Social History* (Orlando, Fla.: Academic Press, 1978), pp. 61–70. All page numbers without a reference citation are to this piece.

Much historical sociology studies long-term cumulative processes that transform social structure: industrialization, bureaucratization, urbanization, and fertility, and mortality decline. But the general principle of cumulative causation operates at smaller time scales as well. The key is that, for some substantial time (whatever *substantial* means in the context), causal forces act in the same way, producing incremental changes in whatever effects they produce. A one percent per year growth of industry, for example, doubles industrial product in seventy years, so approximately doubles the industrial workforce, urbanization of industrial districts, and smoke in the atmosphere. Similarly, a growth of hostility among class parties of one percent per week produces a doubled, and perhaps uncompromising, hostility in seventy weeks, about a year and a half, and the revolution gets harder to stop.

Likewise for slow structural changes: if there is differential slow growth of bureaucratic administration of industry compared to personal small business "entrepreneurial" administration, with one of them growing one percentage point faster per year, then after about seventy years bureaucratic structure will be relatively twice as important compared to small business. More education for bureaucratic industrial posts in business schools, more investments in corporate firms, more pages of writing in union contracts, and other bureaucratic epiphenomena will also grow to correspond.

Whenever a principle of cumulative causation results in the transformation of a social structure from one with one series of characteristics (e.g., a feudal method of administration) into one with another series of characteristics (e.g., a centralized royal bureaucratic method of administration), then each series of characteristics is an "ideal type" which is related to the other by the inherent, or scientific, connection with the transformation process. That is, the connection between feudal administration and royal bureaucratic administration in de Tocqueville (1955 [1856]) is not merely that a bunch of causes happened to institute one of these and not the other in eighteenth-century France, and each might have had different characteristics and the whole analysis will be, in principle, the same. Instead there is a causal process, the growth of royal authority and the attempt by the king to bring administrative authorities under his command, and his command out from under the authority of the law and the [feudal] courts, which tends to transform one system into the other. In this case, then, ideal types are the end states of a causal process and take on their meaning from that process. (p. 62)

Trotsky applied this mode of reasoning to explain why, in Russia, a society introduced into capitalist industrialization late slowly developed into a society in which, during a revolution, class hostility could grow very rapidly, in much the way slow accumulation of dead underbrush produces fast-spreading and very hot forest fires. His concept of "combined and uneven development" relies on differential growth of different aspects of modern capitalist democratic society in underdeveloped countries.

The first part of [Trotsky's] theory has to do with the structural preconditions of intense class conflict, not with explaining why there was more social conflict in Russia before the Revolution than in other places (though this might also be true), but rather why the potentiality for a deep revolutionary class conflict was there. . . . In sketchy form, it says that three ways of organizing society have become archaic [because of being inadequate to new economic systems] and no longer viable, because they cannot solve people's problems and consequently cannot maintain authority.

These three are (a) the absolutist state where the ruling economic interest is property in land and unfree labor on the land—i.e. absolutist feudalism, which was therefore replaced in the more advanced countries by bourgeois parliamentarism and a free peasantry; (b) colonial capitalism with foreign domination of the governments of backward countries, without national independence or with fictional national independence, and government-managed, exporting monopolistic business as the ruling economic interest; and (c) parliamentary industrial capitalism with national independence, parliamentary government, wage labor in privately owned factories as the main labor relation, and the native bourgeoisie as the ruling economic interest. None of these three forms of government or modes of production is supposed [by Trotsky] to be viable in the modern world because none can solve the problems posed by organizing the world its way [in Marxist theory such situations are called "contradictions" of feudalism, colonialism, or capitalism]. But England and France [except for their colonies], at least, do not add to the impossibility of industrial capitalism, also the impossibility of lack of [real] political independence and the impossibility of trying to run a modern country with serf[-like] labor.

But Russia was an extraordinarily fragile social system (as was Austria-Hungary) because it combined all three impossibilities: its modern sector was heavily dominated by foreign capital and its policies closely tied to the policies of the [World War I] alliance; its pattern of land tenure and organization of agriculture still had a great many feudal elements, high concentration of land with little rural wage labor and few independent peasants [in spite of the formal abolition of serfdom in the late nineteenth century]; its government was not even legitimized by bourgeois-democratic methods, let alone by its capacity to solve the problem of proletarian alienation; in fact, it combined the difficulty of being dominated by foreigners with the difficulty of trying to maintain its own domination over minority ethnic groups. This compounding of the problems of development took concrete form in the insertion into the Russian social structure of several kinds of upper classes: a noble and bureaucratic class resting on rural property and nonwage work by peasants; a developing bourgeoisie and political elite in the dominated Central Asian, Caucasian, Baltic, and Balkan nationalities; an industrial bourgeoisie of native Russian production; a foreign banking and investment community with a *comprador* [agency for foreigners] bourgeoisie working for them.

But the political requisites of the forms of domination suitable for each of these types of upper class are in part incompatible. Thus they are only precariously political allies of one another. Further, the forms of oppression compound one another in particular circumstances, as when a feudal landlord commences to regard his feudal privileges exclusively from the point of view of how to extract the greatest commercial profit from them, so that they have neither the legitimacy normal to feudal and traditional relations nor the legitimacy of the "freedom" of a modern worker to move from job to job. Thus the hold of the upper classes on government is precarious and shot through with conflicts of interests, and the consent of the laboring classes is precarious because new oppressions are being added onto the old.

Given this brief summary of what was already a brief summary of a previous book of Trotsky's (see "Peculiarities of Russia's Development," pp. 3–15 in 1960 [1932], vol. 1), Trotsky then undertakes to explain the cumulative intensification of this latent exacerbated conflict in the rest of the three volumes.... During a revolution, there is an explosion of possibilities, an explosion of political groups advocating those possibilities in various localities or in various parts of the society. And at the same time, the cover of legality is taken off of the social mechanisms which ordinarily limit possibilities and make things seem inevitable—the police, the army, and property relations. This means that to stop someone from constructing an alternative social order one has actually to go out and stop him—to rally those whose interests are touched by the question, organize them into an effective force, come to a consensus on policy, and act. That is, class relations are stripped, rendered naked, and hence visible. And the bourgeois that wants to institute regular production under his ownership is doing so against an apparent real possibility of doing so under the workers' ownership....

[A] main feature of Trotsky's analysis, which differentiates him ...from most other historians and social scientists [is] his extreme sensitivity to conditions leading to different rates and directions of change. The army moves slower [toward revolution] than the proletariat; Russia's class tensions grow at a higher speed than England's or Germany's; people who are ambivalent drop out of politics faster in time of revolution than in normal times; the peasantry grows toward anarchic disorganization of the administrative and property system, while the proletariat grows toward the capacity to take power; the masses grow more radical while their leaders elected a few weeks before either grow more conservative, or do not grow radical as fast. That is, Trotsky thinks quite naturally in the form of differential equations, in which the dependent variable is not the [high or low] *value* of another variable, but instead high [or low] rates of change [of it].

Note that this is not the causally thin stuff of the Club of Rome, enchanted to discover that a constant percentage rate of change gives rise to an exponential curve [as I toyed with in introducing this material above]. Instead it is about what causes some exponentials to go up faster than others, or in different directions. The pulse or event conception of cause, popularized by Hume and the psychological experiment, fits very uncomfortably with Trotsky's mode of analysis. There is no event that causes the army to be less ready to go into rebellion than the workers, but "molecular processes" of contrasting speeds. (pp. 65–68)

From the standpoint of this chapter, the central point of the "Stinchcombe Time Short Version" is that there are, in particular, different speeds and patterns of mobilization. Proletarians are mobilized into workers' soviets first, and there more quickly learn to trust Bolsheviks or Mensheviks, with different theories of how to organize a new government. Peasants are mobilized to take landlord property, but not very well to government-creating parties. (The main exception was the Makhno anarchist government in the Ukraine, which was very effective until conquered, with great effort toward the end of the civil war, by the Bolshevik government. Trotsky does not really analyze this exception.)

Ties of Trust

ONE OF THE MOST CRUCIAL PARTS of the frame of the recipient of social movement influence is what sort of person he or she trusts. But there are strong network effects especially on this trusting part of the framework. That is, whom one trusts is determined in large measure by the very network that carries information. For example, doctors adopt new drugs through network ties that have already convinced them that the other doctor will choose well what new drugs to adopt (Coleman, Katz, and Menzel, 1957), built up by a history of interaction among physicians. Though I was inclined to be a socialist and hence not to adopt things from different kinds of reactionaries, I trusted some of my socialist friends a lot more than others, and trusted some liberals more than some of my socialist friends, though they were suspicious of government ownership and strong trade unions. The general point here is that although receptiveness of the general frame of the recipient of influence is crucial, there is a lot left over for personal networks to explain, because a crucial lens through which people view the world is who is trusted.

But it is also crucial for my argument that a network contact itself is *a framework in the mind of the node in the network*, a belief that one is among friends, or that Uncle John is a sweet person and a good father (but a hopeless reactionary), or that Dr. Slaughter practices in a teaching hospital and is really up on all the new drugs but stoutly refuses to change his name. Network nodes can validate cosmopolitan ideas on the local scene only if the people there trust the nodes, and *that* is a quality in the mind of the trusters (though made more likely by such realistic variables as whether Dr. Slaughter really does know what he is doing).

Trust consists of two main components: the other person "being on my side," and the other person "being competent." If people love their two-year-olds madly, and have very strong network contacts with them, they still do not trust them to make investments for them because the children are not competent. Network studies hardly ever notice one's connection to the two-year-old, because that is not a network partner people generally trust (perhaps Tibetan lamas can be two-year-olds trusted in sacred matters).

But the other component, thinking the contact is on one's side, is equally important. People may have thought Jesse Helms was a brilliantly competent politician, without thinking he would probably be on one's side for anything important, unless one were a Cuban émigré or a tobacco farmer.

Competence is where the trust in cosmopolitans usually comes from. If cosmopolitans are tracking the larger world, but nevertheless have local loyalties, then they are more trustworthy on a lot of questions even if a local is closer to some other local person. So cosmopolitans are influential especially in technical matters. I showed in my book on South American steel plants (Stinchcombe, 1974; the book itself is a failed cosmopolitan link) that there is a high correlation between (1) having friends in other places, (2) reading books, (3) having migrated to the locality from elsewhere, (4) other measures of having commitments to outside social systems, and finally (5) the hours per day in a steel plant (in each of the three plants studied) spent developing or otherwise working on innovations. The correlations among the first four (six positive correlations in all), I argued, showed that I was really measuring cosmopolitanism, in accordance with the argument in chapter 4, above. The last was the tie of cosmopolitanism to what I really wanted to explain: why these folks who had never had an integrated steel mill in their country could manage to come closer every year to the steel-producing efficiency of the advanced countries.

To realize the importance of these features of trust, one has to go back to the original situation that we are trying to explain. We are trying to build a mechanism for something complicated (in politics, in technology, in culture) to which people are being mobilized, which the people mostly do not know much about. There are contending parties, as well as contending forces, such as the costs and risks. A potential joiner of a movement will not go out to conduct research on all that, to decide whether to go on a freedom summer project to the South where he or she has never been. Someone who has already decided to go, who reads the *New York Times* at least once a week, who knows the organizer from another university, says that a freedom rider is very unlikely to get killed, and that the movement is likely to get into the newspaper if enough people come. There is basically nothing about this movement that the cosmopolitan does not know more about than the recruit does.

Further, the recruit knows the cosmopolitan well enough to believe she would not con him for some purpose of her own. She doesn't "talk wild," whatever that means to the person being recruited. She takes a recruit, as a first step, to a meeting with somebody from the headquarters of this project in New York, who will tell more about it.

More or less the same thing happens when a successful farmer, who knows a lot about "nontillage" ways of raising corn, also knows about a meeting with the county agent and a researcher from the agriculture department who is going to explain it and answer questions. Questions may run a gamut: "If I am not going to be plowing and harrowing, but instead using herbicides to clear the land and keep the weeds down, can I get a good price for the secondhand tools and tractors that I use for tilling the soil?" "What is the cost per acre of the chemicals for the whole season?" My point is that without friends the farmer trusts on this question, he knows as little about it as the average sociologist, except that the average sociologist probably does not even know "nontillage corn" exists.

The person thinking of giving up plowing and harrowing and running the cultivator through the fields has to go into a world where he does not know the way. He needs someone to guide him until he gains some mastery. But a sociological researcher has to know two main things about such guides: that the recruits believe guides are motivated to tell the truth and will judge the innovation from the point of view of the recruit's own interests, and that they believe guides have ways of finding out the truth.

By and large, then, the information will come to a recruit to a freedom ride or to nontillage corn in a "two-step flow of communication," from the written word legitimated by ultimate creators and marketers of new culture to a cosmopolitan who is competent and on the recruit's side, and then from that cosmopolitan to the recruit. And so the smaller mechanism that explained why people are recruited by people they trust explains the larger finding that everyone is recruited by networks, and that those networks have a two-step flow through the cosmopolitans on the local scene. The upshot is that one needs to develop measures of competence and being on the right side, according to the beliefs of the recruits or adopters, of those who might transmit information. Then one needs measures for the contacts the knowledgeable and appropriately partisan cosmopolitan has, what they think of him or her.

Adoption and Rejection after Adoption: New Things in the Life World

PEOPLE DO NOT NECESSARILY STAY MOBILIZED IN A SOCIAL MOVEMENT, and do not necessarily keep on using nontillage methods for growing corn. For example, a Johns Hopkins dissertation (Goldberg, 1970) showed that the membership of the NAACP (National Association for the Advancement of Colored People) in Baltimore was more or less steady from year to year, while that of Los Angeles fluctuated wildly, apparently according to the salience of racial issues in that city's newspapers.

Baltimore had the sort of "old machine" politics in which a candidate for mayor had to be popular with many ethnic groups, especially blacks, Jews, and Catholics. Los Angeles had a nonpartisan election system with large constituencies and a "clean government" ideology in which it was hard to do favors for leaders of the various ethnicities. This meant that the incorporation of the leadership of an ethnicity (in the relevant case, blacks) into the political leadership of Baltimore came about in a steady fashion, each group getting the mayor to come around, to wear a yarmulke at a Jewish meeting, to eat fish on Friday with the Catholics, and to make speeches about civil rights at an NAACP meeting. He was likely to be introduced by a Jewish alderman in the Jewish districts, by the alderman from a black neighborhood at the NAACP. Political favors did not flow in response to newspaper articles in Baltimore, but in the daily negotiation of whether there were enough black policemen, whether Jews could get a zoning variance for a new synagogue, whether the charitable organizations of the Catholic Church could recommend somebody in deep financial trouble to the social worker in the city welfare system.

A political leader in a large ward in Los Angeles, without even a party apparatus connecting a constituent to the leader, and the leader to the city government, could not manage the party to give a faithful ward heeler a position on the city council, and could not pass out police positions.

In the language we used above, the cosmopolitans in an ethnic group who knew what was going on in Baltimore as a whole got that knowledge through interpersonal ties, shaped by political opportunities, rather than from the newspaper. That is, they were in a network sense "more local" than the cosmopolitans in Los Angeles.

But this in turn meant that lack of newspaper coverage in Los Angeles demobilized the NAACP, except for a small core. The same kind of demobilization did not happen in the NAACP of Baltimore, because the newspaper did not mobilize people in the first place—they learned what they needed to know about politics from their friend who knew the alderman who knew the mayor. But the culture that a Baltimore cosmopolitan gave people was more knowledge of a system of interpersonal patronage relations of continuing usefulness, so producing continuing NAACP memberships. It tended to build into people's minds a conception of the larger world as a set of links among trustworthy people, and other links among enemies. The culture that a cosmopolitan gave people in Los Angeles was whether or not there was a crisis that the NAACP had to act on, which would justify mobilization.

I'm not sure how to go about building the demobilization part of the mechanism, but let me suggest a line of thought that might help us say what evidence one would need in this situation. The less one understands the mechanism, of course, the worse one's search for causal connections, the correct variables, the important context is likely to be. The following is therefore an example of methodology for starting on a subject. But a start toward an understanding is a way to bet on these methodological decisions.

Demobilization and de-adoption come about because the adopter (I'll use that word for both innovations and mobilizations) has to fit a thing whose nature is defined in the "system" into his or her "life world" (the language is from Jürgen Habermas, but the conception of "life world" has a different purpose here). Such system products are *not* actually in the control of a person's interpersonal network. The innovation or mobilization *as it fits*, then, has spikes of uncertainties or faults on it that come from the larger system. The mobilization into the NAACP in Los Angeles had a connection in the larger system to whatever crisis got it into the newspapers. The de-adoption then depended on what happened in that system; the passing of the newsworthiness of the crisis made the mobilization fit uncomfortably in the local life world. Without changing a joiner who had been mobilized all the way into becoming a core member of the NAACP, a dead issue no longer seemed worth staying mobilized for, and mobilization went down.

In Baltimore, the adaptation of ethnic mobilization to the local life world was more continuous. The recruit's network connection was instead to local politics, to a flow of patronage and help in trouble and voting in the next election in the ward, as well as a zoning variance for the synagogue. The conditions on which that network would move out of the life world of an adopter are different from those that would destroy the newsworthiness of an issue in Los Angeles. And so demobilization was slower.

Similarly, for adoption of hybrid corn (maize), as described in detail by Zvi Grilliches (1957), it turned out that when seed that had been developed to maximize production in the core of the corn and hog belt—say, Iowa—was adopted elsewhere, it quite often failed. This meant that to get lasting adoption elsewhere, the complex culture of the technical innovators had to be changed, so the hybrid seed could be grown, say, in the hills of Tennessee, while the first hybrid seed was still used in the plains of Iowa. Similarly, a seed company had to have two different kinds of seed corn in Zimbabwe: one kind for the largely subsistence farms on the infertile lands left to the black farmers during the colonial period, and where the black farmers are still concentrated, and the other kind for the "commercial farmers" on whose harvests the exports of corn mainly depended and still depend (Koponen, 1998). So the innovators had to go back to their complex scientific and experimental farm work, to develop a cosmopolitan item that would fit into hill farmers' or black farmers' life world, and not be de-adopted.

Explicitly, the strategy is as follows:

1. Investigate (theoretically and empirically) which parts of the movement or innovation as a cultural object fits the life world of the adopter.
2. Investigate the forces on the other part of the adopted item, the part "known only to" the developers and core transmitters of the item, that might change the place of the item in the life-space of the adopter.
3. Investigate changes in, or feedback from, the activity involving the adopted item in the experience of the item in the life-world of the adopter.
4. Investigate the consultation of the adopter with the cosmopolitans in his life world who might provide remedies for his troubles, wherever they ultimately come from.

5. Use all this to develop a theory of de-adoption or demobilization.
6. Invent methods to measure the causes and effects of demobilization.
7. Carry out a study on the causes of de-adoption or demobilization, which are likely to be different from the causes of adoption.

Social movements transmit contentious culture. Innovations are new pieces of culture, and so at least contend with old methods. When a new method is on its face superior, explaining its pattern of adoption is merely the transmission of information, which easily goes over networks whose nodes are not classified by competence or by whose side they are on. But the crucial character of networks in social movement recruitment is that they have to translate a larger, "great tradition" culture into the life world of potential recruits, when that culture is contentious. Both the transmitter and the receiver then have to be classified, the first as trustworthy (competent and on the receiver's side), the second by a dimension running from "seeker" to "committed opponent."

Broadly speaking, networks constitute ways of translating causes into effects, because they connect the person or organization or pattern bearing the cause to the person, organization, or pattern showing the effect. Units of analysis within the networks are the nodes, which either transmit or do not transmit the cause, or which either do or do not respond to the cause with the relevant effect, and the channel (or each link in it), which may be described as relations of trust or not. In the first instance, then, the concepts to be improved by data are those describing the nodes and the links—for example, those saying how social movement participation fits into the life world of a (person-) node, or those saying whether a link is to a trusted cosmopolitan or not. But further variables are generated by structural arrangements of the networks, such as the difference between Baltimore's more "ethnic machine" network structure and Los Angeles's "newspaper-responsive" network structure, producing different patterns of mobilization of civil rights organizations.

Comparative Racism: Methods for Sorting Out Mechanisms

IN STUDIES OF RACISM, three main mechanisms have been developed to explain race hatred and discrimination, one of them in three sub-varieties. Historical methods and historical mechanisms are appropriate, because there have been great variations in both the intensity and the organization of American racism, and countries with varying histories have different amounts and kinds of racism.

1. Repressed labor. Example: African Americans, especially up to 1900, more intense before the Civil War.
2. Collective conflict. (2a) In democracies where the minority might become (or has become) the majority. Example: East Indians versus blacks in Guyana or Trinidad. (Note that generally in the Caribbean, *colored* or *coloured* usually means of mixed race and with free parents; *black* usually means either very dark or born a slave—but in this context, as in the United States, the "coloured" and "black" are referred to as "black.") (2b) In "foreign relations" when the "minority" race controls territory the dominant race wants. Example: American Indians or Australian Aborigenes. (2c) Secession of ethnic minorities. Example: the Caucasus.
3. Minority race as "exploitative modernizer." Examples: East European Jews up to about 1930; Chinese in Southeast Asia up to the present.

In the United States it seems that some phenomena of American racism are to be explained by each of these mechanisms. The null hypothesis that all treatment that departs from the norm of equality regardless of descent is racism, *and therefore to be explained the same way,* is to fall into the trap of taking the most null of null hypotheses—a hypothesis that is not really theorized in our theories of racism. That is, the null hypothesis is the weak one that "no sort of racism is going on," rather than, for example, that "no objection to exploitative minorities is going on."

For example, for a long time after the Civil War, there was a very strong correlation between the political support by whites of racist policies and the proportion black in the county in which those whites lived, which looks like mechanism (2a) in the list above: that in a democracy people are most hostile to those races that might be the majority and might make them the minority. The problem is that, for historical reasons, those counties were also the ones that had had the fullest development of the plantation economy, so would also fall into mechanism (1), the "legacy of slavery and continuation of plantation exploitation" explanation. Historically, part of that legacy was, ultimately, that blacks could not vote and so could not form a majority, so the second mechanism of majoritarian collective conflict was not operative between about the 1890s and the 1950s.

If we look *also* at modern Guyana (modern Trinidad would do almost as well) as a place where *both main ethnicities* were subordinate in a plantation economy, we could form a better comparative study of those alternative explanations. That is, in Trinidad and Guyana the races competing in more or less democratic systems for who is in the majority, who in the minority, are both formerly subject races. The "plantation repressive labor system" hypothesis should predict solidarity of the two races, rather than racial conflict between them. So one has to look at the evidence where the explanation from the first mechanism is constant, to sort out the likely effect of sheer numbers of voters in the plantation belt of the old South, versus the single racial divide along the slave-free boundary.

The key purpose in the comparison with Guyana or Trinidad is to figure out what are the symptoms of democratic collective conflict explanations, of which a presumed example is Guyana (Rabushka and Shepsle, 1972), and what are the symptoms most distinctive of the plantation counties of the American South (Key and Heard, 1949).

A sociology dissertation by Sarah Gatson at Northwestern (1999) studied the development of racially tinged citizenship legal cases in Kansas and Missouri in the period just before the Civil War. In Missouri the legal cases were almost all about the freedom of the black people; in Kansas, about the land of the Indians. The treatment of both was racist. But the question of the *freedom* of Indians never came up; rather, the question of the legal standing of their "foreign" land tenure system was the core of court cases. The Indians more or less knew that the land would be taken away from them one way or the other, and they were trying in court to get the most possible out of it. They were a "conquered foreign nation" more nearly than an "oppressed race," and the conception of what had to happen for them to become citizens (give up their "savage" ways, including collective ownership and redistribution of land; become educated and speak English; and preferably then move away from the good land to the desert) was quite different from the conception of black people.

Gatson wanted to use historical information from court cases to see what the difference was in two different mechanisms (2b and 1 in the list above). By sorting out the distinctive features of racism in Missouri and Kansas, then, we get another specification of what is distinctive of racism against African Americans in the United States, and what makes it different from racism against Native Americans.

To some very small extent, the current moderate U.S. sniping at Chinese Americans, Japanese Americans, East Indian Americans, and Jews has more the character of "exploitative modernizers" than oppressed labor or conquered foreigners (both Chinese and Japanese in the United

States were originally oppressed laborers, mainly on plantations or railroads). Jews and Asians are much overrepresented, both as students and faculty, in leading university science departments, and in psychiatry. Jews are overrepresented in the communications industries (in the New York publishing and media industries, and in Hollywood). Asians are overrepresented in Silicon Valley.

These industries and prestige positions tend to dominate the society more over time as development goes on, and the elites of those industries therefore tend to be able to wrest control from traditional authorities (declining industries are disproportionately owned and administered by Protestant white males). Biochemistry, for example, produces more innovations as time goes on than does metallurgical engineering. So the fact that older metallurgical engineers are mostly Protestant, white, and male, while biochemists are much more Asian American and female, tends to create sentiments against the modernizers and map those hostilities onto races and genders. American Jews, Chinese, Japanese, and (in Florida) Cubans are, then, in somewhat the same position as the historical merchant ethnicities, especially Jews, in the countryside in Poland, Byelorus (then known in the West as "White Russia"), and Russia up to World War I.

Insofar as these groups face a distinct kind of racism manifested in the Ivy League ethnic quotas against Jews in order to retain the Protestant, white character of the Ivy League, it is an American manifestation of a kind of racism seen in eastern European pogroms, not that manifested in plantation counties in the American South. We can even look for symptoms of similar antimodernizing racism toward African American professors or African American appeals court lawyers, and toward civil rights leaders from the Harvard Divinity School (like Martin Luther King). We can also imagine that in communities like Los Angeles, where African Americans are more fluent in English, more highly educated, and in other ways more "modern" than most Mexican Americans, we might find a racism against black people among the Los Angeles Hispanics more similar to anti-Semitism than to southern plantation racism.

By looking abroad for purer manifestations of the three main mechanisms, then, we can sort out what are likely to be the symptoms of each kind. That helps us in the analysis of race prejudice and discrimination in the United States, so that we can see that discrimination against Jews, Asians, and Cubans in the United States is likely to be produced by a different set of mechanisms than that against black people, and can see southern (and especially border-state) racism as a mix of the traditions of plantation racism and a hill-country populist racism more similar to that of eastern Europe against Jews.

Why Historical?

I HAVE ALREADY IMPLIED THAT RESEARCHERS NEED to find comparison cases to see what mechanism might be going on. One might, for a first stage, try just to find a "pure case" of each, and see how it generated symptoms of what kind of a "disease" it was, what was its "clinical syndrome," just as one might search for a sample of young people with Alzheimer's disease to unscramble the deep confounding of age with the illness. But then one can go looking in African American history for cases that might fit each mechanism, and look to see if some part of the antiblack racism looks like that. For example, was the assassination of Martin Luther King more like a pogrom of partially urbanized peasants in the Ukraine against Jews, or more like the dignified southern gentleman organizing an orderly lynching in a black belt county of the deep South?

The lynchings in the Appalachians tended to have a disorganized character (Brown, 1954). They were usually not sponsored by the upper classes and not limited to the matter at hand, which caused them to be different from the lynchings of the deep South. In the deep South, repressing labor was the main mechanism producing racism. So we might say, given the character of King's alleged assassin, his social origins, the border-state urban territory in which the killing took place, the assassin's relation to the ruling class of that region, was not this assassination more like a pogrom than like labor repression? Some of the symptoms of that assassination seem more like a pogrom.

First, to see why historical investigation might be necessary, we have to know how to frame the question empirically (see the chapter above on context). First, Memphis, where the assassination took place, is a big city, where African Americans were much more likely to vote and organize into ordinary politics than in rural Mississippi in King's time, and where they were a big part of the population, so the democratic majority-minority racism mechanism (2a) is a reasonable hypothesis. If one didn't know anything about Memphis politics, one might not realize that it is a more or less traditional southern big city. This means in particular that voting of both races was important, and the large black populations in the urban South were a real democratic threat. Thus, the collective conflict of the (2a) kind, political conflict in majoritarian systems, might tie Memphis and the plantation counties together, with similar strategies and rhetoric—but Memphis might be a purer case.

Second, without knowing the history of plantation agriculture, especially its historical geography, the investigator might not realize that the area around Memphis was more like an extension of the Mississippi plantation complex than of hill agriculture; some of the biggest Mississippi plantations were in the Mississippi River valley, near Memphis. And finally, without the history the researcher might not realize that the hills of Tennessee and Kentucky were centers of a populist, anti-big-city, antiplantation, but highly racist culture, with a long history of rather disorganized political violence, KKK organization, and a populist, "congregational" sort of religious tradition. This, like the populist Protestant regions of Germany that voted for the Nazis, might be just the kind of peasantry that might be recruitable to a pogrom and to the disorganized lynchings that characterized the hills. Many of the white poor of Memphis were migrants from the Appalachians. Clearly, the import of mechanisms from Guyana, Poland, or Mississippi into Memphis has to take account of the historical features of the development of Memphis and its relation to its surrounding racial-social systems.

So in the King assassination we have a clear case where each of the three mechanisms of racism outlined above is about equally likely *a priori*; the context doesn't rule out any of these three (1, 2a, 3). We need to sort out the situation by the symptomatology of the assassination, as we started to do above.

In order to get at the symptomatology, an investigator has to modify the cultural and special political elements of the typology, to fit the case. For example, the roughly equal numbers of people of East Indian and black ancestry in Guyana was different than roughly equal numbers of blacks and whites in a black belt county in Mississippi, because neither race had been the plantation elite in Guyana. One would need a detailed understanding of majoritarian democracy in Guyana and Trinidad as well as Mississippi to see whether they looked the same.

Similarly, if the investigator had not read *Huckleberry Finn* (Twain, 1996 [1885], pp. 25–26) since eleventh grade, and only vaguely remembered Mark Twain's portrait of the ignorant ranting of Huck Finn's father against a citified free black person, he or she would need to go back to that source, to see whether it resembled the rhetoric surrounding the King assassination. To refine one's identification of the symbolism of peasant populist racism against successfully modernizing minorities, one could look at the rhetoric of east European pogroms, perhaps nearer the paradigmatic case of populist racism, to see whether the elder Finn sounded anything like a Ukrainian bigot. Differences between that and Twain's account of border-state American racism might suggest how to recognize Memphis's nearness to Mississippi, versus its nearness to the Appalachians. People use a historical imagery from their own history, and that history was different in Memphis versus in the Ukraine, Poland, Russia, and the eastern part of Germany. Thus, taking several examples where one might expect to find the symptomatology of populist racism might give a better idea of what was a general indicator.

So if the King assassination was an attack against an overeducated cosmopolitan from Harvard bringing modern race relations to the Tennessee hill culture, the investigator would have to adjust what he or she was looking for by reviewing the historical rhetoric of that sort of racism in the border states. Huckleberry Finn's father was definitely not a plantation owner, nor were the slave Jim or the visiting citified colored man (*sic*—one sometimes has to use the language of the time when investigating the pattern of rhetoric in that time, in spite of is inappropriateness now) plantation slaves.

This is even more true of the "growth of an opposition ethnic machine" theory. The United States has had many takeovers of central city governments in the North by a minority machine of poorer immigrants (most often Democratic). White upper-class politics was then pushed into the suburbs, and into an alliance of the suburbs with the (often Republican) countryside. That coalition frequently tried to take political power in the state government first, then to take back local autonomy from the cities and relocate power into the state government. For example, once in Boston the police were put under state administration so they would not be a resource for the Irish (with some Italian support) machine. The administration of O'Hare Airport by the city of Chicago, when it is not *in* the city of Chicago, has likewise been quite precarious, as a special grant of power by the state of Illinois to the usually Democratic city of Chicago. There is a tier of counties in the south of the state that usually vote Democratic, so the rural-suburban Republican alliance has been less often victorious than it was in Massachusetts. The point again is that to sort out the mechanisms in a particular case, to see which is dominant, one needs to study more or less pure cases—Guyana and Boston, perhaps—to find the symptoms of majoritarian political systems with ethnic group competition for power.

A historical sociologist making such comparisons has to know that the machines in the South (e.g., in Memphis, the northernmost of Mississippi cities) were not built on an immigrant base. The local city parties do not, therefore, have a well-developed tradition of how the Democratic party (or occasionally the Republican party) "puts together a slate" that represents many ethnicities and bargains internally for patronage for them. That is, an investigator has to be careful to sort out the mechanism of majoritarian collective conflict (2b) from its different historical heritages in northern versus southern cities. Memphis did not get much of the immigration of Jews and Catholics up to 1920; most southern cities did not, because they were not industrializing at that time. This meant that the white population was not split up into many ethnic groups, and that the Democratic party therefore could not easily adjust piecemeal to the growth of the black minority, in a context of incorporation of multiple ethnic groups, so it was not easily prepared for it to become a majority.

The overall point is that if there are different mechanisms producing racism, then racism against each ethnic group will have a different social base, a different rhetoric, a different kind of violence. The different racist mechanisms produce different symptoms. So racism against Asians getting rich in software and physical science professorships or against Jews getting rich in the film industry may not be the same as the racism that creates "American apartheid" (Massey, 1993) for African Americans.

Further, any big, complex, and long-lasting racism is likely to have more than one mechanism driving it, so what drives plantation county Mississippi racism may not be the same mechanism that drives Tennessee hill folks to regard Martin Luther King as a threat. So we can use our theories of mechanisms to create several kinds of measures of racism. That way, we do not confuse our analysis by lumping them all together, and we do not think that all of them ought to be measured by a question about intermarriage (of two) of the races.

When several mechanisms can explain phenomena that, on the surface, have a lot in common, the basic methodological strategy is to search for the distinctive symptoms of the various processes. To do this, it is useful to know a lot about the nearest one can find to "pure cases" where one of the mechanisms is dominant: eastern European (including here Prussian) racism against commercial modernizing Jews, Guyana mutual racism between people of East Indian ancestry and those of African ancestry, or cotton county southern plantation racism or the plantation racism of Jamaica. From these one can pick up the *differentia specifica,* or the defining symptoms of the different mechanisms. Then one can search the data for these symptoms in a particular case, to diagnose it as involving a particular mechanism. After that, one can build a strategic set of variables to measure the specific causes and effects in that mechanism, building up a methodology for the analysis of the case. This strategy is particularly useful in historical sociology, where the most has to be made of each piece of data on a specific case.

Conclusion

A MECHANISM IS A LITTLE THEORETICAL MACHINE, a "mere device," out of which larger structures of theory can be constructed. It translates causes into effects. Thus, one wants to choose concepts of units of analysis in the light of mechanisms, because they translate distances on causes into distances on effects. But conversely, they are keys to the methodology of studying the larger structures. If one can locate mechanisms in them, these generate more specific, but easily graspable, subtheories. These generate a wide variety of causally relevant variables on which one can get measures and locate crucial distances to see if they are having the effects predicted by the mechanisms.

A further advantage is that mechanisms are more transferable to other theoretical structures. For example, thoughts on the sociology of the novel are useful in analyzing variations relevant to the sociology of law or the sociology of science, because they too have worlds of creation with complex products, also received by various kinds of more naive audiences. In all these fields, many of the connections between two worlds involve the transmission of "texts," containing the complexity, from one world to the other—here, through network mechanisms involving cosmopolitans versus locals. The techniques useful for studying the audience of libraries are likely to be useful for studying the reactions of students to a curriculum involving many choices in the sciences because many of the mechanisms have the same structure. Examples have been given for the other two main mechanisms in this chapter, bargains and mobilization, and for various mechanisms specific to theories of racism.

7 Testing Theories by Testing Hypotheses with Data

THE MAIN PURPOSE OF THIS CHAPTER is to connect the logic of the approach of this book to the logic of statistics. I believe that these logics are basically the same, but that statistics textbooks do not ordinarily go into where the numbers they calculate with come from. We have gotten near the end of a long book on method before coming to this point, and I believe that most of what precedes ought to be at the beginning of a good statistics textbook. Only the burden of such a statistics book in the student's backpack justifies omitting it. I have discussed in previous chapters the components of theories that can connect to observations. Statistics, as used in sociology, help us choose among theories. One theory is called, in old-fashioned statistical terminology, "the null hypothesis."

The scientific purpose of most statistical reasoning is "to reject the null hypothesis." The core of the application of statistics to sociology is to so form the null hypothesis so that it is part of a set of null hypotheses, one corresponding to each thing we want to test. Then we need to so shape the data as to test each of these, so that we find out as much as possible about the scientific theory we are working on. The key is the strategic choice of null hypotheses. The rest is calculation and reasoning about probabilities, which we all learn about in statistics courses.

The workhorse of applied statistics for testing social science theories nowadays is the multiple regression equation. Most other statistical methods common in sociology can be thought of as multiple regression equations with transformed variables. To estimate and test these other equations correctly, one usually has to use other parts of probability theory than those commonly used to construct tests in multiple regression equations. But except for developing new methods, most applications do not require one to know these slightly modified branches of statistical theory. I start with the formation of contacts between data and theory by the testing of hypotheses about multiple regression equations, and then go on to some apparently rather different methods that have the same broad structure.

The central idea of this chapter is that one develops the best possible theory of the data, but *without* the specific theory being tested, in order to have a null hypothesis one might possibly believe if one ended up "accepting" it. There is no sense bothering to reject a null hypothesis that no sensible scientist would ever have believed: rejecting a null hypothesis that there is no relation whatever between race and social stratification position in the United States is not worth a serious scientist's effort. A theory that tried to explain why now reservation Native Americans are very much worse off, African Americans fairly much worse off, and Chinese and Japanese somewhat better off, than white people taken as a whole would be the larger theory we would try to build to account for all the data. Each of the tests of that theory might test, as a preliminary, a hypothesis about one of these differences. But to test that larger theory, we should set about explaining that pattern with every other theory in the grab-bag of race theories with some currency, build the best possible alternative theory, and start with that as the null hypothesis. Starting with the theory that any of these well-known effects is zero is only a fiction that might be useful in teaching statistics, not in teaching race relations or improving its theory.

We require that, at the least, our theory should explain some of the race differences that the other theories, taken together, do not, and at best that it does everything the other theories do, as well. If it does not explain everything previously explained, then some sort of pluralistic-mechanisms theory is probably necessary.

This basic mode of reasoning is called "hierarchical" testing in applied statistics in sociology. The key is to have a hypothesis to test that uses the best of available theories as the null hypothesis, and requires that the theory being tested be better. Multiple regression is perhaps the simplest form of such statistical reasoning, except for experiments that positively control or randomize everything but the experimental variables, such as the one examined early in chapter 6. The multiple regression method of forming powerful null hypotheses can best be approached by talking about the "residuals" from two different regression equations.

Regression as Creating a Parameterized Comparison Group, as a "Null Hypothesis" for "Residual Analysis"

....

THE INFORMATION IN PARTIAL REGRESSION COEFFICIENTS all comes from the effect of *residuals of each independent variable*, predicted from the other independent variables, on the *residuals of the dependent variable*, predicted from the other independent variables. That is, one can calculate the partial regression of y on x_n by computing the multiple regression of y (the dependent variable) on x_1 *to* $x_{(n-1)}$, and the regression of x_n on those same $(n-1)$ variables; then subtracting the predicted score of y and x_n from their observed value for every case; then finally running the simple, one-variable regression of the residuals of y on the residuals of x_n. One would never do this except for exploratory purposes (e.g., finding out which of a large variety of variables have strong relations to the residuals, so that one can theorize about what is missing from the main received theories).

Furthermore the significance level of that regression coefficient could be computed (using a different number of degrees of freedom) that would give the correct significance level. The reader does not have to understand how to do this, because one would only do it under very unusual circumstances. What is important is that we have produced a residualized measure of x_n and of y that has already taken into account everything that can be linearly explained by the other $(n-1)$ variables. That is, every theory that has been incorporated into the other variables has been eliminated from the residuals. The new coefficient measures the effect of this purified x variable (purified by taking out all the explanatory force of the x variable that could be explained by the other theories) on this purified y variable. The researcher has actually produced a "hierarchical" test, having one theory that serves as the null hypothesis of $(n-1)$ variables, and then asked whether the theory with x_n also as a predictor is any better than the one with only $(n-1)$ variables.

Students will probably not understand why the degrees of freedom change until they have competency in a linear algebra (matrix algebra) course. This does not matter, because one can follow the recipe. Intuitively one can think of the N (the number of cases used in the regression equation) as the number of "pieces of information" in the original data. By computing the regression equation with $(n-1)$ variables, they have used up n pieces of information—one for the constant (which says how the mean of y is related to the means of the other variables), and one for each of $(n - 1)$ coefficients. The new coefficient uses one more piece by computing the second regression equation on the residuals with x_n and y in it. The statistical test asks whether this one piece extracted last is better than a random piece of information picked out of the residuals. To get the average random piece of information in the residuals, we divide the total information in the residuals by the number of pieces that are left. I imagine this intuitive explanation will confirm students' notion that they never will understand degrees of freedom.

These effects of the theoretically *uninteresting* independent variables are all subtracted off, both from the dependent variable and from the theoretically interesting one; this "purifies" the independent variable of all the influence (but see measurement error, below) of the other measured variables. In other situations—for example, in elaborating one of the theories incorporated in the null hypothesis—one may be very theoretically interested in these coefficients. Now, the hypothesis says the purified independent variable causes the purified dependent variable— a hierarchical test that takes all the theories in the "control" variables and tests the investigator's theory, against all the others, for explaining the last bit. This means we *do not* want to put into the null hypothesis as "control" variables any that measure the forces in the theory the investigator is interested in—one does not, after all, want to eliminate the theory being tested before doing the hierarchical test. Then it will not turn out to add anything, since its effect has been eliminated already. We do not want to know the effect of social class of parents on children's achievement, *net of parents' occupations and wealth*, because we were thinking of social class as parents' occupations and wealth.

The coefficient of the purified dependent variable residuals and the purified independent variable residuals is called the "partial regression coefficient." The statistical t-test of that coefficient (which is equivalent to the test for added variance between the equation without and the equation with the variable being theorized about, and is, in an ordinary multiple regression analysis, the t-test squared, and is then called the F-test) is usually given by the standard programs with the coefficient. Such a "purified" test is actually computed in the usual regression programs for each independent variable, so someone else interested in a theory that predicts an effect for another independent variable (called "uninteresting" above) can use the same equation. In some other versions that are essentially the same in theory as linear regression, a difference of chi-squares test is used; the F-test (and so the t-test in this situation) is a test of the ratios of chi-squares, and the two tests are supposed to give the same answer about probabilities.

So this looks logically just like our residual method for the impact of venereal disease on fertility in central Asia, by comparing the birth rates there with Hutterites who are very monogamous (and who eject from the group those who are not monogamous). But we are not finished with our problems. Suppose that the variable we are analyzing is measured with a quite a bit of random measurement error. Now *the other variables in the equation will not explain that measurement error.* If they do, *then* we ought to develop a theory of the measurement error, because it is evidently a real variable out there in the world, with causes and effects we should understand. So except for chance, the measurement error of that variable will not be incorporated into the predicted part of that variable, and so will not be subtracted off. When we take out all that predicted part, we are taking out (almost entirely) *that part of its variance that was true variance*, that really measured what we were supposed to be measuring. But we have not taken out any substantial part of the measurement error. So we have concentrated almost all the measurement error into the residuals. We can therefore find ourselves trying to explain the dependent variable with a residual that is mostly random numbers. This means that we will underestimate the effect of that variable, if we have measurement error.

Now suppose that there is random measurement error in *another* independent variable—by the same logic as before, *we will have underestimated the effect of that variable.* Then *that variable's effect* on both the dependent variable and the other independent variables will be underestimated. All the variance that is truly variance in that other independent variable—that is, say, truly operating among the Hutterites—is still in that independent variable. This means that part of the effects that are in the residual we are using for estimating the effect of our favorite independent variable (our favorite in sociology is bound to be social class or race) are really the variation that ought to have been included, and so taken out, in the "control" variable. So we are overestimating the effect of our favorite, because we have not really controlled for the variable we think we have controlled for—we did not subtract off enough.

The reason we could get away with using the Hutterites is that they are a numerous group, observed over many years, so that when we take an average of age-specific fertility, we are getting rid of a lot of the random variation in our control, by taking an average of a lot of years of many people. So we have the correct fertility rates (and so postulated fecundity) with very little error, and we really control for them rather than having much measurement error. That is why demographers can do it, and the rest of us usually ought not to use measures with a good deal of error of measurement. We do it anyway, controlling for things that we have measured badly and hoping that our underestimates from measuring social class badly will be just about compensated for by measuring race badly (if race were a genetic concept, we would need to measure the number of "white" versus the number of "black" genes—not a likely achievement— most sociologists think "race" is only very secondarily a genetic concept, although skin color is obviously partly genetic and so partly inherited).

Sociologists measure almost everything pretty badly. Take one of our best measures of social class: namely, occupational prestige as measured by the Duncan-Hauser scale. It turns out that people who are reinterviewed and *have not changed jobs* only give the same answer again about five times out of six. Further, if they give a different occupation, its prestige score is almost uncorrelated with the score of the response they gave before. For example, they may say "barber" the first time and "business owner" (meaning they own or rent a barbershop) the next time. The second is high prestige, the first low. Or suppose in a fit of populism I tell a survey interviewer I'm a schoolteacher one time, a sociologist the next. Now the reader probably will not be able to understand this, but the response "sociologist" has much higher prestige than "schoolteacher."

Similarly, if respondents say, "I shovel shit," one time, and "I'm a horse trainer" another, they get lower status for language, and for occupation, for the first answer. About 20 percent of the standard error of occupational status is then error variance of the most transparent kind, variance that is almost uncorrelated with the respondent's true occupational status, whichever it was. This means that when we control for it in measuring a race effect (say on children's achievement test scores), we will still have some unmeasured social class variation in the race variable because we measured social class badly, though we measured it as well as we know how. So we won't have a "pure race effect." (It is presumably a deeply interesting question why people use different names for their occupations at different times, and why the different name very often has a different prestige value. But if we were studying that question we would use different methods than a survey regression equation.)

The same process works the other way around. We do not understand very well what makes race such a big cause of, say, discrimination. We would have to explain, for example, why on race questions the powerful whites who have the power to hire physicians now discriminate *in favor of* Asians born in the United States and *against* African Americans (part of this, of course, is because relatively fewer African Americans have medical degrees). We often measure discrimination by the residual effect for race, and we measure race by what people call themselves. It is a far stretch to imagine that people discriminate because people call themselves one race at one time, another race at another time. So someone who looks vaguely Italian but calls himself or herself African American or black may not have as much of whatever makes race a cause of discrimination, and a Nigerian-born person who immigrated from England and who looks very black may say he or she is English and yet be more discriminated against.

Similarly, people who read badly were once quite likely on school tests not to understand the question asking if they were Hispanic, perhaps because they only knew the pejorative word *spic* for them. So the cause goes from being a poor reader to checking "Hispanic," and not from being Hispanic and reading badly. The ones who were really Hispanic would do as well as other whites, especially if the sample were taken far from the Mexican border where true Hispanics who read English badly are less common. The ones who mistakenly described themselves as Hispanics were terrible readers on the achievement test, as well as on the ethnicity question. But when one studied the effect of "Hispanic" on achievement tests, one would then really be studying the effect of low reading achievement on reading achievement, and so would overestimate the zero effect and underestimate the effect of everything else. We cannot use the words on the ethnicity question that poor readers might recognize, because they might be insulting.

So the advice here is to pay close attention to whether we think that the measures of independent and control variables are really good measures. One does not "control for" a variable by including a bad measure of it, and regression methods will not work as hierarchical tests if a crucial control variable is badly measured. (There are various ways to test how good the measures of a variable are if we have several measures of the same thing, or if we ask the same questions repeatedly over time of the same people and think that the underlying thing we are trying to measure stays the same [called "reliability"]. There are also various methods in econometrics, sometimes called "instrumental variables" methods, which can get us the right regression coefficient estimates if all their assumptions hold. My own opinion is that they very rarely hold in sociology.)

A Note on R^2

....

TO GET THE TOTAL AMOUNT that *all* the variables explain in the dependent variable, what the programs do is to apply the coefficient that is really based on the residuals of each, and attribute it *also* to all the correlated part that was itself *also* "explained" by the other variables. That is, the "total partial effect" of a variable is that part of its correlation with the dependent variable that would be explained, if the coefficient of the purified part were extended to all of its variance, including the part "shared" with other variables. Put the other way around, if we add up the unique explained variances of all the variables, it will not add up to the total R^2 because each of those coefficients left out of account the part explained by variance they explained jointly.

The common variance of any two variables, as measured by their correlation coefficient, gets multiplied by both coefficients, and then doubled for reasons that we do not need to go into here, to get the total attributable to the parts that are common to both of them together—and the same for every other pair of variables.

The reader may have heard of the problem of collinearity in regression analysis. This is the problem that *if* two variables are very closely correlated, *then* there isn't much information left in the residuals to estimate either of the coefficients accurately. If, in addition, one or both of the variables have substantial random measurement error, then most of that little bit of information will not really be information.

As a practical matter, if we have seven measures of social class (this is quite common in sociological surveys), we should *not* throw them all in and then show that all their partial coefficients are zero. In this situation, we only got the zeroes because almost all that was explained is attributed to a whole bunch (twenty-one, specifically) of "covariance terms" that the seven have in common.

Hierarchical Models

....

THE TERM *HIERARCHICAL MODELS* HAS TWO MEANINGS in sociological methodology. The first is in statistics. If we fit one "model" derived from alternative theories and then get a measure of how well the model "fits" the data, that tells us what the alternative theories tell us. Then we add some more variables from another theory but include all we had before (so the first model is "nested" within the second one). Any test for whether the second model "fits better" than the first is a test of whether there is "added empirical content" in the model involving both theories as compared to the model involving only the first ones. The test is not confused by anything successfully incorporated into the first model. The simplest case of this is the t-test for a partial regression coefficient, as explained above. A common sign of whether we are doing a hierarchical test of this kind is whether the program either subtracts chi-squares to get the chi-squares (or "explained variances," or "error variances," or "between sums of squares") one tests, or alternatively, whether it takes ratios of them. In either case, the computer program thinks it is making a hierarchical test.

(Sometimes the chi-squares that one subtracts are larger if the model fits better; this is more common when one is using maximum likelihood methods of estimation. But sometimes they are measures of "badness of fit," which for some reason is called a "goodness of fit test"—which measures how much information is left in the residuals. The one from maximum likelihood is often labeled "$-2\log$ likelihood," which measures something like "variance explained by the model adjusted for sample size." The chi-square that students may have learned in elementary statistics to analyze cross tabulations was a "badness of fit" chi-square, measuring squared deviations of the data from the model.)

The second sense of *hierarchical models* is that the "parts" of a larger entity are "contained within" or "nested within" the larger entity *in the real world* rather than in our theories, and so the larger entity is hierarchically "superior" to the contained entities. For instance, a "group" is hierarchically superior to "people as individuals" contained within it. Now think back to my laborious attempt to convince readers that the entities "person" and "group," as "units of analysis" on which variables are measured, are also both concepts that "connect causes to effects." We might have two models in which one has *all* the causes that are connected to effects by persons, and one that also had *all* the causes that are connected to effects by the group.

Now suppose that we nest all the models in which persons are the units of analysis *within* all the models that have *either* the person *or* the group as units of analysis. That is, the model we are starting with, the refined "psychological" or "rational action" model, has only "individual effects" in it, and forms the "null hypothesis" for a test of the social model. The second has both "individual effects" and "group effects" in it.

Now we bring these two sorts of hierarchical thinking together, and construct a test of whether *distances between people on causes within groups* are doing the explaining, or whether there is an additional explanatory power of *distances between groups*. For example, distances between individual students are manifested both within schools and between schools. (My own opinion is that most group differences in educational effectiveness are not between schools, but instead between classrooms. There is more difference between teachers than between schools, I believe, and also more distances between any one teacher's "classes that go beautifully" versus "classes that are a disaster" than between teachers. But none of these beliefs is commonly involved in public policy, so there are no regressions involving them.)

School effects involve distances in causes and effects only between schools. We can ask whether the differences of or ratios between chi-squares between the best theory we can construct using distances between individuals (and between classrooms, which are in practice regarded as between-individual effects), and the best theory we can construct using *both* distances between individuals *and* distances between groups are significant.

Notice that there is no real logical difference between partialing all group effects by all individual effects, and partialing each individual effect coefficient by other individual effect variables in a regression equation. However, it requires a lot of mathematical fussing with the data to actually do the comparison and isolate individual and group causes and effects.

The main place we find hierarchical models in this double sense is when investigators are trying to sort out "process" variations over time that involve collective (e.g., labor market) processes versus "inter-individual" variance (e.g., individual people having different preferences and different human resources, constant over the time period being analyzed). In such cases, authors usually use the word *longitudinal* to describe their data. "Longitudinal" data allow one to sort out causes, and therefore effects, that are constant over the period studied, from those whose causes and effects both vary over that period. A labor market sociologist or a labor economist who is doing survey empirical work usually use the terms *longitudinal* and *hierarchical linear models* (or equivalently *fixed effects*) in the text. It is important to realize they are trying to do the same thing that authors in the journal *Symbolic Interaction* are trying to do, except the latter let the individuals change as well. The logic is the same but the statistics are different (none versus some).

Before going further, I want to dwell on the "theoretical power" of observations on the residuals of each individual or group in either sense of *hierarchical,* as compared with observations on the values of the original variables without a hierarchical relation among the models.

Observations on Partial Distances

IN CHAPTER 3 I discussed why we should want to design a study so as to get the maximum orthogonal distances between cases when we had two variables that were causes. I said we would want to get (for example) an oversample of rich African Americans and of poor whites, so as to have the maximum variation in income or wealth that was autonomous from race, and vice versa. This is the same as saying that, after predicting income and wealth from race, we want to oversample the largest residuals to sort out their separate effects. To reformulate this in hierarchical testing terms, we want to oversample the cases that give us the most information about the differences between the theories. So we want to sample in such a way that when we formulate our hierarchical models, we have those distances on the independent variables that will give us the largest residuals from (say) the person-level theory *on the independent variables* of the group theory. If we are trying to see if there are group effects above and beyond individual effects, we want to get the biggest differences among groups that are not due to differences among the individuals.

Let's now look at the logic of *hypotheses.* Hypotheses are theoretical statements, "derived from" or otherwise integral to the theory the investigator is mainly interested in, combined with observational theories and practices, which are *predictions* of what he or she will observe.

This brings up the notion of the "power" of an observational and analytic procedure. *Statistical power* is a subclass of power more generally. Statistical power of a parameter estimate has to do with how much, of *all* the information on a relationship between distances (or other observations) that is in the data, the investigators have extracted into their hypothesis tests. It further analyzes how much *more* power could be extracted from a different data set—for example, one with a larger sample or one with less measurement error. But before I go on to the topic of design for hierarchical modeling and its logic, let me give some rules of thumb about the power of observations with respect to a given theory, *other than* the "crucial experiment" kind of reasoning. These are arranged in what I believe is the correct order of importance.

Rules of Thumb for Increasing Power of Observations
for Causal Studies

....

1. *If possible, an investigator should increase the variance of observations on the causal variable(s).* Ways to do this include sampling extremes, making experimental manipulations more exact in moving only the variable being studied and having bigger movements on that variable, studying more observable ("measurable") phenomena on the extreme cases (e.g., making a special multiple-question interview and observational study of extreme cases), and studying nations that have more inequality on the variable or which "spontaneously" oversample the extremes (e.g., to study the impact of race on politics, one might choose to study Guyana, which is about half black and half East Indian, since a sample evenly split between the two categories maximizes the variance of a dichotomy). Ordinarily in the United States (if we believe that race is the same thing in the United States as in Guyana—I do not), we will get less variance on race, because minority races are such a small part of the population. When whites are a majority, the modal distance between individuals in the population is zero, and one learns nothing about the impact of race from all those zero differences. Choosing a universe to sample from that has large variance is the first and best way to improve observational power.

We will also get more variance by following around, and interviewing on the scene of action, those in a field site whose behavior is more extreme—say, the ones who are more extreme in loudness *and* those most extreme in being quite quiet and unmoved. Remember that in the simple case, it is the square of the distances that tells how much information one has in the sample of distances, so we get much observational power from maximizing variance, because that is a measure of an average of squared distances between observations.

2. *It is okay to sample on the dependent variable to get the extremes, but get both extremes.* The bad reputation of "selecting on the dependent variable" is due to many people's preference for studying only the cases they really want to explain (e.g., frequently poverty-oriented investigators study only poor people), instead of realizing that we also need the cases farthest from them to do the job of causal inference. What is not legitimate is to use, say, only MIT graduate students to study the impact of mathematical talent; we also have to sample the opposite extreme—in this example, perhaps graduate students in the humanities at Brandeis

(to control for average general intelligence), or perhaps students in consumer mathematics in junior high school (to maximize variance in mathematical talent).

3. *An investigator needs a sample (ideally of about the same size) in the middle if he or she thinks the relationship is a simple curve, or is well approximated in the range of the data by a simple curve.*

4. *The more measures of both the independent and the dependent variables an investigator has, the more the power.* The investigator can get multiple tests, one with each pair of measures of independent and dependent; reduce mistakes in the measurement theory; or locate the multidimensionality of a concept he or she thought was all one thing. For example, attitude toward bussing students for integration turns out not to be mainly a measure of racial attitude, but instead mainly a measure of what people think the powers of courts should be; it is more closely related to how much the respondent favors the rights of criminals in courts than to a belief that integrated neighborhoods are ideal. If the investigator did not already know that, and he or she had only bussing attitudes as the measure of prejudice, we would all be out in the cold. So multiple measures help investigators correct their errors about what variations in some of the observations measure.

(*Rule 4a: If the measures can be combined to give a measure of a single dimension of greater accuracy than any one of them, that increases power even more than many "confounded" tests, each of which is weak.* A factor analysis will often help build powerful measures of multiple repeated observations if they are sufficiently standardized. However, properly systematic, overall *gestalt* coding of a whole interview along a given dimension, previously carefully defined, as Heimer and Staffen did (1998c; see "short version" in chapter 8), is much better than a yes or no on whether some bits of behavior were reported.)

5. *The larger the sample, the greater the power.* Against random null hypotheses, the power goes up with the square root of the number of cases, everything else being the same. So whatever the study design, doubling the sample increases power by about 1.4, quadrupling doubles power, and so on. The main reason for putting this sample-size point as the fifth of my rules is that sociologists usually cannot afford to double the data collection costs by getting more people, each of whom takes about ten hours of finding them for each hour of interviewing, unless we are studying something that economists or demographers have persuaded the government to study with big samples. Adding a minute to ask a few

more questions of each respondent on the same topic, without adding a factor of ten to costs, reduces measurement error more cheaply than more cases reduces sampling error, and so increases power more cheaply. For example, by systematically oversampling extremes on the variable I was most interested in, in my buried study of South American steel plants (Stinchcombe, 1974), I found many relationships among variables with samples of about 125 in each place, separately in three different countries. But I would have been even more solidly grounded if I had had 250 in each country; my results would have been 1.4 times as powerful.

6. *If the investigator knows of some alternative theory of the dependent variable, which is not deeply confounded with the one he or she is studying (in the simplest case, another variable that is not correlated with the main variable), and which is known to have a big effect on the dependent variable, then it is wise to control for it even if one is not interested in hierarchical tests.* The reason is that otherwise all the randomness *in that cause* appears as random error in the dependent variable in the study, which makes it harder to find the effect being tested (and conversely makes a nonsignificant result less convincing). So we want good measurements or observations of distances on variables determining what is mainly going on, even if we are studying something more delicate. The higher one pushes the R-square for irrelevant variables (without using up too many degrees of freedom), the more powerful the study.

For example, there is a lot of variance in the abilities of people to do the dissections in medical school—hopefully, with future surgeons surpassing their future psychiatrist colleagues who are all thumbs. If one does not take account of that, one may find what looks like less commitment by future surgeons to the deviant student culture that urges not paying much attention to dissection. They do not dissect carelessly, because it is easy for them to dissect properly, not because surgeons are hard to socialize. (Of course, surgeons may be hard to socialize as well as having an easier way to conform, producing even more deviance from being less socialized to student culture in this case.) Becker and colleagues (1961) would have been more convincing if this confounding factor could have been controlled for by special observations on skilled dissectors.

7. *There is a special consideration on "accepting the null hypothesis."* Obviously the more powerful the study design, the more it means "not to reject the null hypothesis." Concluding that there was no causation going on is a much more powerful conclusion than that a given relation is "not significant" in this study, when unfortunately this particular study was of small power. If a study is so designed so that it would *not* have found

even a big relationship, accepting the null hypothesis is meaningless. This is a difficult topic, so deserves more elaboration.

In sociology many of the causes in major subdisciplines have connections with their effects in the general region of a correlation or a partial standardized regression coefficient of about .2. Unless we make special arrangements in the study design, a truly random sample of one hundred will find a relationship that strong to be significant about half the time. So with a sample of one hundred we will quite often find a relationship of the size we usually regard as important. But we will equally often find that it is not there, "not significant." Thus, a sample of one hundred without especially powerful designs is generally useless in sociology. Partial correlations or partial standardized regression coefficients have about the same distribution. One needs a sample of about four hundred to have a 95 percent chance of finding a true correlation (or standardized partial; in the older literature a standardized partial coefficient was often called a "path coefficient," according to its use in population genetics where the "metric" of a gene was meaningless) of .2 to be significant at the 5 percent level. Presumably, roughly the same lower limit applies to ethnographic or historical studies, so that studies of less than a hundred observations of events, without special designs to increase power, will be of very little use. Becker's paper on participant observation (1958) has some advice on ways of increasing power.

One exception to this should be noted. Usually correlations that we think important for organizations, nations, or other substantial-sized groups are above .4. Therefore, we can have smaller samples and still expect to find the important causal connections, even without special arrangements. For many sociological purposes, studying individual people rather than organizations or groups or communities is scientifically inefficient. The reason the correlations are higher for groups is that usually the measures have less measurement error, so causes with "the same force on individuals" are easier to find. If we take the means of the individuals in groups as our group measure, the standard deviation of measurement error goes down about as the square root of the number of individuals in the groups.

When the measurement error is as large as it usually is in sociology, much of the error variance in an equation is measurement error, not randomness in the world. Similarly, we study the effects of gravitation with planets rather than grains of sand, because it is easier to find big gravitational effects than small ones, and easier to lose what gravity there is between the grains because the wind is blowing them around, creating large error variance. The reasoning behind this is not very difficult, but readers will not need to know it until they are designing a study of a sample of organizations or nations. The general rule of thumb is that one has a more powerful study for statistical tests if the units of analysis are groups, countries, or organizations than if they are people. One can, then, have smaller samples. This rule likewise applies to historical or ethnographic methods.

So what do we do about the fact that with a sample of one hundred individuals, a conclusion that we "accept the null hypothesis" will give sociologists the wrong answer half the time? Either we can choose to conclude nothing, or we go over to confidence interval reasoning. By a *confidence interval* we mean that we describe the result by stating an interval where all the points would not be rejected by the data—at a given significance level. That is, a value of the coefficient anywhere within that interval would be moderately likely to produce the sample we have. Likewise, if we had a larger sample, or observations that measured the variables more accurately, then our sample would have had a more convincing result and a narrower confidence interval. In the usual small-sample study, the largest value of the coefficient that is compatible with the data would be considered an important cause in sociology. So if the strong relationship had been considered as the null hypothesis, it would have been accepted, as well as the zero in accepting the null hypothesis. All of the points in a confidence interval, if they were the null hypothesis, would be accepted.

The general point here is that if we are going to *assert* that there is no important causal impact, then we are *making an estimate* that the correlation or partial regression coefficient is zero. Making an estimate that something is zero is a very different thing from not rejecting a hypothesis that it is zero. We are going over *from* saying that our default null hypothesis is that the relationship might be zero and might not, *to* saying that zero is a number, and zero is what we are asserting. "Accepting the null hypothesis" from a small or otherwise poor sample is forgetting that zero is a number. Asserting there is no relation is saying the writer knows what the number is, and the number is zero. What investigators might be asserting more reasonably is that the causal relation here is *not importantly different from zero*. Since, for a lot of stuff for individuals, what is important to sociological theory is in the region of a correlation of .2, something that might well have been .2 *or* zero is indeterminate. Sociologists generally should *not* accept the null hypothesis if a correlation or standardized partial regression of .2 or −.2 is in the confidence interval. This should be the result if the true correlation or partial is zero and the sample is of the usual size for run-of-the-mill sociological studies, around fifteen hundred.

My ranking of rules of thumb reflects my conviction that the big deals here are increasing variances and increasing measurement efficiency, and especially increasing measurement efficiency for the extreme cases (which we hope we have oversampled in order to increase variance as well). Well-studied extreme cases on both ends of the variables are by far the most useful for the science. Confidence interval reasoning is one of a class of methods for specifying the class of theories compatible with the data. A brief view of some other methods of this kind is given in "Stinchcombe Causes Short Version," below.

Stinchcombe Causes Short Version

Adapted from Arthur L. Stinchcombe, Review of Vaughn
R. McKim and Stephen P. Turner, eds., *Causality in Crisis?*
Contemporary Sociology 27 (1998): 664–666. This is a slightly
expanded version of the original. Page numbers refer to the book
being reviewed.

I take the notion of "cause" to be a particular kind of theory, or a part of a theory, not a fact. Observed facts never "prove" a theory, so one cannot "infer" a theory from a fact; one cannot therefore infer causation from a correlation, or from any other fact.

Facts can be more or less supportive of a theory, according to how improbable they are under plausible alternative theories. So the less likely it is that the coefficient would be observed under any other theory, the more a correlation or a regression coefficient may support a given causal theory.

Causal theories are different from other theories because they predict a rate of change in one variable, as a result of some condition such as the value of another variable. For example, IQ was born as a part of a causal theory, because it was supposed to predict a rate of learning in schooling. IQ at ten years is supposed to measure how much a child has learned in ten years; it estimates then a rate of change of knowledge, cumulated for ten years. One often talks about this by saying that causal theories are about processes, rather than about static comparisons. This is true even if only static comparisons are observed. Causal theories are about underlying generative processes.

In *Causality in Crisis* a frequent line of attack in criticizing inferences on causation from correlations is to invent ["theorize"] alternative processes that might have produced the cumulated change being measured. The critics then want more detail about the temporal process and the underlying "mechanisms" that produce change. They, too, think of causal theories in terms of underlying temporal processes. One is left unsatisfied with correlations between IQ and learning because one is predicting a rate of change from a past [cumulated] rate of change in what looks to be approximately the same variable. We are left wondering what the "real cause" was (e.g., a set of genes or a parent very attentive to homework). But as John Stuart Mill says, such a correlation shows either a cause or an effect or "is connected with it through some fact of causation" (quoted on p. 4). There would never have come to be a difference in the amount learned unless there had been a different rate of change sometime. So something causal is going on, although we may be unsure what exactly it is.

Often we are more satisfied if the condition predicting a higher or lower rate of change was a manipulation applied by an experimenter, and the change is observed to occur between before and after the experimental manipulation.

Some comment in the book is about whether a value of a causal variable observed in the world is a good simulation of experimental manipulation. Is having a real friend similar to being told by an experimenter, "You will probably like the people you will meet here"? This is like imagining that a Bunsen burner is quite like the Sun.

The theme that we know cause if the proposed causal variable was manipulated by an experimenter recurs in this book. Perhaps the search for experimental certainty rests on the uncertainty problem of multiple contending plausible theories in nonexperimental observations. We think we understand a causal process when we apply the supposed cause to only one group and it creates a correlation between the manipulation and the outcome. But whether that manipulation is like anything we might have measured in nature—and so would help us understand any given naturally occurring causal process—depends on a hypothesized analogy between the experimenter's manipulation and nature's manipulations. Thus the experimental design might make us feel more secure, but it should not [until we have calibrated the experimental manipulation by the measures of real-world forces].

Many of the methodologists in this book would like to have the reverse "inference" between an observed fact and a causal theory be much more certain than such connections ever are. Many of the philosophers in this book criticize the regression tradition. They illustrate the logical fact that if "Theory A implies fact a, and fact a is true," it does not imply that "Theory A is true." We have known this at least since Aristotle. Of course Aristotle did not apply it to the case where the fact was a correlation, and Theory A was a causal explanation of correlations between states of variables, from which patterns of rates of change might perhaps be inferred.

This book of essays is largely about approximations to an impossible ideal. It is nevertheless illuminating for scientific strategy, because it shows us how to get nearer to confidence in inferring causation from correlation, even if we must admit that we never quite get there. A good example from the book is the chapter by the late Clifford Clogg and Adamantio Haritou. They explore the consequences of assuming that a multiple regression coefficient of y on x, controlling for some z-variables, correctly represents the [cumulated] causal effect of x. They ask what else is implied, with this added postulate, by a causal theory about the rest of the statistical results in a regression analysis. The assumption that some observed coefficient is truly causal implies that no variation in y actually dependent on the z's is in the residuals of an equation predicting y from those z's (equation 18, p. 103). As Clogg and Haritou stress, for this to be so the z's must be perfectly measured. They remind us that those sociologists publishing regression equations who believe that their ten to twenty control variables are perfectly measured are out of their minds, or at least delusional. Therefore, our causal coefficients are ordinarily biased, usually estimated as larger in absolute value than they are. LISREL, or Clogg and Haritou's suggestion of regressing on principal components of the controls, can get unbiased coefficients. What we usually do cannot. Thus Clogg and Haritou have a critique and a tractable solution.

The problem is a deep one for us particularly, because the central variable in much of sociology is some version of "social class." Social class actually consists of many quite distinct components, which give different kinds of advantage in social life.

For example, perhaps the best measure of social class to explore its impact on school achievement (and on IQ, for that matter) is whether or not there is an encyclopedia in the home. But that does not predict very well whether the child of a family can get rich as a used-car salesman, which probably requires a different set of cultural capital measures. [One does not turn to a reference book to look up how to sell cars.]

Social class is a congeries of variables [which produce different rates of change in different effect variables], including at least father's and mother's occupations, cultural capital and wealth, attentiveness to cognitive development of the child, whether the child is "watched and fed" or guided to enriching activities, whether the parents are respected among their peers so that their authority is legitimated, whether the parents own their own business in such a way that they can place the child in an apprenticeship to running a business and to property management, and so on. It is extremely unlikely that one can control for all the various sources of social class advantage, and they are not terribly highly correlated with each other, so controlling for social class with no measurement error is extremely difficult.

Much of the book is concerned with the fact that "nearby" causal models are also compatible with the observed data. [Much of this is derived from the fundamental work by Glymour et al., 1987.] We are all familiar with this in the form of confidence intervals: a 95 percent confidence interval (or a confidence oval of a pair of coefficients of a cause and its main control) is a list of all the null hypotheses about the coefficient (or the pair of coefficients) that would not be rejected by the data at .05 [two-tailed]. There are always "nearby" theories, compatible with the data [e.g., all those within the confidence intervals or ovals]. Most of the analyses here consider the broader [Glymour] problem of how many different path diagrams are compatible with [an observed] correlation matrix, and particularly with the whole set of partial relations that go to zero (all the pairs of variables that are "conditionally independent").

In some of the applications this knowledge is combined with knowledge of "exogeneity" ("unmoved movers," variables whose rates of change do not vary with the values of other variables within the model), to further reduce the set of compatible causal diagrams. For example, causal arrows cannot go back in time. In general, the authors here are very suspicious of allegations of exogeneity. People's being born African American comes before they are discriminated against, but discrimination is highly correlated with race, including the race of parents: temporal priority may not be sufficient to establish causal priority. Similarly, IQ measured as, say, the cumulated number of words one knows by age ten is presumably correlated with whatever determines the total number of words one has heard (or read) that have been repeated enough times to learn them by age ten. If discrimination takes the form of decreasing African American children's exposure to verbally rich environments, and that discrimination continues to operate, especially in summers and after school, during the eleventh year of age, then the cumulated learning in the IQ score at ten will be measuring the same discriminatory effect as is incorporated in the change in achievement score cumulated during year eleven. Controlling for IQ in an analysis of the impact of race on learning then controls for the discriminatory learning environment in the eleventh year [and so underestimates effective discrimination in that year].

Many of the essays concern [Glymour] computer programs (and related theorems about them) that aim to produce all the causal diagrams that are compatible with all zero partial relations that can be computed from a given correlation or covariance matrix. The main evidence for the effectiveness of these programs comes from their ability to recover the generating model (as one of the possible ones) that produced simulated data. This shows that if a body of data is generated by a given causal structure of the sort the researchers have in mind [e.g., with linear relations only, no measurement errors in the variables], then that causal structure will be among the ones found to be compatible with the data. The more important point is that, like a confidence interval or oval, the programs tend to produce many causal pictures compatible with the data; and without adding exogeneity information, some of those will look pretty silly. I think the computer programs (developed mainly at Carnegie-Mellon University) have the right answer—and, more important, the right view of what the right answer has to look like: the best we can hope for is a list of the causal theories compatible with the correlations in our data (after we have corrected them for measurement error).

I suspect most sociologists think more like the authors criticizing these new methods than like the authors who developed them, and so will reject the right answer because they want to know more than can be known [from a correlation matrix]. The right answer, I believe, is that multiple causal theories will be compatible with the correlations in any body of data. So inferring causal structure will always be problematic. The basic tack the defenders of the methods take is that if some particular causal arrow is in every one of the possible causal theories that might have generated the data, then the evidence for that causal connection is much stronger than it would be if some of the compatible models did, and some did not, have the causal arrow.

A wonderful essay on the problems of causal inferences in macrosociology by Stanley Lieberson shows that some sociologists know what they are doing, and that that is different from our elementary statistics courses.

All teachers of regression methods in sociology should read this book [and Glymour et al., 1987], but [these books are] a good deal harder to read than this review, so expect to work on it.

Strong Hierarchical Reasoning: Statistical Form

THE BASIC IDEA OF HIERARCHICAL REASONING is that we aim to build the main alternative theories of the dependent measures into a model of the data. Then we build an alternative model of the data in which *both* the alternative theories *and* the theory mainly under investigation are true. Finally we see whether the *combination* explains more of the data than the alternatives to our theory.

To put it another way, we shape the null hypothesis *so that it is believable*. Instead of asking the question, "Is there anything at all going on in our data?" we are saying that we know that there is probably something going on in it. And we hope and believe that *two* things are going on there: everything the alternative theories can explain, and more that the new theory can explain. We build the null hypothesis so that the alternative theories have the *best chance possible* to explain the data. We set out to do even better than scholars who believe the other theories in constructing the model for them: we will improve measurement of their variables, get as much variance as we can on the variables *they* are most interested in, put in process data on the mechanisms *they* think generate the results of their theories, and, in short, do a bang-up job of their work for them. They will not be able to say we did not fairly give them a chance to explain everything. But then we will do, as near as we can, equally well for an alternative theory.

In the usual case, however, the reason we are doing the multiple regression or other hierarchical reasoning is that the world is confusing: both theories do explain, and they are highly correlated with each other. Even if the effects of ethnicity or race and social class of parents "only" add to each other, if they are highly correlated, then a great deal of their explanatory power will not be represented by their regression coefficients or the tests of "unique variance" that we get from the tests of each of their coefficients. For example, in the United States parents' occupational standing, income, and wealth are all highly correlated with African

American "race." And both African American "race" and "social class" (some combination of the other three measures) are explanatory of educational achievement, in the hierarchical sense.

But the high correlation between race and social class means that quite a lot of people are poor and black, quite a lot rich and white, so the *addition* of the two forces takes place in large groups of people at both ends of the distribution. The separation of the coefficients depends on the relatively few who are black and rich, or white and poor. But their separation is of small overall importance, when most real folks "live in" the covariance terms. High educational performance, then, will disproportionately be among children of families that are both well off and white, and low performance among those both black and poor. That is what those hidden covariance effects, which do not show up in the tests of the partial coefficients, look like concretely.

This happens with social revolutions, as well as with schooling. In most countries, but especially those with a recent colonial history, ethnicity (e.g., Arabs versus Jews in Palestine) or race (e.g., black versus colored versus white in South Africa) and social class are highly correlated. If both organized poverty and organized race or ethnicity are correlated with revolutionary inclinations (and there is much evidence for this), then countries with large groups of poor Muslims and well-off Jews, or poor blacks and well-off whites will be in political trouble (an example where much of the action is in the covariance terms is the regression analysis of revolution in Boswell and Dixon, 1993).

Somewhere Charles Tilly comments that it is a society that has a revolution, not just groups of people in it. Suppose a society undergoing one kind of revolution—say, one between slave-owning capitalists versus capitalists who either are small farmers or are using free labor, as in the American Civil War. One would not be surprised to find that an ethnicity—black people, for instance—had a lot of reason to join one side rather than another in that rebellion, even if the free-soil farmers were very prejudiced against blacks. That rebellion then became, and still remains, more intense because it was ethnic as well as class conflict. And the key is that one kind of class conflict (slave versus slave owner) had an ethnic dimension that the other class conflict (manufacturers and family farmers versus slave capitalists) did not. Once the society was in revolution, black resistance to slavery took quite different forms. During and after the Civil War, there were battalions of black soldiers (for "menial" soldier work), instead of the prewar resistance of running away to Canada on the "underground railway." (This is an example of the interaction effect of race and temporal context, as analyzed in chapter 5.)

But this means that the very high correlation between race and slavery (though it was, of course, far short of a perfect correlation) was much of the cause of black people taking the side of the Republican government of the North. Blacks' Republican loyalty lasted for much of the late nineteenth century, and in some places well into the twentieth.

Back to the Residuals Method

QUITE OFTEN, EITHER THE ALTERNATIVE THEORY or one's own will be a complex one, not easily represented in regression form. For example, it is deep in the nature of economics that the *effects* of action *cause* it; rational action is undertaking an action because its effects are good. This means that the causes in economics mostly go around in circles, as action causes effects that are the motive of the action. Similarly, if divorce has a certain effect, such as fathers seeing less of their children, one can have an economic theory that whoever initiated the divorce (e.g., by starting an affair) wanted the consequence of seeing less of the children. The most likely person to want that is perhaps the person, usually the male, who gets out of the in-kind costs of raising the children: the work and the worry.

This is more likely if, as Hochschild (1989) has shown, the ones who begin the alienation of affection show every evidence of having been trying to get out of in-kind services to children when they were still married. (Alice Rossi has shown, with Peter Rossi [Rossi and Rossi, 1990], that men's in-kind services to children ["care"] vary a lot among men and that the big variable explaining this is "emotional expressiveness"— but that is a part of the theory we will get to in a minute.) Thus, the simple regression of consequences on their causes is not an adequate representation of the rational-action alternative, because rational action is a mechanism involving many variables whose causation "goes backward in time." Emotional expressiveness is a predispositional cause, and goes from cause to effect forward in time. But wanting a life in the future without children causes the sorts of things the rational actor, in the meantime, thinks will bring that future about.

But if we look at the big alternative theory to rational action, "sensible action on a local scene *that shapes preferences*," sociologists will likely come up with a theory of the character of discourse and "bonding" of people, with variables in it like "trust," "integrity," "dispute resolution," and "responsibility to other people." This theory describes the local scene in terms of social ties, and "sensible action" as action that helps one's friends or one's organization. That is, a sociologist will probably come up with a "network theory" about people learning the bonds, the responsibilities, the trust and trustworthiness, and the integrity.

There may even be a mechanism of the sort of purposeless communion, "phatic communion," that makes up the majority of marriages during the decade or two that they last, on the average. One sits in a room with spouse and children with little other purpose than being there; watching a boring program on TV is something to do to be together. Network ties, especially those of families, are causes that also turn back on themselves, since, for example, competence at living with somebody increases with experience living with them, experience with conflict resolution grows with the number of conflicts resolved, and responsibility to a particular other grows with knowing a lot about the feelings and wants and competencies and minor faults of the other person, so that their "needs" seem real.

So the causes for this mechanism again go around in circles: if one has a good marriage it will last longer, and many of the effects of lasting longer will increase the chances that it will last longer yet. Similarly, the person a child has probably lived most with by the time he or she is twenty is the mother. Given the gender differences in discourse about needs and wants and expressions of emotions, an even larger share of the emotional discourse of a child who has reached twenty is likely to have been with his or her mother. Depending on the mother, that may create different mixes of love and hatred, but what it will not produce is indifference. So, in general, in family relations the theory of a sociologist (specifically, Rossi and Rossi, 1990) is likely to be even more tangled than the rational action theory of an economist. Causes cause themselves, not only through motives, but also through all the various devices of network analysis. Very likely, then, the "emotional expressiveness" that was a straightforward causal link going the right way in time is itself caused by a long history in which emotional expressiveness was a cause of itself, and produced an environment in which expression of emotions "works."

No one sensible thinks that marriage has *nothing* to do with rational action involving getting benefits from living together, or wanting to have kids only if you trust your spouse to help and to be nice to them. That is, the mechanisms of economics help produce marriages, because some kinds of benefits are produced most efficiently within families that love each other, so the equilibrium is often to stay in that marriage. (Coase [1937] originally made this argument for firms, but nothing in his argument makes it inapplicable to families.) If people do not pay attention to whether they get anything out of the marriage, they are not likely to last long in it; for them, there will be uncompensated costs, creating more uncompensated costs, leading to alienation, indignation, and divorce. An investigator does not really want to have a theory of marriage and love that has no rational action in it. "It has to be rational to love you, because it makes me so happy." So network processes have causes that go around in circles because many rational actions are located in networks, and they themselves go around in circles. Partly because one can predict one's spouse's (or even spouses') responses, needs, competencies, and commitments better, it is rational to work with them to satisfy one's own wants.

So the models in these kinds of theories are very complex and "reflexive." They can generate hypotheses that can be tested by multiple regression, but a regression equation is not a natural way of representing the process. If a woman's husband is rational and efficient in changing diapers, it is less costly and more pleasant to live with him, and the couple will have more time for pillow talk on what they should best do with their money. So rationality feeds into the discourse model, and is an outcome of that model. But the discourse model suggests that the baby's happiness will be of more utility to the father if he babbles to the baby while changing its diaper, so that later he will be rational in thinking it worthwhile to pay the cost in time when the kid needs to be held because she missed a crucial goal at a soccer game and "we" lost.

The methodological point of these long digressions is that the usual regression model of the causal system is hopelessly primitive for much of what sociologists care about. This is because the causal picture is badly represented by a theory in which the causal arrows go only one way in time. Economics, which has faced this problem from the beginning, mainly uses "equilibrium" models in theorizing, and builds autoregression effects into the equations. Sociology's regression equations also do not represent causes that are involved in self-replication of social relations well.

Sometimes the methodological solution is to exclude all self-replicating causes by controlling for "autocorrelation." But in my opinion, that is usually throwing out the baby with the bath. Autocorrelation is the center of evolutionary biology, and also of sociology. It is the absolute causal center of the fruitfulness of network analysis. Furthermore, it is especially causes that go backward in time that tend to produce high autocorrelation: hoping to own one's own house someday explains the autocorrelation of paying the mortgage every year for thirty years.

Building the most powerful rational action model to test the discourse model against, and the most powerful discourse model to test the rational model, is a deep problem. Making such comparisons of rational action and network processes "hierarchical" will be very difficult with regression equations, though that is the way we try (and, I believe, nearly always fail) to do it.

The general point here is that when we are confronted with a problem where we have complex theories, especially theories where the causes and effects go around in circles, regression methods are too crude. Whenever one naturally talks about "planning," and when we confront self-reinforcing social ties and loyalties, regressions are a clumsy tool. Similarly, when we believe that discourse and debate in legislatures is central to political bargaining, in order to render political action rational, it is hard to sort out the rationality from all the determinants of rational discourse, such as the way seating in the House of Representatives is arranged, and why the committees of the House meet separately in other rooms. We have to work hard before we get to a null hypothesis (e.g., a particular rational action "null hypothesis") against which we can test our (e.g., discourse) "experimental" hypothesis. And the "experimental treatment" of the discourse hypothesis (e.g., that in families people have more caring relationships if they exchange their emotions accurately) is perhaps more difficult yet.

This means that the multiple regression equation that we have taken to represent the core "crucial experiment" logic of turning causal theories into hypotheses that can be "tested" with the data is only the simplest of the quantitative methods. Therefore, it is the easiest one to give seven rules of thumb for, on how to design studies for such data analyses to be fruitful. The hierarchical or "crucial experiment" style of thought is, however, the main philosophical underpinning of most methods, and is more prominent in quantitative methods exactly because it is easier to see what is going on there.

But another deep practical problem that is conventionally buried in the folklore of traditions of empirical work in sociology is the problem of getting "high resolution" in the data. Study design not only has to have hypotheses that throw a lot of light on the theoretical meaning of the data, but also both the theory and the data have to be "on the right scale."

The Character of "Resolution" as a Methodological Criterion

....

THE BASIC NOTION OF THIS SECTION IS THAT, as one homes in on an area of research, by eliminating as many alternative theories as possible, then one knows more and more about what one is supposed to be observing. Then, by "controlling for" some more alternatives (or supplements to one's main theory to take care of special circumstances) by one of the broad residual methods, such as multiple regression, comparative historical ideal typologies, or hierarchical linear models, one gets closer to the point of doing the main theoretical development. The more the investigator knows what he or she should be observing, the finer the detail he or she can plan to get about what is really going on. This problem of "where to think" is the logical source of the methodological problem of "getting the right resolution." One wants data on the processes that are crucial to improving the theory, and that means getting data on the right scale.

This, then, is the time and place to hone one's ideas about mechanisms and to think about how one would observe them, in their place in macroscopic processes. One can observe the causes flowing from the bigger structure, and the effects going back to that structure from the mechanism, if one can have detailed observations simultaneously on the small scale and on the flows from and to the large scale. This is the time and the place to develop scales made up of multiple observations of variables instead of single questions or single observations. This is the place in the research process to go back to the comparative cases and refine one's observations, to get a deeper understanding of the context. When the microscope can be reliably directed at the right place and time to observe a phenomenon, that is the time to turn up the magnification of the microscope; conversely, one may build a telescope to rapidly scan the whole sky for tiny variations in the background radiation. The problem of "resolution" is that sometimes one needs the microscope, sometimes the scanning telescope.

The more refined the observations at the right scale, the fewer alternative theories they will be compatible with, and the more likely they are to reject the currently favored theory, requiring further theory development. Probably nothing contributes more to the speeding-up of scientific theoretical innovation than higher resolution of instruments that can be precisely aimed at the central phenomena. So the finer an investigator's resolution of observations, the more "exact" the empirical content that is being added to his or her theory. But if the "exactness" of the theory predicts a large structure, efficient scanning for tiny (by the time they get to us) variations on a large scale produces the highest resolution *for the theory.*

Refining Fieldwork Observations

SOMETIMES THE REFINEMENTS THAT GIVE ADDED RESOLUTION, more of a close-up, are quite simple. Suppose, for example, investigators are ethnomethodologists. The original idea of the name is that one studies the methodology by which the *people (ethno-) themselves* decide what is true about social life, and one regards this as the basic mechanism by which social life is constituted—and hence the central "truth" the sociologist has to grasp. Ethnomethodologists were especially interested in the dynamics of conversations (how people figure out what other people mean, in the context of what has just been said, and how they establish something as valid for the purposes of the discussion). The particular theory being studied might be that "successful interruptions" are a sensitive indicator of relative status, temporally refined enough to indicate changes in status over the course of a conversation. One's theory of status, then, has to have been developed to the point at which it can be illuminated by detailed observations of indicators at a very small social scale and over a very small time period.

To have a successful interruption, the interrupter has to start talking while someone else is talking. Further, he (or she—but we usually find that successful interruptions are less often carried out by women in mixed groups) has to keep talking until the interrupted person quits talking. The length of time the interrupted person keeps talking measures, perhaps, the strength of the denial of the claim of the interrupter to higher status. Perhaps the interrupted person raising his or her voice to override the interruption would be a further measure of denial of a claim to higher status. The speed with which people turn their eyes to the interrupter, leaving the interrupted person talking to himself or herself, would be a wider measure of the success of interruption. A woman who says, later in the meeting, "Would some man make the following suggestion [that will resolve this particular problem], because I have said it three times and no one paid any attention," would be an extreme indicator, perhaps supported (finally) by the turning of eyes toward her.

We have various other measures of higher or lower status: total proportion of the conversation occupied by different people, a poll afterward about who had the best ideas, formal rank in the organization in which the conversation is embedded, the time and situation when a person starts the move toward a decision by saying something like "Shall we take a vote?" or "It seems to me that we all could agree to the following compromise ... Does anyone object to that, or can we move on?" All these, if they cohere, might be a more reliable indicator of relative status, confirming or denying that "length of time after an attempted interruption that the interrupted person still holds the floor" is an accurate measure of status.

Now the problem is to get the detailed measures, for the period of conversational overlap, on the volume of each speaker, the time when the attempted interruption began, the length of time they were both speaking, who stopped, who shifted their eyes to the interrupter, and so on. If one videotapes a conversation, and then locates the attempted interruptions, one can play them over and over again while coding times, volumes, and focus of attention of the audience. By collecting a poll afterward, doing a rough coding of who "held the floor" for how long for the whole conversation, who initiated the process of deciding after a patch of conversation that the discussion should end with a decision, and so on, one can get the other measures of status.

But most of the measures of status that the investigator has used to validate attempted interruptions, and success of interruptions, are at a longer time scale than the interruptions themselves. Since interruptions are a fairly frequent feature of conversations, the frequency of attempts by a given person with respect to another person talking may be mappable onto fairly short time intervals, and similarly for the success of overcoming an attempted interruption. This gives a finer temporal resolution to the measurement of conversational status, and one can use it to elucidate the fine-grained structure of gaining and losing status.

With such resolution, one also may discover that hierarchical rank in the organization in which the conversation is embedded counts more when it is status internal to the department whose main problem is being discussed, so that outsiders of higher rank have trouble getting a word in edgewise. Repeated failed attempts to interrupt may measure a person who thinks he or she deserves a higher status than the local conversation would provide. Then, if higher status women have more attempts and failures, it may reflect the greater vulnerability of women's high status to status degradation outside their immediate bailiwick. In general, as we develop greater density of observations on a conversation and the conversational measures of status, we have higher resolution on what determines when and where people of high formal status cannot get a look in.

Now suppose that this works, and we get the idea that people put themselves at risk of interruption if they pause—a tiny, nearly instantaneous, change of status. And we suspect that the length of pauses predicts the likelihood of interruptions. Back to the videotape. By now we are starting to have fine-grained observation with a high degree of resolution on the subject of how status is manifested in "holding the floor" and "interruption" norms. We perhaps previously did not even think of one's status as changing at the microtempo of fractions of a second of pauses. But all we have done is look at a videotape, which is actually of lower resolution than the original conversation, but which a researcher can look at again and again. Allen Grimshaw (1989) organized a book in which a tape recording of an oral examination of a sociology student was analyzed by many people with different approaches to conversational analysis. Of course, he had to get everybody to agree to this beforehand, not only for human subjects purposes (some poor student having his or her answers judged by many sociologists for years afterward, and similarly for the questions of the faculty members), but also for having the different people paying attention to the same conversation.

Now, the investigator cannot tell without trying whether he or she has come into an area where finer resolution will produce new knowledge that requires new theorizing, and whether his or her colleagues will recognize the work as sociology or say, "Maybe you could get tenure in linguistics, instead." It may be that we already knew everything about status that is manifested in interrupting behavior, from the gross measures we used to validate the new one. Maybe we find that novelists have been putting in "hesitantly" to describe a person speaking in exactly the situations in which people get interrupted. And perhaps novelists are taking hesitating as a measure of their character's status in the conversation. If all good novelists already knew it, the investigator will not show how powerful sociology is by showing what "we humanists" already knew. If now we know down to a tenth of a second of pauses what a novelist's "hesitantly" means and that is all, then the added resolution was of no use. People in real life didn't need it down to a tenth of a second, or they would not have known they could get away with interrupting someone successfully.

Resolution on a Grand Scale

NOW LET'S LOOK AT THE OPPOSITE EXTREME: finding the right resolution to look at large-scale social structures. One does not look at a mountain range through a microscope to see what structure it has. Similarly, we will not want to know whether George III of England got interrupted a lot when he was stuttering and it sounded like a pause, to find the causes of the American Revolution. The revolution is "not on the scale of" an ethnomethodological investigation.

For example, one can look at a map of the king's roads in eighteenth-century France, and (if the map isn't too big or too detailed) see that there was a dense network of roads on the plains of the Seine and Loire valleys. This was the main grain-growing area of France at that time. If we look instead at the design of a bridge in the famous *Encyclopédie*, we will not see where those bridges are probably being built, because at the scale of an etching of a bridge we would not see the network that is being connected across rivers.

Suppose the same book happened to have a map on about the same scale of the proportion of all men who could sign their own names to the marriage register in different parts of France. We would see that this same plain that had a dense road network also had a high level of literacy.

André Siegfried (1975 [1933]) showed that this same region regularly voted "red" (at that time, meaning a vote for secular and republican government and policy) in the tradition of the Revolution. He also showed that inhabitants of the river valleys between the plain and the sea tended to vote red during the nineteenth century. Combining this with the fact that the roads tended to run along the rivers, one might connect the whole complex of easy communication, literacy, and republican spirit to the northern plains, and to the roads and rivers that connected it to international commerce.

The reason the red streaks can be identified in the west of France along the rivers is that the hills are reactionary, black, while the roads connect the red plain to the sea. None of that can be seen at the level of resolution of the bridge over one of the streams. So we need different levels of resolution to study things on different scales, and we may refine the scale to the best resolution by looking at fractions of a second of pauses, or by looking at all France at once, described only by the paths of roads. We should use the level of resolution that best illuminates our theoretical problems.

The same thing applies to the other sciences. For example, in order to identify that the structure of DNA was a helix, Rosalind Franklin, who did the X-ray diffraction studies, had to use a frequency of X-rays that would find a structure *on the scale of* the spirals of the helix. If she had used a shorter frequency, she would have gotten a good picture of the molecules that make up the helix. If she had used a longer frequency, for instance, light, she would have gotten whole chromosomes. Neither of the other scales of resolution would show that the structure was a helix. (See Watson, 1980 [1968]; especially the papers in that volume by Klug, pp. 153–158, and Franklin and Gosling, pp. 252–257; also the account of the Cochrane, Crick, and Vand paper cited on p. 257 at pp. 40–43; also pp. 239, 262.)

But physicists cannot use X-ray diffraction at all unless they can make those tiny molecules line up with each other in repetitive patterns, unless they can "crystallize" or "gel" them. Some of the estimates of structures were crystallized in relatively dry conditions, gelled in relatively wet conditions—the latter were more stable and in an environment more similar to physiological conditions. Crystallizing or gelling anything requires one to set up the conditions so that the molecules will move around a bit, but not with such energy as to make them break up quickly if forced by the others to line up. They have to line up ions (or be isolated from ionized orienting by water or other insulation) in such a way that forces on each pair of molecules cause them to line up with the ones next to them, in a regular fashion. Discovering what makes them crystallize is therefore the preliminary phase of X-ray diffraction, unless such conditions can be found naturally occurring. Watson calls this part of the process the "witchcraftlike technique of the biochemist" (Watson, 1980 [1968], p. 46; for the importance of this to the research, see pp. 37, 48, 240, 252–253, 261).

Crystallizing fragile molecules such as proteins or nucleic acids is actually a big trick in finding molecular structures; Franklin and her colleagues did a considerable part of their research on the wrong form of the crystal-gel complex. To find the helices, one must not only find the scale on which they exist, but also figure out how to make the molecules line up with each other so that millions of X-rays can be deflected in the same ways by one molecule after another, since the patterns of deflections are what shows helices. In other words, one has to increase the resolution of molecular structure both by making the molecules line up so the diffraction is repetitive, and by shooting the right part of the spectrum at them so that the diffraction will tell about the right aspects of the structure.

The "Preferences" of Organizations

LET ME TAKE UP AN EXAMPLE where it is hard to see what the right scale of analysis is. If we study individual people too closely, we find that their preferences are not very stable, though population averages may have a simple, stable structure. Sometimes people want money, and sometimes they will give up a lot of money for regular sex; sometimes they pay a lot for French beans in a restaurant, and sometimes they look around the produce section to see what is in season because that's always both better and cheaper. (Incidentally, one can disprove the economists' proposition that people will pay more for something better by the right resolution; if one uses seasons [e.g., months] when a given kind of produce is best versus worst, one will find that at the season when produce is best, people pay less for it, because there is lots of it.) Sometimes people want to move up the hierarchy in the university, and then sometimes they get bored because a department chair's power and status is experientially lower than it looks on the organization chart. Clearly, individuals do not have stable preferences, and so most economic reasoning, which depends on the stability of preferences, is a poor predictor of individual behavior.

Investigators like Gary Becker (1981; and Becker and Tomes, 1986), extending economic reasoning to subjects like divorce, get multiple regression R-squares (variance explained) of about .04. That is a correlation between the predicted value and the actual observed value of about .2, a reputable number in sociology but not in economics. To get a point of comparison, the correlation between husband's and wife's years of education is about .6, or a variance explained (r-square) of about .36. The correlation of a father's occupational prestige with a son's occupational prestige is about .4, for an r-square of about .16. A scale of liberal values on equality of legal rights of the races and a scale of civil liberties attitudes are likely to be correlated around .3 (or perhaps .4—it varies with the scales), or a variance explained of .09. So this multiple correlation is toward the low end of the correlations that sociologists concern themselves with. It's not bad, but is no particular advertisement for the superiority of economic reasoning over sociological reasoning. This is partly because Becker is assuming constant preferences in an animal that does not have them, and insofar as it does, one does better by estimating their stability from observations over time, rather than assuming them. In particular, the preferences that led one originally to marry the spouse one just divorced do not predict very well that one will marry him or her again.

But if an investigator looks at the behavior of a corporation—say, its preference for money over all other good things—it turns out to be very stable indeed. A corporation's informal internal rate of return (how much an investment has to pay before the organization will decide it's rational) or its risk preference function (whether it would buy blue-sky, gold-prospecting stocks, for example) also turns out to be quite stable. Hospitals likewise have about a constant mix of spending on research versus patient care, percentages of Medicare and Medicaid patients, number of diagnostic tests done before assigning a diagnosis, and so on, indicating a rather stable utility function. (A utility function is the set of rates in various tradeoffs between different goods that a person or organization could choose—that is, at different levels at which they already have two goods, how much of one would they give up to get more of the other?) If a university already had about 30 percent expenditure on research, how far would it take students of lower ability in order to skim off more tuitions for supporting research (to move to 35 percent for research, for instance)? The criteria for admissions are remarkably stable, showing a relatively stable preference function.

So we find that organizations have much more stable preferences than people do. If one wants to apply economic reasoning assuming stable preferences, one ought to take the scale of analysis to be firms rather than individuals, because corporations and businesses have more stable preferences than individuals. Economics pretends philosophically that it is about individuals, but economists' resolution in their strongest findings is at the level of firms or countries, not individuals. The philosophers within a discipline do not always know what the discipline is good at. The key is to look at this problem at the right scale. One cannot go around asking individuals in a university what they think the right tradeoff is between research and, say, committee work and filling out administrative memos.

Northwestern University, for example, is in a runaway process of increasing the ratio of administration to faculty, but is adding no increases of faculty to decrease student-faculty ratios. So what is making tuition there so expensive, growing faster than inflation, is not hiring fancy professors, but hiring fancy administrators. Then the administrators have to have something to analyze, and another administrator to send their decisions back to, to say they are not well enough justified yet. Then the lower administrator in turn asks a faculty member to write a longer memo. No particular person is sitting anywhere deciding that faculty should spend more of their time serving on committees or writing memos. If not in meetings, the faculty would be writing obscure papers that would be read by a hundred or so people, some of them not even of high prestige; better a memo that is valuable to an associate dean, than a paper of such low prestige that only a hundred people think it valuable.

This is a stably increasing preference function for a higher ratio of memos to students. No one would make a speech to justify such a preference function (not even to write a memo, unless they could publish it in a methods book). This increased relative preference for memos grinds slowly, but grinds exceedingly fine.

The preference function on this tradeoff of the organization is constructed by *not paying attention to it when committees are being formed.* The "curriculum review committee" tends to be dominated by departments that depend heavily on required courses to fill classrooms. *No one has the job of asking* whether the committee is more valuable than the sacrificed number of (say) foreign language humanities papers that could have been written. Investigators have to go to where committees are generated, where a position is created that requires memos and reports from scholars or departments, where faculty are seconded to committees that read and summarize memos to write the results into memos that go on up the line (and to carefully edit out the recommendations they think might be unacceptable above), where outside authorities get the ability to require more memos and reports of time spent (because those who give money want to pay only for memos to them, not memos on other problems). That is, investigators have to find places where demands are made on faculty time that are not thought through. One can only find silences by ethnographic work, and silences are the central way that tradeoffs are not posed as problems. Probably the best place to do that is in the deans' offices where demands for more administrative knowledge are translated into demands for more memos from faculty. One cannot interview them, because they actually do not believe they want faculty writing memos instead of doing teaching and research.

The structure that investigators of requirements for memos are observing consists of the *relations between positions,* those who can call committees and those who might, but do not, protest, or not come to meetings, or retire, or otherwise protect their research time. So we have to look at the phenomenon *on the right scale* to observe it (and at that scale we need methods that can locate silences about costs). We could go around all day talking to faculty, and they would say that they were pestered with committees. We could go to the dean's office, and they would say that scholarship and teaching are core to the university. Nobody wants increasing tuitions to pay the deans and their subordinates to read the memos (and, to be fair, to write each other memos—they oppress each other, as well as us).

There is a saying among historians that "the beauty is in the details." Scientists talk about the same thing as "increasing the resolution" of their measurement and observation procedures. But just as the scale of details for bacteriology is not the same as the scale for geology, so the scale for studying status systems by the details of pauses, time spent in simultaneous talk, and so on, is not the same as studying the details of the flow of committee appointments in deans' offices to study the implicit politics of the tradeoff preferences between memos and research articles. The details have to get the beauty on the right scale, or it will not do any good.

Strategic Questions in "Testing" Theories

LET ME START THIS SUMMARY of the theoretical half of getting hypotheses of the right kind for data of the right resolution by a list of advice to researchers designing hypotheses to test theories with observations:

1. Investigators should provide as good theorizing of hypotheses from alternative theories as they do for their own.
2. They should increase the *power* of observations to test their theories: by increasing variance on the causes or, if need be, on the effects; by using multiple measures of both causes and effects; by increasing the number of observations. The basic idea is that investigators want to make the observations such that *if* their theory is true, there is a high probability that they will observe something very unlikely under the alternative, and *if* their theory is false, they will observe something very unlikely under their theory.
3. Investigators should regard their problem of having a single case or a few cases to observe as demanding studying *mechanisms* within the case(s) that produce multiple and repeated phenomena, which are then subject to all the considerations of power in (2) above.
4. One alternative theory is always that they have observed a bunch of random numbers, so very generally a minimum test is that their observations could not have been generated by chance (at least if they are due to chance, that the chance pattern observed is the one predicted rather than random variation not obeying the chance law the investigator theorized).
5. Investigators should use hierarchical thinking *and* hierarchical tests to specify "subtracting off" the variations predicted by alternative theories.

5a. "Real" models to subtract off: Hutterites in fertility studies, Polish peasant anti-Semitism as a predictor of reaction to Martin Luther King in Memphis; ideal type (i.e., in Weber, Prussian) bureaucracy to identify what makes American municipal government efficient or inefficient.

5b. Specifying all the "control variables" measuring a complex model of alternatives, with one (or more) regression (or other similar) coefficients explaining the "residuals" from a regression equation with only the alternatives in it being tested.

5c. Comparing, in "hierarchical linear models": e.g., all cross sectional variation between people subtracted out, to isolate temporal causation, "process," or study processes over time within "the same" group(s) by ethnographic or historical methods

5d. Noting that an "ideal type" that might predict a good deal of what investigators find serves as an alternative theory, from which the "residual," if probable under the investigator's theory, is evidence of added empirical content.

6. As investigators home in on where the troubles lie with their theory, they should increase the *resolution* of their observations. For example, code videotapes for measures of interrupting behavior (who tries interruptions, who wins out, how long two or more people talk at once, when the attention shifts to the interrupter); or code in detail the requests of dean's offices for formation of new committees or new administratively required memos from faculty, to study the shifting preference function of the university in the tradeoff between administrative memos and scholarly papers.

An Overall View of What These Strategies Do

WHAT ALL THESE STRATEGIES DO, it seems to me, is to multiply the number and variety of hypotheses to which investigators can give powerful tests. That is, they allow investigators to step back from the theory under investigation and ask what they can do to give themselves what I would call *focused flexibility* in investigation. Investigators want multiple measures on extreme cases (e.g., on the Sun and on the planets) because they don't know exactly what hypotheses are going to turn out to be relevant, what mechanisms of producing "weather" on the Sun (e.g., sunspots) they are going to need to study that differentiate weather there from weather on Jupiter or on Earth. So investigators want to measure everything they can about sunspots, everything they can about the red spot on Jupiter, and everything they can about hurricanes on Earth. When they find out something new about one of them, they should go observe that with multiple measures on the other cases.

When investigators first get the rough notion that spots might be storms, they want to home in on things that have to do with heat, motion, concentration into spots and sometimes circular motions identifying the spot, and instability of layering of atmospheres. At that "notions" point of the investigation, investigators do not know which of those hypotheses are going to be relevant, so they want to increase their "general strength" of observational discrimination, of observations relevant to a lot of alternative theories. For example, magnetic variations on the scale of the storm may have a lot to do with sunspots, but relatively little with storms on the Earth.

The outline here of main points on testing is largely about methods. But I started off by emphasizing that investigators want the same sort of power for theories. That is, in the first place, investigators want to develop the alternatives to the theory they are currently favoring until they are as good as possible. Investigators do not want to knock down straw men, except for rhetorical purposes. And they want to be very careful indeed with straw men even for rhetorical purposes, because being obviously stupid about what their opponents think and say is not rhetorically effective. So they want the alternatives to be as strong as they can make them, both for scientific and for rhetorical purposes.

But then for each of the theories, investigators want to derive hypotheses that are as discriminating as possible between the theories. Obviously, the most discriminating kind of derivation is to predict that under some new conditions, a variable can be observed that the theory predicts will be between 1.5 and 1.6, or some such. And it is even more discriminating if the theory predicts it will be between 1.56 and 1.57. Fewer alternative theories will predict the more precise constant. Of course, in general, sociology does not have such precise predictions, and does not even give the regression coefficients, units of measurement, the population on which it was measured, precisely enough so that an investigator could compare the coefficients across studies. The main exceptions to this are studies that attempt to combine results across many small studies to get more solid results for policy purposes (Cook, 1991; or large sequences of survey analyses of changes in attitudes over time, carried out at National Opinion Research Center in connection with the General Social Survey [Smith, 1996]).

But aside from that, the more *different* hypotheses investigators have, still in the area of focus, the better. So to go back to the observation of interrupting behavior, an investigator might have the initial hypothesis that higher status people would interrupt more successfully, in the sense of ending up with the other person silent and the eyes turned toward himself (or, more rarely, herself). But then, with high-resolution observations, one might predict that the more nearly equal the status of the interrupter and of the interrupted, the longer the period of both talking should be (and perhaps if the interrupter stops first, he or she will mumble, "Oh, sorry," if the two are of equal status). That is, with more resolution, there are more consequences of the investigator's theory, and more especially of alternative theories, that an investigator can test.

But higher resolution means, too, that one is more likely to be able to find smaller effects, perhaps of the alternative theories. One might expect as an alternative that interruptions would be more successful if they are on the same topic, less successful if they introduce a new topic. Thus, one might predict that the status differences producing a given effect would have to be larger if the interruption was off the topic, that the person on the topic would keep talking for longer even if the other kept talking, or might even say, "Excuse *me*!" There might be special rituals for interrupting an interrupter who is "off the topic," such as shouting, "Point of order!" We would expect status equals of the speaker to be more likely to speak up. Bodies of peers, such as the House of Representatives, should have more "point of order" shouts. The higher one's resolution, still in the area of focus of the set of theories one is working with or against, the more all the theories will yield hypotheses that can be tested, even in the face of the noise of a dominant theory.

Recall the Lévi-Strauss image (1969 [1964]) of his method of studying a complex of myths, of a cloud ("nebula") of symbols in myths, where he looked for contrasts among symbols anywhere in the body of myths, starting from the symbols near the center of his investigations. He imagined each contrast or opposition connected by a line. As he followed the symbols out, finding more contrasts with the ones the starting symbol was contrasted with, and so on, the mesh of the lines remained sparse on the far-away symbols in the cloud, toward the periphery, but got more and more dense toward the middle. He is describing perfectly the main point here, that he became more and more able to do fine discriminations among the symbols toward the center of his cloud and so to check more and more subtle hypotheses there. His resolution came to be higher toward the center, while remaining at its original, lower level toward the periphery of the cloud. The better one's theory, the better one can choose the right methods to test it, and the more delicate and numerous the observations one can make at the focus of the theory, the more one can increase the testability of the theory. Theory and data thus combine to tell us how to improve resolution of observations at the focus of a theory.

Variances, Interactions, Boundaries, Scope Conditions, and General Complexification

LET ME POINT OUT three kinds of enrichment of hypotheses: (1) variations across groups in variances (heteroscedasticity—not as a statistical problem investigators want to get rid of, but as a hypothesis); (2) interaction effects, or "conditional causation"; (3) boundaries of the operation of mechanisms in theories; (4) all of these three adding up to "scope conditions" of any particular theory; and (5) the general complexification of theory in a "fish scale model" of science, where scopes overlap.

Variances

Let me start talking about variances with a very simple example of migration to and from cities. If investigators count the absolute numbers of people who move out of a city (with "city" defined in some sensible way, which is not at all a simple problem), then the bigger a city, the more people move out of it; the number of movers is larger for larger cities. This means that for cities to preserve their large size (and the relative stability of rank ordering of cities shows there is something of this), then the larger the city, the more people, in absolute numbers now, it has to attract. The larger the city, on the average, the larger the number of people who move into the city.

Now, suppose there is an influence on the probability of being attracted to a city, such as the general decline in manufacturing employment that affects particularly cities in the manufacturing industrial belt stretching roughly from a line connecting Boston to Charlotte, North Carolina, sweeping west to a line connecting Milwaukee to St. Louis. All across this area all sizes of cities have been becoming less attractive. The more metropolitan of them (e.g., as measured by amount of wholesaling and financial employment) have been less affected, but relative to the growth of other U.S. metropolises, their growth has been reduced. Investigators would expect that the probabilities of someone chosen at random to be attracted to any of these cities would be reduced. But in a gross way the bigger cities would attract more people, still, than the littler ones.

This would mean that the *distance* that deindustrialization would produce in the *gross* number of people moving in would be larger for the big cities than for the little cities. Chicago would have a bigger gross decline in attractiveness than Peoria, and Detroit a bigger gross decline in attractiveness than Bay City. But roughly speaking the relative sizes of Chicago, Detroit, Bay City, and Peoria are likely to remain the same. So we have here a relatively small cause, this year's deindustrialization, of the size of growth or decline of cities. But this cause of change apparently usually comes out to be roughly proportional to the size the city already has. That is, what happens to individuals who might migrate in, in order for the autocorrelation of city size to be as high as it is, has to be proportional to city size.

It is not well understood why the attractive force of a city has usually been proportional to the size of the city, or what are the mechanisms that bring it about. But since the rank ordering of cities tends to stay fairly stable, in the face of a relatively high probability of people moving out of a city, the causes of in-migration at the individual level have to be more or less proportional to city size. It must, I suppose, be something that makes the number of vacancies of jobs created in a city be roughly proportional to the number of jobs already filled there. It's a scandal that we do not have a theory of why, for example, the variance from year to year in the gross size of in-migration is larger for bigger cities.

When the size of the small causes producing variation in a variable is proportional to the size of the value that variable already has at the aggregate level, the *statistics*, but not the causal substance, are straightened out by taking logs of everything first. We used to take logs to the base 10. But now we take logs to the base e, because if an investigator ever had a theory with differential equations in it, that is the kind of logs we would want. Only a few of us have theories that have differential equations in them, but those who do have dominated those who do not. Presumably, there is a differential of city size, namely, the rate of creation of new jobs, that is a function of city size, which indeed creates a differential equation in the probability of attracting a country boy or girl, so creating a theory that might have an e in it.

But using the base e is only a trick to make the mathematics behave. It does not tell an investigator why little causes have bigger gross effects on the bigger cities, why *each person's* probability of being attracted to Detroit in a given year goes down at about the same percentage as manufacturing employment, as is true of *each person's* probability of being attracted to Bay City. In particular, past causes of in-migration, as well as this one, have been roughly proportional to city size, so that they replaced one of the many more out-migrants in Detroit than there were in Bay City. So the explanation of why Detroit is historically bigger than Bay City is probably roughly the same as the reason it attracts more replacements for its out-migrants than Bay City does—perhaps we need base *e* rather than base 10.

We have a problem, then, of explaining the larger variance of net migration to or from larger cities than from smaller cities, and we tend to bury it in a mathematics that makes the variances equal, rather than causally explaining the higher variances. But we will never know why bigger cities are by and large more attractive than little cities to the average person ready to migrate from central Iowa, until we notice it. Whenever investigators have to take logs to straighten out the statistics, they probably have bigger variances among big things than among little things. They should be able to give an explanation of that, instead of just burying it in a mathematical operation "for methodological purposes," "to reduce skew."

For another example, the biggest inequality in most less developed countries is between people who work in urban industries and people who work in agriculture. If we measure this urban-rural inequality by the ratio of incomes, (or by taking logs in the first place, which is the same thing), we find that the ratio is much larger in poorer countries. Thus, while farmers in the United States are nearly as rich, educated, and highly capitalized (or more highly capitalized, if we count the land value) as urban workers, in Africa south of the Sahara the farmers are much poorer than the urban workers, on average. (South Africa is a funny case, more or less one small rich country and one large poor country, with the same international boundaries and same government; it has very large variances for somewhat different reasons.) Mexico will be in between. So we cannot get rid of *this* difference in variances within by taking logs, because the logs vary, too. The variance of logarithms (and so the ratios) is larger in poorer countries, mainly due to a very large ratio of urban versus rural families.

The absolute differences in incomes are generally larger in richer countries, which means there is an interaction effect on absolute income between richness of countries and whatever puts people on top of the stratification system. The very rich in rich countries have a greater absolute income as a difference from the poor of their own country, and consequently of the world. In the literature people find out again and again that as a country gets richer, the dollar or pound or mark difference between the upper and lower classes gets bigger. We do not have a theory of why that is generally true. One's education, for example, is worth more dollars, but a smaller percentage of GNP per capita, in the United States than in India.

We need a causal theory that would explain why inequality is greater between rural and urban industries in poorer countries, and if it has wide enough scope, it will also explain why one's education would not do one as much good in absolute terms in India as in the United States. So we look at variances, and *if* we find variations in the variances, variations in the amount of inequality, then we need to think about them. We need to study the mechanisms that seem to be at work in the extreme cases—small and big cities, the poor agricultural areas versus the cities in poor countries and in rich ones.

But the fruitfulness of this advice depends on two things. First, people used to thinking with regression equations, which means the majority of sociologists, do not easily think about interaction effects; their method discourages them from it. Second, it is easy to obscure a process that produces interaction effects by taking logarithms (i.e., studying ratios rather than differences), without thinking why ratios are a better measure of distances than differences. Both will be remedied by thinking about the causes of variations in variances, the mechanisms that create larger differences in some places or times than others.

Interaction Effects and Boundaries

By an interaction effect, we mean essentially that some cause has a bigger effect when another variable is high rather than low (or vice versa): a cause has a bigger (or smaller) effect, for instance, if the people studied are black rather than white, dead rather than alive, and so on. An interaction effect is a "conditional" effect of a variable, conditioned on the value of another variable. A particular kind of effect that we call a "boundary" is an interaction effect that is enormous at a given point of a line or surface (or more usually, "has a steep slope" near a line or a surface). A teacher's voice, for example, has a large effect on what students write down up to the walls and doors of the classroom, but no further. So a condition for the teacher's voice to have its effect is that it be within the boundary, marked out by the barriers to perception that we carefully put around this room to produce that boundary effect. Think how hard it would be to learn statistics while listening to a lecture on Russian verbs (a much more difficult subject) going on at the back of the room.

Another example of interaction effects marking boundaries of a given causal system is found in Paige (1999). Jeffery Paige's basic argument is that many variables important in historical analysis of whole societies are simultaneously ones that vary over time *and* that make other causes differentially effective. For example, during modernization of economies, the size of the urban manual manufacturing, construction, and transportation working class first increases as the society industrializes, then decreases again as its economy becomes dominantly a "service" economy. Obviously, the effect of mobilizing the urban manual working class on political issues is larger if there is a higher proportion of such workers. Thus, we would expect the origin of working-class parties in western Europe and Anglo North America to be a powerful effect on politics in the last quarter of the nineteenth century and the first half of the twentieth century (a bit earlier in England, a bit later in Italy and Spain). But we should find very few large working-class parties before about 1875, many starting after that but before 1950, and then few or none starting after 1950. If we are looking at the effect of "industrial rather than craft" unions on Anglo-American national politics, we would want to draw the time boundary of the main effect of this contrast later—say, about 1900. But if we wanted to see the effect of the anarchism of "agricultural proletarians," we would put the boundary earlier—say, 1800. We would expect continuing effects of that anarchism later in later industrializing countries—say, in Spain up to about 1940, but in England only until about 1900. The radicalism of white southern rural proletarians up to about 1920 in the American South, but disappearing much earlier in the northern prairie states, was a within-country effect of industrialization and modernization.

This looks like an interaction effect between time and mobilization, so mobilization of industrial workers has big effects during one time period, of agricultural workers earlier, of public school teachers later. It is sensible, then, to distinguish the "context" by time boundaries, with the "industrial age" of the United States, Britain, France, and Germany being between about 1875 and 1950. But really we are using time as a measure of the proportion of the population who are urban manual working-class employed workers, especially manual workers employed in big bureaucratic "assembly line" organizations. This makes mobilization of workers have big effects in one time period, but not before or after.

By and large, when investigators find interaction effects being quite strong in social life, we will find that social life, so to speak, "makes use of" them. Barriers to perception are deep parts of that. A door is an important *legal entity* because it allows the norms unique to a family or a business to govern interaction within it, but allows norms of "public spaces" to govern activity outside. The law says breaking and entering is a crime; the law says a police officer cannot *come in the door* unless invited or unless a warrant has been obtained; the law then gives an American the right to lock or barricade the door, if the door is on one's own property or property one rents. The law also says that if the meter reader cannot get in without breaking and entering to read the meter, the householder has to arrange to permit a reading; the law will not give the meter reader the right to break down the door to read the meter, or to wake the householder with a siren early on Saturday to read it; the law says that in case of fire, a fireman can break and enter.

All these rules are organized around the door as a legal entity. But if we set out to analyze the deep sociological structure behind the legal importance of doors, we find that they are crucial because barriers to perception and to entry produce interaction effects, so that some causes from outside cannot work inside, and some inside do not work outside. We make multiple social uses of those things—of doors, for example—because we want some causes to have private effects, some public effects. That is, *because* doors have interaction effects on the causal reach of speech or other action, laws to protect family privacy use doors as a crucial legal entity.

So interaction effects are especially likely to be surrounded by social forces that *increase* their boundary-making effects. Lots of mechanisms have their boundaries where there are deliberately created social boundaries, within which some causes have their effects, outside which *other* causes have *their* effects. The same is true of a person's skin, and also clothing—penetration of either is strongly socially controlled, but skin had an enormous interaction effect even before it was socially reinforced (e.g., with clothing). Clothing makes access of cold winds difficult, as well as being a reasonably effective contraceptive because the penetration of clothing is socially controlled. Skin and clothing are natural boundaries creating interaction effects of many variables inside and outside them. But those boundary functions are used and magnified by social life, and rendered impotent by special arrangements to weaken them—for example, in the operating room and in the marital bed.

I emphasize the difficulty of regression equation thinking to deal with interaction effects because ethnography and history have much less trouble with this. One need not be a gifted ethnographer to see that a teacher's voice has a different effect inside than outside the classroom. One has to be a very gifted survey researcher to find this obvious effect, inventing new measurements and new statistical procedures.

Similarly, one does not need deep historical talents to see that industrial workers were mobilized into unions very rapidly in the Great Depression of the 1930s in the United States, but that teachers and other national and local civil servants were mobilized very rapidly from about 1960 to about 1990. Finding the causes of this interaction effect of mobilizing efforts by survey research methods would be very difficult indeed.

I would say that on the average, a well-documented interaction effect is about four times as likely to be published as a well-documented unconditional cause. This is partly for aesthetic reasons, that an interaction effect is more entrancing. This, combined with the ease with which many interaction effects are found by ethnographic or historical work, is part of the explanation of why ethnography and history are more fun to read. But also an interaction effect is often something that is socially important, because somebody *wanted* to keep some causes within bounds, or to keep other causes out, or both. An investigator, at least in theory, should home in on interaction effects, especially ones that are obvious "assumptions" of social life, such as the social effects of barriers to perception. Goffman did, and look where it got him: famous.

Scope

Sometimes the core processes that an investigator wants to theorize about have more or less natural boundary conditions, within which the causes are important and connect causes to outcomes, while outside them, they work fitfully or not at all. The theory of hurricanes, for example, works when the change of seasons produces a large-scale inversion of temperatures, with warmer air near the ground or near the sea surface, warmer so it is lighter than the colder layers above it. (Air gets thinner naturally at altitude. The surface air is ordinarily warmer than the higher layers. If the temperature gradient is not too steep, the density of air closer to the ground compensates for it being warmer, and the whole weather system is reasonably stable.) When the water gets warmer in summer, but the higher air does not warm as much (because the conversion of light energy from the Sun into heat is done by the water or ground absorbing light and emitting heat, and air is transparent to much of the Sun's energy), it produces instability.

This instability makes any hole "punched" in the cold, heavy layer an escape valve for all the air that "wants to rise." The surrounding higher, dense cold air is then a source of pressure on the other, hot air beneath it but away from the hole, forcing it to flow rapidly toward the low pressure under the hole. The hole, the warm air below, and the developing hurricane all gather force as more and more air flows up through the hole, and so in toward the hole at the surface; the process goes on as long as the hurricane travels over the warm water. One gets the big hurricanes on the east coast of the Americas and Asia, where the summer sun has heated the sea nearest the Tropic of Cancer—namely, the Caribbean and the South China Sea—and the prevailing winds drive it across the warm sea toward the west.

Sociologists are not interested in this unless they study the sociology of disaster. But the methodological point is that this particular theory of weather will be relevant mostly in July, August, and September in the Caribbean and the Atlantic Ocean to the east of the Caribbean, and over the same months in Taiwan, the Philippines, and South China and the ocean east of them. The *scope* of the theory, then, is quite restricted, because the mechanism of the inversions, the holes, the accumulation of energy as the storm moves over warm seas, the dissipation of that energy as the storm moves north over colder seas or over the land. It is an elegant theory, but it is definitively local because it relies on an interaction of heating with layering that depends on seasonal variations in the angle of the Sun.

It is inherent in the theory of the stability of layers of air (or of magma, the semi-molten stone under the Earth's crust) of different densities and different temperatures that heat inversions in stable density-heat layering create instabilities. So there is a general theory of stability (and so of instability) of such systems that applies to all the atmosphere, all the oceans, and all the magma of the Earth, and presumably to the Sun and other stars. But the location of these inversions in the atmosphere over oceans, having stronger effects on wind patterns on the western sides of those oceans in the northern hemisphere in the months of late summer and early fall, is a specification of that general theory, which makes hurricanes grow there and decline elsewhere. The specification applies only to atmospheres, only in the subtropics, only in the hurricane season.

This lengthy example is meant to illustrate why theories that are very valuable and elegant are not important to the great variety of scientists. Quite often the scope of a theory is defined by where the mechanisms in it have boundary conditions, so it really amounts to an interaction effect causing a given kind of cause to "die out" as investigators get outside its "scope." For the application of this notion to something more social than a hurricane, consult Paige (1999) or the "Clemens Time Short Version" in chapter 5.

The hurricane mechanism is a convenient model for illustrating how scope conditions for theories are created by interaction effects because the scope conditions themselves vary in a regular, repeated pattern. Warmer seas (seas stay warm longer because water holds more heat energy) with denser, higher layers of colder air create inversions regularly in the same places at the same seasons, and the prevailing winds carry the conditions across the oceans long enough for hurricanes to build up. The storms regularly break up shortly after hitting the land on the other side, as the scope conditions of the hurricane mechanism disappear. The exposition of these special theories can be found in elementary textbooks in the physical sciences.

Similar scope conditions govern the processes of centralization of "national" governments during wartime, with the accompanying changes in stratification systems, labor relations, growth of administrative capacity for centralized taxation, rationing, industrial development, and other such mechanisms; after the wars centralization tends to slow down or stop, or even occasionally to reverse itself. Labor history, for example, ordinarily skips over the wars, because the history becomes one of government regulation rather than mobilization for organizing conflicts. It is relatively hard to find out from a reading of labor history of the United States that the big booms in unionization of the labor force took place during the two world wars. That is, with the beginning of a war the scope conditions implicit in labor history's "radicalism of workers" mechanism are crossed, and other conditions embedded in national reorganization of stratification processes and the suppression of some kinds of internal conflict, but not suppression of "bargaining," determine union growth rates.

Similarly, the rate of increase of educational achievement scores drops sharply in the summertime, actually going negative for some social groups. Much of the gap in the United States between the achievements of the social classes and races occurs during the summer rather than during the school year. In public policy Americans blame the schools for the outcomes of summer vacation. It is very hard to find out the summer effect, and the causes of educational achievement in summer, by reading educational sociology (but see Heyns, 1978). The scope conditions for educational sociology's mechanisms are not met in summer, so we do not study learning in the summer. Learning in the summer presumably goes on, but it is not well measured by the achievement tests we use. Heat differences drive winds in the winter as well as in the hurricane season, but the methods of satellite photography that show us the hurricane results of late summer and early fall seasons do not show as much in the winter. Summer produces racial and class gaps in achievement test scores and produces hurricanes. Seasonal boundaries in both cases are produced by obvious interaction effects that create scope boundaries of the relevant theories.

Complexification and Fish Scale Models of Science

This analysis of scope conditions for theories suggests that the best social organization of science might be a patchwork, created by the boundary conditions for mechanisms, in turn created by interaction effects. This means that the boundary effects themselves tend to disappear theoretically in the cracks between disciplines. One methodological consequence of this is the loss of much of the creativity and intellectual excitement that comes from studying interaction effects. Economists compute their regression equations without organizational variables. Labor historians' stories of dramatic class conflict stop with the onset of war. Educational sociologists compute regression equations or randomized experiments on teaching methods during the school year. Tropical storm specialists fly instrumented planes into hurricanes only during the hurricane season. While disciplines are primarily social structures that make very little scientific sense, some disciplinary boundaries represent boundaries in the world between which mechanisms work at specific times and places. The boundary between planetologists and solar physicists, for example, is such a sensible boundary based on different mechanisms. But there is a lot of scientific mileage where the interaction effects dominate, as when the solar wind hits the upper atmosphere, and they meld solar theory and planetology.

Lévi-Strauss (1969 [1964]) urges that archival ethnographic analysts of myths should push their way toward the periphery, *in order to* understand what is going on in the center of their field of study. Outside the scope of the kind of theories such analysts usually work with, there will be other theories whose scope is outside theirs: on a larger scale or a smaller scale, with different mechanisms dominating, accessible with different methodologies for summer learning than for school-year learning. By tracing education into the summer, they learn more about what is distinctive of schools.

When investigators come toward the edge of *their* cloud, they will *also* be coming into the edge of another scientist's cloud. As we go down from the world-system, for example, we come to the point where we have to know something about how the State Department works, how the CIA works, what their interrelation is, which one deals with trade policy, or which one has better lines into the Department of Defense and its intelligence apparatus.

Now, while world-system theory more or less originated in sociology, with Immanuel Wallerstein at the historical end and with John Meyer at the contemporary world government end, as investigators work toward the periphery of global forces toward the level of nations, they will approach the work of nationally oriented political scientists. As world-systems sociologists study the interrelations of Wallerstein's core and periphery (richer versus poorer countries), they will be over against the international trade economists, pushing into the edge of their cloud. In the internal developments in poorer countries as the world-system penetrates, they will be coming up against the economic development field, a subfield of economics, sociology, and history where the disciplines have routinely talked across boundaries. And they may get as far as the anthropology of contact between "primitive" and "advanced" societies: Pierre Bourdieu in his early studies of Morocco, or Clifford Geertz in his studies in Morocco and Indonesia, both examined economic development and influences from outside. World-systems sociologists have to learn from all these people, to be any good at world-systems theory. But the total theory of all the world has to have all of these things in it. One investigator cannot work on everything. If an investigator starts in the seventeenth-century Netherlands or in Poland, as Wallerstein did, he or she is probably not ever going to become enough of an expert on the CIA to compete with somebody who specializes in it.

It seems to me that "scope" and "complexity" intertwine here. Methodologically we ought not to stay out of other disciplines. We need to read their regression equations to figure out why they do not apply in our bailiwick. Otherwise we will be too ignorant to do our work. But also, since both the seventeenth-century Netherlands and the CIA are immensely complex, we cannot expect to become a core member of the other discipline. So *both* we and they have to cover the fringes of our and their respective Lévi-Strauss clouds, or the edges of our and their respective fish scales (Campbell, 1969). And both of the subdisciplines will have to rely for the center of the other cloud on the next fish scale over on the other discipline.

If something is properly described, especially in its scope conditions, and if it is true in one discipline, then it is true in another. One cannot theorize Jupiter as one theorizes the Sun, but what is true about the Sun is still true when it comes to the Sun's interaction with Jupiter.

Now, back to testing hypotheses. It is perfectly all right to do the most complex of hierarchical statistical tests about alternative theories of learning during the school year, or historical comparative tests in different industries' workers' mobilization of organizing strikes toward the end of the Great Depression in the United States. It is not appropriate to think that the regression equation of test scores holds during summer, or that the causes of unionization during the Depression explain unionization during the two great wars of the twentieth century. That is because the interaction effects between season and learning mechanisms, or between union organizing mechanisms and peacetime versus wartime, are so strong that all but the best scholars are simply bewildered that their theories and methods do not work across scope boundaries. Nothing in the logic of hierarchical testing on an investigator's own scale of the fish implies it will work on another fish scale.

The general point about alternative theories and deriving the best alternative theory as a null hypothesis is to look for boundary conditions or other symptoms of interaction effects. It may be wise to look for them in neighboring disciplines. The sociology of culture extends "below" the texts, and much of the relevant knowledge and hypotheses are in linguistics; the sociology of organizations extends "above and before" current organizations, in the historical process building institutions and nation states; the sociology of social movements has as its lowest social-psychological elements the cognition of competences of cosmopolitans by recruits who are only locally competent. Each of these boundaries shows strong interaction effects at the boundary, and different kinds of hypotheses studied by different disciplines lie across the boundary. New alternatives to the standard hypotheses can often be easily derived by going near a disciplinary boundary.

Summary on Testing

....

STATISTICS IS THE SCIENCE OF RANDOM PROCESSES, the standard alternative theory suggested by the phrase "null hypothesis." It has the basic form: "there is nothing going on here but the generation of random motions in what the investigator thought was a causal space." Because there is a great deal of random motion in social life, and because there is a great deal of random noise in social science techniques of observation, every social science finding has to show that it is not likely to be simply noise. Because that alternative theory is one of the few in social science that is well formulated mathematically, it is in general the hardest for ordinary social scientists to learn. We spend much of our teaching time on methods in statistics because mathematical theories are hard for us. It is also required because randomness is the most pervasive alternative theory.

But this has the unfortunate side effect that the word *hypothesis* hardly occurs outside statistics courses. The "power" of a hypothesis, for example, is hardly ever analyzed except against a random alternative, as in "statistical power." The basic argument of this chapter is that this is nearly always a mistake, because sociology is now empirically and theoretically strong enough that we can almost always design a better null hypothesis. This is easiest to see when we notice that our first statistics courses very often focus on estimating the sampling variation of a mean—something that never occurs again in one's methodological reading until one has to teach elementary statistics. Because a multiple regression equation is a hierarchical test of one theory against a substantive alternative, the lowest level of statistical test actually used in routine social science is a test of a partial regression coefficient.

The main exception is in experimental work, where alternative theories are eliminated instead, or also, by experimental design. In that case there may be only a single coefficient (e.g., a difference between means of experimental versus control groups—this is equivalent to a regression coefficient of the outcome on a single variable without statistical controls) estimated and tested against random alternatives.

But the observational power of a hypothesis is a function of the overall theoretical situation, and depends as well on exactness of concepts and mechanisms and observational procedures for both the theory being tested and its main substantive alternatives. As a rule of thumb, one should spend as much time learning the alternative theories of the phenomena one is studying as one spends learning the statistical theories that are the minimum standard. A really beautiful test of new hypotheses (such as Roger V. Gould's *Collision of Wills* [2003]) can use very simple statistics, because it is so well designed theoretically and the observations are so exactly relevant to the theory that the result in the table leaps to the eye, then the next table confirms it. One may occasionally notice that there are asterisks where there are supposed to be, showing that the result is not random noise.

This chapter examines the logic of several alternative ways of designing observational tests of whether a given theory has more information in it about the phenomena being investigated than the extant alternatives. The workhorse is the multiple regression equation, in which we summarize the alternative theories by a set of variables that act as causes of the phenomenon we are trying to explain. The simplest alternative theory then might be called "a congeries of simple alternative causes," usually assumed to be linearly related to the outcome, additive in their effects, and perfectly (or at least very well) measured. Even if one does not believe all these assumptions about the alternative theories, the results are often sufficiently illuminating to be worthwhile. The main practical trouble is that sociologists measure everything badly, so that the residuals from the alternative theories are really not cleaned of the alternatives, and they may still be operating in the measured partial cause. Various devices are useful for improving the alternatives, but the most fruitful one is to better theorize each theory represented by a variable and then measure them better.

A slightly more complex system for eliminating alternatives occurs when one wants to test against the alternatives of all theories or mechanisms that operate within units of analysis at one level (e.g., individual adult people) against mechanisms at a different level (e.g., organizational mechanisms). A closely related problem is to eliminate all dispositional characteristics of the people involved in a process, from the effects of variability in the process itself. Various devices for such tests can be constructed. The first kind are often called "hierarchical linear modeling," the second kind "fixed effect models." The theory of what one is trying to do is not difficult, but the statistical procedures tend to get hairy.

A third major technique is to use the principle of orthogonal design to provide more information to start with on the differences between theories. Oversampling the big positive and negative residuals (e.g., rich blacks and poor whites) is an example of such methods. The basic idea is to design the study so as to maximize the information on the difference between the theory being mainly tested and its alternatives.

A fourth major technique is to scan nearby disciplines for alternative theories not prevalent in the investigator's own discipline, and to look for boundary conditions of the process being studied. This tends to produce more theories about conditional (or "interaction effect") theories, which allows the investigator to multiply tests of whether the mechanism works where he or she theorizes it works, by showing that when the conditions for the mechanism to work do not exist, the effects do not exist either.

8   Improving Theories with Data

To conclude, I will try to outline and illustrate what a major research program looks like. It is on the level of a research program, with several papers or a book as an outcome, that the back-and-forth movement between the improvement of methods, then the resulting improvement of theory, and then back to improving methods and then theory again, becomes clear. Such a research program may take from five to ten years, and may result in a new line of research, built on a solid empirical foundation and a theoretical apparatus suited to the empirical terrain.

I will first develop the notion, borrowed from C. Wright Mills (1959), that the process of developing such a program is one of simultaneously developing the methods and the theory in a fashion that he calls "crafting." This means fitting the theory to the truths shown by the methods, then sharpening the methods to tell more about the theory, then improving the theory again, and so on, not quite indefinitely.

Then I will propose three standards by which one can keep track of failures and successes in this process as it develops: elegance, power, and economy. The three-concept phrase is common in describing mathematical beauty, but I will try to twist it to guide the messy business of social science advance. The process of finding a proof in mathematics is not as beautiful as the end result, so the analogy is not as distant as it seems (Polya, 1954). But first, a brief description of the criteria.

By "elegance" I mean the experience of things starting to "click into place." The fact fits exactly into the theory, and the theory fits the fact exactly. Bertrand Russell somewhere describes it as the "Aha!" experience. It makes one understand why Archimedes might have jumped from his bath shouting, "Eureka! I have found it," when he recognized that the volume of water displaced by his body must equal the volume of the rise in the water level (perhaps spilling over the edge of a full bath). Then the theory of the way to get the volume of a supposedly gold object so that its weight would tell the gold content, and the theory of buoyancy and why intact boats float, followed neatly.

I know of no way to define elegance other than by example, and the resulting responses of "Aha!" and "Eureka!" The contrast between my own laboriously crafted fit of method to the degree of oppression of slaves, versus the neatness of using the "No answer" to a paper-and-pencil survey that was using classroom authority to get an answer, as a measure of school rebellion, does not measure up to Archimedes, but I hope it will do.

By "power" I mean the sort of thing that Archimedes saw as the consequence of being able to estimate the amount of gold in a crown for why boats float, and float lower when loaded. That is, the principle of displacement of water by an object had many consequences, tying together seemingly disparate facts. This illustrates power for explaining a lot of things with a few principles. I will give illustrations of power from Heimer and Staffen's (1998b) development of the concept of "responsibility," which ties together rational action theory in changing situations with the generosity of care for the utilities of others. They apply it to many problems in the uncertain areas related to the care of badly damaged newborn infants in the family and the hospital. See the "Heimer and Staffen Responsibility Short Version," below.

Purely intellectual economy is illustrated in a small intellectual area by the power of the extensions of displacement to buoyancy by Archimedes. He needs very little more than his displacement observation to encompass a great deal. Some of the comments on mechanisms in chapter 6 also illustrate the principle of economy. For example, the export of Griswold mechanisms to a wide variety of high-culture fields shows a general intellectual economizing effect of getting the right oversimplification, so that it has wide applicability. In the "Stinchcombe Information Short Version," below, the discussion of the economical fit between the nature of the theory and the choice of the department within the organization as the unit of analysis illustrates the concept. The motto form of the principle of economy is Occam's razor: Do not multiply entities needlessly. We are interested in the economy of methods as distinct from theories, and much of the book has been devoted to getting as much information as possible about a theory from as few well-designed observations as possible.

Theories as Crafted

THE USUAL METAPHOR IN SOCIOLOGY for the connection of theory with data is "derived." We have a general theory, then we specify its "operational definitions," and derive empirical results from the two sorts of things. Theory comes from some vague place outside the research process; its components are sometimes called "axioms," with the vague notion that they might be like the axioms of geometry in Euclid. Another metaphor is "generalization"—the notion that we observe a pattern in the facts, then generalize tentatively to a universe to which it might apply. We then look for the pattern in a sample from the universe, and either confirm or deny the hypothesis that our pattern was "general." In this mode of thought, the "universe" to which we are trying to generalize, and the units of analysis that make it up, are often the main representation of theory in the investigation. We know the causation from the pattern, and the scope of the theory from the definition of the universe, and the relation of the facts to the theory is defined by the sample representing the universe correctly. The first of these styles is usually called "deductive," the second "inductive." I will urge a middle ground, with the right metaphor being that theories are "crafted" in the course of the investigation (Mills, 1959).

Facts, in this view, may show investigators where there is a gap in the theory, exploratory methods show us the approximate size and shape of the gap, and the theory is crafted to fit that shape. The improbability *a priori* of exactly fitting the gap gives some credibility to the theory so crafted, and insofar as it suggests the shape of other gaps or anomalies, and these improbably shaped gaps turn out to be exactly fitted, then it both becomes more credible and gives greater empirical content to the theory. The metaphor of crafting theories to the exact factual shape of a theoretical and factual gap seems to fit my experience as a methodologist and as a theorist better than either the deductive (or "Euclidean") or the inductive (or "sampling a universe") metaphors.

The big problem with the crafting metaphor, however, is commonly called the "degrees of freedom" problem, or the *post hoc, ergo propter hoc* problem (roughly, "After we know what a theory had to fit, it is often easy to fit any theory to it"). Suppose one has a hole in a brick wall, and a quantity of wet mortar. One then wets the hole so the mortar will make a bond, stuffs the hole full of the mortar, smoothes it off, and lets it "set," keeping it damp. The mortar exactly fits the gap, so is an elegant solution to the theoretical problem. The problem is that mortar is deliberately made so it will fit all shapes and kinds of wall anomalies, so it does not actually tell anything about what the problem of the wall was. It has too many degrees of freedom, so it can fit anything.

In my early book *Constructing Social Theories* (Stinchcombe, 1968), whose title also suggests the crafting metaphor, I said that if students had a correlation they were interested in, and they could not think of at least three theories that might explain it, they should choose another profession. One's mind, then, has too many degrees of freedom in being able to construct several theories to fit. That a particular one, which the student crafted to fit, does fit, is not much evidence against the others. Or otherwise put, exactly because the student did not craft any theories that failed to fill the gap, the fit was a condition of even considering the theory.

The empiricist way out of this—a good way—is to take a sample twice as big as needed in the first place, split it in half, develop the theory on the first half, then "test" it on the second half. This at least shows that one is not exactly filling a gap that only occurred once through sampling variation. But an even better strategy when doing ethnographic fieldwork is to develop the theory by the iterative method suggested by Becker (see the "short version" in chapter 3; or Becker, 1958) and then choose a case to study further that differs on some variables thought to be crucial to the operation of the mechanisms in the theory.

Suppose one has a theory developed to fit ethnographic fieldwork in one urban NICU (neonatal intensive care unit; Heimer and Staffen, 1998c; or see the "short version," below), then has tested it by doing fieldwork in another. There is, then, a neat fit of the theory to the first NICU with one-third single mothers, half without private health insurance, in an environment in which the hospital's liability for releasing a child to a family that cannot take care of it is very salient. But theories of the mechanisms of dealing with uncertainties of the responsibility of families developed in such an environment may not generalize to an NICU where most of the parents are married, have insurance, and have a car to make visiting the hospital easy. For example, a very big predictor of the level of responsibility of the baby's father to the baby is whether or not he is married to the mother; in the first NICU this was a massive problem, in the other a minor one. In the first hospital, then, many of the mothers had to take all the hard knocks; in the other they took "only" most of them.

Thus, picking an NICU as different as possible in its client base is justified by the nature of the mechanisms located in the first one. It should be
as different as possible *on the variables that are central to the mechanism
being theorized*. If there is a gap in the theory of the relationship between
organizations and people assuming responsibility, and one has a theory
that fits that gap in one setting, seeing whether it applies in a maximally
theoretically different setting is a strong test of generalizability. Crafting the theory to fit the gap allows one to theorize about where would
be the best case to test the theory for generality. If the answer is that the
theory is like wet mortar, suitable for any gap, then it is a bad theory; it
has no empirical content. If it fits carefully crafted data or another quite
different unit, it is powerful.

What Does Crafting Mean?

MORE THAN 90 PERCENT of what we sociologists write will be borrowed
from someone else, and that will be especially true of the theory and
methods part of a paper (or book). This leads to the most important methodological principle of all: Know a lot about the subject and what other
people (especially people who have thought deeply) think about it. The
implicit action implication of chapter 3 on economy is that the library is
the most economical source of data and theories. When one spends less
than about half of one's research time reading, one is very often wasting
a lot of time showing what is already known. It is, of course, an economy
in looking for sources in a library if one already has a very good idea of
what is probably true. But it is even more likely that one will design a
study efficiently if one knows a big chunk of what is in the library about
it. Crafting is noticing, for example, that a great deal of the activity of the
king of Poland in early modern times had to do with managing the duties
and privileges of Jews rather than of the cities they lived in, and so going
to find the books on Polish and Ukrainian Jews (in early modern times a
crucial fact is that much of the Ukraine was part of Poland or Lithuania,
an important guide to what to look for in libraries), as well as reading
the books on cities. The ratio of reading to investigation will often be
somewhat less if the researcher plans to write ethnography papers.

Perhaps the best analogy for building a research program is that in
technological advance, most of the parts are "off the shelf." The advantage of such parts is that they are known to work and have been perfected
by many minor improvements before they became standard enough to
be reliably on the shelf. Of course, an innovation is more likely to have

already been made if the parts central to it have been around for a long time, and so it will not be an innovation. The same with scholarship: the borrowed parts of a real innovation are fairly likely to be themselves newly developed; innovations of substantial magnitude are likely to combine the more fundamental innovations of the distant past (which became fundamental because they were widely useful) with what just came into the inventory of methods or theories.

For example, the JAVA programming language for the Internet could not conveniently be written until the UNIX operating system had developed many subvarieties, all of which might use it on the Internet. UNIX was designed to work in many different computers, so was a convenient place to start to write a programming language that would run on those many machines. This was essential for a language for programming for an Internet that would connect Sun, Macintosh, Hewlett-Packard, and Windows. Then again, because UNIX and JAVA were both open systems (that is, having publicly available, often free, codes that programmers could improve), people could figure out how to make new programming for the Internet function efficiently with them. Microsoft stumbled along afterward trying to develop code borrowed from UNIX and JAVA so it could monopolize it. In general, software one can monopolize is not very good for communication systems. If Microsoft had a patent on English, and one bought a license to translate *War and Peace*, and translated it into the English of Bill Gates, Tolstoy would be to us a minor Russian count, himself patented by the Orthodox Church.

The negative impact of secrecy on the advance of knowledge is illustrated by a deep dip in new physics in the early 1940s, when secrecy reigned because radar and the atom bomb were military secrets; one was forbidden to take a piece of a radar machine to design something else, even a laboratory machine. The fact that 90 percent of a person's innovation is part of the common heritage means that monopolies on that heritage are bad methodology.

So when students doing a Ph.D. fit their particular gap, many of the parts that fit will be in the journals and in graduate textbooks, though some of the best parts will be in recent articles, and in the classics. The fruitfulness of using *mechanisms* to build theories (discussed in detail in chapter 6) depends on this: a mechanism is a ready-made part that may fit as a part of an investigator's theory in his or her gap. Investigators, of course, would rather have a mechanism that they know works, has empirical and theoretical support on other problems, or has a literature dedicated to the mechanism itself.

Theoretical craftsmanship mainly works like the cultural *bricoleur* that Lévi-Strauss talks about as an analogy for creation of new myths from the symbols of the old. A *bricoleur* in southern France was a craftsman who would put together a machine for one purpose (say, a lamp) by using a part made for another purpose (say, a shell casing made to fit flat at the back in the breech of a gun), because some feature of that part was useful in the new purpose (e.g., the flatness made it rest nicely on a flat table); it might have incidental features that were very convenient (e.g., the lamp wire could go through the hole made for the shell's firing mechanism); and its structure was adequate to the purpose (a strong shell casing would make a very durable lamp, though originally meant for confining the explosive).

Lévi-Strauss first points out that investigators will not understand the lamp, and where it comes from, without understanding something about artillery. But also they will not understand the craftsman's creativity unless they understand that the world is made up of usable pieces, already formed. And culture (including science) is made up of creations, much of whose creativity is the new use of old parts.

When I am in one of my moods, I urge that Ph.D. examinations have the purpose of certifying that it is okay for a student to be ignorant the rest of his life of all things that were not on the exam. My argument here is that the part one needs to build a lamp may be over there in artillery engineering. To be a theorist, and so to be a good methodologist because methodology is good if it solves deep theoretical problems, one needs to borrow from all over.

The place I have most systematically tried to exemplify this is in *Constructing Social Theories* (1968), which is all about theories available in the early 1960s, so has few new ideas for students today. It was accurately criticized for being shamelessly eclectic by a brilliant Marxist anthropologist, Marvin Harris. He did not like the notion that Marxism was merely a mine in which a non-Marxist theorist could find materials that might be used in a theory being built for whatever was being explained. More particularly, I suppose, such eclecticism might be applied to politics as an excuse for theorizing how a compromise with the bourgeoisie might work. To have them in the same theory book as a geopolitical mechanism for explaining the distribution of things like military boundaries, or network theories of why the Port of New York made a metropolis out of New York City, while equal tonnage going through Norfolk, Virginia, still made Norfolk a small provincial city, undermined the political function of Marxist theories.

Now readers may not want to know why the boundary between Spain and France falls in the Pyrenees, or why Norfolk is a little city although many big ports are big cities, but both facts are theorized in the book. And readers may not want to know that Marxism looks, on the surface, different from Parsonianism, *even though* both are built with functionalist mechanisms. But I was trying to show how we should act *if* we had any of those problems. And the answer I gave was, "Borrow whatever works to build a theory for wherever one needs it." The argument of this book is that the same advice can be applied to methods.

Crafting Methods

OBVIOUSLY SOME LARGE PART of methods consists of formulating what sort of observable phenomena are implied by a substantive theory. I have developed this idea in chapter 7 under the label of the "power" of a hypothesis to accept or refute a theory. The theoretical concepts will often be connected to observable phenomena by "observational theories" of various degrees of complexity. For example, when a culture of the impossibility of learning everything in the curriculum, combined with a student model of what a general practitioner would have to know, is supposed to be connected to cutting corners in first-year medical school, the *saliency* of that corners-cutting culture in the concrete reality is a central concept. So Becker and colleagues (1961; also Becker, 1958) developed a theory of observation that describes an observational variable that we might call "number of spontaneous mentions." The central methodological contribution is to offer a theory of various ways of observing more versus less spontaneous mentions. This is true methodological craftsmanship, because it gives a situationally specific measure of saliency, uncorrupted by the researcher artificially increasing saliency by asking a question about the matter whose saliency is being observed.

Similarly, I observe that in the Caribbean (see the "short version" of my methodological appendix [Stinchcombe, 1995c], in chapter 3) nearly all "colored people" (people of European ancestry among people also with slave ancestors) were born in the islands. In the color of individuals or color composition of populations, then, I have a very rough measure of assimilation to European culture among slaves and ex-slaves. This is because sex between whites and blacks more often happened in the islands, where Europeans ran things, than in Africa, where there had been few Europeans. So if I want to know what sort of activities are more common among slaves who are born on the islands, I might look for activities more common among colored rather than black people. For archival purposes, the color of slaves (or of free people) was much more salient and more often mentioned than their occupations, or how well they spoke the conqueror's language.

For women, there were three big activities more common among colored than black people: colored women were more often mistresses or prostitutes, more often household servants, and more often petty traders. They were also much more often manumitted, set free from slavery. Colored men were, much more often than blacks, gang bosses or managers, craftsmen, and household servants. They, too, were much more often manumitted. That is, the "colored" of both sexes were more likely to do activities that required regular and nuanced communication with white people, and receive the great reward that they could be legally free even in a slave society. All these things make it essential that one keep colored slaves and colored free people separate from those called black or white, though in America now the use of the word *colored* is considered demeaning.

So methodologically I had an empirically well-defined gap in the theory of slavery and manumission: colored people were more often manumitted, and more often had jobs that required communication with whites. By observing that the distinctive biography of colored people required that they (most likely) be born in the islands, of slave mothers with more contact with whites, I had also a potential explanation. The methodological craftsmanship depends on looking for all sorts of data on differences between colored and black that bear on the various elements of that theory, because the theoretical gap is well defined by the preliminary data.

Creoles (in the Caribbean this usually means people with at least partial African ancestry who were born in the islands; in Spanish islands it also sometimes means white people born in the islands; in Caribbean parts of Louisiana creoles were and are very often white) are evidently more likely to be in occupations that involve social interaction with whites, being more or less autonomous agents of whites, or being people whose skills whites rely on. The kinds of people who get manumitted tend to have the same characteristics that we have just identified among the occupations colored people occupy.

The only one that really surprised me was that mistresses and prostitutes were often manumitted. While there would not have been many colored slaves to start with if there had to be a lot of communication to start a plantation owner–black slave sexual relation, evidently even slave owners wanted slave mistresses and prostitutes they could talk to. And they seem to have been more likely to free those of their mistresses (and the children) whom they could talk to. My theory of slavery has somehow to squeak into that gap of sexuality leading to intimacy, and by way of intimacy to freedom: morally suspicious, but then the craft of research sometimes has morally suspicious requirements. The "Stinchcombe Slavery Short Version" presents part of the theory this methodological trick helped build.

Stinchcombe Slavery Short Version

Summarized from Arthur L. Stinchcombe, "Planter Power, Freedom, and Oppression of Slaves in the 18th Century Caribbean," in *Sugar Island Slavery in the Age of Enlightenment: The Political Economy of the Caribbean World* (Princeton: Princeton University Press, 1995), pp. 125–152. All page numbers with no further identification are to this source. Original table numbers are preserved.

In the late eighteenth century Caribbean variations in the intensity of slavery had two classes of causes. The first class of causes was variations in the political power of slave owners, a social structural determinant. The political power of planters was probably greatest in Barbados and perhaps weakest in the Bahamas. So Bahamas slavery was not very intense, in the sense that liberties of slaves were not very restricted; Barbados slavery was very restrictive. The three main causes of sugar planter power were the degree to which the island economy was completely dominated by sugar plantations, the solid formation of class solidarity among them by long-continued sugar dominance, and less interference in slave owner local government by the colonial empires. Barbados was the earliest sugar island, had almost no other major products, had an elected council that advised the governor and on occasion sent a recalcitrant governor back to England, and had an appeals court on the island itself that handled plantation bankruptcies. Thus, the causes of exclusive devotion of governments to the oppression of slaves reached its highest pitch in Barbados.

The second class of causes applied to individual slave-master relations, which tempered the owner's use of government-guaranteed power in his or her own interest. The more a slave owner wanted voluntary compliance from the slave, the more he or she tended to treat the slave as almost free, and in fact the more likely he or she was to free the slave. The lowest requirement of voluntary compliance was gang labor in sugar plantation fields—simple, repetitive labor easily monitored by a man with a whip. The extreme of wanting voluntary compliance was perhaps slave pearl diving off Isla Margarita, where the slave could not be monitored except by a diving slave master, and finding pearls required skill and intelligence. Long-term mistress is a family-like relationship to slave masters; these women likewise made a better home for the master if their action was governed by their purposive considerateness rather than the slavemaster's close monitoring and coercion. Both kinds of slave were often freed.

Tables 4.1 and 5.1 [the numbering is from the book, pp. 95 and 138] present the structural analysis of islands. In Table 4.1 the islands

Table 4.1   Period of Sugar Frontier by Degree of Dominance of Sugar, for Caribbean Islands. (Highest planter power is in upper left.)

	Period of Frontier[a]		
Sugar Dominance[b]	Before 1750	1750–1800	After 1800
80% or more	Barbados Antigua Martinique	St. Croix (Danish) Guadeloupe	Tobago
50 to 80%	St. Kitts	Jamaica[c] Haiti Grenada	Trinidad
50% or Less	Nevis	St. Vincent St. Lucia Tortola (British)	Cuba Puerto Rico Santo Domingo (Dominican Rep.)

Never Really Sugar Islands: (British in 1800s) Caymans, Bahamas, Dominica, Montserrat, Anegada, Barbuda; (Dutch in 1800s) Saba, Curaçao, Aruba, St. Eustatius; (Spanish and Venezuelan in 1800s) Isla Margarita; (Danish in 1800s) St. Thomas, St. Johns; (Swedish and French in 1800s) St. Bartélemy.

[a]The best measure of the peak of the sugar frontier period is the point at which the number of slaves equals half of what it reached when African slaves or indentured immigrants stopped being imported faster than the maintenance by natural births and deaths. All the elements of this estimate are rarely available. In such cases I have guessed from slave populations, 19th-century immigration figures, land clearing, sex ratios of the white population, percent African of slaves, or other indicators. See the appendix to Chapter 5.

[b]By sugar dominance, I mean the proportion of the labor force occupied in sugar after the period when this labor force stopped growing rapidly. Being lower in the table means either that there were other major agricultural crops, that there were relatively large urban populations, or that nothing much would grow on the island. The estimates are guesses based on scattered export data, agricultural land use, etc. Since sugar used from five to ten times as much labor as other crops, acreage has to be adjusted to estimate labor force composition.

[c]Jamaica had considerable coffee and livestock, and may belong below.

Table 5.1   Factors Leading to High Planter Power

Planter Solidarity[b]	Planter Representation and Island Autonomy 1780[a] (Planter power high in upper left)		
	Autonomous Assembly, Justice of Peace	Governor-chosen Council	Urban Cabildos, Strong Bureaucracy
Settler planters with few other crops	Barbados	Martinique Guadeloupe Br. Leewards	
Adventurer bachelor planters or other crops prevalent	Jamaica Surinam	Br. Windwards Haiti (St. Dom.) Guyana (Eng) Trinidad (Eng) St. Croix (Dan)	Trinidad (Sp) Cuba[c]
Few planters, many ranchers, peasants, and merchants	Curaçao	Dominica Bahamas, Caymans St. Johns (Dan) St. Thomas (Dan) St. Eustatius (Du)	Puerto Rico Santo Domingo (Dominican Rep)

[a]In the columns of the body of the table, autonomy and control over administration of the law leads to high planter power on the left, urban representation and strong bureaucracy leads to low planter power on the right. The classification is impressionistic, and I have taken account of factors not mentioned explicitly in the table showing high island power in empire policy as applied to the island.

[b]When there were fewer planters and when they were birds of passage developing a frontier who did not form local families to use power consistently (when they were "bachelor adventurer planters") then planter power was lower. If settler planters dominated the economy on the islands where they had greatest organizing capacity developed over historical time, they had greater power. Again the judgments are impressionistic, but the sex-ratio among whites and a low reported amount of absentee ownership, where available, were decisive in distinguishing adventurer planters from settlers. See Appendix Ch. 5.

[c]Cuba taken as a whole was never dominated by sugar, and Trinidad was not so dominated in the 18th century. Both had politically powerful sections dominated by sugar in the early 19th century, and most of the literature on slavery on those islands deals with that period. I have moved them up to make their slave society politics of the early 19th century understandable. They should be in the lower right corner in the late 18th century.

most dominated by sugar plantations are in the top row, and the ones with longest such dominance are on the left. Thus Barbados in the upper left had the conditions for greatest planter dominance and most developed planter class consciousness, while Cuba, Puerto Rico, and Santo Domingo had the lowest preconditions for planter dominance. Sugar developed much after the eighteenth century in the big Spanish islands. The diagonal from most planter power from upper left to least on the lower right is collapsed in the stub of Table 5.1, so the top row has the highest economic conditions for planter power. The left column has the most local government power in the empires (the empires of importance were British, French, Spanish, Dutch, and Danish), the right column the least, that is, the most direct intervention of empire officials, often against local island economic interests.

Given different island propensities to make slavery oppressive and to leave all decisions about slave privileges and freedoms in the hands of the slave owner, we then have to ask how many liberties individual slave owners were to grant slaves. The furthest extreme is granting slaves the full freedoms of nonslaves on the islands. It is important to remember that working-class people (as most ex-slaves were) did not have as many freedoms as we are used to in the modern world, but those freedoms were ordinarily greater than those of even the most free slaves, as is indicated by the fact that virtually all slaves with any chances to be free, took them, and often fought for them. To be granted freedom by manumission (as opposed to general emancipation) a slave had to form a relation with powerful whites (or occasionally colored slave owners). The most widely available data on the freedoms slaves enjoyed are data on manumissions, though even these are very problematic on islands where slavery was weakest, where informal manumission was apparently common. From these data, it seems that the most important ties leading to freedom were sex, agency of the slave in cooperative work maintaining an establishment, commerce (including prostitution), and politics (especially slave military service).

Sexual ties between slave and free were mostly between white men and black or colored slave women.

Higman says:

> [Slaves manumitted] tended to be female, creole, young, and colored, and to work as domestics. In the [British] sugar colonies females were roughly twice as likely to be manumitted as males in the period before 1820.... Females, however, more often obtained manumission through sexual relationships with whites or freedmen, and such relationships were by no means confined to the towns. (Higman, 1984, p. 383) (p. 144)

The children of such unions were also often manumitted, and sometimes even inherited part of the estate of their planter illegitimate father. Higman also observes that "the highest manumission rates occurred where freedmen were already relatively numerous, for example in Trinidad, St. Lucia, the [British] Virgin islands, and the Bahamas (1984, p. 385) (p. 145).

By "domestic and managerial," I mean the ties that involve close and continuing contact between a white owner and a slave who has to be trusted to achieve objectives that cannot sensibly be monitored as "gang labor." Domestic servants who were not sexual partners were more likely to be manumitted than field hands, as were drivers, skilled workers, or stockmen. Such people were often born in the islands and often colored, so more exposed to European culture, and more able to communicate about managerial and domestic purposes and priorities. Herd management is difficult to monitor, so in the Spanish islands "the rate of 'manumission' was much higher, though it left a large free colored population rather than manumission documents as testimony" (p. 146). Overall managerial responsibilities in either the home or the business tended to result in manumission and apparently other treatment as "nearly free people" before manumission.

> By "commercial" ties I mean master-slave relations whose basic form was the exploitation of the slave by a formal contract with the slave.... The slave generally exploited commercial opportunities on his or her own discretion: sometimes by women's carrying on a huckstering enterprise in the market; sometimes by men's hiring themselves out for episodic transportation work on the docks; sometimes by prostitution; sometimes by manufacturing or providing laundry services. The commercial opportunities that could be exploited by slaves were mostly urban. (p. 146)

Slave political services that elicited treatment as "almost free" and often led to manumission were largely military and police services. "The more monocultural in sugar an island was, the fewer whites there were to defend it, yet the more valuable it was to an empire [and to the competing empires]" (p. 148). Often slave troops were more valuable in the islands, because they were the survivors of childhood bouts of tropical diseases, which killed up to one-third of white troops sent from the empire center. Thus, they tended to be recruited, and in some empires promoted to officers and even generals, late in the campaigns when the white empire troops were crippled by disease. Sometimes slaves were also used as "intelligence agents" to find out about rebellions or to hunt down runaways. At any rate, an armed and militarily trained slave with solidarities with other such armed slaves was a different problem of control than gang labor in the fields, and they were often given their freedom and land somewhere far from the centers of power.

In daily life, then, the high point of slavery was among the highly class-conscious and oppressive large sugar planters' field labor. Hardly anyone in field sugar plantation labor got manumitted; hardly anyone had intimate relations with whites, though they sometimes became pregnant in a nonintimate relation; hardly any managed work on a collegial basis with the owner or owner's agents; hardly any sought out commercial opportunities with autonomy and discretion; hardly any earned freedom as a reward from governments for loyalty and bravery; and all were subject to the most class-conscious slave owners, those most interested in the "health" of the slave system as a whole.

> As the sugar plantation core of slave society sloped off into slave mistresses; slaves owned by freedmen; creole slaves in domestic service, skilled work, and first-line management; slaves in cities and especially in urban commerce; slaves in smaller enterprises; slaves of masters to whom the maintenance of the whole slave system was a secondary consideration, the slave relation became more like the relations among free unequals in eighteenth-century urban society, or those between free peasants and landlords in western European countries. And that slope also led to the boundary between slave and free for some manumitted slaves. (p. 149)

Neither of these "observational theories" is very complicated or surprising. When Howard S. Becker wrote about spontaneous mentions as a better measure of situated saliency in his and others' study of first-year medical students (1961), it was about how we could use that fact for a methodological purpose, on which the more traditional methods might well get the wrong answer. It was not a deep social-psychological principle that people to whom something is salient will often talk about it a lot. When I wrote about colored people's occupations and combined that with the methodologically useful fact that basically all colored slaves were creoles while many black slaves were African-born, I was not telling anyone anything new about the relative racial purity of African blacks. (I would have had to do that if the Western slave traders had bought many slaves from the high Ethiopian plateau, where racial mixture is evidently ancient.) The "theory" of the correlation between birth in the islands and the color of slaves was only a methodological convenience, not a sociological finding.

But then the craftsmanship is to combine the trivial "theory" in the measurement with three features:

1. The theories of the other observational devices, such as classifying slave occupations by their interaction with whites, or the observations by Becker, Geer, and colleagues (1961) of the excessive demands to learn everything, put on medical students by their professors. The more the trivial theory agrees with other measures, the greater its value.

2. *System* in the overall plan of observation, especially being sure to observe systematically when something is present versus absent, high versus low, or some other distance (for the colored, freedom by manumission is higher, for field slavery, lower—but one wants to know whether that is everywhere or only on sugar islands still importing African slaves, in urban life as well as rural, and so on).

3. A close connection of the observation with the theory, so, for example, one knows to look for relatively less oppression of slaves where they are in occupations that have more interaction and more intimate communication with whites.

For example, in the novel *Texaco* (Chamoiseau, 1997 [1992]), mentioned earlier (in connection with squatting), there is a lovely account of the relative freedom of a Martinican slave carpenter in the period leading up to general emancipation, because he was rented out to people he himself had found who needed carpenters' services, and his owners knew less than he did about what the requirements for building things were. The point about him (he was not the main focus of the novel) was that he already knew how to make a living as a free man when emancipation came. Scattered data on color, on skilled work, on mistresses and prostitutes were crafted into a theory of the "assimilation of immigrants" tending to lead to the first element of citizenship, legal freedom, even when the immigrants and then their children were slaves.

The "Stinchcombe Information Short Version," below, looks back on a book that had several case studies of organizational forms. It represents the finished form of theory and method, crafted out of those case analyses. There is no easy way in which hypotheses about when a department in an organization will have a rubber stamp to print "Bullshit" on a memo, and when a university department will carefully document the citation counts of second authors, because a particular person's first authors raised the money rather than doing the hypothesis construction and testing. Only the theory crafted in the book shows the comparability of those cases. That comparability had to be crafted out of the analysis of observations on uncertainties, on information processing systems, and on decisions, in subunits of organizations.

Stinchcombe Information Short Version

Reprinted from Arthur L. Stinchcombe, "Restructuring Research on Organizations," in *Information and Organizations* (Berkeley: University of California Press, 1990), pp. 358–362. References have been omitted, as well as a few short text passages, the latter indicated by ellipses.

By units of analysis I mean those units on which data are typically collected. That is, should one collect data on individuals, departments, transactions, organizations, systems [or fields] of organizations, or what? The central criterion for determining appropriate units of analysis is that, with respect to the theory at stake, they should be strongly causally connected internally. The units of analysis have to be chosen so that they are the place where causes are connected to effects—functions to needs, decisions to situations, flows to stocks, structures to environments. The central argument of this book is that units of analysis should be subparts of organizations that deal with distinctive sorts of uncertainties, that are responsible for securing effective responses to different sorts of news. Whole organizations may sometimes be proxies for the right units of analysis when they are dominated by a single type of information-processing system, as when universities are dominated by departments in various branches of scholarship. But even in this case one gets stronger and cleaner results if one distinguishes faculties from buildings and grounds departments.

Ordinarily organizations themselves, because they have had to build different substructures to deal with different sorts of uncertainty, will themselves provide guides to the right units. Universities will tend to locate buildings and grounds far from the faculty in the administrative system, but will tend to locate sociology moderately near to physics, because estimating the reputation of a physicist is the same general sort of problem as estimating the reputation of a sociologist.... Quite often, whatever is called a "department" in an organization will be the right unit of analysis; but if the uncertainty in question has to do with investments or other matters with a longer time horizon, divisions or subsidiaries may be the right units. But since we have been arguing that features of the social organization of news processing are to be the main variables, we do not want to have units that cannot have social organization with a high degree of continuity through time. We therefore do not want to have either individuals or decisions as the central units of analysis.

Since in the theory a social structure relates decisions to news about uncertainties, the units chosen have to be those that tie news to decisions. Consequently, we need to so choose the units that they have authority (with review, to be sure) over a class of decisions that is served by a common news-collecting structure. Since authority is very generally divided in much the same way as specialized departments are distinguished from each other (we rarely find departments that do not make—or at least recommend—important decisions), this criterion usually coincides with the one that tells us to choose as units of analysis specialized sub-units. But it draws attention to the volume of the flow of information, short periods between transmissions of information, and the like, as a criterion for what is a unit of analysis. Thus, if it is true that some drug companies have a "vice president in charge of going to jail," who is responsible for everything affecting the quality of drugs but gets very little information about those things and makes very few decisions about them (John Braithwaite, personal communication), we would not want the different departments for which he or she is "responsible" to be a unit of analysis for our theory [though if we were interested in organizational deviance it *would* be a unit]. His job is to go to jail when low quality is to be punished by the courts, not to unify quality control. [That is, it is a "department" that does not satisfy our criteria for a unit of analysis, for it does not respond to news of quality by taking decisions about quality.]

Units of analysis are fundamental aspects of the strategy of scientific inquiry and scientific theorizing. If people do not typically look at the units that connect a given kind of uncertainty to decisions, their theory is unlikely to be about such connections. Since our units do not have the natural skins that serve as boundaries around the units of analysis in much of psychology, and do not necessarily have legal existence as separate organizations as the units in ecological organizational theory have, we have to tell how to recognize those units in some detail. That makes the definition of units of analysis itself into a theoretical question. Our suggestion that one normally will not go too far wrong by using whatever is called a "department" as a unit of analysis is merely an empirical convenience. But that empirical convenience comes about because of an observation that connects it to the core of our theory—that usually departments connect news about a distinctive sort of uncertainty to the authority required to make decisions, just as a thing with a skin is a unit in psychology because it happens that things with skins are what connect motives to individual actions.

Types of Variables

The argument of this book implies that we need to look at two broad types of variables, one describing the variations in the kinds of uncertainty that affect the units of analysis, another describing variations in the information and decision structure of the parts of the organization that form the units. For example, the service provided by a university faculty member is more valuable and has a higher price if the university has a good reputation, a fact that describes one type of uncertainty, about how to estimate reputation, while customer satisfaction and the capacity to get the job done right are more important in a service like that of barbers or beauticians. The complicated structure of peer evaluation, and the system of paying faculty members for research work that is monitored, not inside the university, but in the researcher's own field, reflect (or so we have argued) the fact that it is uncertainty of reputation that determines the price a university can charge for its teaching. We therefore expect peer review when such renting of reputations is rational, because news of reputations cannot reliably be collected by other means (or course, it is not all that reliable when collected by these means either).

Similarly, hospitals that depend on referrals to their physicians by primary-care physicians or by other hospitals should be expected to use peer review and investment in future reputations of their staff in much the way universities do. Of course, such hospitals are often university teaching hospitals and so find it easy to adopt variations of usual university personnel procedures. But, to return to the point made above about units of analysis, we will not expect much peer review in the hiring of nurses in that hospital, nor in the buildings and grounds department of the university, because neither service becomes much more valuable by increasing the reputation of the service givers.

We have given many examples of such variables [in the book]: whether or not the structure of the program governing a worker's handling of uncertainty is analogous to a batch program or to an interactive program, and the corresponding skill level of the worker (higher for interactive, lower for batch ...); whether the accounts have to provide for comparisons among firms by outsiders and honesty of reporting to those outsiders rather than provide materials to analyze cost reduction projects, and the corresponding standard codes versus specialized detail and rigidity versus flexibility of the accounting structures ... ; whether a firm is in several markets or a single market ... and the corresponding divisionalization; whether the subpart of the organization is trying to maintain the monopoly position derived from having introduced a product innovation, and the corresponding network structure connecting users to the marketing department and the close integration of engineering with marketing and manufacturing.... Many more examples are scattered throughout the book.

Forms of Theory

The definition of the variables and units of analysis involves a simultaneous orientation of the theory to three main domains of fact: the sources of uncertainty outside the organization; the organizational objectives that make the uncertainty important to the organization; and the volume, error, and bias of the flow of information about the uncertainty. The theory connects the larger social structure and the available productive technology to the microstructure of the organizations. But it does not connect every part of the larger structure to every micropart of the organizational structure.

The crucial indicator that some uncertainty outside the organization is shaping a part of an organization is that information or news about that uncertainty is flowing through that part and being reshaped into such a form that it can serve as the basis of a decision. The citations to a faculty member's work in the scholarly literature are processed into an overall ranking of the impact that scholar has on his or her field, as required by the dean's office; that is, departments must demonstrate the distinction of a given faculty member, as compared with alternative candidates who might be hired instead. This indicates that the information in the scientific or scholarly community shapes the personnel process of the university. Similarly, the fact that the well plan for a given well is shaped in detail by the well reports for neighboring wells is what indicates that drillers care a lot about the information from neighboring drill crews and drilling engineers, and makes it less surprising that they stamp *Bullshit!* on information from purchasing on how they might save money buying spare parts.

The theory, then, is about a flow of interactions between the environment and the subpart of the organization. Further, the argument is that the *main thing* that is going on in those interactions, the part that matters, is what will shape the main outlines of the subpart's structure. Sometimes the theory will be about variations in what matters in the interaction. For example, the argument of Chapter 5 is that the things that matter when one is trying to preserve the monopoly advantage to be got from a product innovation are quite different from those that matter when one is selling competitive products in a straightforward way. Sometimes the theory will be about variations in the temporal aspects of the interaction flow, as when the information for the general office of a multidivisional firm is abstracted into longer-period measures of performance, because the temporal structure of investment and return is slower than the temporal structure of market variations and response.... Sometimes the theory will be about variations in the degree to which one has unanalyzed information indicating that everything seems to be going all right, as when personnel systems make great use of seniority criteria....

But the basic presumption of all the sub-varieties of the theory is that it is massive flows of interaction between an organizational part and the uncertainties of the environment that shape organizational structure. All the theoretical structures, then, are not so much about critical events as they are about flows of interaction, flows of information about uncertainty, flows of impacts of uncertainty on important continuing objectives, flows of outcomes that show that things are (or are not) being handled by the system. The overall theory of this book, then, is about all the different sorts of things a flow of interaction between an organization and its environment brings in, and how that flow of interaction affects the structure of work flow in different subparts of the organization.

As a final example of what crafting looks like, the "Heimer and Staffen Methods Short Version," below, is more concentrated on the difficult problem of measuring properly a concept central to fitting human capacities for being rational to human capacities to care for others ("responsibility"). Heimer and Staffen simultaneously had to develop ways to identify a variable with at least five major components (all necessary for it to fill its role in the theory) with the logistics of fieldwork in two hospitals; this resulted in a set of methods more or less unique to the research (though each of their components is fairly well known somewhere in the social science literature).

Heimer and Staffen Methods Short Version

Summarized from Carol A. Heimer and Lisa R. Staffen, "Appendix on Methods," in *For the Sake of the Children: The Social Organization of Responsibility in the Hospital and the Home* (Chicago: University of Chicago Press, 1998), pp. 375–388. All page numbers without citations are to this source.

"Discussing methodology is like playing the slide trombone. It has to be
done extraordinarily well if it is not to be more interesting to the person
who does it than to others who listen to it," the economist Frank
Knight once observed (cited in Merton, Sills, and Stigler 1984:331).
(p. 375)

Heimer and Staffen believe that to interview people about organizational processes and their reactions in them, one has to understand
a lot about those processes and the actions in them first. When they
discovered an inoffensive physician they had observed in the unit was
known in a support group as "Dr. Death," they did not understand
enough about the Neonatal Intensive Care Unit (NICU) to see where
this could come from. They went back to observe more.

> That decision [to spend much more time in the NICU before interviewing
> parents was] very important. Without [it] we would not have been able
> to write chapters 5 and 6. The fieldwork provided a crucial context for
> the parent interviews but also let us see for ourselves how and why
> parent and staff perspectives are so different. (p. 376)

In commenting on how they tried similarly to observe the social setting and interactions in households during interviews, they comment
on justifying the observer to the observed.

> Here we believe we made a virtue [to have one researcher observe the
> household and the interaction during the interview] of necessity. Because
> all of the parents we interviewed had small children, we had to devise
> some way to conduct lengthy interviews in the face of the very
> substantial capacity of toddlers to disrupt any adult social interaction
> [which the observer could do by babysitting as well as observing]. . . .
>   We wish here not simply to sing the praises [of combining
> observation with interviewing] but also to underscore the importance of
> a flexible research design. Methods, after all, are the tools of the
> sociologist's trade, and different jobs require different tools. (p. 377)

The hospital had its own distinctive social setting, and the observer
had to take up a different role there. In neither setting could the researcher monopolize the attention of those interviewed or observed,
or control the setting of the information collection.

> Although the NICU staff members usually were quite willing to let us
> observe their activities and share their experiences in formal and
> informal interviews, helping us with our research was a low priority

compared with caring for sick babies, tending to anxious parents, and even completing administrative work. Interviews were postponed—or just delayed several hours, people forgot to inform us when meetings with parents were scheduled or rescheduled, and more than once we arrived for a regularly occurring meeting only to learn that everyone else knew it wouldn't occur on a holiday. (p. 379)

The social system of the university and hospital research branches also shaped the setting and the method of the interview, sometimes reducing the scientific value of the data and the consent of the interviewee.

Such letters [informing parents that the authors would be calling to arrange an interview] were a mixed blessing, it turns out, but one about which we had little choice. Both the university and hospital human subjects committees required them and placed some constraints on their content. Although some groups of people found the letters a reasonable introduction, other respondents had clearly been put off by them. Despite the university letterhead, they were convinced we were in some way or other out to deprive them of their welfare checks, Medicaid cards, disability payments, or even of their child. Official letters are not always reassuring. As field workers have long known, official endorsements do not always help and often harm a research project, and we were often required to do repair work when contact was later made over the telephone or in person.

We were also required to have interview respondents sign informed consent forms, indicating their participation had not been coerced.... One of the institutional review boards even went so far as to ask us to get witnesses to add their signatures to the consent forms along with ours and those of our respondents. We dissuaded them from this by pointing out that it was difficult simultaneously to promise confidentiality and to arrange... a signing ceremony at the beginning of the interview. (p. 380)

Promises of confidentiality also had to be adapted to the situation. An account of an incident in an NICU disappeared from a researcher's mailbox. In attempting damage control, the authors talked to an NICU worker.

We... describ[ed the] particular incidents in the NICU and had been asking for guidance [from an NICU informant] specifically about these passages. But our informant reassured us that only if you knew the location of the NICU and had observed these particular incidents would you be able to identify the location and participants. It was a vivid portrait, but not one that revealed the participants' identities. (p. 381)

Selection into the sample of people interviewed became highly positively correlated with the dependent variable, responsible action on behalf of the child. For example, poorer and more transient people have uncertain relations to phones, and fathers who had little to do with the mother or the child were hard to find and hard to get to consent to the interview.

The phone number in a medical record may be for a neighbor's phone, and so of no use if the woman has moved.... [A relative] who can be relied on to transmit a message about an emergency... justifiably may not wish to make a special effort to transmit a message about scheduling an interview appointment. And if the message is transmitted, why should anyone return the call? Typically a message will not supply sufficient context to make it meaningful, and it is nearly impossible to be persuasive about an interview second- or third-hand. Our observations (mainly in Chapter 6) about principal/agent relations apply well here—we were the weakest of principals to induce intermediaries to act on our behalf in arranging interviews....

We had special difficulties locating fathers who were no longer attached to the mothers of their children. We often could not rely on the medical record to have information about the names and addresses of fathers who were not married to the mothers of their children. And if the parents were no longer involved with each other, mothers were often able to give us only very little to go on in our search. In one instance, the mother had some contact with the father even though they were no longer involved, and she provided his name and a work telephone and address where we could contact him. Unfortunately, the nature of his business required him to be out of the office most of the time, and we never successfully contacted him. We sent a letter to the small shop he owned and left messages on his answering machine, but he never returned our calls. We even drove to his place of business several times hoping to catch him there, but we never did....

Non custodial fathers were not only more difficult to locate, but they were also considerably less likely to agree to be interviewed even if we did locate them. Because their ties with their children were tenuous at best, we found it very difficult to coax these fathers into talking.... And once again, our difficulties in locating fathers and cajoling them into talking with us might be regarded as information about the kinds of troubles teachers and social service workers might encounter in attempting to incorporate fathers in decision making about their children. And in the most extreme cases, our difficulties gave some hints about why couple relationships might have been difficult to sustain. (pp. 382–383)

But figuring out how to measure something like responsibility is only half the problem. We also needed to convince ourselves and our readers that we were not merely social scientists spouting societal prejudices in dressed-up form. For this reason, we have highlighted the ways in which our findings do not fit with common prejudices. Not all young, unmarried, poor, or minority parents are irresponsible, and not all older, married, middle-class or white parents are responsible. Some of these characteristics are correlated with responsibility, but there are important intervening variables, and these are where our story is focused. We have tried to provide as much raw data as possible in the text so that readers can assess for themselves the appropriateness of our conclusions.

The point is that in this kind of research [seeing how people dealt with problems that elicited strong emotions and developed over time in contingent ways], one never really knows where the question [asked by an interviewer] is going to lead and what it will be strategic to ask next given the answer that respondents give. For these reasons, the interviewing could not be "farmed out." We had to have a deep understanding of what the research was about to make any sensible judgment about when to probe, when to try to "get back to the subject," and when to let the respondent keep talking.

People do not talk about responsibility in the same way, and often we did not fully understand the significance of some fact [missed in previous coding of an interview] until we had reread the interview several times. It is for this reason that on key points (e.g. the coding that underlies the categorization of families in chapter 3 [summarized by ALS elsewhere in this chapter]), we worked out careful coding instructions and consulted frequently about the appropriate coding of particular statements. In addition, some time after the interviews were complete, transcribed, and corrected, we had research assistants go through the interviews compiling information about key topics. Later we had them sort for information on specific points so that we could check the representativeness of the quotations and examples we had selected for use in the text.

Finally, we should note that conducting the interviews and working with them afterward are a highly emotional enterprise. Our respondents often cried during the interviews. We often cried with them, and we learned to bring tissues, along with tape recorders and spare batteries, to interviews.... We have [each] been sustained by having [our coauthor] who also carries with her vivid mental images of people who are unknown to our friends, colleagues, and families. But, of course, the object here is not to keep these families secret. Although we have worried a great deal about issues of confidentiality, we nevertheless want others to know the essential parts of their stories. We have therefore been gratified when our research assistants commented on the interviews or on parts of the manuscript in ways that suggested that not only did they understand the argument we were making but that they also were moved. If as Zajonc (1980) suggests, feelings typically precede cognitive responses, we hope to grab people's minds by first grabbing their hearts (p. 385).

Methodology also requires its authors to select those findings of most interest to readers, because the readers are interested in the theories on which they bear. Aiming for many audiences creates trouble in planning, financing, and research design, as well as in writing.

Our research has been hampered by the tendency of social scientists to categorize research more by substance than by theoretical questions. What makes our contribution important, we believe, is not so much its substantive focus as the questions it poses in those settings. But that means that at the stage when we needed research support to get the project started, [support] was hard to find. Sociologists of the family did not always sympathize with our focus. Medical specialists thought we drew too little on the work of medical researchers, and there weren't any researchers who specialized in the study of responsibility. There is no way to state this complaint that doesn't sound like sour grapes, of course, and we do not wish to dwell on this point beyond noting that the organization of the discipline and of research funding may discourage some kinds of work. At some point people have to choose for themselves whether they will do a piece of work even without funding and the legitimacy that funding brings. We ultimately chose to get on with the work rather than to submit more proposals.

As a project nears completion, the balkanization of academic disciplines leads to parallel problems in the dissemination of research results. We are eager for our work to be read by medical sociologists and sociologists of the family, but we believe that our findings are equally important to those interested in questions about the relationship between law and other normative systems, the persistence of gender inequality, incentive systems inside and on the boundaries of organizations, the social psychology of the diffusion of responsibility, and the place of moral discourse in an organizational world. Because we believe that the social organization of responsibility is of fundamental importance to both social theory and social policy, we have tried to pitch our work to a variety of audiences. While we believe that this was the responsible thing to do, we are aware that by attempting to speak to many, we run the risk of speaking to none. (pp. 386–387)

Elegance, Power, and Economy

I DISCUSS TWO EXAMPLES in which data were used to improve concepts. One of mine that I want to discuss I have labeled "Stinchcombe Rebellion No Answer Short Version," and I think it's the most elegant piece of methodological analysis I have done. It shows that the pattern of no-answers on the survey itself is evidence for the theory of the book. I am one of the many mathematicians *manqués* in sociology, and from that background I developed a feel for the central virtues of proofs in mathematics, "elegance, power, and economy." The one I discuss from my own book below is quite trivial, but shows something about how *elegance* is done right, I think. The one that illustrates *power* will be "Heimer and Staffen Responsibility Short Version." I think the reader will see from this example what I mean by power: that responsibility is a very important concept and that good solid methodological work (see above) has contributed to the meaning of the concept, made it a lot clearer, and provided measures of it simultaneously. The first of these is quantitative, the second almost entirely qualitative. I will not give a separate example here of economy, since I have discussed economy above, though in a different sense than mathematicians use it. By "economy" mathematicians mean making use of the fewest axioms possible, and the fewest intermediate results possible, to reach a proof. I am not a very economical thinker, and have a taste for too many nice empirical examples to have good aesthetic sense for mathematical economy So I will not provide an example that is very likely to be a bad one. If I had been Euclid, I would have given too many examples of triangles, not enough proofs.

My favorite example of an elegant simple proof in mathematics is the proof that there is an infinite number of prime numbers. For if there were a finite number, there must be a largest one. Take that one, multiply it sequentially by all the numbers below it (that is, call it *P*, compute *P* factorial), and then add one. Then the number computed is not divisible by any number smaller than or equal to *P*. Therefore, either it is a prime, or if it is divisible, it must be by a prime number larger than *P*, so *P*, whatever it is, is never the largest prime. Beautiful.

Stinchcombe Rebellion No Answers Short Version

Reprinted from Arthur L. Stinchcombe, "Appendix on Method," in *Rebellion in a High School* (Chicago: Quadrangle, 1964; reprint, New York: New York Times Press), pp. 186–191.

The interviewing on which the analysis was based was done by a pencil and paper schedule, a copy of which is included in Appendix II [in the original book]. Interview schedules were passed out to the teachers of the social science classes, which also function as "home-rooms." Most of a class hour was given over to administering the questionnaire. In the mentally retarded classes, two or three class hours were used. All interview schedules were considered "usable" and were transferred to IBM cards, even if most of the responses were "No Answer" (or worse).

Administered as part of the school program by school authorities, the interview itself is a relatively close replica of the classroom situation it studies. Not obeying the implicit command to "answer the question" is, therefore, a measure of rebellion, correlated with other types of rebellion (see Table I).

[One reads the table as follows. There were thirty-six out of the fifty-two questions where rebels had more no-answers than the well-behaved. Many of these had very small differences in the no-answer rate, less than one percent. These are in the bottom row of Table I.

Table I On Most Items, Rebels Have Higher Non-response Rates than Conforming Students

Size of Differences in No-Answer Rate	#Items Rebels More No-Answers	#Items Conformers More No-Answers
More than 3%	7	0
From 2% to 3%	3	1
From 1% to 2%	13	6
Less than 1%	13	9
Total	36	16

We see that on questions with little distance between rebels and well-behaved, just about as many items (9) had the well-behaved with higher rates, as the number of questions where rebels had more (13). For those items where there was a high difference (3 percent or more), seven had higher no-answers among the rebels, none had higher no-answers among the well-behaved.]

That is, rebels had a higher non-response rate on thirty-six of the fifty-two items that could be analyzed for non-response. This is true even though those who did not answer the questions on rebellion were classified as "conformers." Some of the other questions could not be used to compute a non-response rate, either because they were designed not to be answered by some people or because of peculiarities of the coding scheme. (A Wilcoxon matched-pairs-signed-ranks test applied to the percentage differences in non-response rate between rebels and non-rebels gives a one-tailed probability of the null hypothesis of approximately 0.0005. Such a test assumes that nonresponse is independent among items, which is almost certainly not true.)

This association between rebellion and non-response holds, even when curriculum interest is held constant, leading us to suspect that it is not merely the lesser sophistication of rebels which accounts for their non-response (see Table II).

[Thus in the upper left cell there were 196 well-behaved college-preparatory girls, who therefore had 50 × 196 or 9,800 opportunities not to answer a question. Of these occasions, only 0.72 percent, or

Table II   Percentage of No-Answer Responses to 50 Items, by Sex, Curriculum Interest, and Rebellion (Numbers in parentheses are numbers of respondents. The base for the percentage is this number times 50.)

Sex* and Rebellion**	Curriculum Interest*** College Preparatory	Curriculum Interest Other
Girls, well-behaved	0.72% (196)	1.22% (314)
Rebellious	0.79% (29)	1.78% (119)
Boys, well-behaved	1.06% (173)	2.30% (242)
Rebellious	1.41% (75)	2.41% (249)

*Those who did not answer the question on sex are omitted.

**Rebellious students either skipped with a group or were sent out of class. A "No-Answer" response was treated as indicating good behavior on an item to which no answer was given, so that any relation between rebellion and non-response would not be produced by a relation between non-responses on different items.

***Those who did not answer the curriculum interest question are omitted. In the body of the book, they are included among those giving "ambiguous" answers. This explains the different numbers of respondents here.

71, gave rise to a no-answer. In the lower right cell, there were 249 rebellious boys on noncollege curricula, giving rise to 12,450 opportunities not to answer. Of those about 1 in 40 gave rise to no-answer, for about 300 no-answers, or just over one apiece. The key finding for this comparison is that boys who have little to gain from high school are, on the average, less likely to answer the questions posed to them in a classroom. They are somewhat more likely not to answer if they have already shown disobedience as measured by skipping school, being sent out of class, or getting a grade below passing.]

In addition, Table II shows that non-response, like rebellion, is more common among boys than girls, and more common among those not on college preparatory curricula. The "No Answer" responses for sex and curriculum interest have been eliminated from Table II, giving fifty instead of fifty-two items.

Boys' non-response rate is higher than girls' in each curriculum interest group, and among both rebels and well-behaved. Among boys and girls, rebellious and well-behaved, those on college preparatory curricula are more likely to answer the questions. And in three out of four cases, rebels are more likely not to respond than well-behaved students, whatever their sex or curriculum interest. Only college preparatory girls depart from this pattern.

The pattern of Table II, then, is essentially similar to the pattern of some tables in chapter 4 [in the book being quoted], in which some attitude indicating expressive alienation was shown to be related to articulation, whether or not students had become rebellious in behavior. Though in a slightly different format, the essential result of Table II is that sex and curriculum interest are closely related to non-response, just as they are, for example, to short-run hedonism, whether or not the alienated attitude that non-response has yet resulted in behavioral rebellion.

In other words, non-responses do not appreciably confuse the inferences drawn in the main body of the book, but rather serve as an independent test of the main hypothesis. Rebels, and those who, on theoretical grounds, we expect to be expressively alienated, do not obey the command to answer the question when it is given in a classroom-like interviewing situation, which uses the authority system of high school to secure answers.

The passage reprinted in "Stinchcombe Rebellion No Answers Short Version" is intended to have two virtues for our purposes here. The first is to establish that the number of no-answers measures rebellion against the classroom authority structure that administered the questionnaire. The second is to establish that as such a measure, it has the same causes as I argued in the rest of that book cause rebellion against school authority structures. That this material occurs in an appendix on method shows that the study of the method of concept formation, and of nonresponse as a measure of the concept of expressive alienation, reveals something also about the method of classroom administration of surveys. The finding presumably applies to tests and other such "measuring instruments"—the "standards" tests that have become common recently are administered in much the same way. Scores should be influenced moderately by expressive alienation. Managing to confirm a theory as part of a discussion of what the interviewing situation was seems to me elegant. But to understand what that elegance means, it is useful to have some background, some of which is in the "Stinchcombe Rebellion Short Version" given in chapter 4.

So in the appendix I went through the same operations of chapters 3–5 that defined and operationalized expressive alienation and rebellion, and showed that they were caused by being on tracks in high school that did not lead anywhere. They were abbreviated in the appendix selection above, to show that not answering the questions was indeed part of the clinical entity, by being correlated with other rebellion and with the relevant attitudes. Not only was it part of the same dependent variable by the coherence criterion, then, but it turned out the same causes tended to cause it. This is further evidence that the complex of attitudes and behavior was indeed a clinical entity, and that the same germs of not thinking they were going to get anything out of high school were at the core of its causes.

Perhaps the central thing I established in that book is that it is anticipated own future social class, *not social class of parents*, that explains rebellion against authority in high schools. Since then studies in Norway and in Japan have indicated that in those societies, in which secondary school tracks headed for the working class do indeed get graduates a good job in the working class if they do well in them, future working-class students are not rebellious against the secondary school. In those societies employers are more or less forced into a sort of "contract" with the "vocational" tracks in the secondary schools, and pretty much have to hire their working class from the schools. Something like that also happens in Germany, but replications of my study have not been done there.

The only point that is of more general interest here is that sociologists' observations are created by social relations. If those social relations are distinctive in terms of the variables of their theory, or of some other theory important more generally in sociology, then sociologists should think through the impact of the mechanisms in the social relations of data collection on what sort of data they are generating.

Mostly what the human subjects committee requires of us is that we create a voluntary relationship with the people we are inquiring about, and that we ask their consent on a sort of "do good" basis: thus, we really need to have a representative sample and their dropping out would hurt it; their answers will be reported as aggregate information only, which will be available to everybody; we will not tell the FBI about their crimes. So the kinds of people more generally who are willing to answer our survey questions are the ones who believe that kind of voluntary "good-government-if-men-and-women-of-good-will-work-together-and-participate-properly" ideology.

I would expect that members of the League of Women Voters would be at the very high end of answering our questionnaires and all the questions within them, and those who think it's all a shuck, to do poor people in, will not answer as often or as fully. Sociologists really care that we undercount young black men in our surveys, but they do not really care that we undercount those who think sociology is just part of a bigger shuck. Quite a lot of the people who do not answer because they do not believe in us do-gooders are themselves elderly, well-behaved, often rural people who think that we irreligious young people from the university are sapping our moral fiber, if we aren't actually on the take.

Responsibility

WELL, SO MUCH FOR NEAT LITTLE ELEGANT RESULTS on methods confirming a concept by showing that *methodological artifacts* can be created *by the same mechanism as the theory alleged*, and the mechanism works the way it's supposed to work to explain the methodological artifacts as well. But that is not a finding of much intellectual power. Now to "power" of concepts, in Heimer and Staffen (1998b). The basic idea of power is generativity, that a great many results that would be difficult to arrive at or to understand become easy with concepts that have power. So by "power" in an empirical science, we mean that deep concepts organize a lot of phenomena into a variable so that all are explained by, or all explain, the same process. We can then explain a lot simply.

The basic idea behind the concept of responsibility in Heimer and Staffen, originally anticipated in an unpublished paper by Heimer called "Producing Responsible Behavior in Order to Produce Oil" (1986), is that a lot of rational behavior, behavior of an "agent," is oriented to accomplishing some goals of someone else (e.g., of a neonate with medical problems), or of some organization (e.g., the state oil company [called "Statoil"] of Norway), or of goals justified by some higher value (e.g., the advance of sociology).

So, on the one hand, responsibility is flexible and rational adaptation to the world, and, on the other hand, it is deeply social and normative. Heimer and Staffen argue that a lot of social life cannot be explained solely by people being selfish, though of course they would like to be rewarded for what they do for the organization or the higher value, or be rewarded by the reassurance that their baby with neonatal troubles will be able to make it in the world in spite of its difficulties. But doing the things that are responsible requires rationality—so the identification of rationality with selfishness is all wrong for these situations. The problem is how to get people to fulfill their social responsibilities flexibly, using perhaps resources granted by organizations to be devoted to that purpose, taking risks in order to accomplish the values including perhaps risks that will cost themselves something, producing as a result commitment to the responsibility and to whatever reasonable efforts are needed to accomplish the goals of others.

Another way they describe it is that a lot of norms require more than "conformity," more than simply "not being deviant." The norm to "take care of your child" does not demand just conformity, but the best parents can do under the circumstances: bearing responsibility, which means that if their baby is damaged, they pay a lot more effort for the baby and get a lot less out of it, at least in the obvious ways.

Similarly the norm to "advance sociological knowledge" may require working about a decade (and having other people think in the meantime that they—for example, Heimer and Staffen—do not really produce enough) in order to bring the best possible information to bear on the definition and empirical realization of the concept of rational action on behalf of someone or something else, and to figure out its place in the causal order (what conditions encourage it, what conditions discourage it). Similarly, the norm to "advance knowledge" does not just require learning the right answers on a test. It means here, "Do whatever is necessary so we really understand responsibility." How can one define responsibility at all, if the resources that have to be used are under the control of someone else (e.g., the medical insurance company and the neonatal intensive care physicians and nurses), but the parents have to make sure they are mobilized on behalf of their baby? To advance knowledge of why a neonatal intensive care unit tries to send a baby home to parents who will be responsible, and why those parents (at least some of them) care for the child with competence and generosity, the concept has to be powerful.

Heimer and Staffen Responsibility Short Version

Summarized from Carol A. Heimer and Lisa R. Staffen, "What Do We Mean by Responsibility?" in *For the Sake of the Children: The Social Organization of Responsibility in the Hospital and the Home* (Chicago: University of Chicago Press, 1998), pp. 77–136. Page numbers with no further identification are to this source.

We may specify the components of a complex mechanism of "responsibility" from its definition as rational action on behalf of another person or some organization or institution. We can specify five dimensions of the variable of the degree to which this mechanism dominates a person or a role (pp. 80–81):

> People who take more responsibility can be differentiated from those taking less along five dimensions: (1) More responsible people tend to take account of others' interests as well as their own, balancing those interests against pleasures and interests of their own. Either the utility function being maximized is that of another person, or some institution, rather than the person's own, or at the very least it includes arguments describing others' interests as well [footnote omitted]. (2) More responsible people think about long-term outcomes and maximize the utility function over a longer time horizon. (3) More responsible people tend to define their roles more diffusely. That is, such a person will maximize a utility function, trading off between many values, all of which he or she is responsible for, rather than a single value. (4) More responsible people use more discretion. The person chooses how to maximize the utility function rather than follows a rule or prescribed procedure. And (5) more responsible people cope with whatever contingencies arise. The person accepts the obligation to maximize the utility function under conditions of uncertainty about what exactly is entailed and what costs and benefits will accrue to him or her.

For example, the "long-term outcomes" component of responsibility is clearly laid out by Elliott Jaques:

> In one of the very few social science investigations of responsibility, Elliott Jaques (1972 [1956]) specifically linked responsibility to planning for the future. Pointing to the intimate connection between long-term performance and hierarchical differences in responsibility in industry, Jaques argued that higher-ranked employees are reviewed at longer intervals because short-run measures of performance distract executives from using long-term objectives to set priorities. Thus the more responsible the role, the more the performance measures embedded in the incentive and authority systems of industrial hierarchies will focus on distant outcomes.

Because the demands of responsibility for an infant are greater if the child has more severe problems, we cannot judge responsibility without taking account of the child's needs. Thus a child may have few troubles, but the parents plan badly for the few. A child may have severe troubles and the parents move mountains to see he or she gets the best future possible. Or parents may do wonderfully taking care of minor problems, or give minimal and short-term care for children with major problems. Responsibility creates much more work and more use of resources when the burden of need is severe—this adjustability of costs when the need is greater is perhaps the core of responsibility as a moral concept. Thus the symptoms of responsibility vary with the heaviness of the burden of need.

Because responsibility is rationality on behalf of the child (or institution), it rationally demands more for greater emergencies. But whatever the level of the child's need, rationality on his or her behalf requires taking account of the child's interest, orientation to the child's long-term future, thinking diffusely of all aspects of the child's interests rather than just food, shelter, and doctor visits, being flexible in adapting to changing situations and needs rather than following rules, and coping with whatever contingencies arise even if it costs one's own time or money.

We find that a separate coding of the five elements of responsibility, when averaged, agrees well with an independent coding of the overall interview schedule for responsibility. This allows us to see quickly some of the main correlates of parental responsibility toward newborns (pp. 133–134 and p. 132).

First, we found that there is significant variation in the amount of responsibility parents assume and that this variation can be measured systematically. Second, women were on average more responsible than men. And third, the larger the magnitude of the burden parents faced, the more responsible they were likely to be. [These differences between parents whose children are relatively healthy and those whose children remain quite ill are only a bit larger than the differences between mothers and fathers. Fathers' mean scores are all very close to the mean scores for the parents of healthier children (p. 132).] These last two findings together suggest that while part of taking responsibility is undoubtedly linked to persistent cultural notions about gender, another part of taking responsibility is emergent, demonstrating that many parents use their agency to meet unexpected contingencies as they arise. And finally, we found that some parts of taking responsibility are more difficult than others. As our empirical analysis shows, while most parents took their child's needs seriously, far fewer of them demonstrated that they used their discretion to adjust means to ends. Attachment to their child is not the stumbling block for assuming responsibility for most parents [especially for most mothers]. The stumbling block is translating that attachment into meaningful action on the child's behalf.

So how do Heimer and Staffen describe the norms that require responsibility, when we are used to thinking of norms as requiring "obeying the rules"? The parents are not merely "obeying the rules" when they notice that their child is curious and will lift her head, thereby strengthening the neck muscles (damaged by having a machine attached to the artery in the neck), if she is put so that she has to use those muscles to see what is going on. *We* never heard that rule, no one told the mother that was the rule, other mothers didn't do it, but *it got the job done*. That social life can make a mother invent the rule for her own behavior is not just a problem of explaining why the mother was not deviant. It's a problem of investigating why the mother used creativity and intelligence to solve her child's *particular* problem, and to solve it for the benefit of the baby even when it cost her a lot.

Now if Heimer and Staffen are right, this will be a big thing. So they start off with a notion of the components required for such a set of phenomena to be observed. The components are derived from the theoretical problem of conceiving rationality on someone else's behalf. In the first place, they cannot ask standard questions or use experimental methods because their whole notion is that people have to figure out, *in the world*, where resources and problems are thrown up as chance brings them in, and where therefore *what they have to do varies with the situation*. Otherwise the investigators cannot observe responsibility as they have conceived it.

Second, the concept itself requires that responsible people organize a lot of things on into the future. It is central to all rational action that it is not oriented to the past, but to the future, and that the future is always uncertain. (The future orientation of rationality partly explains why economic historians are wise to get jobs in history departments rather than economics departments; their economist colleagues are, by their choice of their central mechanism, interested in the future rather than the past.) The parents do not know what is going to be required until they see how the world is, and that is why they have to be rational at that future time, not now. If they are producing the same thing day after day with the same resources reliably delivered to their work station on the assembly line, they only have to be responsible when something unexpected happens. In a chemical plant, sometimes a worker's job is just to wait for something to go wrong—all the work is routinely done by the machines themselves, and the people are there to put out the fires (often literal, not metaphorical).

So when Heimer and Staffen interview people about the real world, they are looking for them to do or fail to do the responsible thing about organizing resources, many of which are, in the modern world, under the control of organizations. So they have to interview them about how they interact with the nurses and doctors and other specialists in the neonatal intensive care unit, how they deal with insurance providers or welfare officials, how they negotiate with their employers so they can come visit their babies and bond with them, besides collecting information about the baby's needs and mobilizing resources. That is, in order to locate the concept accurately, the investigators have to interview parents (or observe the parents doing it) so that *they know the connections the people make or fail to make* among the components of rational action on someone else's behalf.

But to do that, the investigators need to figure out how to classify, at least crudely, the phenomena in the real world that create the need for responsible behavior. If a child needs to be in the hospital a few days before going home normal, if it needs to be hospitalized for a long time and then to go home on a ventilator; if it needs to have an incision for feeding or breathing cared for and kept clean and functional, and might have to come back into the hospital on an emergency basis: these are all quite different situations. So in order to develop the concept, the investigators have to find out enough about the contingencies the world brings to these babies, so they can figure out what it takes for the parents to be rational on their behalf.

What the investigators hope they come out with, first of all, is confirmation or doubts about whether they chose right about the main things that responsibility entails. A big part of this—which the authors did not anticipate very well, so it was something *they* had to learn about responsibility—was that people had to learn *what organizations* had the resources they needed, what they had to do to get them, and then when it did not work, they had to make up for the failures of the organization and go back and forth until they finally got what was needed. They had to try again if the doctor wouldn't listen to their account of the symptoms, because she had already made up her mind what was the matter and felt that what the parent said was irrelevant. So responsible parents had to go and recruit the nurse to notice more authoritatively for them, so as to get through to the doctor.

To grasp all that, Heimer and Staffen had to theorize the task of "client social control" of organizational participants. For example, a long hospital stay for the baby implies more parental need to learn to be a responsible manipulator of hospital procedures and personnel. The long stay also decreases the "one-time participant meeting the full-time professional" social distance in the patient-hospital relationship; increases the parent's medical competence as compared to average parental medical competence, especially on the problem that their child has; clears away a lot of the startup costs of getting coverage arranged with the insurers or the welfare office, and so on. That is, the parent of a severely damaged child is a lot better prepared to be a rational agent of the child in this interorganizational environment, as well as needing to be a more rational agent because it matters more. Take the task of maintaining a child on a ventilator. By the time the caretaker has to do that, and to get a nurse in to do it when he or she has to be gone, he or she knows a lot more about how to do it, and how to fill in the gaps if the nurse has not learned how to do it. The hospital organization has many motives to try to get the mother or someone trained to be a rational agent for a ventilator-dependent child, or the child will occupy a ten-thousand-dollar-a-month bed while the hospital nurse manages it.

Complex Causal Roles of Concepts, Complex Concepts, and Complex Fieldwork Studies

....

WHAT WE WANT HERE is a concept that can do a certain job—namely, to identify variations in how well people (or organizational roles or organizations or populations of organizations subject to a given regulatory regime) act rationally on behalf of others. First, we have the variation in the others on whose behalf action is supposed to take place, or in the relation of the values to be served (such as advancing knowledge) to the private interests (such as getting promoted before the argument of a paper is perfect) of the person or organization(s) acting. Second, we have the contingencies that determine what needs to be done, and the variation, in the world, of those contingencies. Third, we have the derived "needs" of the other, the organization, and so on. Fourth, we have the resources needed to satisfy that need, and under what conditions they are needed. Fifth, all this has to be organized on a long time scale, rather than only a short-run responsiveness, so that we take account, for example, of what will happen to the child when he or she is an adult.

We want a variable, responsible versus irresponsible, to play a complex causal role, which varies with the situation in the world. Rationality *is always* such a complex entity, which is why we have a whole discipline, economics, to deal with just the selfish case; the "on behalf of" makes responsible rationality a lot more complicated, as is indicated by the trouble economists have with using the concept of "altruism" to explain why parents leave money to their children instead of consuming all of it, or why they do not. Specialists in selfish rationality turn out not to be much good at explaining unselfish rationality. Of course, if all the people in all the firms are always maximizing their own selfish, short-run benefits, the rational firm behavior needed to make economics of real markets (that is, ones dominated by firms) run will not work.

At the very least we need responsible managers to design the incentive system that makes organizational maximization rational for all the members of the organization. Part of what Heimer and Staffen have to explain is why an organization, the hospital, puts so much effort into saving these babies, a subject not treated above. Part of the answer is that the hospital is liable for negligence if it turns a baby over to a person who cannot take care of it, but a lot of it is because hospitals, and the people who work in them, do not like babies to die, for the sake of the children.

Then we need to be able to collect information or observations on the indicators of this entity, responsibility, its essential components, and so on. That is, we need to be able to observe this thing. To observe it in the real world (and we only care about what it takes to adapt to the real world on somebody's behalf), we need to collect a lot of information about what world it is *for each individual*—say, a nurse or a mother—how they think about that world (and how that thinking departs from rationality), and how they manipulate the world by mobilizing resources on behalf of the child, or on behalf of an organization.

It is hard to imagine a neat little way to show here that, for example, the no-answers measure of fathers measures irresponsibility. (It is probably right that Heimer and Staffen no-answers measure irresponsibility—they had a lot of trouble even asking *any* questions of the unmarried fathers, because they couldn't be found or would not cooperate, and there was lots of indirect evidence that most of them were very irresponsible. What we cannot get very easily is evidence of what psychologically accompanies an unmarried father's irresponsibility.) Given the difficulty of the task, it is no wonder that the investigators needed a couple of person-years of fieldwork in hospitals, a couple or three years of thinking about the whole problem, and about four person-years of writing (all this while supporting themselves by teaching and other university duties, because no foundation, with the partial exception of the American Bar Foundation, would believe they could actually do it).

Now, the test a student should apply to this chapter is that one ought to be able to take the concept, design a study on the responsibility in the teaching process of the faculty and graduate students in the department where they study, and come up with a way to analyze the following: how rationally the people analyze the contingencies that come up, how they adapt to them, on whose behalf they act, how they make the tradeoffs between uses of resources in a responsible way, how they develop their competence to mobilize the resources they need, and how they think about the long-run benefit to the students and to the collective intelligence of sociology as a whole. The student should be able to observe people in such a way as to classify them by how hard it is to do the various things they have to do to be rational, what the risks involved are and how willing they are to bear them, and how they connect all these to the long-run future of their students or of the discipline, and in other ways to rank them into groups by levels of responsibility. If Heimer and Staffen have done their work responsibly, they should have done a good job of showing how that could be done. *I'm convinced*, but then I've had a decade of learning about responsibility in neonatal intensive care units, at close range.

Conclusion

THIS LAST CHAPTER has been as much a sermon on the life of research as an attempt to explicate the logic of inquiry into social causation. It has been an essay and exemplification of Virgil's observation, "Happy he who can find out the causes of things." The examples not only demonstrate attempts to do what the book tells one to do, but they also have the implicit message, "Go thou and do likewise."

A responsible author of such a book must eventually stop because even he or she knows that students have other altruistic utilities besides finding out the causes of things: peace, justice, mercy, love of children. And students also have some of the more private utilities that rebellious high school students wanted in place of an extended adolescence: sex, cars, their own money to spend, and a bit of fun in the interstices of responsibility.

The core of scientific method, even before learning a lot in libraries about the subject of research, is a moral choice, a choice to prefer a closer approximation to truth over disprovable falsehood. But the core of life as a scientist is to balance that preference for truth, still imperfect, with the other good things of life, as imperfect as they, too, may be. An author also ends a book because he has other things he wants to do.

References

Abbott, Andrew. 1992. "What Do Cases Do? Some Notes on Activity in Sociological Analysis." Pp. 53–82, 228–230 in Ragin and Becker, 1992.

Albrecht. G., Hans-Uwe Otto, S. Karstedt-Henke, and K. Bollert, eds. 1991. *Social Prevention and the Social Sciences: Theoretical Controversies, Research Problems, and Evaluation Strategies.* New York: Walter de Gruyter.

Baker, Wayne E. 1984. "The Social Structure of a National Securities Market." *American Journal of Sociology* 89: 775–811.

Bearman, Peter, Robert Faris, and James Moody. 1999. "Blocking the Future: New Solutions for Old Problems in Historical Social Science." *Social Science History* 23, no. 4: 501–533.

Becker, Gary. 1981. *A Treatise on the Family.* Cambridge: Harvard University Press.

Becker, Gary, and Nigel Tomes. 1986. "Human Capital and the Rise and Fall of Families." *Journal of Labor Economics* 4: S1–39.

Becker, Howard S. 1958. "Problems of Inference and Proof in Participant Observation." *American Sociological Review* 23: 652–660.

———. 1963a. *Outsiders: Studies in the Sociology of Deviance.* New York: Free Press.

———. 1963b. "The Culture of a Deviant Group: Dance Musicians." Pp. 79–100 in Becker, 1963a.

———. 1963c [1953]. "Becoming a Marijuana User." Originally published in *American Journal of Sociology* 59: 235–242. Reprinted as pp. 41–58 in Becker 1963a.

Becker, Howard S., Blanche Geer, Everett C. Hughes, and Anselm Strauss. 1961. *Boys in White: Student Culture in Medical School.* New York: Transaction.

Blumer, Herbert. 1954. "What Is Wrong with Social Theory?" *American Journal of Sociology* 19: 3–10.

Boswell, Terry, and William Dixon. 1993. "Marx's Theory of Rebellion: A Cross-National Analysis of Class Exploitation, Economic Development, and Violent Revolt." *American Sociological Review* 58, no. 5: 681–702.

Breiger, Ronald L., ed. 1990. *Social Mobility and Social Structure*. Cambridge: Cambridge University Press.

Bridges, William P., and Robert L. Nelson. 1989. "Markets in Hierarchies." *American Journal of Sociology* 95: 616–658.

Brown, Roger. 1954. "Mass Phenomena." Pp. 833–876 in Lindzey, 1954.

Campbell, Donald T[homas]. 1969. "Ethnocentrism of Disciplines and the Fish-Scale Model of Omniscience." Pp. 328–348 in Sherif and Sherif, 1969.

Carruthers, Bruce G. 1996. *City of Capital: Politics and Markets in the English Financial Revolution*. Princeton: Princeton University Press.

Carruthers, Bruce G., and Terry Halliday. 1998. *Rescuing Business: The Making of Corporate Bankruptcy Law in England and the United States*. New York: Oxford University Press.

Carruthers, Bruce G., and Arthur L. Stinchcombe. 1999. "The Social Structure of Liquidity: Flexibility, Markets, and States." *Theory and Society* 28: 353–382.

Cavan, Sherri. 1966. *Liquor License: An Ethnography of Bar Behavior*. Chicago: Aldine.

Chamoiseau, Patrick. 1997 [1992]. *Texaco*. Trans. Rose-Myriam Réjouis and Val Vinokurov. New York: Viking.

Chandler, Alfred D. 1962. *Strategy and Structure: Chapters in the History of Industrial Enterprise*. Cambridge: MIT Press.

Charrad, Mounira M. 2001. *States and Women's Rights: The Making of Postcolonial Tunisia, Algeria, and Morocco*. Berkeley: University of California Press.

Clemens, Elisabeth. 1992. *The People's Lobby: Organizational Innovation and the Rise of Interest Group Politics in the United States, 1890–1925*. Chicago: University of Chicago Press.

———. 1999. "Continuity and Coherence: Periodization and the Problem of Institutional Change." Pp. 62–83 in Engelstad and Kalleberg, 1999.

Clemens, Elisabeth, Walter W. Powell, Kris McIlwaine, and Dina Okamoto. 1995. "Careers in Print: Books, Journals and Scholarly Reputations." *American Journal of Sociology* 101, no. 2 (September): 433–494.

Clemens, Samuel. *See* Twain, Mark.

Coase, R. H. 1937. "The Nature of the Firm." *Economica* 4: 386–405.

Coleman, James S. 1964. *Introduction to Mathematical Sociology.* New York: Free Press.

———. 1990. *Foundations of Social Theory.* Cambridge: Belknap Press of Harvard University Press.

Coleman, James S., Elihu Katz, and Herbert Menzel. 1957. "The Diffusion of a New Drug among Physicians." *Sociometry* 20: 253–270.

Collins, Randall. 1998. *The Sociology of Philosophies: A Global Theory of Intellectual Change.* Cambridge: Belknap Press of Harvard University Press.

Cook, Thomas D[ixon], ed. 1992a. (With Harris Cooper, David S. Corday, Heidi Hartman, Larry V. Hedges, Richard J. Light, Thomas A. Louis, and Fred Mosteller.) *Meta-Analysis for Explanation: A Casebook.* New York: Russell Sage Foundation.

———. 1992b. "The Meta-Analytic Perspective," and "Explanation in Meta-Analysis." Pp. 1–33 in Cook, 1992a.

Darwin, Charles. 1872 [1859]. *The Origin of Species by Means of Natural Selection, or Preservation of Favored Races in the Struggle for Life.* 6th ed. London: Murray.

Dewey, John. 1938. *Logic: The Theory of Inquiry.* New York: Holt.

Dimaggio, Paul J., and Walter W. Powell. 1983. "The Iron Cage Revisited: Institutional Isomorphism and Collective Rationality in Organizational Fields." *American Sociological Review* 48: 147–160.

Dobbin, Frank, John R. Sutton, John W. Meyer, and W. Richard Scott. 1994. "Equal Opportunity Law and the Construction of Internal Labor Markets." Pp. 272–300 in Scott, Meyer et al., 1994.

Dyson-Hudson, Neville. 1966. *Karimojong Politics.* Oxford: Clarendon Press.

Edelman, Lauren B. 1990. "Legal Environments and Organizational Governance: The Expansions of Due Process in the American Workplace." *American Journal of Sociology* 95: 1401–1440.

Edge, David O., and Michael J. Mulkay. 1976. *Astronomy Transformed: The Emergence of Radio Astronomy in Britain.* New York: John Wiley.

Egeberg, Morten, and Per Lægreid, eds. 1999. *Organizing Political Institutions: Essays for Johan P. Olsen.* Oslo: Scandinavian University Press.

Elster, Jon. 1987. *Nuts and Bolts for the Social Sciences.* Chicago: University of Chicago Press.

Engelstad, Fredrik, and Ragnvald Kalleberg, eds. 1999. *Social Time and Social Change: Perspectives on Sociology and History.* Oslo: Scandinavian University Press.

Fisher, R. A. 1937. *The Design of Experiments.* 2d ed. Edinburgh: Oliver & Boyd.

Fligstein, Neil. 1990. *The Transformation of Corporate Control.* Cambridge: Harvard University Press.

Fouraker, Lawrence E., and Sidney Siegel. 1963. *Bargaining Behavior.* New York: McGraw-Hill.

Fox, Renée. 1974 [1959]. *Experiment Perilous: Physicians and Patients Facing the Unknown.* Philadelphia: University of Pennsylvania Press.

Gatson, Sarah. 1999. "Fanatics, Farmers, Politicians, and Slaves: Racial Citizenship in U.S. Communities." Ph.D. diss., Northwestern University.

Geertz, Clifford 1973a. *Interpretation of Cultures: Selected Essays.* New York: Basic Books.

———. 1973b [1959]. "Ritual and Social Change: A Javanese Example." *American Anthropologist* 61: 991–1012. Reprinted as pp. 142–169 in Geertz 1973a.

Gilbert, G. Nigel, and Michael Mulkay. 1984. *Opening Pandora's Box: A Sociological Analysis of Scientists' Discourse.* Cambridge: Cambridge University Press.

Glymour, Clark, Richard Scheines, Peter Spirtes, and Kevin Kelly. 1987. *Discovering Causal Structure: Artificial Intelligence, Philosophy of Science, and Statistical Modeling.* San Diego: Academic Press.

Goffman, Erving. 1959. *The Presentation of Self in Everyday Life.* Garden City, N.Y.: Doubleday.

———. 1963. *Behavior in Public Places: Notes on the Social Organization of Gatherings.* New York: Free Press.

———. 1967a. *Interaction Ritual: Essays on Face-to-Face Behavior.* Garden City, N.Y.: Doubleday.

———. 1967b. "Where the Action Is." Pp. 149–270 in Goffman, 1967a.

Goldberg, Louis C. 1970. "A Social History of the Organizational Dilemmas of the Congress of Racial Equality Target City Project in Baltimore, 1965–1967." Ph.D. diss., Johns Hopkins University.

Gould, Roger V. 2003. *Collision of Wills: How Ambiguity about Social Rank Breeds Conflict.* Chicago: University of Chicago Press.

Granovetter, Mark S. 1974. *Getting a Job: A Study of Contacts and Careers.* Cambridge: Harvard University Press.

Grilliches, Zvi. 1957. "Hybrid Corn: An Exploration in the Economics of Technological Change." *Econometrica* 254: 501–522.

Grimshaw, Allen. 1989. *College Discourse: Professional Conversation among Peers.* Norwood, N.J.: Ablex Publishing.

Griswold, Wendy. 1987. "A Methodological Framework for the Sociology of Culture." *Sociological Methodology* 17: 1–35.

Halaby, Charles N., and David L. Weakliem. 1989. "Worker Control and Attachment to the Firm." *American Journal of Sociology* 95: 549–591.

Heimer, Carol A. 1985. *Reactive Risk and Rational Action: Managing Moral Hazard in Insurance Contracts.* Berkeley: University of California Press.

———. 1986. "Producing Responsible Behavior in Order to Produce Oil: Bringing Obligations, Rights, Incentives, and Resources Together in the Norwegian State Oil Company." Institute of Industrial Economics, Bergen, Norway, Report No. 76. Also issued as a working paper at Center for Urban Affairs and Policy Research, Northwestern University.

———. 1988. "Social Structure, Psychology, and the Estimation of Risk." *Annual Review of Sociology* 24: 491–519.

———. 2001. "Cases and Biographies: An Essay on Routinization and the Nature of Comparison." *Annual Review of Sociology* 27: 47–76.

Heimer, Carol A., and Lisa R. Staffen. 1998a. *For the Sake of the Children: The Social Organization of Responsibility in the Hospital and the Home.* Chicago: University of Chicago Press.

———. 1998b. "What Do We Mean by Responsibility?" Pp. 77–136 in Heimer and Staffen, 1998a.

———. 1998c. "Appendix on Methods." Pp. 375–388 in Heimer and Staffen, 1998a.

Heimer, Carol A., and Arthur L. Stinchcombe. 1999. "Remodeling the Garbage Can: Implications of the Origins of Items in Decision Streams." Pp. 25–57 in Egeberg and Lægreid, 1999.

Heyns, Barbara. 1978. *Summer Learning and the Effects of Schooling.* New York: Academic Press.

Higman, Barry W. 1984. *Slave Populations of the British Caribbean 1807–1834.* Baltimore: Johns Hopkins University Press.

Hochschild, Arlie Russell. 1989. *The Second Shift: Working Parents and the Revolution at Home.* New York: Viking.

Homans, George Caspar. 1974. *Social Behavior: Its Elementary Forms.* Rev. ed. New York: Harcourt Brace Jovanovich.

Jaques, Elliott. 1972 [1956]. *Measurement of Responsibility: A Study of Work, Payment, and Individual Capacity.* New York: John Wiley.

Jauss, Hans Robert. 1982. *Toward an Aesthetic of Reception.* Trans. Timothy Bahti. Minneapolis: University of Minnesota Press.

Kagan, Robert A. 2001. *Adversarial Legalism: The American Way of Law.* Cambridge: Harvard University Press.

Kahneman, Daniel, Paul Slovic, and Amos Tversky, eds. 1982. *Judgment under Uncertainty: Heuristics and Biases.* Cambridge: Cambridge University Press.

Kahneman, Daniel, and Amos Tversky. 1982. "The Psychology of Preferences." *Scientific American* 246, no. 1: 160–173.

Key, V[aldimer] O[rlando], Jr., and Alexander Heard. 1949. *Southern Politics in State and Nation.* New York: Alfred A. Knopf.

Kingsolver, Barbara. 1998. *The Poisonwood Bible.* New York: Harper Flamingo.

Klatzky, Sheila R. 1972. *Patterns of Contact with Relatives.* Arnold and Caroline Rose Monograph Series in Sociology. Washington, D.C.: American Sociological Association.

Koponen, Timothy. 1998. "Zimbabwe's Maize Commodity Chain: Embedding the Economy of Food in Race and Science." Ph.D. diss., Northwestern University.

Kubler, George. 1962. *The Shape of Time: Remarks on the History of Things.* New Haven: Yale University Press.

Kuhn, Thomas. 1970 [1966]. *The Structure of Scientific Revolutions.* Chicago: University of Chicago Press.

———. 1978. *Black Body Theory and the Quantum Discontinuity 1894–1912.* New York: Oxford University Press.

Latour, Bruno, and Steve Woolgar. 1979. *Laboratory Life: The Social Construction of Scientific Facts.* Beverly Hills: Sage Publications.

Lattimore, Owen. 1967 [1940]. *Inner Asian Frontiers of China.* 2d ed. Boston: Beacon Press.

Lawler, Edward, and Jeongkoo Yoon. 1998. "Network Structure and Emotion in Exchange Relations." *American Sociological Review* 63: 871–894.

Lazarsfeld, Paul, and Frank Stanton, eds. 1949. *Communications Research.* New York: Harper & Brothers.

Lévi-Strauss, Claude. 1969 [1964]. *The Raw and the Cooked: Introduction to a Science of Mythology: I.* Trans. John and Doreen Weightman. New York: Harper & Row.

Lindzey, Gardner. 1954. *Handbook of Social Psychology, Vol. 2.* Reading, Mass.: Addison Wesley.

Lounsbury, Michael, and Marc Ventreska. 1999. *Social Structure and Organizations Revisited, Vol. 19.* Amsterdam: JAI Elsevier.

Markoff, John. 1996. *The Abolition of Feudalism: Peasants, Lords, and Legislators in the French Revolution.* University Park: University of Pennsylvania Press.

Massey, Douglas S. 1993. *American Apartheid: Segregation and the Making of the Underclass.* Cambridge: Harvard University Press.

McAdam, Doug. 1986. "Recruitment to High-Risk Activism: The Case of Freedom Summer." *American Journal of Sociology* 92: 64–90.

McAdam, Doug, and Roberto Fernandez. 1988. "Social Networks and Social Movements: Multi-organizational Fields and Recruitment to Mississippi Freedom Summer." *Sociological Forum* 92: 64–90.

McKim, Vaughn R., and Stephen P. Turner, eds. 1997. *Causality in Crisis? Statistical Methods and the Search for Causal Knowledge in the Social Sciences.* Notre Dame, Ind.: University of Notre Dame Press.

McNeely, Connie L. 1995. "Prescribing National Educational Policies: The Role of International Organizations." *Comparative Education Review* 39: 483–507.

Menger, Pierre-Michel. 2002. *Portrait de l'artiste en travailleur.* [Portrait of the artist as a worker.] Paris: Editions du Seuil.

Merton, Robert K. 1949. "Patterns of Influence." Pp. 189–202 in Lazarsfeld and Stanton, 1949.

Merton, Robert K., Marjorie Fiske, and Alberta Curtis. 1946. *Mass Persuasion: The Social Psychology of a War Bond Drive.* New York: Harper.

Merton, Robert K., David Sills, and Stephen Stigler. 1984. "The Kelvin Dictum and Social Science: An Excursion into the History of an Idea." *Journal of the History of the Behavioral Sciences* 20: 319–336.

Mills, C[harles] Wright. 1959. *The Sociological Imagination.* New York: Oxford University Press.

Morris, Aldon D. 1984. *Origins of the Civil Rights Movement: Black Communities Organizing for Change.* New York: Free Press.

Mulkay, Michael. *See* Edgerton and Mulkay 1976; Gilbert and Mulkay 1984.

Padgett, John. 1990. "Mobility as Control: Congressmen through Committees." Pp. 27–58 in Breiger, 1990.

Paige, Jeffery M. 1999. "Conjuncture, Comparison, and Conditional Theory in Macrosocial Inquiry." *American Journal of Sociology* 105: 781–800.

Papandreou, Andreas G. 1958. *Economics as a Science*. Chicago: Lippincott.

Patillo-McCoy, Mary. 1998. *American Sociological Review* 63: 767–784.

Pinard, Maurice, Jerome Kirk, and Donald Von Eschen. 1968. "Processes of Recruitment in the Sit-In Movement." *Public Opinion Quarterly* 33, no. 3: 355–369.

Polya, George. 1954. *Mathematics and Plausible Reasonsing*. Princeton: Princeton University Press.

Powell, Walter W., and Paul J. DiMaggio, eds. 1991a. *The New Institutionalism in Organizational Analysis*. Chicago: University of Chicago Press.

————. 1991b. "Introduction." Pp. 1–38 in Powell and DiMaggio, 1991a.

Powell, Walter W., and Dan L. Jones, eds. Forthcoming, 2004. *How Institutions Change*. Chicago: University of Chicago Press.

Rabushka, Alvin, and Kenneth A. Shepsle. 1972. *Politics in Plural Societies: A Theory of Democratic Instability*. Columbus, Ohio: Merrill.

Ragin, Charles, and Howard S. Becker, eds. 1992. *What Is a Case? Exploring the Foundations of Social Inquiry*. Cambridge: Cambridge University Press.

Redfield, Robert. 1971. *The Little Community* and *Peasant Society and Culture*. Chicago: University of Chicago Press.

Rosmarin, Addena. 1985. *The Power of Genre*. Minneapolis: University of Minnesota Press.

Rossi, Alice S., with Peter H. Rossi. 1990. *Of Human Bonding: Parent-Child Relations across the Life Course*. Hawthorne, N.Y.: Aldine de Gruyter.

Schneiberg, Marc. 1999. "Organizational Heterogeneity and the Production of New Forms: Politics, Social Movements and Mutual Companies in American Fire Insurance." Pp. 39–89 in Lounsbury and Ventresca, 1999.

Schneiberg, Marc, and Elisabeth Clemens. Forthcoming, 2004. "The Typical Tools for the Job: Research Strategies in Institutional Analysis." In Powell and Jones, forthcoming, 2004.

Scott, W[illiam] Richard, John W. Meyer & Associates. 1994. *Institutional Environments and Organizations: Structural Complexity and Individualism*. Thousand Oaks, Calif.: Sage.

Sewell, William. 1992. "A Theory of Structure: Duality, Agency and Transformation." *American Journal of Sociology* 98, no. 1: 1–29.

Sherif, M., and C. W. Sherif, eds. 1969. *Interdisciplinary Relationships in the Social Sciences.* Chicago: Aldine.

Siegfried, André. 1975 [1933]. *Tableau politique de la France de l'ouest sous la troisième république.* [Political description of the west of France during the Third Republic.] Reprint. New York: Arno Press.

Smith, Tom W. 1996. *General Social Surveys, 1972–1996: Cumulative Codebook.* Chicago: National Opinion Research Center.

Sørensen, Aage B., and Seymour Spilerman, eds. 1993. *Social Theory and Social Policy: Essays in Honor of James S. Coleman.* Westport, Conn.: Praeger.

Stinchcombe, Arthur L. 1964a. *Rebellion in a High School.* Chicago: Quadrangle. Reprint. New York: New York Times Press.

———. 1964b. "The Psychological Quality of Adolescent Rebellion" and "Appendix on Method." Pp. 15–48 and 186–191 in Stinchcombe, 1964a.

———. 1968. *Constructing Social Theories.* Chicago: University of Chicago Press.

———. 1974. *Creating Efficient Industrial Administrations.* With the assistance of Zahava Blum and Rene Marder. New York: Academic Press.

———. 1978a. *Theoretical Methods in Social History.* Orlando, Fla.: Academic Press.

———. 1978b. "Technical Appendix: The Logic of Analogy." Pp. 25–29 in Stinchcombe, 1978a.

———. 1978c. "Principles of Cumulative Causation." Pp. 61–70 in Stinchcombe, 1978a.

———. 1983. *Economic Sociology.* New York: Academic Press.

———. 1990a. *Information and Organizations.* Berkeley: University of California Press.

———. 1990b. "Restructuring Research on Organizations." Pp. 358–362 in Stinchcombe, 1990a.

———. 1991. "The Conditions of Fruitfulness of Theorizing about Mechanisms in Social Science." *Philosophy of the Social Sciences* 21, no. 3: 367–388. Reprinted in Sorensen and Spilerman 1993, pp. 23–41.

———. 1995a. *Sugar Island Slavery in the Age of Enlightenment: The Political Economy of the Caribbean World.* Princeton: Princeton University Press.

———. 1995b. "Planter Power, Freedom, and Oppression of Slaves in the 18th Century Caribbean." Pp. 125–152 in Stinchcombe, 1995a.

———. 1995c. "The Constitution of the Data." Pp. 152–158 in Stinchcombe, 1995a.

———. 1998. Review of Vaughn R. McKim and Stephen P. Turner, eds., *Causality in Crisis? Contemporary Sociology* 27: 664–666.

———. 1999. "Ending Revolutions and Building New Governments." *Annual Review of Political Science 1999*: 49–73.

———. 2001. *When Formality Works: Authority and Abstraction in Law and Organizations*. Chicago: University of Chicago Press.

Stouffer, Samuel A. 1955. *Communism, Conformity, and Civil Liberties*. Garden City, N.Y.: Doubleday.

Sutton, John R., and Frank Dobbin. 1996. "The Two Faces of Governance: Responses to Legal Uncertainty in U.S. firms, 1955–1985." *American Sociological Review* 99: 944–971.

Thomas, W[illiam] I[saac]. 1967a [1923]. *The Unadjusted Girl*. New York: Harper Torchbooks. Originally published in Boston: Little Brown.

———. 1967b [1923]. "The Definition of the Situation." Pp. 42–52 in Thomas, 1967a [1923].

Thurstone, L[ouis] L[eon]. 1935. *Vectors of the Mind: Multiple Factor Analysis for the Isolation of Primary Traits*. Chicago: University of Chicago Press.

Tilly, Charles. 1964. *The Vendée*. New York: John Wiley.

Tocqueville, Alexis de. 1955 [1856]. *The Old Regime and the French Revolution*. New York: Doubleday.

Trotsky, Leon. 1960 [1932]. *History of the Russian Revolution*. Trans. Max Eastman. Ann Arbor: University of Michigan Press. Reprinted in 1 vol. with the original 3-vol. pagination.

Tuma, Nancy Brandon, and Michael Hannan. 1984. *Social Dynamics: Models and Methods*. Orlando, Fla.: Academic Press.

Twain, Mark. 1996 [1885]. *The Adventures of Huckleberry Finn*. New York: Barnes & Noble.

U.S. Department of Commerce. Various years. *Historical Statistics & Statistical Abstract*. Washington: U.S. Government Printing Office.

Watson, James D. 1980 [1968]. *The Double Helix: A Personal Account of the Discovery of the Structure of DNA*. Ed. Gunther S. Stent. Norton Critical Edition. New York: W. W. Norton.

Weber, Max. 1924 [1889]. "Zur Geschichte der Handelsgesellschaften im Mittelalter nach sudeuropaïschen Quellen." [On the history of business associations in the Middle Ages according to southern European sources.] Pp. 312–443 in Weber, *Gesammelte Aufsätze zur Sozial- und Wirtschaftsgeschichte* [Collected essays on social and economic history]. Tübingen: G. C. B. Mohr and Stuttgart: Ferdinand Enke.

———. 1968a [1921–1922]. *Economy and Society: An Outline of Interpretive Sociology.* 3 vols. Ed. Gunther Roth and Klaus Wittich. New York: Bedminster Press. Originally published in German.

———. 1968b [1921–1922]. "Cities." Vol. 3, pp. 1212–1372, in Weber 1968a [1921–1922].

———. 1981 [Ger. 1923, Eng. 1927]. *General Economic History.* Ed. S. Hellmann and M. Palyi, trans. Frank H. Knight. New Brunswick, N.J.: Transaction.

White, Cynthia A., and Harrison White. 1965. *Canvases and Careers: Institutional Change in the French Painting World.* New York: John Wiley.

Whiting, William. N.d. [19th c.]. "Eternal Father Strong to Save." Hymn.

Wright, Erik O. 1978. *Class Structure and Income Inequality.* Orlando, Fla.: Academic Press.

Zablocki, Benjamin. 1971. *The Joyful Community: An Account of the Bruderhof.* Baltimore: Penguin Books.

———. 1980. *Alienation and Charisma: A Study of Contemporary American Communes.* New York: Free Press.

Zajonc, Robert B. 1980. "Feeling and Thinking: Preferences Need No Inferences." *American Psychologist* 35, no. 2: 151–175.

Zuckerman, Harriet. 1977. *Scientific Elite: Nobel Laureates in the United States.* New York: Free Press.

Index